Intelligence

The Eye,
the Brain,
and the
Computer

Intelligence

The Eye, the Brain, and the Computer

Martin A. Fischler

SRI International

Oscar Firschein

SRI International

ADDISON-WESLEY PUBLISHING COMPANY

Reading, Massachusetts • Menlo Park, California • Don Mills, Ontario
Wokingham, England • Amsterdam • Sydney • Singapore • Tokyo
Madrid • Bogotá • Santiago • San Juan

Sponsoring Editor • Peter S. Gordon
Production Supervisor • Bette J. Aaronson
Copy Editor • G. W. Helfrich
Text Designer and Art Coordinator • Geri Davis, Quadrata Inc.
Cover Designer • Marshall Henrichs
Manufacturing Supervisor • Hugh Crawford

Library of Congress Cataloging-in-Publication Data

Fischler, Martin A.
   Intelligence : the eye, the brain, and the computer.

   Bibliography: p.
   Includes index.
   1. Artificial intelligence. 2. Machine learning.
3. Cognition. 4. Perception. I. Firschein, Oscar.
II. Title.
Q335.F57 1987   006.3   86-3557
ISBN 0-201-12001-1

Reprinted with corrections April, 1987

   BCDEFGHIJ-HA-8987

Preface

This book is intended to be an intellectual journey into the domain of human and machine intelligence. The subject matter has been approached from a conceptual and sometimes even philosophical point of view, one biased by our experience in that branch of computer and cognitive science called artificial intelligence (AI). On this journey we will often be dealing with topics, such as the operation of the brain, where knowledge is lacking, and where there are only vague conjectures as to possible mechanisms. In our review of machine intelligence, we will discuss both the present-day and ultimate limits of machine performance.

We intend the book to provide the *Scientific American* level reader with an understanding of the concept of intelligence, the nature of the cognitive and perceptual capabilities of people and machines, and the representations and algorithms used to attain intelligent behavior. While we have attempted to make the material understandable by an educated layman, we are equally concerned with having something important to say to our professional colleagues and peers.

"Boxes" have been used to augment the text. These boxes, and longer appendices, present material of interest that expand on the topics being discussed, and sometimes they may contain technical material of more interest to the specialist. It is intended that the text should stand on its own; the reader can usually omit the boxes until a later reading.

PREFACE

A unifying theme in our exposition is the critically important concept of representation. Issues related to this and other important concepts may be raised in an earlier chapter, our position stated, and then elaborated and supported in later chapters. If our initial discussion on some important point appears to be brief or unsupported, have faith, since we will probably return to this topic many times before your journey through the book is completed.

Our primary purpose in the first part of this book is to provide a basis for understanding the nature of intelligence and intelligent behavior: (a) as it exists in man and higher animals, (b) as it could exist in a machine, and (c) as a scientific discipline concerned with the mechanisms and limits involved in acquiring, representing, and applying knowledge.

The last part of the book deals with perception and primarily vision, the means by which knowledge about our physical environment is acquired. We will see that perceptual behavior, far from being passive or mechanical, requires a reasoning ability at least equal to that needed for the most difficult problem-solving tasks.

The flavor of this book can be gleaned from the following brief description of chapter topics.

Intelligence

This chapter discusses the nature of intelligence, indicating its characteristics or components. We examine the issue of whether intelligence is primarily associated with functional behavior (performance) or with the structures and machinery that give rise to behavior (competence). The role of language in intelligence is explored and we speculate about the role of emotion (pain, pleasure), aesthetic appreciation, and physical interaction with the external world, in achieving intelligent behavior. The subject of artificial (machine) intelligence is introduced and something of its history, goals, and approach is indicated. Finally, the problem of measuring or evaluating intelligence is treated.

The Brain and the Computer

We examine the ultimate capacity of the computer as an *intelligence engine* and whether man can create a machine more intelligent than himself. Are there components of man's intelligence which cannot be found in any animal or duplicated in a machine? Are there essential differences between the architecture of the human brain and the digital computer which imply a difference in capacity or competence? Are there problems that cannot in theory be solved by a machine?

The Representation of Knowledge

We explore the concept of *knowledge*, and note that the nature of the physical encoding of knowledge is an important consideration in achieving intelligent behavior. We describe how knowledge can be represented in the memory of a computer and raise the question as to whether there are elements of knowledge that cannot be described or discussed.

PREFACE

Reasoning

This chapter discusses the role of reasoning in intelligent behavior. We describe how a reasoning system can use a formal language to represent things in the world and their relationships, and how it can solve problems using such a representation. The limits of formal representations in their ability to solve problems and to deal with vaguely formulated problems are indicated. The crucial difficulty arises of how a reasoning system might select the best representation for a given problem, since how can a reasoning system know which facts in its database are relevant to the problem at hand?

Learning

While a primary attribute of learning is the formulation of concepts and representations to deal effectively with new situations, an important aspect of the learning process is the identification of a particular situation as being an instance of an already-learned concept. We will find that the noting of such similarities is far from trivial, and that *analogy* lies at the heart of much of the learning process. This chapter examines the different modes of learning, and indicates the extent of present-day machine learning.

Language and Communication

This chapter examines the purpose of language and methods of communicating, and explores the role of language in intelligent behavior. The question arises as to whether man is the only organism with a true capacity for language. Finally, we discuss the approaches used for machine "understanding" of natural language.

Expert Systems

We describe *expert systems*, programs that duplicate human expertise in a specialized field such as medicine or engineering. These systems are of interest because they can act at a high level of competence by relying on a detailed *knowledge base* of information, despite a rather limited reasoning ability.

Biological Vision

Visual perception is one of the most difficult tasks yet faced in attempting to design machines that can duplicate human behavior. The relationship between the evolutionary development of vision in organisms and their needs and limitations is explored. We examine the universal mechanisms that nature has devised and which offer a solution to the problem of visual understanding of the world.

Computational Vision

This chapter describes the representations and algorithms that are used in computer analysis of images. We indicate how sensor information is converted to an array of numbers and the problems involved in deducing a model of the three-dimensional world by means of operations carried out on such image arrays. The major problems and paradigms underlying current attempts to achieve machine vision are discussed.

Epilogue

In this concluding chapter we restate and summarize the most important views and arguments relevant to the modeling of intelligence as an information processing activity that can be carried out by a machine. We discuss whether it is possible to construct an intelligent machine that can function in the world.

Acknowledgments

We owe a major debt to three people for their extensive help with respect to both technical and organizational aspects of this book: Professor Walter Gong, San Jose State University; Dr. Richard Duda, Syntelligence; and Professor Nils Nilsson, Stanford University.

The Addison-Wesley reviewers, Anthony Pasera and Werner Feibel, were masterful in their criticisms, not only pointing out deficiencies, but also providing the references that broadened our thinking on a number of topics. Chris Varley, our original editor at Addison-Wesley, was very enthusiastic about the project, and we greatly appreciate the continuing support of Peter Gordon, our current editor.

Various chapters of the book were reviewed by the following people, but we take full blame for any remaining errors in the text: James Dolby, Martin Billik, and Jon Pearce, San Jose State University; Gordon Uber, Lockheed Palo Alto Research Laboratory; Peter Cheeseman, NASA Ames; Hugh Crane, Don Kelly, Michael Georgeff, Ray Perrault, Jerry Hobbs, Phil Cohen, and Enrique Ruspini, all of SRI. SRI colleagues who helped in other ways include Ken Laws, Grahame Smith, Lynn Quam, Helen Wolf, Steve Barnard, Bob Bolles, Alex (Sandy) Pentland, and Andrew Hanson.

We are grateful for the environment of the SRI Artificial Intelligence Center made possible by the past leadership of Peter Hart and Nils Nilsson, and now by Stan Rosenschein. We acknowledge the earlier influence on our thinking by Russell Kirsch and David Willis.

We wish explicitly to acknowledge the contribution made by DARPA, whose enlightened support at the national level was critical to the development of artificial intelligence as a scientific discipline. In particular, we cite those technical monitors with whom we had direct contact with in our work in machine vision: Dave Carlstrom, Larry Druffel, Ron Ohlander, Bob Simpson, and (at a higher management level) Bob Kahn and Saul Amarel.

Our families served as intelligent lay reviewers: Beverly, Sharon, and Ron Fischler; and Ben, Joseph, and Theda Firschein. Sharon Fischler also contributed some of the ideas for the final artwork.

Menlo Park, CA

M.A.F.
O.F.

Contents

CONTENTS

Part Two

Cognition   81

CONTENTS

CONTENTS

Part One

Foundations

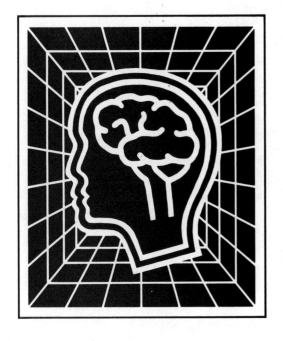

In the first portion of this book we examine, in a very general way, the nature of intelligence and the principal mechanisms by which it is achieved.

Our subject matter includes the attributes of intelligent behavior, the structure of the "reasoning engines" devised by both nature and man, and the critical role played by the way in which knowledge is encoded. These topics provide a foundation for our discussion, in Parts II and III, of cognition and perception, the two major faculties by which intelligence is exhibited.

1

1

Intelligence

In this book we will explore some of the central aspects of intelligent behavior, and the approaches employed in creating machines that can exhibit such behavior. Our purpose in this chapter is to address three broad questions about the nature of intelligence:

- What is intelligence, and to what extent is it a unique attribute of the human species?
- How can intelligence be measured or evaluated?
- What is the nature of the mechanisms that are capable of intelligent behavior? In particular, can a machine be designed to display intelligent behavior?

WHAT IS INTELLIGENCE?

Intelligence is easier to recognize than to define or measure. While the word "intelligence" is used in ordinary conversation, and has a dictionary definition, it has no agreed-upon scientific meaning, and no quantitative natural laws relating to intelligence have as yet been discovered. In view of this situation, the concept of intelligence is subject to change as our understanding of human intelligence increases. Further, without a scientific definition, much of the social debate over matters relating to intelligence (e.g., contentions about racial differences with respect to intelligence) cannot be rationally resolved.

A dictionary definition of intelligence

includes statements such as *(1) the ability to meet (novel) situations successfully by proper behavior adjustments*; or *(2) the ability to perceive the interrelationships of presented facts in such a way as to guide action toward a desired goal.* We can associate the word "learning" with the first statement, and goal-oriented behavior, problem solving, and understanding with the second. Some additional attributes of intelligence (see Tables 1-1 and 1-2) include reasoning, common sense, planning, perception, creativity, and memory retention and recall.

Theories of Intelligence

Theories of intelligence are primarily concerned with identifying the major independent components of intelligent behavior, and determining the importance of, and interactions between mechanism, process, knowledge, representation, and goals. In particular, such theories address the following issues:

- *Performance theories*: How can one test for the presence or degree of intelligence? What are the essential func-

---

TABLE 1-1 ■ Attributes of an Intelligent Agent

We expect an intelligent agent to be able to:

- Have mental attitudes (beliefs, desires, and intentions)
- Learn (ability to acquire new knowledge)
- Solve problems, including the ability to break complex problems into simpler parts
- Understand, including the ability to make sense out of ambiguous or contradictory information
- Plan and predict the consequences of contemplated actions, including the ability to compare and evaluate alternatives
- Know the limits of its knowledge and abilities
- Draw distinctions between situations despite similarities
- Be original, synthesize new concepts and ideas, and acquire and employ analogies
- Generalize (find a common underlying pattern in superficially distinct situations)
- Perceive and model the external world (see Box 1-1)
- Understand and use language and related symbolic tools

TABLE 1-2 ■ Attributes Related to, but Distinct from, Intelligence

There are a number of human attributes that are related to the concept of intelligence, but are normally considered distinct from it:

- Awareness (consciousness)
- Aesthetic appreciation (art, music)
- Emotion (anger, sorrow, pain, pleasure, love, hate)
- Sensory acuteness
- Muscular coordination (motor skills)

tional components of a system capable of exhibiting intelligent behavior?

- *Structural/function theories*: What are the mechanisms by which intelligence is achieved?
- *Contextual theories*: What is the relationship between intelligent behavior and the environment with which an organism must contend?
- *Existence theories*: What are the necessary and/or sufficient conditions for intelligent behavior to be possible?

(A separate set of issues is associated with the question of how theories of intelligence can be validated.)

Theories are statements, circumscribed by definitions, about objects and their relationships that are implicit in a body of knowledge. Thus, definitions and theories of intelligence cannot be separated. Quantitative definitions of intelligence range from implicitly defining intelligence as that human attribute which is measured by IQ tests, to assuming that the total information processing capacity of the brain is measured by its size.[1] However, the dimension along which definitions of intelligence differ most is the structural (internal) versus the contextual (external). At the structural extreme, intelligence is viewed as the competence of the human (or animal) nervous system to reason, while at the contextual extreme, intelligence is viewed as the ability of an organism to adapt to its physical and social environment. In the latter case, goals, expectations, stored knowledge,

---

[1]Beyond that needed to support normal body functions.

 BOX 1-1   **Visual Thinking**

The idea that "visual thinking" and artistic creation are part of intelligent behavior has been discussed by Arnheim as follows [Arnheim 69]:

My contention is that the cognitive operations called thinking are not the privilege of mental processes above and beyond perception but the esssential ingredients of perception itself. I am referring to such operations as active exploration, selection, grasping of essentials, simplification, abstraction, analysis and synthesis, completion, correction, comparison, problem solving, as well as combining, separating, putting into context. These operations are not the prerogative of any one mental function; they are the manner in which the minds of both man and animal treat cognitive material at any level. There is no basic difference in this respect between what happens when a person looks at the world directly, and when he sits with his eyes closed and "thinks."

Another aspect of visual thinking is the concept that the artist constructs his drawings by a reasoning process. Gombrich [Gombrich 61] describes the task of setting down a pictorial likeness on a flat surface as resembling the method used by scientists in arriving at a theoretical description of the natural world. The artist does not simply trace an outline of their visual contours to represent the appearance of things, but instead prepares a hypothetical construction to be matched and then modified in the light of further evaluation. Through an iterative process, the artist gradually eliminates the discrepancies between what is seen and what is drawn, until the image on the flat surface begins to resemble a view of the world as it might be seen through a pane of glass. The iterative process of the artist corresponds to the conjectures and refutations of the scientist in creating a theory of nature.

and prior experience are as important and relevant as the internal reasoning machinery.

Theories of intelligence are largely dependent on whether we define intelligence to be a natural phenomenon appearing in living organisms (especially man), or whether we define it to be an abstract facility with certain specified properties. If intelligence is viewed as an outgrowth of specific biological structures, then it is reasonable to ask whether a single or coherent mechanism produces intelligent behavior, or whether intelligence is the result of a number of relatively independent processes. From a practical standpoint, we might also ask what kinds of measurements are needed to predict human performance in specified tasks requiring intelligence.

For example, if intelligence is a highly integrated process, then it is quite

---

 ## BOX 1-2 Psychological/Performance Theories of Intelligence

Plato drew a distinction between the cognitive aspects of human nature (thinking, reasoning, problem solving) and what he termed the *hormic* aspects (emotions, feelings, passions, and the will). He theorized on the cause of individual differences in intellect and personality: *The God who created you has put different metals into your composition—gold into those who are fit to be rulers, silver into those who are to act as their executives, and a mixture of iron and brass into those whose task it will be to cultivate the soil or manufacture goods.*

The modern concept of intelligence was formulated by Herbert Spencer and Sir Francis Galton in the nineteenth century—they believed in the existence of a general ability distinct from, and in addition to, more specialized cognitive abilities. Galton also introduced some of the tools and methodology by which statistical correlation between tests of performance became the basis for answering questions about the relationships between different cognitive skills and general intelligence. Galton, and in 1890, James Cattell devised "intelligence tests" based largely on sensory and motor functions (e.g., color discrimination, time perception, accuracy of hand movement, description of imagery) under the assumption that these easily measured quantities were highly correlated with intelligence. In 1895, Alfred Binet argued for more direct testing of cognitive skills (e.g., verbal comprehension, moral sensibility, aesthetic appreciation). Binet, in 1904, also introduced the concept of "mental age," closely related to the idea of intelligence quotient (IQ: 100 times mental age divided by chronological age).

Early in this century, C. Spearman employed a technique called "factor analysis" to provide statistical evidence for the predominance of a general cognitive ability. Spearman proposed a "two-factor" theory of intelligence: Every intellectual activity has two underlying components, one specific to that particular activity, and one common to all intellectual activities. This second factor was called "general intelligence" or *g*. Following Spearman, L.L. Thurstone developed and employed a more advanced form of factor analysis to argue that Spearman's general factor *g* might be an artifact arising out of a set of primary mental abilities: spatial visualization, perceptual ability, verbal comprehension, numerical ability, memory, word fluency, and inductive and deductive reasoning. There was also evidence that these primary mental abilities were the base of a hierarchy in which the primary abilities first cluster into verbal, numerical, and logical groupings, and then finally into Spearman's *g*.

In the same time period as the work of Thurstone (1930–1950), Cyril Burt* used new statistical methods in an attempt to determine the relative contributions of heredity and environment to IQ test perform-

---

*See "The Real Error of Cyril Burt" in Gould (Gould 81) for a description of how Burt faked some of his data.

possible that a single number, such as an IQ test score, could be a good predictor of a human's ability to perform in almost any intellectual task domain. To the extent that intelligence arises from a loosely integrated combination of different mechanisms, prediction of human performance would depend on tests much more closely related to the specific task of interest. Most psychological theories of intelligence, and intelligence tests that implicitly arise from these theories, assume that intelligence is a composite of a relatively small number of component factors, possibly dominated by a single integrating factor. These theories can be called "performance theories," since they are based on measurements of performance and make assertions about relationships and correlations between different tests of performance (see Box 1-2). Such theories are largely empirical and, while they have

---

BOX 1-2 *(continued)*

ance, and by implication, to human intelligence.

Between 1950 and 1980, Guilford [Guilford1967] formulated what was intended to be a comprehensive theory of the structure of human intellect. He identified three classes of variables:

1. The five activities or operations performed—cognition (immediate awareness of information), memory, convergent (logical) thinking, divergent (creative) thinking, and evaluation
2. The material or content on which the operations are performed—images, symbols, concepts, and nonverbal social perceptions
3. The six products which result from the operations—unitary items, classes, relations, systems, transformations, and implications

Guilford's system results in $5 \times 4 \times 6 = 120$ separate factors or abilities contributing to intelligence. There is no general factor. Guilford and his associates used factor analytic methods on performance tests

to prove the existence of many (but not all) of the factors he defined.

Raymond Cattell (no relation to James Cattell, circa 1890), working in the same time frame as that of Guilford, proposed and provided statistical tests for an alternative theory of intelligence in which g combined two distinct general abilities: "crystallized" and "fluid" intelligence. Crystallized abilities are based on learned cultural knowledge (vocabulary, numerical skills, mechanical knowledge), while fluid intelligence relates to innate perceptual and reasoning abilities.

Most of the above work used statistical methods to determine how mental processes vary from individual to individual, and to study the relationships among these mental processes in a single individual. One exception to such studies, which are based largely on statistical analysis of performance tests, is the work of Piaget (described in Chapter 5) who proposed a qualitative theory of how intelligence evolves in an individual—from "sensory," "concrete," and "subjective" in the child, to "abstract" and "objective" in the adult. There are also the more

cognitive-type theories of G.H. Thomson and E.L. Thorndike (1920–1940) who hypothesized that general intelligence is a function of the number of structural bonds (or stimulus-response connections) that have been formed between specific mental abilities. Performance on any one task would be the result of activation of many of these bonds.

In retrospect, as noted by Butcher [Butcher 73]: "During the first forty years of this century, the idea of intelligence or general mental ability was found to be useful and important by psychologists. . . . Recently, however, the concept has become less generally acceptable and more exposed to various kinds of criticism."

Almost all psychological investigators employ a paradigm based on statistical testing for the existence of presupposed intellectual structures. We believe that the study of the *computational requirements* for intelligent behavior—the underlying theme of work in the field of artificial intelligence—will provide a more productive means for understanding the nature of both human and machine intelligence.

significant practical utility, they offer very little insight into the nature of intelligence. As noted by Butcher [Butcher 73],

> The study of human intelligence has yielded a large accumulation of knowledge about individual differences, but very little about the basic laws of cognitive functioning. . . . For a concept to be valuable it should have more than purely statistical support, and be more than a blind abstraction from a set of correlated performances.

Most of our concern in subsequent chapters will be with what might be called structural/function theories of intelligence. These are theories that propose certain physical or formal structures as the basis for intelligent behavior, and then examine the functionality that results. For example, if we assume that intelligence is a result of formal logical inference, then we might ask if there are human capabilities that could be shown to be unachievable in the formal system because of limitations inherent in logical reasoning. In Chapters 2 and 4 we show that logical systems do indeed have limitations we do not usually ascribe to people.

Finally, there are (largely philosophical) theories about the physical conditions necessary for the mechanization of intelligence; we call these existence theories. For example, there is a school of thought that asserts that intelligence is a nonphysical property of living organisms, and cannot be re-created in a machine. Another school holds that intelligence is an emergent property of organic matter—silicon[2] is inadequate, but when we eventually

---

[2]"Silicon" is a shorthand way of referring to silicon-based microcircuits that are used in digital computers.

learn how to build machines out of organic compounds, we might have a chance of inducing intelligent behavior. One other school believes that intelligence is a functional property of formal systems, and is completely independent of any physical embodiment. This latter viewpoint is the one with which we will be primarily concerned.

Theories of Mind

As previously noted, we will extensively discuss the attributes of intelligence and intelligent behavior, describing mechanisms that are capable of achieving such behavior in both living organisms and machines. However, we will not provide a precise definition of intelligence; this book as a whole is our contribution in this regard. Nor will we do much to "explain" or elucidate the conscious awareness that seems to be an essential component of human intelligence. Introspectively, there appears to be an "inner entity," the *mind*, which views the world through the body's sensory organs, "thinks," "understands," and causes the body to react in an appropriate manner.

A primary concern of philosophy is the attempt to understand the relationship between the internal world of our conscious awareness and the external physical world. Plato (c.428–c.348 B.C.) held that the mind (*psyche*) was in charge of the body and directed its movements. In the *Phaedrus* Plato spoke of the mind as having both *appetitive desires* and *higher desires*, and having also a rational capacity to control, direct, and adjudicate between these two types of desires. Later theories held that man was made of two substances, mind and matter. The theory that the mind and body are distinct, known as "dualism," was given its classical formulation by Descartes in the seventeenth century. In his *Discourse on Method* (1637) he argued that the universe consists of two different substances: mind, or thinking substance, and matter, which can be explained by science and mathematics. Only in man are mind and matter joined together. His concept was that mind was an immaterial nonextended substance that engages in rational thought, feeling, and willing. Matter conforms to the laws of physics with the exception of the human body, which Descartes believed is causally affected by the mind, and which causally produces certain mental events. A basic problem that must be dealt with in this theory is how interaction can occur between the nonphysical and the physical.

The current dominant school of thought[3] regards mind as being a purely physical phenomenon. Sagan [Sagan 78] sums up this view succinctly: "My fundamental premise about the brain is that its workings—what we sometimes call 'mind'—are a consequence of anatomy and physiology and nothing else." A similar view by Restak [Restak 84] is based on a belief that signals from the brain will some day be understood:

> Since the development of appropriate technologies, it has become obvious that thoughts, emotions, and even elementary sensations are accompanied by changes in the state of the brain . . . a thought without a change in brain activity is

impossible . . . to understand the "mind," therefore, it is necessary to understand the brain—how concepts are arrived at, the mechanisms underlying perceptions, memory, the neuro-chemistry of our emotions, and so on.

Searle [Searle 84] comments on the mind-body problem: "Mental phenomena, all mental phenomena whether conscious or unconscious, visual or auditory, pains, tickles, itches, thoughts, indeed, all of our mental life are caused by processes going on in the brain."

The *information processing model* is used by Newell and Simon [Newell 72]. They view formal logic as a way of capturing ideas by symbols, and the algorithmic alteration of such symbols as leading to mindlike activity: "The persistence of concern with the mind-body problem can be attributed in part to the apparent radical incongruity and incommensurability of 'ideas'—the material of thought—with the tangible biological substances of the nervous system."

Those who take the above computational point of view feel that the mind-body problem will disappear when we have demonstrated the operation of mind using formalisms and algorithms for manipulating symbols.

One should not think that all modern researchers look at duality with scorn. In his final book, *The Mystery of the Mind*, the famous neurosurgeon Wilder Penfield [Penfield 78] doubts that an understanding of the brain will ever lead to an explanation of the mind: "Consciousness of man, the mind, is something not to be reduced to brain mechanisms." Another example of this point of view is contained in *The Self and the Brain* by Karl Popper

---

[3]Thomas Hobbes (1588–1679), John Locke (1632–1704), and David Hume (1711–1776) originated the idea that thoughts obey physical laws and can be characterized as computational processes.

and John Eccles [Popper 77], an updated plea for dualism, the belief that the brain and the mind are distinct entities.

Until someone provides convincing proof of the physical basis of mind, we can expect the mind-body debate to continue.

HOW CAN INTELLIGENCE BE MEASURED OR EVALUATED?

Assessing Human Intelligence

As noted in the previous section, while an intuitive concept of intelligence exists, there is no formal or scientific definition of intelligence that is widely accepted. If intelligence cannot be defined, then it certainly cannot be measured in any precise or comprehensive manner. If intelligence tests do not measure *intelligence*, what do they measure? The purpose of most of these tests is to predict the future performance of the person being tested with respect to an ability to compete or perform in an academic program or in a skilled work task. Whether or not an "intelligence test" actually does have the required predictive power can only be determined by extensive testing in the specific application area.

There are a number of intelligence tests in widespread use, one of the most popular being the Terman-Merrill revision of the Binet-Simon intelligence scale. The original Binet-Simon work was performed in the period 1905–1911. Binet insisted on three cardinal principles for using his test:

1. The scores are a practical device and are not intended as the basis for a theory of intellect. They do not de-fine anything innate or permanent. What they measure is not "intelligence."
2. The scale is a rough, empirical guide for identifying mildly retarded and learning-disabled children who need special help. It is not a device for ranking normal children.
3. Whatever the cause of difficulty in children identified for help, emphasis should be placed on improvement through special training. Low scores should not be used to mark children as innately incapable.

All of his warnings were disregarded, and his scale was used as a routine device for testing all children [Gould 81]. The Binet-Simon test was superseded by Terman's 1916 standard version, and then by the Terman-Merrill revision of 1937, and by a later revision in 1960. Table 1-3 lists some of the categories of items found in the 1960 revision. It is interesting to note that the procedure for selecting questions for this test was that the questions had to satisfy certain preconceived notions of what results the test should produce. This is standard practice in all intelligence test construction. For example, questions that yield systematically higher scores for either boys or girls are eliminated. By use of question selection and scoring procedures, the test was constructed so that for the white American population, biased somewhat toward urban and above-average socioeconomic level persons, the scores would have a *normal distribution* with an average score of 100, and a standard deviation of 16. This means that 50 percent of the reference group (white Americans) would score under 100; 85 percent would score

---

> TABLE 1-3 ■ Categories of Questions that Appear in the Terman-Merrill Version of Binet-Simon Intelligence Scales
>
> | | |
> |---|---|
> | Obey simple commands | Comprehension |
> | Identify object by use | Opposite analogies |
> | Repeat digits | Pictures alike and different |
> | Response to pictures | Memory for sentences |
> | Repeat digits reversed | Vocabulary |
> | Memory for stories | Picture completion (picture of a man) |
> | Find absurdities in pictures | Discriminate animal pictures |
> | Picture vocabulary (recognize pictorial objects) | |

under 116; 97.5 percent would score under 132, etc.

Another commonly used intelligence test, the Wechsler intelligence scale, uses separate tests for adults and for children. This test is divided into two main parts, one to test predominantly verbal ability, and a second to test performance (see Table 1-4). Even though the Wechsler and the Binet tests have somewhat different philosophies and different categories of questions, they use similar principles of test construction and produce scores that are in reasonable agreement.

Starting in the 1960s, the role and value of intelligence tests have been seriously challenged. In particular, critics have argued that these tests take too narrow a view of intelligence, and that they are based on such dubious assumptions as: (a) A child is born with a fixed or predetermined level of intelligence; (b) IQ tests can measure this intelligence; (c) IQ scores will show little variation from early childhood to old age; and (d) the tests employed, relatively unchanged since their introduction in the early 1900s, are good predictors of human performance. Not surprisingly, political and social concerns have been intermixed with issues of scien-

> TABLE 1-4 ■ Categories of Questions that Appear in the Wechsler Intelligence Scale
>
> **I. Verbal Tests**
>
> General information (who is President of the United States?)
> General comprehension (what would you do if? . . . Why do we usually? . . .)
> Arithmetic reasoning (simple mental arithmetic)
> Remember series of digits forward and backward
> Similarities (pairs of words: subject has to tell how they are alike)
> Vocabulary (explain meaning of words)
>
> **II. Performance Tests**
>
> Digit symbol coding (subject must assign digits and symbols to pictures)
> Picture completion (subject must detect nose missing from face)
> Block design (construct color-pattern designs in duplication of given patterns)
> Picture arrangement (subject arranges pictures to tell a story)

tific validity in addressing the question of what is reasonable and meaningful in regard to the testing of human intelligence.

Assessing Machine Intelligence

If one were offered a machine purported to be intelligent, what would be an appropriate method of evaluating this claim? The most obvious approach might be to give the machine an IQ test. As will be seen in later chapters, we already know how to build machines that can perform quite well on selected portions of such a test. For example, machines can currently solve high school algebra problems, solve the type of geometric analogy problems used on IQ tests, answer questions about the content of a simple story, parse English sentences, etc. However, none of this would be completely satisfactory because the machine would have to be specially prepared for any specific task that it was asked to perform. The task could not be described to the machine in a normal conversation (verbal or written) if the specific nature of the task was not already programmed into the machine. Such considerations led many people to believe that the ability to communicate freely using some form of natural language is an essential attribute of an intelligent entity.

In 1950, Alan Turing proposed an "imitation game" to provide an operational answer to the question, "Can a machine think?" [Dennett 85, Hodges 83, Turing 50]. The game is played with three people, a man, a woman, and an interrogator who may be of either sex. The interrogator stays in a room apart from the other two, and attempts to determine which of the other two is the man and which is the woman. The man tries to convince the interrogator that he is the woman. Communication between the interrogator and each person is by teleprinter, and the interrogator is free to ask any question of the participants.

Suppose we now ask the question, "What will happen when a machine takes the part of the man in this game?" Turing felt that a machine could be considered "intelligent" when the interrogator decides wrongly as often when the game is played with the machine as when the game is played between a man and woman. It should be noted that to accomplish this, the machine must be able to carry out a dialogue in natural language and reason using an enormous database of "world knowledge." The "man-woman" formulation proposed by Turing is not usually stressed in describing the imitation game. Instead, the theme is usually the idea of a machine convincing an interrogator that it is a person.

The Turing test has more historical and philosophical importance than practical value; Turing did not design the test as a useful tool for psychologists. For example, failing the test does not imply lack of intelligence. The important central idea is that the ability to successfully communicate with a discerning person in a free and unbounded conversation is a better indication of intelligence than any other attribute accessible to measurement.

IS MAN THE ONLY INTELLIGENT ANIMAL?

If we examine the attributes of intelligent behavior that were presented in Table 1-1, we can find examples of superior animal performance in each of the attribute categories. Until recently, however, it was believed that only man, of all animals, could produce (as opposed to understand) structured linguistic phrases to communicate meaning. Experiments more fully described in Chapter 6 (Language and Communication) have demonstrated that chimpanzees can learn American Sign Language (ASL) and can learn to assign word meanings to physical tokens (e.g., small colored plastic disks), and then arrange these tokens into structured sentences to communicate with their trainers. Thus in an objective sense, it appears possible that man differs from the higher mammals mainly in degree of intellectual ability rather than in having some unique and unshared capability.

In a related sense, recent work by Gordon Gallup [Gallup 77] addresses the question: "Do minds exist in species other than our own?" Gallup defines "mind," "consciousness," and "self-awareness" to mean essentially the same thing. His operational test for self-awareness is that an organism can identify itself in a mirror; for example, a child can recognize his reflection at approximately a year and one half to two years of age. Gallup discovered that while humans, chimpanzees, and orangutans can learn to recognize themselves in mirrors, no other primates can! Thus even though gorillas appear to possess some degree of linguistic competence (see Patterson's work with Koko [Patterson 78]), gorillas fail this particular test for self-awareness. Our understanding of the relationship between self-awareness, language, and intelligence is still at a very primitive stage.

THE MACHINERY OF INTELLIGENCE

Reliance on Paradigms

It would appear that we deal with the world by relying on *paradigms*, overall strategies or frameworks that we use as the high-level plan for solving various problems. The use of paradigms allows us to reduce the complexity of our environment by discarding most sensory data and selecting only that which is relevant. Thus, we are usually unconscious of breathing, body support pressures, background hums and noises, but any of these could become important in special situations; e.g., consciousness of breathing could be important to an astronaut in a space suit. If the paradigm for dealing with a situation is not adequate, then performance will be poor: *If the only tool you have is a hammer, you tend to treat everything as if it were a nail.* For example, the city dweller may not have the proper paradigms for dealing with a jungle environment. His "city paradigms" would not help him to focus on the necessary sensory data; he would not be able to properly interpret the jungle environment data being received, and he would not be able to invoke the appropriate actions for survival.

Two Basic Paradigms

There is evidence to show that the two hemispheres of the human brain are specialized to deal with problems in different ways by the use of two distinct types of paradigms. The sequential (or logical) paradigm is based on a problem solving

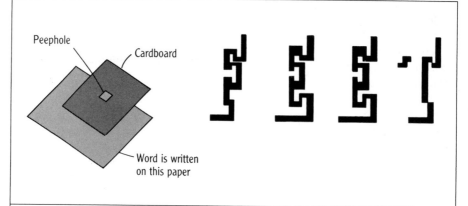

FIGURE 1-1   Experiment Illustrating the Distinction Between the Sequential and
Gestalt Paradigms for Problem Solving and Perception.

Subject is asked to read a word. Subject is not permitted to see the word as a whole, but must examine it by looking through a small peephole in a piece of cardboard that he or she can slide over the paper on which the word is written.

approach that considers only a small portion of the available data at any given time, while the parallel (or *gestalt)* paradigm processes data on a global basis, or *all at once.* That these are fundamentally different capabilities can be seen from the experiment offered in Fig. 1-1. A human subject is given an opaque card with a small window in it and asked to explore an English word (printed in a rather unusual type font) by moving the card over it. The subject will not be able to perceive the word because all of the pattern data must be viewed at once to reveal the structure. The important point here is that problems that can be successively decomposed into simple and relatively independent parts can be effectively solved using the sequential/logical paradigm. On the other hand, many problems, especially those of a perceptual nature as in the example, do not permit decomposi-

tion, and can be effectively solved only by employing the gestalt paradigm that can deal with global information.

In most normal people, the left hemisphere of the brain is specialized to deal with tasks amenable to a sequential paradigm. These include language understanding and production, logical reasoning, planning, and time sense. The right hemisphere of the brain is more competent to deal with spatial tasks and tasks requiring a global (gestalt) synthesis. These include comparing and identifying visual imagery,[4] visual and analogic reasoning (including,

---

[4]There is evidence to support the surprising discovery that mental images are neither generated nor manipulated by the normal sensory-based visual system; a module in the left hemisphere, but not language-based, appears to provide the necessary competence. There is no similar module in the right hemisphere [Gazzaniga 85, p. 134]

perhaps, dreaming), and body sense and coordination.

Some of the evidence supporting the concept of specialization of the two brain hemispheres with respect to the gestalt and sequential paradigms has come from *split brain* experiments with subjects who have had brain surgery to control epilepsy. The connection between the right and left hemispheres is severed so that signals no longer flow between the hemispheres. By examining the subjects of such experiments, it has been found that the human brain can support two separate and distinct "personalities," one in each hemisphere, as described in Box 1-3. The philosophical implications of this finding are rather staggering and are still being investigated.

ARTIFICIAL INTELLIGENCE (AI)

The Mechanization of Thought

The idea of man converting an inanimate object into a "human-like" thinking entity is an old one. In Greek myth we have the story of Pygmalion, a king of Cyprus who fashions a female figure of ivory that was brought to life by Aphrodite. In the Golem legend of the late sixteenth century, Rabbi Löw of Prague breathes life into a figure of clay. In the nineteenth century there is the story of the scientist Frankenstein, who creates a living creature.

During the seventeenth century, the idea arose of converting thought into a formal notation and using a calculating device to carry out the reasoning operations. In 1650, the English philosopher Thomas Hobbes proposed the idea that thinking is a rule-based computational process, analogous to arithmetic. Gottfried Wilhelm Leibnitz (1646–1716) describes his book *De Arte Combinatorica* (1661) as containing "a general method in which all truths would be reduced to a kind of calculation." Much later, in 1854, George Boole published *An Investigation of the Laws of Thought, on which are Founded the Mathematical Theories of Logic and Probabilities*. In the first chapter he states, "The design of the following treatise is to investigate the fundamental operations of the mind by which *reasoning* is performed."

The dream of devising a formal system that could be a basis for all reasoning seemed to be almost at hand with the publication of Russell and Whitehead's *Principia Mathematica* (1910–1913). The codification of logic and the reduction of significant portions of mathematics to the language of logic appeared to provide the means by which people (or machines) could do mathematics without having to understand what was actually happening; it would be sufficient to manipulate the symbols according to permissible logical transformations. Even the sequencing of the transformations could be done "blindly" (mechanically).

It even seemed possible that all questions of philosophy could be phrased and answered in such a logical language. The logical positivists, extending the empiricism of David Hume, believed that only within the framework of a logical language could philosophical problems be raised with any degree of precision: All problems are either questions of fact or questions of logic; the former are properly relegated to the sciences and philosophy simply becomes a form of logical analysis. Thus,

| BOX 1-3   Split-Brain Experiments

If we were to cut in half a complicated mechanism, such as a car, a computer, or a person, we would certainly not expect each of the halves to continue to function. Nevertheless, when the human brain is cut in half by severing the major connecting bundle of nerve fibers linking the two hemispheres, the *corpus callosum* (see Fig. 1-2), the two resulting pieces continue to operate independently, as if two separate personalities now exist in place of the original individual (see [Ornstein 73] and [Gazzaniga 85]).

Since we devote a significant portion of Chapter 2 to a discussion of the structure and functioning of the brain, here we merely note the following facts. The brain, in terms of its outward appearance, is bilaterally symmetrical. The two similar appearing "hemispheres" of brain tissue are spatially separated, and normally communicate through the *corpus callosum*. Each half of the brain controls muscles on only one side of the body, and receives direct sensory inputs from sense organs monitoring only the left or right half of the physical space surrounding the individual. For example, nerve cells in each eye that monitor the left half of the visual field have direct connections only to the right hemisphere. (This right-left "crossover," which also occurs in muscular control, has no special implications for this discussion.)

In a *cerebral commissurotomy* operation, performed to alleviate severe epileptic seizures in some patients who did not respond to medication or other forms of treatment, the *corpus callosum* is cut to prevent

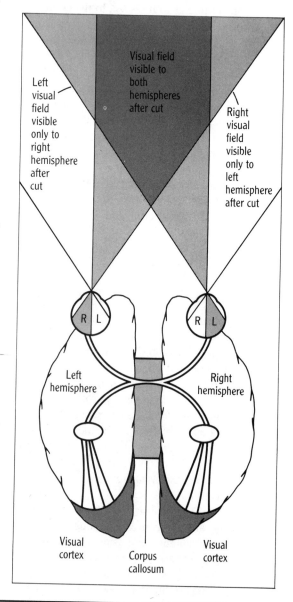

FIGURE 1-2   The Split Brain.

Cutting the corpus callosum effectively separates the two hemispheres of the human brain.

Localized functions relevant to the split-brain experiments: *Left hemisphere*: right visual half-field; right hand; right ear; left nostril; main language center. *Right hemisphere*: left visual half-field; left hand; left ear; right nostril; simple language communication.

as Barrett [Barrett 79] notes, ". . .when Philosophy, which was supposed to question everything, turns to questioning itself, it finds that it has vanished," i.e., it is reduced to physics and logic. However, at least in part for reasons touched on below, the dream of a formal system for reasoning began to fade in the 1930s.

Formal investigation of the limits of mechanical reasoning did not occur until the twentieth century. Alan Turing, a British mathematician, carried out investigations using a conceptual model that he called an automaton (now known as a Turing machine). In the 1950s, Turing was able to prove formally that there is a "universal automaton" that can simulate the performance of any other automaton if it is given an appropriate description of that automaton.[5] In addition, Turing proved that certain types of automata could never be built, e.g., one that could tell whether an arbitrary program run on an arbitrary automaton would ever halt. Results concerning the limitations of automata are described in Chapter 2.

Also in this era, John von Neumann dealt with the questions of how complex a device or construct need be in order to be self-reproductive, i.e., to make a copy of itself. He also investigated the problem of how to design reliable devices that must be made from parts that can malfunction [von Neuman 56a]. He surmised that autom-

---

[5]Simulation of one computer type by another is now quite common. In fact, one often simulates a computer on another type of computer in order to verify the design prior to fabrication.

BOX 1-3 (continued)

a seizure starting in one hemisphere from spreading to the other. Although it first appeared that there were no undesirable aftereffects, tests later showed that "split-brain" patients were indeed different after the operation.

In one test situation, the split-brain subject is seated in front of a screen that hides his hands from his direct view. His gaze is fixed at a spot on the center of the screen and the word "nut" is flashed very briefly on the left half of the screen. This image goes to the right hemisphere of his brain which controls the left side of his body. The subject then uses his left hand to pick out (by sense of touch) a nut from a pile of objects hidden from his view. But he cannot verbally report what word was flashed on the screen because the image (of the word "nut") could not reach the left-brain hemisphere where the main centers for language production are located and the left hemisphere receives no direct sensory inputs from the left hand. The language portion of the subject's brain controlling conversation with the experimenter seems unaware of what the subject's left hand is doing. If the word flashed on the screen remains longer than one tenth of a second, the subject can move his eyes so that the word is also projected to the left hemisphere. If the subject can move his eyes freely, information goes to both hemispheres, and this is why the deficiencies caused by severing the hemispheric connections are not readily apparent in daily activities.

Experiments with split-brain patients tend to confirm knowledge obtained through other means in normal human subjects. These results indicate the separation, or at least dominance of skills, to individual hemispheres, based on whether they are sequential/analytic (left hemisphere) or spatial/gestalt (right hemisphere). While there is still some controversy regarding the precise nature of such specialization (Gardner82), there can be little argument with the finding that split-brain patients exhibit two distinct streams of consciousness. It is reasonable to ask whether *cerebral commissurotomy* produces a splitting or doubling of the mind, or whether it exposes a multiplicity previously present.

ata whose "complexity" is below a certain level can only produce less complicated offspring, whereas those above a certain level can reproduce themselves or even construct higher entities.

In recent years, the information processing paradigm has become a popular model for explaining the reasoning ability of the human mind. As stated by Simon [Simon 81], "At the root of intelligence are symbols, with their denotative power and their susceptibility to manipulation . . . and symbols can be manufactured of almost anything that can be arranged and patterned and combined." This view, that intelligence is independent of the mechanisms by which the symbol processing is accomplished, is held by most researchers in the field of artificial intelligence.

The Computer and the Two Paradigms

The digital computer is the only device that has been used to achieve any significant degree of artificial (machine) intelligence. However, the conventional digital computer is a sequential symbol manipulator, and is primarily suitable for tasks that can be broken down into a series of simple steps. Thus, it is only effective for realizing one of the two basic paradigms employed in human intelligence: the sequential paradigm. Attempts to duplicate human abilities involving the global (gestalt) paradigm, such as visual perception, have been strikingly inferior, even for visual tasks that people consider extremely simple.

At the present time there is a vast difference in favor of the human brain, as compared to the computer, with respect to logical complexity, memory characteristics, and learning ability. Computer-based AI must be specialized to very restricted domains to be at all comparable to human performance. For example, games with a limited number of positions and possible moves are well matched to the computer's great search speed and infallible memory.

How can we Distinguish between Mechanical and Intelligent Behavior?

Two basic attributes of intelligence are learning and understanding. One might think that an artificial device possessing these capabilities is indeed intelligent. However, we can illustrate the presence of both of these attributes in the very limited context of a coin-matching game (Box 1-4). In this example, the computer *learns* the playing pattern of its opponent, and in practice will beat almost all human opponents who are not familiar with the details of the program. The computer demonstrates its *understanding* of the game situation by its outstanding ability to predict the opponent's moves. However, the computer starts with the key elements of its later understanding, since the programmer has provided the model of choosing heads or tails based on the statistics of the opponent's previous four-move patterns. The only active role played by the program is to collect the statistics of play, and to make choices based on these statistical data. To the outside observer the program seems intelligent, but once we examine its actual details we see that it is quite simple and mechanical. Some might point out that this same argument can also be applied to human performance; it is conceivable that most of the basic models necessary for intelli-

BOX 1-4   A Coin-Matching Program

The following computer program for playing a coin-matching game seems to the external observer to be intelligent, but turns out to be quite simple and mechanical in design. This illustrates the point that it is difficult to judge intelligence based strictly on observed performance on a specific task.

The computer plays against a single opponent in a game of "matching coins." On each play of the game, the computer makes a choice between heads (H) or tails (T), and indicates its choice by printing H or T. Before looking at the computer's choice the human also decides on H or T, trying to match the choice of the computer. After making a decision, the human opponent pushes either the H or T button on the computer console. If the human matches the computer, he gains one point, if not he loses one point. If the score reaches +25 the human wins, if the score reaches −25, the computer wins. The human is not allowed to flip a coin or use some other random device in making his choice.

Typically, when the game first begins, the score stays close to zero. Then, as the computer observes the behavior of its nonrandom human opponent it finds certain regularities in his play, and is able to predict his moves in advance well enough to beat almost every human player. Even if the human tries to act randomly, he cannot accomplish this well enough to fool the computer.

Thus, this program exhibits the two main attributes of intelligent behavior: (1) it learns, i.e., modifies its own strategy of play to take advantage of the way its opponent is playing, and (2) it understands, i.e., it knows the rules of the game, and after a learning period, it predicts how its opponent will behave, and acts appropriately.

The way the computer accomplishes this apparently sophisticated behavior is actually rather simple: the program forms a table of all possible four-move sequences (there are 16 such sequences), as shown in Fig. 1-3. During the course of play, each time a particular four-move sequence by the opponent is followed by an H, the count in the H column in that row of the table is incremented, and similarly for a T. Thus, after a sufficiently long period of play, the computer can predict the most likely next move of its opponent based on his last four moves.

The basic approach described above can be augmented with a number of additional features designed to keep the human from guessing how the program works and for making it look human in its performance. For example, every once in a while, based on a random process within the program, the computer will make a move which is less likely to win. Obviously, this type of bluffing cannot be done too often.

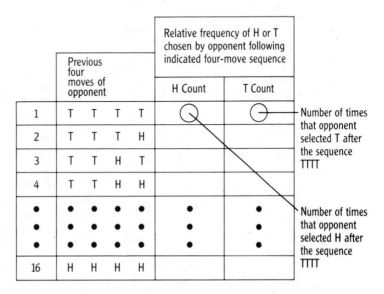

FIGURE 1-3   Prediction Table Developed by the Program for Playing the Coin-Matching Game.

gent performance are inborn, and all we do is select the proper model and adjust the parameters.

The Role of Representation in Intelligent Behavior

As indicated in the previous section, a paradigm is an overall approach for dealing with a class of problems. One of the most critical elements in the specific realization of a paradigm is the *form* in which the relevant knowledge is encoded; we devote all of Chapter 3 to this important subject. To illustrate the role played by the selected representation in solving a problem, consider the example depicted in Fig. 1-4, which shows a configuration of 17 sticks. The problem is to remove five sticks so as to leave three squares with no extra sticks remaining. You are required to find all such solutions! You might try to find one such solution before you read further.

    If the primitive element you manipulate in searching for a solution is the individual stick, and you remove five sticks at a time and check the result, then even if you are careful not to repeat a particular trial twice, you must make over 6000 trials to be sure that you have found all possible solutions. (There are about 6000 combinations of 17 sticks taken 5 at a time.)

    If the primitive element you manipulate is a square, you can select three squares at a time and retain the configuration if there are exactly five sticks left to be removed. Then there are only 20 unique configurations that must be examined to find all solutions, and there is a 300:1 reduction in the number of trials over the approach based on representing

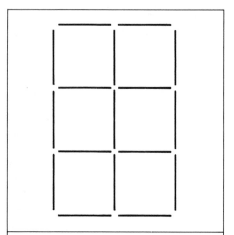

FIGURE 1-4

The Stick Configuration Problem: the Role of Representation in Problem Solving.

The problem is to remove five sticks so as to leave three of the original squares with no extra sticks, and to do this in all possible ways.

the given configuration as a collection of individual sticks. (There are 20 combinations of 6 squares taken 3 at a time.)

    Finally, we note that there are 17 sticks, and after removing five, the remaining 12 can form three squares only if these squares are noncontiguous (i.e., have no sides in common). It is easily seen that there are only two configurations of three noncontiguous squares, and both of these are valid solutions. Here, by using a representation that allowed us to employ deductive reasoning, the required effort is reduced by a factor of 3000:1.

SUMMARY AND DISCUSSION

Intelligence is more an open collection of attributes than it is a single well-defined entity. Some of the attributes most closely identified with intelligence are learning, reasoning, understanding, linguistic competence, purposeful behavior, and effective interaction with the environment (including perception). Since intelligence has no clear definition, differing theories of intelligence are not necessarily in conflict, but often differ mainly in the assumed definition of intelligence as either (1) a natural phenomenon appearing in living organisms, especially man, or (2) an arbitrarily specified set of abilities.

Most psychological theories of intelligence are what might be called "performance theories" since they are based on measurements of performance in specified skills, and make assertions about the relationships and correlations between different tests of performance. For example, correlations between tests have been used by investigators attempting to determine if human intelligence is the result of a single coherent mechanism or a collection of loosely integrated independent processes. Such theories are largely empirical and offer very little insight into the nature of intelligence. Most of our concern in the later portions of this book is with understanding how specified abstract structures can produce intelligent behavior.

Intelligence tests, whether for people or machines, have some practical utility, but cannot be expected to accurately measure an undefinable quantity. Another complicating factor in our understanding of intelligence is the role played by consciousness, and the relation between mind and brain.

It is possible to assume that most intelligent behavior arises from one of two distinct paradigms (strategies): In the sequential (or logical) paradigm, a single path is found which links available knowledge and evidence to some desired conclusion; in the parallel (gestalt) paradigm, all connections between evidence and possible conclusions are appraised simultaneously. There is some evidence that the human brain has separate specialized machinery for each of these two paradigms.

A key insight provided by work in artificial intelligence is that intelligent behavior not only requires stored knowledge and methods for manipulating this knowledge, but is critically dependent on the relationship between the specific encoding of the knowledge and the purpose for which this knowledge is used. This concept, the central role of representation in intelligent behavior, is one of our major themes.

The Ultimate Limits of AI. We have briefly sketched the nature of human and machine intelligence. In later chapters we will repeatedly return to the questions, "What can a machine know about the world in which it exists?" and "What are the mechanisms needed to acquire, understand, and employ such knowledge?" We will also address a number of basic questions concerning the limits and ultimate role of machine intelligence:

- Can man create a machine more intelligent than himself?
- Are there components of man's intelligence that cannot be found in any animal or duplicated in a machine?
- Can all intelligent behavior be duplicated by the current approach to AI, namely by decomposing a given problem into a sequence of simple tasks

or subproblems that can be precisely stated and solved?

- Can a machine ever exhibit fully human behavior without having been human and thus properly socialized? In a more limited sense, is human intelligence in some way bound up in the *human experience* or even human heredity?
- Is intelligent behavior realizable, or even conceivable, with the type of computing instruments currently available?
- Is intelligent behavior in some way a property of organic structure, and thus not achievable by nonorganic machinery?

To illustrate how far we still have to go to achieve a human level of performance, consider how much information would have to be stored in a machine to answer random questions of the following type:

If a young man of 20 can gather 10 pounds of blackberries in one day, and a young woman of 18 can gather 9, how many will they gather if they go out in the woods together?

2

The Brain
and the Computer

The human brain is the most highly organized and complex structure in the known universe. What do we really know about this remarkable organ and 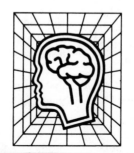 where does this knowledge come from?

Our understanding of the human brain is based on:

1. Physiological and psychological investigations, going back at least 2500 years[6] to the work of Hippocrates, that attempt to catalog and relate brain structure and function by experiment and direct observation

2. Analogy to the mechanical devices built by man that attempt to duplicate some of the brain's functional abilities

We will review some of the anatomical knowledge about the brain's architecture, but there is little hope that the structures we can currently observe and describe will shed much light on how the brain really functions. In a device as complex as the brain, function is too deeply encoded in structure to be deciphered without already knowing the relationships for which we are searching. We can trace some of the sensory and motor pathways for a short distance into the brain, but once we pass beyond the point of direct sensor signal transmission, conditioning, and reflex behavior, we have

---

[6]Knowledge of the neurological symptoms resulting from specific brain injuries existed as early as 3000 B.C. For example, the Edward Smith Papyrus, a surgical treatise, describes the location of certain sensory and motor control areas in the brain.

little understanding of what the brain is actually doing.

At present, our best hope for understanding the brain and the nature of human intelligence appears to be through analogy with the computer and the associated mathematical theory of computation. This may be a false hope, both with respect to understanding and to man's attempts to build an intelligent device in his own image. Historically, attempts have been made to explain the brain's behavior in terms of the most advanced artifacts of the time: in terms of clockwork mechanisms, telephone switchboard analogies, and now the digital computer.

One of our main goals in this chapter is to address the question of whether there are essential differences between the brain and the computer that will prevent machine intelligence from reaching human levels of achievement. In particular, we examine the ultimate capacity of the computer as an intelligence engine:

(a) To what extent is the computer an adequate model for explaining the functioning and competence of the brain?

(b) Are there problems that cannot be solved (in practice or in theory) by a logical device?

(c) Is there a limit to the complexity of a physical device beyond which unreliability renders it successively less (rather than more) competent?

THE HUMAN BRAIN

The human brain is constructed out of more than 10 billion individual components (nerve cells). Can we really hope to understand how something so complex operates, or even determine what it is doing or trying to accomplish? Our current view, that the brain controls the body and is the seat of consciousness, and our understanding of the nature of intelligence and intelligent behavior, is still developing.

In this section we first discuss the evolution of the brain and present a model of its organization based on an evolutionary perspective, the so-called triune brain of MacLean. Next, we describe the architecture of the brain and present two functionally oriented models, one due to Luria, and the second, with more of a philosophical flavor, due to Penfield.

Evolution of the Brain

How did the brain evolve? Is there a continuous spectrum of elaboration reaching from the simplest organisms to man, or is there a sequence of distinct "inventions" that sharply partitions the competence of the organisms with brains incorporating these inventions?

Living organisms have evolved two distinct strategies for obtaining the food and energy necessary to sustain life. Plants are stationary factories that exploit the largely renewable nonliving resources in their environment. Animals eat other living things and must be capable of both finding and catching their prey—i.e., of perception and motion. The physiological correlates of purposive movement through the environment are sensors, muscles, and an effective apparatus for interpretation, coordination, and control.

The essential invention that allowed higher-level animal life to evolve was the nerve cell (Appendix 2-1), and indeed, one of the most important distinctions between animal and plant life (once we pass beyond the most primitive organisms) is that animals possess nervous tissue and plants do not. The nerve cell provides a way of rapidly transmitting sensed information and muscular control commands using a unique combination of electrical and chemical signals, while in plant life, coordination of activity is accomplished exclusively by much slower chemical messages. In addition to a speed advantage, nervous tissue possesses an unusual degree of "plasticity" (modification of function due to environmental influences) that seems to provide the basis for learning.

The first simple animals, like plants, were passive organisms, either stationary or drifters—moved mostly by wind or tide. It is believed that one of man's most distant ancestors was a miniscule wormlike creature that floated in the surface layers of the warm Cambrian seas some 500 million years ago, and that a strip of light-sensing cells and associated neurons developed on its dorsal (back) surface to improve its ability to properly orient and position itself relative to the surface illumination. This strip of nerve cells, by creasing and folding inward (invaginating), first formed a tubular nerve cord and eventually evolved into the spinal cord that distinguishes the vertebrates, including the higher forms of animal life, and ultimately man. (See Table 2-1, Fig. 2-1

TABLE 2-1 ■ The Evolution of Animal Life				
Era	Period	Epoch	Years Before Present (millions)	Life Forms
Cenozoic	Quaternary	Holocene Pleistocene	3	Modern man Early man
	Tertiary	Pliocene Miocene Oligocene Eocene Paleocene	70	Large carnivores Grazing mammals Large mammals Modern mammals Early mammals, modern birds
Mesozoic	Cretaceous		130	Climax of reptiles, conifers, first flowering plants
	Jurassic		165	First true mammals, first birds
	Triassic		200	First dinosaurs, amphibians
Paleozoic	Permian		230	Abundant insect life
	Pennsylvanian		300	First reptiles
	Mississippian		320	Sharks
	Devonian		360	First amphibians
	Silurian		400	First land plants
	Ordovician		480	First fishes
	Cambrian		550	Abundant marine life
Precambrian			600	Very primitive organisms (Few fossils found)

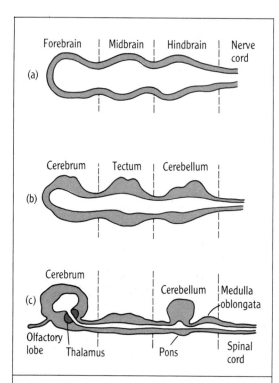

FIGURE 2-1

Evolution of the Vertebrate Brain.

(a) Diagrammatic depiction of the three primary swellings of the neural tube as it is believed to exist in aboriginal chordates, and as it appears in embryonic development of the human brain. (b) Evolutionary developments believed to have occurred in the roof of the primitive neural tube. (After C. M. U. Smith. *The Brain, Towards an Understanding*. Capricorn Books, New York, 1972.) (c) Elaboration of the neural tube in embryonic development of the human brain.

the overall data transmission requirements and time delays, a process called "neurobiotaxis."

It appears that the aboriginal vertebrate brain (the somewhat enlarged anterior end of the spinal cord) underwent a series of three evolutionary expansions to permit the development of the three main distance receptors (See Fig. 2-1): the hindbrain for vibration and sound, the midbrain for vision, and the forebrain for olfaction (smell). In the higher vertebrates, and especially man with his elaborated cortex, the sensory interpretation functions migrated from the lower centers where they originally evolved, and now mainly reside in the cortex itself. Nevertheless, in the growth of the individual, the vastly more complex modern chordate brain still develops from these three bulges in the embryonic neural tube (Fig. 2-1 and 2-2). The hindbrain gives rise to the cerebellum, the main center for muscular coordination; the midbrain enlarges into the optic tectum, which still serves as the main visual center in birds and fish; and the forebrain, which grows into the large multifunction cerebrum in man, is an inconspicuous swelling in many lower vertebrates that is employed to analyze the inputs from their olfactory organs (Color Plate 1). It should be noted that olfaction is the dominant sense in most mammals. Food selection, hunting, socializing, mating, and navigation can all be effectively based on a keen sense of smell. Almost alone among mammals, vision dominates smell in the primates. This is undoubtedly due to the fact that the primates evolved in the trees where three-dimensional vision is critical to survival, and scents quickly fade.

and 2-2, and Box 2-1). In the course of evolutionary development, sense organs tended to develop on the forward (anterior) end of the organisms, for that is the end that first penetrates new environments. Nerve centers concerned with analysis of data from these sensory organs also moved forward to minimize

FIGURE 2-2
Part I: Embryonic Development of the Nervous System.

(a) Ectodermal cells form a neural plate in the midline, and proliferate to form a multicellular layer. (b) As cells at each side of the neural plate proliferate, the sides are elevated (arrows) to form neural folds enclosing a groove. (c) The neural groove deepens and the neural folds come together in the midline (arrows), fuse, and form the neural tube. (d) The neural tube forms the primitive central nervous system. The overlying neural crest will form the peripheral nervous system and related cells. (From E. L. Weinreb. *Anatomy and Physiology*. Addison-Wesley, Reading, Mass., 1984, p.158, with permission.)

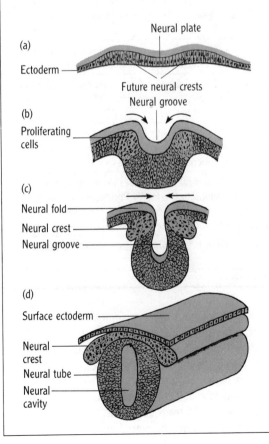

(a)

Neural plate

Ectoderm

Future neural crests
Neural groove

(b)

Proliferating cells

(c)

Neural fold
Neural crest
Neural groove

(d)

Surface ectoderm

Neural crest
Neural tube
Neural cavity

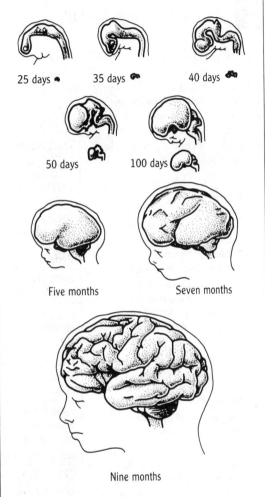

25 days   35 days   40 days

50 days   100 days

Five months   Seven months

Nine months

Part II: Embryonic Development of the Human Brain.

The three main parts of the brain (the forebrain, the midbrain and the hindbrain) originate as prominent swellings at the head end of the early neural tube. The cerebral hemispheres eventually overgrow the midbrain and the hind brain and also partly obscure the cerebellum. The characteristic convolutions and invaginations of the brain's surface do not begin to appear until about the middle of pregnancy. (From *Scientific American*, 1979. Reprinted by permission.)

BOX 2-1   Animal Evolution

The human brain developed in the context of animal evolution. The story of this evolution can be told in terms of a series of "inventions" involving not only sensory and integrative systems (based on the original invention of the nerve cell), but also inventions with respect to:

1. Heredity and reproduction— e.g., DNA, sex
2. Skeletal, effector, and locomotion systems—e.g., bones, muscles, skin, hair, spinal column and vertebrae, legs, arms, fingers, opposing thumb
3. Energy acquisition and utilization via internal transport systems—e.g., ATP, lungs, blood, digestive enzymes, alimentary tract
4. Systems for internal regulation and body maintenance—e.g., the immune system, control of temperature, breathing, heart rate and blood flow, thirst, hunger, emotions

While no one invention stands by itself, a system of classification based on some of the more obvious and easily observable inventions has been devised to distinguish the various life forms and their evolutionary progression. The classification of man is shown in the Table 2-2. Further discussion can be found in Wasserman [Wasserman 73].

TABLE 2-2 ■ Classification of Man
ORGANISM: Man
KINGDOM: Animal (Other kingdoms are plant, Protista, Monera.)
PHYLUM: Chordata (Distinguished by a backbone or notochord, a longitudinal stiffening rod which lies between the central nervous system and the alimentary canal; a hollow, dorsal nerve cord; and embryonic gill slits. The chordates include over 70,000 species distributed over four subphyla. Other major phyla include the Arthropoda, Mollusca, and Echinodermata.
SUBPHYLUM: Vertebrata (The embryonic notochord is replaced by a backbone of vertebrae as the central axis of the endoskeleton.)
CLASS: Mammalia (Warm-blooded; air-breathing; milk-producing; four-chambered heart; possesses hair; young born alive. Other classes include fish, amphibians, reptiles, and birds.)
ORDER: Primates (Enlarged cranium with eyes located on front of head; stands erect; thumbs opposing the fingers; fingers have nails instead of claws. Other orders include rodents and carnivores.)
FAMILY: Hominidae (Large cerebral hemispheres overhanging the cerebellum and medulla. Apes belong to the family Pongidae which consists of the gorilla, chimpanzee, orangutan, and gibbon. There are two separate families of monkeys that also include the baboons.)
SPECIES: *Homo sapiens* (Man is the only living species of the family Hominidae.)

One of the more interesting accounts of the present structure of the human brain, based on evolutionary development, is due to MacLean [MacLean 73]. He hypothesizes that the brain consists of three interconnected biological computers (the "triune brain," Fig. 2-3), each with its own type of intelligence, subjectivity, sense of time and space, memory, motor, and other functions. Each of these three brains (known to be distinct anatomically, chemically, and functionally) corresponds to a separate evolutionary step. The combination of spinal cord, hindbrain, and midbrain (collectively called the "neural chassis") contains the neural machinery

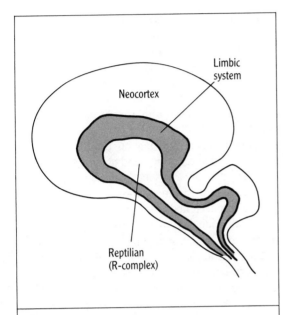

FIGURE 2-3   The Triune Brain.

General schematic of the three major components of the triune brain. (After P. D. MacLean. *A Triune Concept of Brain and Behavior.* University of Toronto Press, Toronto, 1973.)

necessary for reproduction and self-preservation, including control of temperature, muscle tone, sleep rhythm, blood circulation, and respiratory functions. In a fish or amphibian, this is almost all the brain there is; however, more highly evolved organisms are animated by "superior" brain structures, and are reduced to a vegetative state when these higher brain structures are rendered inoperative. Mac-Lean distinguishes three separate drivers of the neural chassis:

1. The reptilian or R-complex, which probably evolved 200 to 300 million years ago, consists of the structures immediately surrounding the midbrain (*corpus striatum, globus pallidus*). We share this complex with other mammals and reptiles. It plays a major role in aggressive behavior, territoriality, ritual, and the establishment of social hierarchies. It is surprising how much of modern human conduct can be ascribed to these primitive behavior patterns.

2. The limbic system (*thalamus, hypothalamus, hippocampus, amygdala, pituitary*), which evolved more than 150 million years ago, is located on top of the R-complex. We share the limbic system with other mammals, but some of its structures are not possessed by reptiles. The limbic system appears to be the site of emotional response (fear, love, hate, pleasure and especially sexual pleasure, pain, altruism, sentiment) and is a major center for memory storage and recall. The oldest part of the limbic system, the olfactory cortex, which originally evolved to analyze scents and smells, still serves in this capacity. The role of smell in sexual behavior, and its involvement in memory, is not accidental.

3. The neocortex, sitting like a cap on the rest of the brain, evolved in the last 50 million years, but the rate of its evolutionary growth increased dramatically in the last few million years in the primates and especially in man.

MacLean has based his theory on years of careful study of the behavior of animals, ranging from lizards to squirrel monkeys, in which he determined which parts of the brain control what types of behavior. Further, his theory of evolution by addition and preservation of pre-existing structure is also justified, in part, by the argument that it is very difficult to evolve by randomly altering a complex system—any such change is likely to be lethal. However, fundamental change can be accomplished by the addition of new systems to the old ones.

Architecture of the Brain

The human brain (See Box 2-2, Table 2-3, and Color Plate 1) is dominated by a massive cortex, which is bilaterally symmetrical in structure. Each cortical hemisphere is composed of four major regions or lobes. These are named the *frontal, parietal, temporal,* and *occipital* lobes.

While it is clear that these lobes do not act as independent functional units, (most higher level functions are known to be distributed across more than one region of the cortex), it is still the case that many human attributes and functions appear to be strongly associated with a single lobe.

The frontal lobes appear to be associated with initiative, anticipation, caution, and the general regulation and planning of action; the temporal lobes with the integration of perceptual information, especially speech and vision; the parietal lobes with symbolic processes (reading, writing, arithmetic), spatial perception, and motor control; and the occipital lobes with vision, the dominant sense in humans and other primates.

Man has convolutions in his cerebral

TABLE 2-3 ■ Physical Attributes of the Human Brain	
Attribute	The Brain
Types of processing elements	Neuron: up to 100 distinct classes; functional differences not known
Number of elements	10^{10} to 10^{12} neurons
Size/volume	Brain volume (man) = 1500 cc Neuron (cell) body diameter = 0.004 in. Axon length: up to a few feet
Weight	3.3 lb
Power	10 watts
Transmission and switching speed	Transmission speed: function of axon diameter and insulation, ranges from 30 to 360 ft/sec Maximum switching speed 0.5×10^{-3} sec
Interconnection complexity per computing element	Up to 200,000 connections (for Purkinje cell)
Reliability	Component reliability: low, neurons dying continuously System reliability: high, design life 70+ yr
Information coding	Digital: frequency modulation

BOX 2-2   Structural Organization of the Mammalian Neocortex

The neocortex is remarkably similar in the brains of all mammals, including man. The same cell types are found and the same stratified structure with six parallel layers* is observed.

Numbered from one to six from the surface inward, layer 1 contains mostly fibers from neurons in other layers; layers 2, 3, and the upper portion of layer 5 deal with internal processing; layer 4 is largely involved in receiving sensory information; and the lower portion of layer 5 and all of layer 6 are concerned with muscle control. The

*From a functional standpoint, the vertical organization of the cortex is as important as the layered horizontal organization: the entire neocortex seems to consist of a mosaic of overlapping functional columns. The vertical organization is described in Chapter 8 for the visual system.

thickness of the neocortex varies somewhat in different brain regions ranging between 50 to 100 cells in depth.

The number of cells lying beneath a fixed-size patch of surface area is essentially constant for all areas of the neocortex: 140,000 neurons per square millimeter of surface with the exception of the visual area where primates have 2.5 times as many cells as in other areas. The human neocortex has a surface area of about 2200 cm² and is estimated to contain 30 billion neurons. The corresponding numbers for the chimp and gorilla are 500 cm² and 7.5 billion cortical neurons; the cat has 4 to 5 cm² of cortex containing 65 million neurons. The average thickness of the neocortex increases by a factor of three in the evolutionary progression from rat to man, reflecting an in-

crease in the amount of "wiring" needed to interconnect the larger number of neurons; however, the density of synapses seems to have remained unchanged.

Thus, the human brain is not visibly distinguished in either gross structural formation, cell type, cell distribution, cell density, or density of synapses, as we ascend the evolutionary scale from the lower mammals. The major visible evolutionary change is the continuous quantitative increase in neocortex surface area, thickness, total number of neurons, and the total number of connections between neurons. From fish to man, the brain assumes an increasingly greater fraction of body weight. In mammals, the neocortex size (or equivalent surface area) shows a similar evolutionary increase relative to the total brain size [Changeux 85, Smith 72].

cortex that are new from the point of view of evolution, and not committed to motor or sensory functions. These areas, which are "programmed" to function after birth, are primarily in the prefrontal and temporal lobes. During childhood, some of this uncommitted area on one side or the other (but usually the left side) of the temporal lobes will be programmed for speech. The remaining area, called the interpretation cortex, is apparently reserved for the interpretation of present events in the light of past experience.

A theory that attempts to character-

ize the functional organization of the brain is due to Luria [Luria 73]. He describes three main functional units. The first unit, centered mainly in the upper brain stem (especially the reticular formation) and in the limbic region, is concerned with the maintenance and regulation of the general "tone" or level of activity in the brain, and more generally, with consciousness and emotion.

The second unit is concerned with modeling the relation of the organism to the external world, and thus with the interpretation and storage of sensory information. This second unit is composed of independent subsystems for each of the different sensory modalities (e.g., visual, auditory, cutaneous, and kinesthetic senses). However, each of these subsystems is organized along similar architectural lines: each sensory modality has a primary reception area that organizes information received directly from the sensory organs. A secondary region, also specific to each sensory modality, appears to interpret the primary sensory output in the light of stored knowledge and past experience, and is responsible for the symbolic encoding of the sensory signals. Finally, a tertiary area, shared among the different senses, integrates symbolic information from the different sensory modalities in creating a composite model of the world. Luria asserts that this tertiary area is a unique human brain structure that converts concrete perception into abstract verbal thinking employing some of the same machinery associated with the speech function.

Luria's third unit, centered largely in the frontal lobes, is concerned with the formation of intentions, the creation of plans, and the monitoring of performance. The third unit controls the actions and thus the motor systems of the organism. Again, Luria asserts that the frontal (prefrontal) lobes, much more highly developed in man than in any other animal (occupying up to one quarter of the total mass of the human brain), are organized to employ symbols and speech processes in their functioning.

Rather than continuing to catalog our admittedly limited knowledge of the relationships between brain structure and function, in the remainder of this subsection we will give a brief specula-tive account of what is known about the highest and most fascinating brain functions: mind, consciousness, personality, pleasure and pain, learning and memory, and reasoning. Perception is discussed extensively in a later chapter.

Mind, Personality, Consciousness, and the Soul. Each human brain appears to house a single individual, although there are rare pathological cases of multiple personalities alternately manifesting their presence in a single body. How do 10 billion nerve cells interact to produce a single consciousness? Where is the site of the "I," conscious awareness, or even the mind or soul should one or the other exist independent of the physical structures of the brain?

In a view contrary to that of the "triune brain" as hypothesized by Mac-Lean, and also distinct from that of Luria, Wilder Penfield [Penfield 78] believes that the brain is a tightly integrated whole, and that conscious awareness resides not in the new brain (neocortex) but rather in the old (the brain stem). In Penfield's theory, the brain consists of two major systems, (1) the mechanisms associated with the existence and maintenance of conscious awareness, the mind, and (2) the mechanisms involved in sensory-motor coordination, called the central integrating system.

Penfield, one of the world's foremost neurologists/neurosurgeons at the time of his death in 1976, formulated his views after a lifetime of studying how the brain functions and malfunctions, especially in the presence of epilepsy. He observed that epileptic fits, abnormal and uncontrolled electrical discharges in the brain that disable the affected areas, generally limit themselves to one functional system. One such type of epileptic fit, called a *petit mal*,[7] converts the individual into an automaton. The patient becomes unconscious, but may wander about in an aimless manner or he may continue to carry out whatever task he had started before the attack, following a stereotyped pattern of behavior. He can make few, if any, decisions for which there has been no precedent, and makes no record of a stream of consciousness—he will have complete amnesia for the period of epileptic discharge. The regions of the brain affected by petit mal are the prefrontal and temporal lobes and the gray matter in the higher brain stem. When an epileptic discharge occurs in the cerebral cortex in any of the sensory or motor areas (e.g., in the parietal or occipital lobes), and spreads to the higher brain stem, the result is always a major convulsive attack (*grand mal*), never an attack of "automatism."

We note that both the central integrating system (essentially a computer) and the mechanisms responsible for mind (consciousness, awareness) have primary, but distinct, centers in the gray matter of the higher brain stem (diencephalon) where they engage in a close functional relationship. With the exception of pain and possibly smell sensations, which make no detour to the cerebral cortex, all sensory signals come first to the higher brain stem, and then continue on to an appropriate region of the cerebral cortex; from there, they return to specific areas of the diencephalon. Thus, according to Penfield, the cerebral cortex, instead of being the highest level of integration, is an elaboration layer, partitioned into distinct functional areas.

The indispensable machinery that supports consciousness lies outside of the cerebral cortex: removal of large portions of the cerebral cortex does not cause loss of consciousness, but injury or interference with function in the higher brain stem, even in small areas, abolishes consciousness completely.

In summary, Penfield views the sensory interpretation and motor control areas of the cerebrum as a "computer" that operates in the service of the "mind." The structures that support the highest function of the brain, conscious awareness, are thought to be located primarily in the higher brain stem and in the "uncommitted areas" of the cerebrum (especially the prefrontal and temporal lobes). Even if Penfield is correct, we still understand very little about the nature of conscious awareness, nor do we have any definitive way of answering questions such as: At what point in evolutionary development did conscious awareness first arise, and at what point in the debilitation of the human brain does it finally depart? Speculative discussion pertaining to these matters is presented in Box 2-3.

Pleasure, Pain, and the Emotions.   The emotions of pleasure and pain appear to be such deep integral parts of the human experience that it is difficult to believe that all that is happening within the brain is the firing of a few specific neurons. Yet, it can be demonstrated that in some sense this is indeed the case.

In experiments performed in 1939

---

[7] We use Penfield's terminology, even though it is now considered obsolete.

BOX 2-3   The Origins and Machinery of Consciousness

When and how did consciousness evolve, and where does it reside in the human brain? Three books addressing these questions all suggest that consciousness is a recent biological invention, closely linked to linguistic competence.

Julian Jaynes [Jaynes 77] offers the strange and somewhat unbelievable thesis that consciousness was first "invented" in Mesopotamia around 1300 B.C. He associates consciousness with the ability to think, plan, desire, hope, and deceive, and asserts that these attributes were lacking in early man and lower animals who were only capable of a stimulus-response pattern of behavior. He believes that the brain was originally organized into two functional components, an executive part called a "god" and a follower part called a "man," neither of which were conscious in the sense given above. Jaynes's main argument in support of his theory is that early man ascribed his actions to the inner voice of the god telling him what to do (e.g., Odysseus in the *Iliad*). Consciousness, according to Jaynes, was invented by man coming to the explicit realization that it is he, and not the gods, who directs his actions. With a different view of his thought processes, man's behavior itself changed from reflexive to introspective awareness.

Curtis Smith [Smith 85] argues that biological mechanisms created a linguistic capability before human language was invented, and that both language and consciousness are related evolutionary conse-quences of purely neurological developments. These critical biological inventions, specifically the development of a mental capacity for manipulation of information in the form of a general symbolic code, were required to integrate information from different sensory modali-ties* each describing the perceived world in a different "language." The evolutionary changes supposedly occurred with the emergence of Cro-Magnon man as a replacement for the prelinguistic preconscious Nean-derthal man on the order of 50,000 to 100,000 years ago. (Neanderthal man, the first representative of our species, appeared approximately 150,000 years ago, but non-ape hominoids who made tools and used fire had already existed for more than 2½ million years.) Language allowed Cro-Magnon man to rise above the limitations of sensory experience, enabling him to possess an internal conscious world with the capacity to dream, imagine, remem-ber,† and create.

Michael Gazzaniga [Gazzaniga 85], a key scientist in the split-brain experiments described in Box 1-3, offers a unique and extremely provocative theory of consciousness. Like C.G. Smith, he believes that

---

*Such an integrative ability is completely lacking in lower animals.

---

†Memory and consciousness are inti-mately related; in a sense, memory retrieval is consciousness. It follow that memory retrieval in lower animals that lack language must be a simpler and more sensory-oriented phenomena.

consciousness is only possible in man, and only developed after the evolution of both language and reasoning ability. However, he asserts that the brain is composed of multiple independent nonverbal modules and a single verbal module. The verbal module, which is the seat of consciousness, "observes" and attempts to explain the actions of the other modules:

It has been commonplace to think that our conscious cognitive self is organized and exists in such a way that our language system is always in complete touch with all our thoughts. It knows where in our brains to find all information we have stored there, and it assists in all computations or problem-solving activities we engage in. Indeed, the strong subjective sense we all possess of our-selves is that we are a single, unified, conscious agent con-trolling life's events with a singular integrated purpose. . . . And it is not true. . . . There are a vast number of relatively independent systems in the brain that compute data from the outside world. These inde-pendent systems can deliver the results of these computations to the conscious verbal system, or they can express their reactions by actually controlling the body and affecting real behaviors.

Thus, according to Gazzaniga, conscious beliefs are explanations (devised by the verbal module) of the behavior of the independent entities constituting the brain viewed as a social system.

Shark (Fish)

Cerebellum
Optic lobe
Cerebrum
Brain stem (medulla)
Olfactory bulbs
Thalamus
Optic nerves

Frog (Amphibian)

Alligator (Reptile)

Pigeon (Bird)

Cat (Mammal)

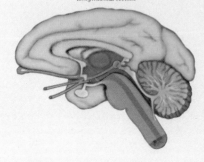

Monkey (Primate)
Longitudinal section

Man
Longitudinal section

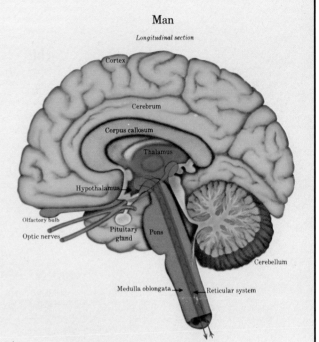

Cortex
Cerebrum
Corpus callosum
Thalamus
Hypothalamus
Olfactory bulb
Optic nerves
Pituitary gland
Pons
Cerebellum
Medulla oblongata
Reticular system

Drawings by Max Gschwind

COLOR PLATE 1(a)
Comparative Anatomy of the Vertebrate Brain

As indicated by the diagrams on this page, the evolution of the human brain has been a process of rearranging and augmenting the basic parts of the brains of lower vertebrate animals. Each of the brains that has developed has been appropriate to the survival of its particular species. For example, the shark, which hunts with its nose, has a brain devoted predominantly to the sense of smell. As perception becomes more versatile in higher animals, the smell brain (green) shrinks in relative size. Patterns of instinctive behavior involved in fleeing, fighting, feeding, and mating are controlled by the hypothalmus (magenta) and associated nerve centers; these man has inherited virtually intact from lower mammals. The thalamus (orange), which serves as a final staging area for messages to the cerebrum (yellow), has grown roughly in parallel with the growth of the cerebrum. A relatively late evolutionary development has been the growth of the cerebral cortex (deep yellow), which plays a major role in reasoned behavior. In fact, the most striking difference between man's brain and those of other mammals is the extent of his cortex. If spread out flat, this thin covering of the brain would be the size of a newspaper page. It fits into the human skull only by being crumpled and wrapped around the rest of the brain like an umbrella. (Max Geschwind in G. Boehm article, *Fortune*, Feb. 1986, with permission.)

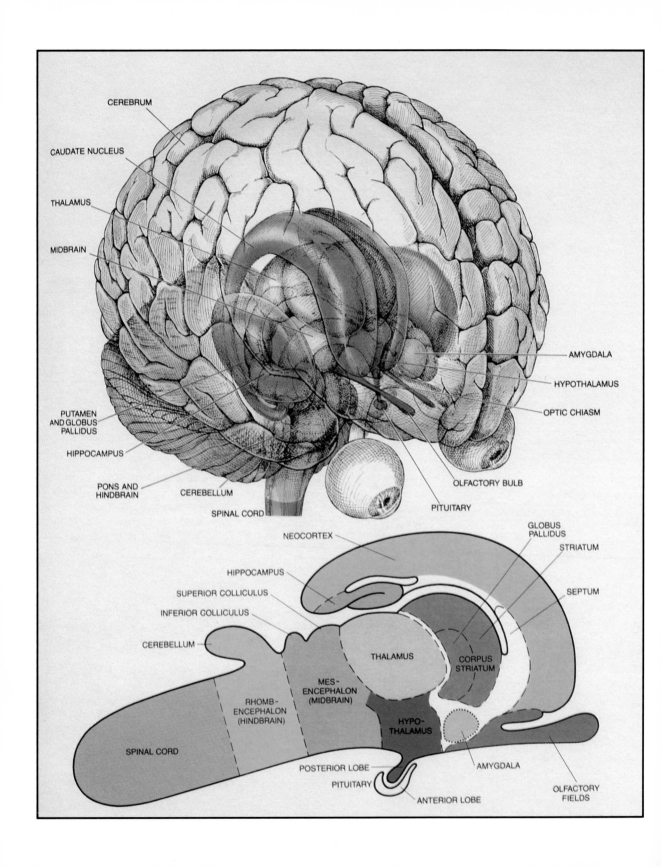

CEREBRUM

CAUDATE NUCLEUS

THALAMUS

MIDBRAIN

PUTAMEN
AND GLOBUS
PALLIDUS

HIPPOCAMPUS

PONS AND
HINDBRAIN

CEREBELLUM

SPINAL CORD

AMYGDALA

HYPOTHALAMUS

OPTIC CHIASM

OLFACTORY BULB

PITUITARY

NEOCORTEX

GLOBUS
PALLIDUS

STRIATUM

HIPPOCAMPUS

SEPTUM

SUPERIOR COLLICULUS

INFERIOR COLLICULUS

CEREBELLUM

THALAMUS

CORPUS
STRIATUM

MES-
ENCEPHALON
(MIDBRAIN)

RHOMB-
ENCEPHALON
(HINDBRAIN)

HYPO-
THALAMUS

SPINAL CORD

POSTERIOR LOBE

PITUITARY

ANTERIOR LOBE

AMYGDALA

OLFACTORY
FIELDS

◀ COLOR PLATE 1(b)
Comparative Anatomy of the Vertebrate Brain (*continued*)

As indicated by the diagrams on this page, the evolution of the Brain and spinal chord of human beings and other mammals can be subdivided into smaller regions according to gross appearance, embyology, or cellular organization. At the top a human brain has been drawn so that its internal structures are visible through "transparent" outer layers of the cerebrum. At the bottom, a generalized mammalian brain is shown in a highly schematic view. Corresponding structures in the realistic and schematic models are the same color. The most general way of dividing the brain is into hindbrain, midbrain, and forebrain. The hindbrain includes the cerebellum. The midbrain includes the two elevations known as the inferior and superior colliculi. The fore-brain is more complex. Its outer part is the cerebral hemisphere, the surface of which is the convoluted sheet of the cerebral cortex, which incorporates the hippocampus, the neocortex, and the olfactory fields. Within the hemisphere are the amygdala and corpus striatum, which includes the globus pallidus and striatum. The rest of the forebrain is the diencephalon: the upper two thirds comprises the thalamus (which has numerous subdivisions) and the lower third the hypothalamus (which connects to pituitary complex). (From W. Nanta and M. Feirtag, *Scientific American*, Sept. 1979, with permission.)

COLOR PLATE 2
A Synthetic Scene Generated using Fractal Textures.

(Fractal landscape rendering by R.F. Voss. From B. Mandelbrot. *The Fractal Geometry of Nature*. W. H. Freeman, San Francisco, © 1982 with permission.)

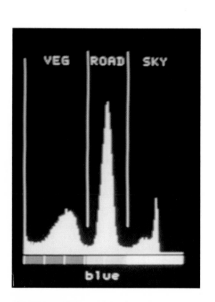

COLOR PLATE 3
Histogram Analysis for Automatic
Threshold Setting.

Top right: Color image of a road scene.
Middle right: Blue component of color image.
Bottom right: Partitioned image, showing road,
  vegetation, and sky.
Above left: Histogram of blue component of color
  image, showing threshold settings.
(Photos courtesy of SRI International,
  Menlo Park, Calif.)

by Klüver and Bucy at the University of Chicago, it was discovered that when the region of the brain lying between the outer cortex and the center of the brain was damaged, monkeys behaved as if their emotional and motivational machinery was destroyed: they ate nuts and bolts as happily as raisins and randomly and inappropriately intermixed pleasure and fear responses to test situations.

More recent attempts to locate the emotional centers of the brain have narrowed the search to the hypothalamus, known (in addition to other functions) to control feeding, drinking, and sexual behavior. In 1953, James Olds discovered a region near the anterior hypothalamus of the rat that, when stimulated with an electrical current introduced through a "brain probe," provided such a high level of gratification that to get this reward rats would cross an electrified grid that previously had stopped rats starved for 24 hours from running for food.

While the positive response[8] to electrical stimulation of the hypothalamus has been demonstrated in rats, fish, birds, cats, dogs, monkeys, porpoises, and man, the interpretation of what is actually happening is not completely clear. In some cases it appears that the stimulation prevents termination or enhances the currently ongoing activity, rather than providing the subject with a pleasure reward. However, human subjects experiencing the positive effect, generally report that the stimulation caused reduction of anxiety or pain, or pleasurable feelings related to sex. One implication of these findings is that in spite of the complexity of human behavior, simple switches in the brain can turn on or off some of our strongest drives and motivating mechanisms.

Memory.   Memory, nominally the ability to store and recall past events, is a critical component of human intelligence; after all, most of our reasoning deals with our previously stored knowledge of the world rather than exclusively with currently sensed data—defective memory is one of the most frequently observed symptoms of impaired brain function. What kinds of memory are there? How long can different kinds of things (a picture, a sound, a word, a story) be remembered? Does the human memory span exceed that of most other organisms? Is indeed memory simply a matter of storage and recall? Or is it a more complex function? What do memory defects tell us about the nature of normal human memory?

The first significant modern study of the psychology of memory was published by Hermann Ebbinghaus in 1885. He addressed such issues as the rate of forgetting (memory loss occurs quickly at first, then more slowly); "overmemorizing" and relearning ("each repetition engraved the material more and more deeply on the nervous system"); the amount of material that can be memorized (the learning time for n nonsense syllables is proportional to $n \log n$ for lists shorter than the immediate memory span); the effect of how the learning time is distributed (it is better to have several short learning sessions spaced out at intervals than to have one unbroken period of work), and a host of similar items.

Since memory was known to be strongly influenced by the meaning and novelty that the material has for the memorizer, the Ebbinghaus and most subse-

---

[8]Regions of negative response have also been found.

quent formal memory experiments attempted to achieve generality by employing nonsense syllables as data to be memorized. This approach masks the fact that, except in rare cases, the symbolic information memorized is an abstraction of the originally sensed data, rather than an exact copy. Thus, in normal situations memory is not simply a matter of storage and recall, but rather a complex process involving a considerable amount of cognitive processing.

The portions of the human brain thought to be involved with memory are the association areas of the frontal, parietal, occipital, and temporal lobes, and parts of the limbic system, especially the hippocampus. Little is known about the actual storage mechanisms and even less is known about the following ability which has no counterpart in computer memory systems: A person knows when something is stored in his memory, and when it is not. Thus, we will exert much effort to recall something that we "know we know," while we will make no effort to recall something that we know we do not know. For example, given the question, "What was Benjamin Franklin's telephone number?," we will not try to recall all of the telephone numbers that we know, but immediately conclude that no such number is stored in our memory.

Human memory is not a monolithic function—many different kinds of processes are involved and there are at least three[9] different types of memory: memory

for sensed data, short-term memory, and long-term memory. The designation "short-term memory" is used to denote the ability to recall information presented a short time previously—short-term memory leaves no permanent imprint on the brain. One theory of short-term memory is based on the idea of "reverberation" of neuronal circuits in which an impulse travels through a closed circuit of neurons again and again. In this view, an incoming thought can be recalled while the reverberation continues. "Long-term memory," the indefinite retention of a memory trace, cannot be explained by reverberation. Rather, the concept of "facilitation" at synapses is used: when incoming information enters a neuronal circuit, the synapses in the circuit become "facilitated" for the passage of a similar signal later (triggered by some portion of the new signal which duplicates the original stimulus). Another theory suggests that long-term memory is related to protein synthesis by RNA: memory results from the production by RNA of specific proteins for each recorded event.

Each sensory modality (e.g., vision or speech) appears to incorporate a means of storing the complete incoming signal for on the order of 0.10 to 1.0 second. For example, we have all had the experience of not immediately understanding a spoken phrase, but by "replaying it" in our "mind's ear," we can recover the intended meaning. There are also visual "afterimages" which occur in a very short interval after the withdrawal of the stimulus, and are distinguished from other forms of visual memory in that these afterimages are not under voluntary control. We can inspect afterimages with our "mind's eye" and "see" things we did not observe

---

[9]There may be additional types of memory, e.g., Gazzaniga [Gazzaniga 85] describes evidence for the existence of memory mechanisms for storing procedural knowledge (such as motor skills) as distinct from mechanisms for storing declarative knowledge (facts or events).

when the visual stimulus was physically present.

In addition to very short-term sensory memory, there appears to be another form of short-term memory which lasts anywhere from 30 seconds to a few hours. Retaining a telephone number "in our heads" until we can complete the dialing —the number is typically forgotten almost immediately afterward—is an example of this type of memory.

Important information that is retained over long periods of time appears to be stored by a completely different mechanism from that used for the various types of short-term memory. But even here, more than one facility is involved. For example, there are memory disabilities in human patients that affect their ability to store and recall verbal material, while leaving intact their memory ability for nonverbal material.

Many other types of memory disorders are known that shed light on the multifaceted nature of human memory. For example, traumatic amnesia can be experienced by a person who has been knocked out by a blow on the head. In a confusional state lasting from days to weeks, the individual is unable to store new memories, and on recovery reports total amnesia for that period. Anterograde amnesia is the impaired ability to store memories of new experiences. (It is interesting to note that short term memory is typically intact among most amnesia sufferers. Some experimental psychologists believe that the primary factor in amnesia is the inability to transfer information from short-term to long-term storage.) Korsakoff's syndrome is a gross defect of short-term memory in which the sufferer may have access to memories of events

occuring prior to the onset of the syndrome, but now immediately forgets each new experience; he lives only in the immediate present with no continuity between one experience and the next.

To summarize our main observation, except for very short-term sensory storage, the memory function is a complex activity that involves distinct modes of information partitioning, selection, and abstraction. It has all of the attributes of perception, and in fact, memory recall can be viewed as a form of internal perception. We do not generally retrieve a unique "token" in the exact form in which it was stored, but rather synthesize a "mental construct" (possibly from many different brain storage modalities) that is relevant to some purpose or ongoing process. The designation of perception, learning, and memory as distinct brain functions is a simplification which masks the true nature and interrelations of these activities.

Reasoning. Man has the ability to use current and past events to foresee possible futures, to plan and judge alternative courses of action, to deduce new facts from stored knowledge, and to reconstruct his environment from sensory data. Where and how does the human brain perform these functions which we ascribe to the general faculty called reasoning? It is in this particular matter that we least understand the machinery of the brain.

From a functional standpoint, we have already seen that reasoning is not a monolithic activity, but rather that there are at least two distinct paradigms the brain employs to solve the problems posed to it. The left hemisphere appears to be especially adept at solving problems

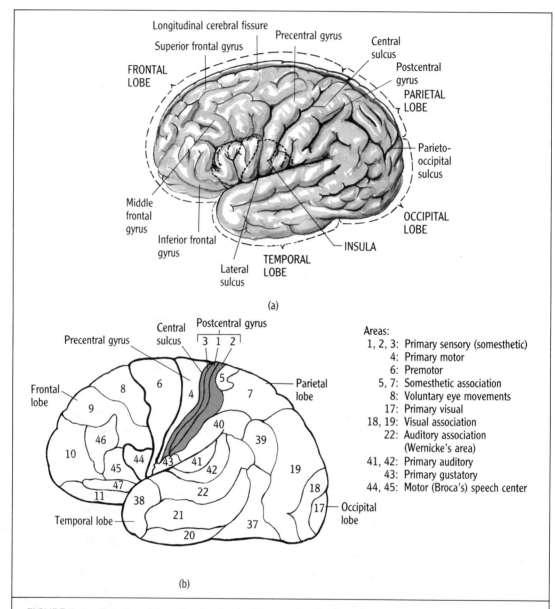

FIGURE 2-4 Functional Localization in the Human Cerebral Cortex.

(a) External anatomy of the cerebral hemisphere. Lobes, gyri, fissure, and sulci of the left cerebral hemisphere. The insula (indicated by broken lines) is hidden by the overlying lobes. (b) Functional areas of the cerebral cortex. The general area is shaded black. (From E. L. Weinreb. *Anatomy and Physiology*. Addison-Wesley, Reading, Mass., 1984, pp. 166,167, with permission.)

having a sequential/logical character, while the right hemisphere is superior in dealing with problems having a spatial/gestalt character. Other than the centers specialized to deal with data from specific motor and sensory systems (Fig. 2-4), no additional localization of the reasoning machinery is known. The computer analogy suggests that assemblies of neurons, individually capable of acting as both the logical switches and memory cells of a digital computer, indeed act as components in a distributed general-purpose computational engine executing relocatable algorithms recalled from memory as the need arises. There is no way at present to either verify or falsify this conjecture. In our current state of knowledge, we know as much (or as little) about reasoning in the brain as we do about the location and functioning of the human soul.

The Brain and the Computer. Before we move on to the computer portion of this chapter, let us examine where we have been and where we want to go. We studied the brain with the goal of learning more about intelligence. We discussed the physical structure of the brain, what the effects of damage are, and what we can introspect about human intelligence. Although these topics are of great intellectual interest, they do not provide the insights about intelligence that we originally hoped to attain.

We therefore turn to the computer with the expectation that, because we can analyze its structure and functioning in a way we cannot hope to do with the brain, we may be able to resolve some of our still-unanswered questions about intelligence.

THE COMPUTER

In its most basic sense, the computer is a machine that operates on information; it takes in information (or data) and transforms it in some specific way. As a physical device, the computer acts on physical quantities, and the assertion that it actually transforms information is an interpretation we impose on its behavior. Thus any physical system (the human brain, a dust cloud, a pocket calculator) is capable of being viewed as a computer.

To understand the behavior of a physical system viewed as a computer, and to determine what it is actually or ultimately capable of, a number of abstractions have been created that attempt to capture the essence of the concepts "computer" and "computation." It should be realized that the conclusions we draw by analyzing these abstractions—for example, conclusions about limits of performance—are valid assertions about the physical system only when viewed in the context of the abstraction; i.e., the limits are those of the abstraction. The most useful and powerful abstractions we have devised for formalizing the concepts of information, computer, and computation are based on the following two ideas:

1. The computer is an instruction follower.
2. The most complex set of instructions can be rewritten in a very simple language; i.e., a language which has an alphabet of only two letters (0,1) and a vocabulary of less than twenty distinct operations for altering strings of 1's and 0's.

The *Turing machine*, an abstraction based on these concepts, is described later in this chapter. It will be seen that while the Turing machine does not lead to practical ideas about how to construct useful computers, it allows us to understand the limitations of all computer systems viewed as symbolic information processors (instruction followers that transform strings of symbols).

The Nature of Computer Programs and Algorithms

The *digital computer* (Appendix 2-2), the most widely used form of the computer, can be considered to be an instruction-following device, with the instructions presented in the form of a *program*. In most current computer systems, the hardware is controlled by a special internal program known as the *operating system*, which keeps track of how the computer resources are being used, and how the work is progressing. The user-provided programs to be processed are known as the *applications* programs. However, from the standpoint of the user, the separation between the hardware and the operating system is unimportant and often invisible; the combination forms the computer which "understands" instructions presented in one or more specialized languages.

Procedures must be described to an instruction follower in terms that are understandable to it. The instruction follower must be physically able to carry out the procedures, want to, or be made to, carry out the instructions in a practical amount of time, and be able to monitor progress and have a way of determining when the task has been completed. These requirements, assumed to be satisfied

when we communicate with a person, must be explicitly met when communicating with a robot or computer.

Natural vs. Formal (Computer) Languages. Procedures are described to computers by means of *programming languages*, which have very precise rules of syntax and use. Such formal languages differ from *natural languages* such as English or French in the following ways:

- *Ambiguity*. A programming language is designed so as to avoid ambiguity; a single meaning can be found for each expression. On the other hand, natural language is often ambiguous: "I saw the orange truck."
- *Context dependency*. The meaning of a programming language expression is minimally dependent on its context; its meaning is almost always the same regardless of what its surrounding expressions are. In natural language, a sentence such as "I disapprove of your drinking" is changed in meaning when we add "so much milk."
- *Well-formedness*. In writing a programming language expression, one must follow the syntax rules exactly, otherwise the instructions will not be accepted by the system. In natural language, especially the spoken form, violations of syntax generally do not affect a person's comprehension of the expression.

Procedural vs. Nonprocedural Instructions. When presenting instructions to an instruction follower, we often specify both what we want done and specifically how we want the task carried out. This is known as providing *procedural* instructions. If, on the other hand, we indicate what we want done, but do not specify "how," this is called a *nonprocedural* or declarative instruction. An example of a nonprocedural instruction is, "Buy a loaf of bread on your way home"; the desired end-effect is specified, but no specific instructions as to how to attain the goal are given. It is quite difficult to devise nonprocedural language systems, because the interpretation system within the computer must supply the 'how' by itself. The interpretive system must know about the "world" it is dealing with, and the effects of actions on this world. It must also understand the nature of the problem being solved. Using this knowledge, the system must devise a *plan*, a sequence of steps that must be performed to attain the goal. Because of these difficulties, only a few languages have been developed that have nonprocedural capabilities and these are generally limited to some specific domain.

Representation of Data in a Computer.
A computer can be based on two distinct types of data representation: isomorphic or symbolic. In the "isomorphic" representation, data is modeled by a quantity which has a "natural" functional and possibly physical resemblance to the original data itself. For example, beads are used in the abacus to represent numbers, and the beads are physically moved to perform the computations. In the "symbolic" representation, the nature of the symbols used to represent the data is completely independent of the characteristics of the data being represented; the desired correspondence is established by a subsidiary set of rules. Thus, if we represent a number by its binary form, there is no natural relationship between the number and the form of its representation.

In current computer technology, the isomorphic representation is employed in the analog computer, which is fast and useful for dealing with certain physical problems, but has limited accuracy and flexibility. The symbolic representation is employed in the digital computer, which is extremely flexible and has unlimited numerical accuracy, but is comparatively slow and presents significant practical problems in accurately modeling many physical situations. For example, since the relationship between the physical situation and the computer representation is completely arbitrary, only those aspects of the physical situation that are both understood and can be described in a formal manner are capable of being modeled. Thus, a complete representation of an outdoor scene in a symbolic language would be an almost impossible task.

The Turing Machine

In order to prove formally what tasks can and cannot be performed by a computing device, Alan Turing, a British mathematician (1912–1954), postulated an abstraction, now called a "Turing machine," that is functionally equivalent to any computer. Turing's thesis was that any process that can be called an 'effective procedure' can be realized by his machine.

An effective procedure is a set of formal rules that tell a device from moment to moment precisely what operations to perform. (A computer program is an example of an effective procedure.) Turing's thesis cannot be established by proof—it is actually a definition of the intuitive concept of a computable function, i.e., a function that can be evaluated by some finite algorithm. All attempts to define computability in some reasonable way have been shown to be equivalent to Turing computability.

In the Turing machine, the reduction of a process to elementary operations is carried to its limit. Even a simple operation such as addition is broken down into a chain of far simpler operations. This increases the number of steps in the computations carried out by the machine, but simplifies the logical structure for theoretical investigations.

As shown in Fig. 2-5, the Turing machine consists of a linear tape, assumed to be infinite in both directions, which is ruled into a sequence of boxes, or cells. The machine has a read/write head that can move from cell to cell of the tape, and can read or write symbols. At each moment of time, the machine is assumed to be in one of a finite number of internal "states" that are identified by the numbers 0, 1, 2, . . . The machine operation is controlled by a "state table" stored within the machine that specifies (1) the symbol to be "overprinted" at the current tape location (i.e., the old symbol is erased and a new symbol written), (2) the direction of head movement, and (3) the next state of the machine. The symbol printed, head movement direction, and the next state are determined by the current state of the machine, and the symbol that is on the cell of the tape currently being scanned.

The various operations that the machine can carry out are: the machine can halt; the previous symbol in a cell can be replaced by a new symbol; the read/write head can move one unit to the right or left; and the state number of the machine can be changed.

The state table 'instructions' are in the form of rows, each of which contains five elements: (1) old state, (2) symbol now being read, (3) symbol to be overprinted, (4) direction of head movement, and (5) new state. Thus, a state table entry [3,#,*,R,7] asserts, "If the old state is state 3, and the symbol being read is #, then the symbol * should be overprinted, the head should be moved one cell to the right, and the machine should go to the new state 7." Note that the first two symbols of a row cannot be the same as another row, since that would mean that there would be more than one operation specified for a given state and input symbol.

Turing showed that a state table could be prepared for each of the common operators such as addition, multiplication, and division, that more complex

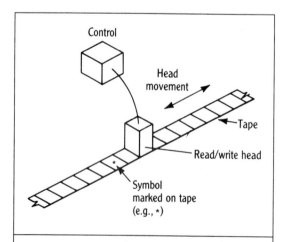

Control

Head movement

Tape

Read/write head

Symbol marked on tape (e.g., *)

FIGURE 2-5   The Turing Machine.

operations could be composed from simple ones in a formal manner, and that his simple machine could carry out effective procedures equivalent to that possible on any computing device. Thus, anything proved about the ultimate capability of a Turing machine will hold for all computers. Box 2-4 shows a complete state table and how the corresponding Turing machine operates on a tape.

The Universal Turing Machine

It is possible to convert the entire state table of a Turing machine into a single number such that the original table can be recovered by decoding this number. A technique for performing this coding and decoding is shown in Box 2-5. We can thus say that the complete description of a Turing machine is given by its code number.

A "universal Turing machine" is a Turing machine that can take such a code number, decode it to obtain the state table of the original machine, and then execute that table. Thus, the universal Turing machine can simulate the operation of any Turing machine, given the code number of the machine.

LIMITATIONS ON THE COMPUTATIONAL ABILITY OF A LOGICAL DEVICE

A machine that operates on the basis of formal logical rules can be shown to have theoretical limits on its problem solving ability: there are certain well-posed problems for which no algorithm is possible, using the formal rules. In other words, we can prove that it is impossible for the machine to solve such problems!

The Gödel Incompleteness Theorem

At the beginning of this century, it was expected that mathematics would soon be mechanical in nature. Given a set of axioms and deduction rules, new mathematics would be produced by "blindly" applying the deduction rules to the ever-increasing set of mathematical truths. This mathematics would be consistent (no two statements produced would contradict each other), and it would be complete (every truth would be producible). Thus, one could eventually produce all true statements and never produce a falsehood.

This expectation was destroyed in 1931 by Kurt Gödel who showed that there are true statements in mathematics that a consistent formal system will not produce, i.e., that it is impossible to alter the foundations of mathematics to exclude unprovable propositions. Gödel showed how to produce a true statement, S, that could not be proved by a consistent system, F, using a set of axioms and a proof procedure. He did this by showing that if S could be proved, then a contradiction would arise. F is therefore "incomplete" since it does not produce all true statements. The approach is a formal treatment of the "liar's paradox":

Given the statement S: *This statement is a lie*. Then if S is true, S is false, while if S is false, then S is true. Gödel's approach used the form:

S: *This statement is not provable*. Then if S is provable, S is not true, and our formal system has produced a falsehood. If S is not provable, then we have a statement that is true, but not provable in the system, and the system is incomplete.

Gödel's approach to proving the

BOX 2-4 **Programming a Turing Machine: The Parity Problem**

Programming a Turing machine with "alphabet" [0,1] consists of preparing a control table that will cause it to operate on a binary input tape in a desired manner. Numbers on the tape can be represented as strings of "1" marks (the number 5 = "11111"), and if we have two numbers we can separate them by a cell that has a zero in it, e.g. 2,5 would be represented as "...001101111100...". Adding two numbers consists of preparing a control table that removes the zero between the strings; subtraction consists of shuttling back and forth between the two strings, stripping off 1's alternately for each until no 1's remain in the smaller string. Multiplication of a string m 1's long by one n 1's long consists of replacing each 1 of n by m 1's.

We will assume that the machine must shift left or right after performing an overprint and prior to entering its next state. The machine is always started at a specific position on the tape in control state 1. If the machine enters the zero state, it halts without performing any further operations.

The parity problem discussed below requires the machine to determine whether there is an even or odd number of 1's on a tape. Conceptually, a control table could be set up so as to toggle between the two states as the head moves along the tape. When a zero cell is encountered, the machine reports in some specified manner and halts. We will examine several forms of the problem.

Parity Problem (P1)

1. Input consists of string of consecutive 1's with start position at the rightmost 1 of string. The machine starts in state 1.

2. For odd parity (odd number of 1's in input string) we require the machine to stop at the leftmost 1 of the input string as shown in the example below:

    input string   ... 0011100 ...
            ↑

    output string ... 0011100 ...
            ↑

3. For even parity (even number of 1's in input string) we require the machine to stop under the second 0 to the left of the input string as in the example below:

    input string   ... 001100 ...
            ↑

    output string ... 001100 ...
            ↑

A control table to solve the above parity problem is shown in Fig. 2-6. It is obvious that the P1 parity problem cannot be solved by a

FIGURE 2-6 Turing Machine for Solving the Parity Problem.

Control state	Present symbol	Overprint	Move	New state
1	0	0	0 (left)	0 (halt)
1	1	1	0 (left)	2
2	0	0	1 (right)	0 (halt)
2	1	1	0 (left)	1

(a)

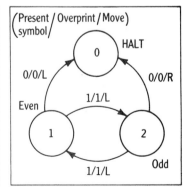

(b)

BOX 2-4   *(continued)*

machine with a single control state. Thus, the above machine is optimal since it solves the parity problem with the minimum possible number of control states.

Now consider an apparently trivial variation of the parity problem in which we merely change the reporting requirements:

Parity Problem (P2)

1. For odd parity, print a 1 on the second square to the left of the input string and stop at this location:

input string   ...0011100...
                          ↑
output string   ...001011100...
                              ↑

2. For even parity, print 1's in the second and third squares to the left of the input string and stop at the second square:

input string   ...001100...
                              ↑
output string   ...001101100...
                          ↑

Try to find a machine that will solve the P2 problem. It should be easy to find a six-state machine; if you are very clever and are willing to spend a lot of time, you may even find a four-state machine [Rado 62].

Nobody has yet found a three-state solution to P2, nor do we know if one exists. It might seem feasible to resolve the issue of the existence of a three-state machine by writing a conventional computer program to exhaustively try out all possibilities. We note that there are more than 16 million three-state machines, and for each such machine we would have to determine if it will report parity correctly, and halt, for every possible input string. As discussed earlier in this chapter, and in Box 2-6, even deciding whether a machine will halt, given an all-zero input tape, is a generally undecidable problem. Thus, while intuitive or heuristic search techniques could conceivably produce a three-state solution to the P2 problem, failure to find such a solution does not imply that one does not exist, nor do we have a formal method, at present, to resolve this issue.

---

general existence of unsolvable problems has subsequently been used to show that specific problems are unsolvable. For example, Hilbert's tenth problem, one of the famous problems of mathematics, has been shown to be unsolvable. (This problem is to find a general algorithm that could determine in a finite number of steps whether or not a given Diophantine equation has an integer solution.) This has been shown to be unsolvable by using a proof that involves Gödel numbering of a statement related to Diophantine equations, and demonstrating the Gödel contradiction.

Unsolvability by Machine

The Gödel concepts carry over into machine unsolvability, since once we have the idea of a single number representing an entire machine (see "The Turing Machine" above), we can prove theorems about unsolvability. For example, Box 2-6 presents an informal proof for the *halting problem*: there cannot be a machine X that when given the state table of an arbitrary machine Y and its starting tape, is able to tell whether machine Y will ever stop. Box 2-7 discusses the *busy beaver problem*, which demonstrates noncomputability. Other examples of unsolvable problems for a Turing machine (thus any computer) are:

- *Machine equivalence.* It is impossible to have a machine that, given the state tables of any two Turing machines, S and T, always can tell whether S is equivalent to T.

BOX 2-5   Gödel Coding: Coding a State Table into a Single Number

There are many ways of coding a sequence of numbers into a single number so that the number can be uniquely decoded back into the original sequence. The one used by the mathematician Kurt Gödel in his original work on undecidability is based on prime factors. If we have a sequence of non-zero integers $S = a, b, c, \ldots n_k$, we can form the product, $N = (2^a)(3^b)(5^c) \ldots (p_k{}^{n_k})$, where $2, 3, 5, \ldots p_k$ are all prime numbers, and p_k is the kth prime number. N is then the code number of the original sequence, and since N was formed from the product of primes raised to a power, we can uniquely determine the power of each prime and hence can recover the original sequence of numbers.

Given a control table of a Turing machine, we first convert all the entries to numbers and eliminate any zeros in the table:

- Right, left, and halt are denoted by some numbers, say 1,2,3, respectively
- Any symbols to be printed are represented by a number
- If any state is labeled as 0, add 1 to all states

We now have a set of five numbers in each row of

the control table, and we can concatenate rows to form a long sequence of numbers. The sequence can be converted into a single number using the prime number encoding approach described above. We can then talk about the Turing machine N, meaning the control table of the machine coded into the number N using Gödel coding.* As an example of this, consider the control table used in Box 2-4. We first eliminate the 0 values by adding one to all numbers. We then obtain a Gödel number for each row:

$$10000 \rightarrow 21111 \rightarrow 2^2 \times 3 \times 5 \times 7 \times 9 = A$$
$$11102 \rightarrow 22213 \rightarrow 2^2 \times 3^2 \times 5^2 \times 7 \times 9^3 = B$$
$$20010 \rightarrow 31121 \rightarrow 2^3 \times 3 \times 5 \times 7^2 \times 9 = C$$
$$21101 \rightarrow 32212 \rightarrow 2^3 \times 3^2 \times 5^2 \times 7 \times 9^2 = D$$

If we call the row Gödel numbers A, B, C, and D, then we can code the entire table into the number $N = 2^A \times 3^B \times 5^C \times 7^D$. Since N encodes the original control table, we can then use the designation "machine N."

---

*Note that this coding approach is conceptual, rather than practical, since the product of the primes raised to a power is an impractically large number.

- *Symbol prediction.* It is impossible to have a machine that can determine whether an arbitrary machine A will ever write the symbol S when started on tape B.

Implications of Gödel's Theorem

Gödel's theorem, showing that in any formal system there are true statements that are unprovable in the system, has had a profound effect on the philosophy of mind. Some see the theorem as indicating a basic limitation on both human and machine intelligence, while others see the

human as somehow escaping the Gödelian limitation. There is also the view that Gödel's theorem has little relevance to the issue of achieving intelligent behavior. The arguments are as follows:

Man and machine limitation. Both people and machines consist of "hardware" that operates according to strict mechanical laws. In the case of computers, the electronic mechanism constitutes the formal system, while for the human, the formal system is the neural structure. Therefore, there will be truths unknowable by both man and machine.

Only machine limitation. People are not machines—they exceed strictly mechanical limits by their ability to introspect and to interpret experience. The powers of mind exceed those of a logical inference machine.

Neither man nor machine. The importance of proof techniques in consistent systems has been overrated. Most of our knowledge about the world comes from inductive methods that operate in inconsistent systems. Gödel's incompleteness theorem simply places a limit on one mode of obtaining new knowledge.

Computational Complexity—the Existence of Solvable but Intrinsically Difficult Problems

We have already observed that there are some well-posed problems in mathematics and logic for which no algorithm can ever be written (e.g., the halting problem)—thus there exists a set of theoretically unsolvable problems. However, even for problems that have solutions, there is a subclass of intrinsically difficult problems —problems for which there cannot exist an efficient algorithm. Intrinsically difficult problems are characterized by the fact that their solution time grows (at least) exponentially with some parameter indicative of problem size (e.g., the number of Turing machine control states in the case of the busy beaver problem discussed in Box 2-7). Such intractable problems often arise from the need to exhaustively search a solution space which grows exponentially with problem size; many optimization problems for which no solution space gradient exists (and

can only be solved by the equivalent of a "backtrack" search algorithm) have this characteristic. Thus in addition to theoretically unsolvable problems, we also have a class of computationally unsolvable problems.

Between those problems for which we have efficient (polynomial time[10]) solutions, and those problems known to be intractable, there exists a large class of problems with the following interesting set of characteristics:

(a) There is no currently known polynomial time sequential algorithm for any of these problems; we suspect that they are all intractable, but cannot prove it.

(b) They are all equivalent to the satisfiability problem (Does a given Boolean or logical expression have an assignment of its variables that makes it "true?" See Chapter 4). If a polynomial time algorithm could be found for any one of these problems, then they could all be solved with polynomial time algorithms.

(c) While the size of their solution space grows exponentially, the number of operations needed to find a solution to any of these problems is polynomial if we choose all the correct alternatives. Thus, with enough computers running in parallel, each checking a different alternative at each decision point, we can achieve polynomial time solutions with an exponentially large amount of hard-

---

[10]The number of computational steps needed to assure a solution is expressible as a polynomial in one or more of the main variables in which the problem is posed.

BOX 2-6   The Halting Problem

The following dialogue is an informal proof of the impossibility of having a machine that can tell in general whether another machine will ever halt.

John: I've written a program called TESTER that tells when another program has an endless loop in it.

Mary: How does it work?

John: I have a way of uniquely assigning a number that represents an entire program. For example, if you give me a program, I first compute the number of the program. Then you give me the number that you would input to that program. Suppose I am given a program whose number I find to be 397 and you want to know whether it will halt if you feed in the number 14 to it. I feed these two numbers into TESTER, and if program 397 would halt given an input 14, then TESTER will output a 1, otherwise it will output a 0. TESTER has the form (see Fig. 2-7a):

TESTER(N,D) :
If Program N would halt on input D,
RETURN 1;
else return 0

Mary: Is it O.K. for me to write the following program? (see Fig. 2-7b):

TRYOUT(X) :
Label L: If TESTER(X,X) = 1
then go to Label L;
else RETURN X

John: TRYOUT seems to be O.K. It says that if TESTER using the program numbered X and input data X causes TESTER to output a 1, then TRYOUT will loop endlessly to L, otherwise TRYOUT returns X.

Mary: Does TRYOUT have a number?

John: Of course, every program has a number. Let's see, it comes out to 4,396. So TRYOUT(4,396) would say that if TESTER(4,396, 4,396) = 1 then go to L; else RETURN (4,396).

Mary: I think that something is wrong. If the output of TESTER is 1, then the program being tested is a program that would halt.

John: Right.

ware. Further, for all of these problems, if we could somehow guess the correct answer, we could check the validity of the answer in polynomial time.

This class of problems, called the *NP*-complete class, includes such well-known problems as the "traveling salesman problem" (find the shortest closed route over a given set of roads that passes exactly once through each of a given set of cities) and the "Steiner minimal tree problem" (design the shortest network of roads that connects a given set of cities).

The existence of intrinsically difficult problems indicates the need to employ representations and algorithms that can find approximate solutions, i.e., representations that embody the concept of distance to a solution. We note that some of our most powerful "exact" techniques (such as the logical formalism, Chapter 4) do not have a natural way of representing solution space distance.

An important question left unanswered in this subsection is whether the

BOX 2-6   (*continued*)

Mary: But if TESTER outputs a 1 when using my
program TRYOUT having a number 4,396, that
means that TESTER thinks that my program
should halt.

John: Right.

Mary: But look at my program. With a 1 output from
TESTER, my program loops! What's more, if
TESTER outputs a 0, that means my program
doesn't halt, but if you look at my program you see

that with a 0 output from TESTER my program
halts (see Fig. 2-7c).

John: That seems a lot like the paradox, "This statement is a lie." If the statement is true, then it's
false, and if it's false, it's true.

Mary: That's right, this proof of the halting problem
uses that general approach.

A rigorous treatment of the above Turing machine
proof can be found in Minsky [Minsky 67].

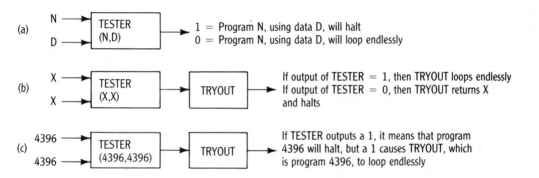

FIGURE 2-7   Programs for Illustrating the Unsolvability of the Halting Problem.

(a) Program TESTER. (b) Program TRYOUT. (c) The paradox.

classification of a problem as tractable or
intractable[11] is a function of the representation employed. This question can be
answered for the case of Turing machine
equivalent computers—any reasonable
problem encoding does not alter tractability—but what happens if we employ
an analog device that is not equivalent
to a Turing machine (see Box 2-8)? While
we do not yet know the answer, it is

interesting to observe that no analog
solutions have been found for intractable
problems.

LIMITATIONS ON THE COMPUTATIONAL ABILITY OF A PHYSICAL DEVICE

From the day of birth, and probably before, but certainly every day afterward,
upward of 1000 neurons die in the human
brain and are not replaced. How can the

---

[11]Whether the problem has a polynomial time solution or not.

BOX 2-7 Nonsolvability, Noncomputability, and the Busy Beaver Problem

It has been known for some time that unsolvable problems exist within specific mathematical systems. For example, it can be shown to be impossible to trisect an arbitrary angle using only a straightedge and compass. There are also undecidable questions: for example, Lobachevsky proved that the parallel postulate in geometry is independent of Euclid's axioms, and thus, neither it, nor its negation, can be proved within a Euclidean system. While the above specific examples are easily dealt with by extending the axiom systems in which these problems are embedded,* there are also problems that are absolutely unsolvable in the sense that there is no finite algorithm for dealing with them. Such problems, first introduced by Church, Gödel, and Turing, are called "recursively unsolvable."

There is a close relationship between the incompleteness theorems of Gödel and the noncomputability results of Turing. Both rely on a form of Gödel coding to make self-referring statements in a modified version of the "liar's paradox"; the proofs are then established by contradiction. While mathematically sound, these methods do not provide an intuitive explanation as to why, for example, there should be well-defined numerical values that cannot be computed, or the relation-

*Though, as Gödel showed, such extensions introduce new undecidable problems

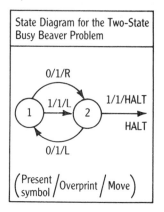

State Table for the Two-State Busy Beaver Problem

Control state	Present symbol	Overprint	Move	New state
1	0	1	R	2
1	1	1	L	2
2	0	1	L	1
2	1	1	Halt	—

(a)

State Diagram for the Two-State Busy Beaver Problem

$\left(\dfrac{\text{Present}}{\text{symbol}}\Big/\text{Overprint}\Big/\text{Move}\right)$

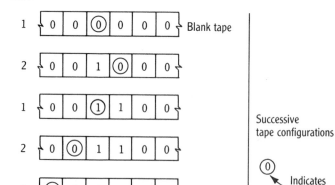

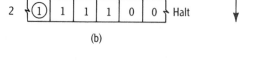

(b)

FIGURE 2-8

Turing Machine Solution for the Two-State Busy Beaver Problem.

(a) State table and state diagram. (b) Starting with a blank tape, the machine writes four 1's and then halts. (After A. K. Dewdney. *Scientific American* 251:19-23, 1984.)

BOX 2-7 *(continued)*

ship between noncomputability and intrinsically difficult problems. The busy beaver problem discussed below will clarify some of these issues.

Consider the problem of determining the maximum number of 1's that can be written on an initially blank tape by a Turing machine (Box 2-4) having an n-state control table. We will call this the busy beaver-n problem, and will let b(n) designate a solution machine and g(n) the corresponding number of 1's. We will only consider as valid solutions machines that halt after writing their tape. Figure 2-8 shows a two-state busy beaver machine that begins with a blank tape, writes four 1's, and then stops.

It can be shown that there are $m(n) = [4(n+1)]^{2n}$ machines having n states, and since we must

examine each machine to determine b(n) and g(n), then the busy beaver problem is intrinsically hard since m(n) grows exponentially with n.

For example, we have:

$$m(1) = 64$$
$$m(2) = 21(10^3)$$
$$m(3) = 17(10^6)$$
$$m(4) = 26(10^9)$$
$$m(5) = 63(10^{12})$$

Thus, m(n) is of astronomical size, even for low values of n. The number of 1's, g(n), ultimately grows at a much faster rate—in fact, it can be proved that for any computable function f(n) there is a value of n beyond which the value of g exceeds that of f. Since g grows faster than every computable function, g(n) cannot be computed; i.e., a finite algorithm cannot be formulated that will produce correct values for g(n).

For small values of n we can explicitly evaluate g as shown below:

g(1) = 1	g(5) < 17
g(2) = 4	g(6) < 36
g(3) = 6	g(7) < 23,000
g(4) < 14	g(8) < 10^{42}

Intuitively, it appears that we can ascribe noncomputability (at least in the above case) to the inability of finite algorithms, based on primitive arithmetic operations, to express all possible functions, especially those with a sufficiently fast rate of growth. However, we cannot ignore the fact that the busy beaver problem includes the halting problem (i.e., we must examine both the number of 1's produced by every potential solution machine and also assure ourselves that it stops), and the halting problem again implies the presence of the Gödelian paradox [Jones 74].

brain continue to function under such conditions, since the loss of even a single component in a modern digital computer will typically render it inoperative? Even more to the point, some biological mechanisms appear to be deliberately designed to take advantage of failure and error in their physical components—one such example is the paradigm for evolution employed by DNA (mutation and natural selection). It is believed that DNA actually adjusts its error rate to produce a percentage of mutations appropriate for current environmental conditions. Under less favorable conditions, a higher rate of mutation has an improved survival value for the species.

Reliable Computation with Unreliable Components

Below a certain level of complexity, things tend to break down—to become more random in their organization. This observation is important enough to have been elevated to a basic law of physics (the second law of thermodynamics). However, very complex systems can be organized so that in spite of the breakdown of their individual components, they continue to function; most living organisms have this characteristic.

In 1952, John von Neumann showed that if the neurons of the brain could be considered to behave as logical switches,

BOX 2-8   Avoiding the Apparent Bounds on Computational Complexity

The Turing machine is more than an abstraction of the digital computer, it is actually a formalization of the sequential logical paradigm—in a sense, it can be taken as an abstraction of the conscious mode of human thinking. Thus it comes as a surprise that complexity bounds, derived for sequential algorithmic computation, can be violated by using a different underlying representation.

For example, consider the problem of sorting a set of numbers. In order to put the numbers into sequential order, the basic operation to be performed is that of comparison, and it has been proved that at least "on the order of" $n\log n$ comparisons are required to sort n numbers; i.e., that computation time must grow faster than a linear function of n. Now consider performing the same sorting task on the "spaghetti computer" [Dewdney 84]. We first cut n pieces of uncooked spaghetti so that each piece has a length proportional to one of the numbers to be sorted; this requires a time proportional to n. Next, loosely holding all the cut pieces of spa-

ghetti in one hand, bring the bundle sharply down on a flat horizontal surface, thus aligning the ends of all the pieces of spaghetti—a single operation. Finally, obtain the desired sorted sequence by first removing the tallest (most protruding) piece; then the tallest of the remaining pieces, and so on until the bundle is exhausted. As each piece is removed from the bundle, it is measured and the resulting number is recorded; this set of operations is linear in n. Thus, the entire sorting operation done on the spaghetti computer requires a series of linear time operations and can be accomplished in linear time—violating the $n\log n$ computational bound on sorting derived for sequential machines.

Two additional examples of how computation in an appropriately chosen analog (isomorphic) representation can violate a bound on sequential computation are:

(a) The "convex hull" of n points is the smallest convex region containing all n points. The convex hull is a polygon, each of whose vertices corresponds

to one of the extreme points of the set of points. While there is a $n\log n$ bound on finding a planar convex hull, this sequential machine bound can be violated by using the "rubber band computer" (Fig. 2-9). When stretched to fit over all the pins and then released, the rubber band will form the convex hull of the points.

(b) The problem of finding the shortest path joining two selected vertices of a graph has a sequential machine complexity of order n^2. We can violate the

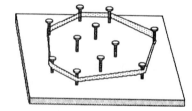

FIGURE 2-9
The Rubber Band Computer.

This computer determines the convex hull of a planar set of points. (After A. K. Dewdney. *Scientific American* 250:19-26, 1984.)

as in a computer, then an arbitrary degree of failure tolerant operation could be achieved at a cost of massive redundancy or repetition; i.e., by employing switches/neurons wired in parallel and performing the same function (see Box 2-9). In 1948, Claude Shannon proposed a more sophisticated scheme for using redundancy in

the context of achieving reliable transmission or storage of information. He showed that rather than just repeating the message many times, it was more efficient to encode the message so that each valid message had no close "neighbors" in "message space." Thus, if a message was slightly altered by noise or transmission

BOX 2-8 (*continued*)

n^2 bound on finding a shortest path in a graph using the "string computer" (Fig. 2-10). Each vertex is represented by

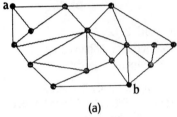

(a)

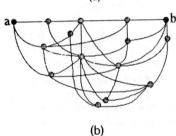

(b)

FIGURE 2-10
The String Computer.

This computer finds the shortest path between two specified vertices in a graph. (a) String analog of a given network. We are required to find the shortest path between the two darkened vertices. (b) The solution path found by grasping the selected vertices, and pulling in opposite directions.

a ring or knot, and if two vertices are joined by an edge, the corresponding rings are connected by a piece of string cut to the correct length and tied to the rings. To find the shortest path between vertices *a* and *b*, pick up the network by the rings *a* and *b* and pull the network taut. The shortest path is the sequence of taut strings. (As an interesting aside, if we pull hard enough to break the strings, the last set of strings that retains the connectivity between rings *a* and *b* is usually the longest path between these rings. It can also be shown that the longest path between any two vertexes can be found by first picking up the tree by any ring, and then holding the tree by the lowest dangling ring; the longest path runs from the ring being held to the one that now hangs lowest [Dewdney 85].)

While no examples of analog computation are known to provide a complete effective solution to intrinsically difficult problems, the "soap film computer" (Fig. 2-11) can find individual potentially optimal solutions to the *NP*-complete Steiner minimal tree problem in linear time. The Steiner-tree problem asks that *n* points in the plane be connected by a graph of minimum overall length. One is allowed to take as vertices of the graph not only the original *n* points, but additional ones as well. The soap film computer consists of two sheets of rigid plastic with pins between the sheets to represent the points to be spanned. When this device is dipped into a soap solution, the soap film connects the *n* pins in a Steiner-tree network.

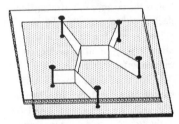

FIGURE 2-11
The Soap Film Computer.

This computer finds the solution for the shortest path connecting a planar set of points (the minimum Steiner-tree problem). (After R. Courant and H. Robbins. *What is Mathematics?* Oxford University Press, London, 1941.)

error, the resulting message would likely correspond to a point in message space that was near the original message but which itself did not correspond to another valid message. The original message could then be recovered from a received erroneous message by finding the nearest valid message in message space. Figure 2-13 shows the "space" of all conceivable messages, and the legal messages are indicated as distinguished points in that space. A message containing an error will not coincide with any of the distinguished points, but if it lies within the shaded sphere surrounding a legal message, then it is assigned to that legal message.

BOX 2-9 The Use of Redundancy to Achieve Fault Tolerant Computing

We are so used to the idea that the transcription of symbolic information and the operations performed in mathematics and logic can and must be error free, that it is easy to lose sight of the fact that perfection is almost never present in the physical artifacts that man constructs.* Yet, machines capable of formal symbolic computation must be perfect in the way they represent and transform information. As we will see in our discussion of logical reasoning in Chapter 4, such perfection is the essence of a strategy for dealing with complexity. The machines we build must employ some other strategy to attain perfection with imperfect components.

It is possible to obtain a reliable computing system using components that are subject to failure by using *redundancy*, i.e., more components than are necessary to accomplish the task. In addition to redundancy, it is also necessary to employ a connection or control scheme that takes into account the nature of the computation and the failure modes of the components. Redundancy can be utilized at various levels in the design hierarchy: at the level of the single component, at the subsystem level, and at

---

*Haugeland [Haugeland 85] in a relevant discussion contrasts the fate of Rembrandt's paintings, which are slowly deteriorating, with Shakespeare's sonnets which, as symbolic constructs, can be preserved exactly the way the author wrote them.

the level of completely functioning systems. Two of the many different approaches to fault-tolerant computing are described below.

Component Replication

Suppose we have a simple component, designated as ▶|, that permits electrical current to flow in one direction, but not in the other. Thus a circuit, A—▶|—B would permit current to flow from A to B but not from B to A. The ▶| component can fail "open" and not permit any current flow, or fail "shorted" and allow the current to flow in either direction. We want to design a circuit that operates properly despite these types of failure. Note that placing two or more ▶| in parallel will not solve the problem, because a short in any ▶| will cause the circuit to fail. Instead, we must use the "series-parallel" circuit shown in Fig. 2-12, which can operate properly even though a short has occurred in a single ▶| in all of the N parallel paths. It can also operate properly even if $(N-1)$ of the paths contain open ▶| elements.

In the 1950s, the mathematician John von Neumann showed how reliable organisms could be synthesized from unreliable components. Since in a complicated network the probability of errors in the basic processors could make the response of the final output unreliable, he sought some control mechanism to prevent the accumulation of these errors. The approach that he

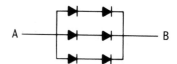

FIGURE 2-12
Redundancy Achieved by
Component Replication.

developed, similar in concept to that shown in Figure 2-12, uses N redundant paths for all operations. Thus, each input line is replicated N times and fed into N identical computing elements; this replication continues throughout the entire system. At the output of the system we have N output lines, and the final result will be accepted if a certain percentage of the output lines agree. For example, in a biological system, the N parallel outputs could be N distinct muscle strands comprising a single muscle. The muscle will flex if a certain percentage of strands agree.

Duplicative redundancy is innately inefficient. For example, suppose we have unreliable computing elements with failure rates of one failure every 200 operations. Using the von Neumann approach, a computing machine with 2500 such elements being actuated every five microseconds would require replication by a factor of 20,000 to obtain eight hours of error-free operation!

Cooperating Redundant Systems

If a set of processors has sufficient freedom to communicate, then we can develop a reliable system whose

BOX 2-9 (*continued*)

operation corresponds to a group of people working jointly on a problem. Certain controls must be incorporated into the system so that there is an effective way of partitioning the work, and so that a deviant processor does not write into the memory of another processor, does not tie up the communications channels, and does not seize the output mechanism. Processors can report to one another concerning their opinion on the "health" of any of the processors, and processors can ignore and redistribute the work of a processor that a consensus of the processors believes is unreliable. The type of "software implemented" fault tolerance has been used as the basis for computer systems that are required to have high degrees of reliability.

An example of message error detection and correction is presented in Fig. 2-14. Figure 2-14(a) uses a Venn diagram to show how three parity bits can provide single error detection and correction of a four-bit message. Figure 2-14(b) shows a code based on this concept.

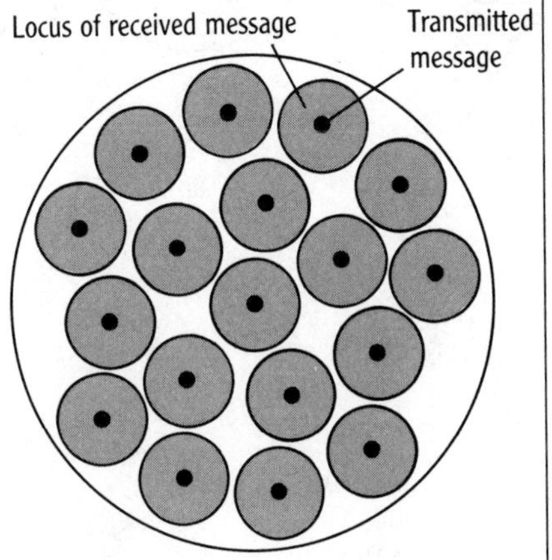

The above (and later) schemes developed to enhance computer and communication reliability do not really provide an adequate explanation of how the brain operates in the presence of failure, and they certainly do not explain the ultra-reliable "operation" of whole species or societies of intelligent organisms. In a sense, these "fault tolerant" schemes slow the effects of degeneration; they do not provide a mechanism for compensation, regeneration, or evolutionary improvement.

It has been suggested ([H. Crane, in press] and Box 2-3) that the brain is literally a collection of intelligent agents operating as a tightly knit social system, and that the same dynamics that allows for the malfunction or even death of individuals in society underlies the ability of the brain to function in the presence of cell death and local processing errors.

DISCUSSION

The brain is a mystery we may never succeed in penetrating—in addition to the obvious difficulties of discovering

Locus of received message

Transmitted message

FIGURE 2-13
Message-Space Representation of a Fault-Tolerant Coding Technique.

Any received message falling into a shaded sphere is assigned to the single legal message located at the center of the sphere (dot). Messages falling into the unshaded regions cannot be corrected.

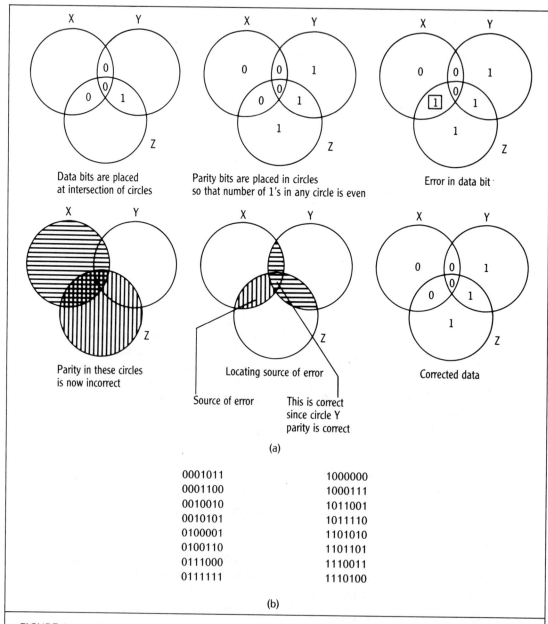

Data bits are placed
at intersection of circles

Parity bits are placed in circles
so that number of 1's in any circle is even

Error in data bit

Parity in these circles
is now incorrect

Locating source of error

Corrected data

Source of error

This is correct
since circle Y
parity is correct

(a)

0001011	1000000
0001100	1000111
0010010	1011001
0010101	1011110
0100001	1101010
0100110	1101101
0111000	1110011
0111111	1110100

(b)

FIGURE 2-14   Using Parity for Single Error Detection and Correction of a Message.

(a) Venn diagram explanation of a message coding scheme. (b) A set of messages for four data bits and three parity bits. The set of 16 messages shown can be correctly decoded even if a single binary symbol is incorrectly received in any transmitted message. If instead, we use simple replication of a four-bit code for each of the 16 possible messages, then three replications requiring 12 bits must be employed to achieve the same level of error recovery.

the nature of such an amazingly complex system, mathematics teaches us that fallacies and paradoxes are introduced into any analytical framework that is capable of discussing or examining itself. As Hofstadter has said [Hofstadter 79]:

> All the limitative theorems of metamathematics and the theory of computation suggest that once the ability to represent your own structure has reached a certain critical point, that is the kiss of death; it guarantees that you can never represent yourself totally. Gödel's Incompleteness Theorem, Church's Undecidability Theorem, Turing's Halting Theorem, Tarski's Truth Theorem—all have the flavor of some ancient fairy tale which warns you that, *To seek self-knowledge is to embark on a journey which . . . will always be incomplete, cannot be charted on any map, will never halt, cannot be described.* [p.697]

We might then ask how human intelligence can seemingly bypass the barriers imposed by logical proofs of unsolvability and noncomputability—or even those of intrinsically difficult (though solvable) problems. We note that it is often easier to prove the correctness of a result than to find the correct answer in the first place. If an "illogical" system, employing induction and analogy (see Chapter 4), can make a sufficiently high percentage of good guesses and pass them on to a logically correct checking device, the combination may be capable of effective operation even in situations where a logically consistent mechanical system will fail. The parity problem (Box 2-4) is an example where human intuition can easily find an answer, while no mechanical procedure has yet been devised to solve this particular formulation of the problem.

However, both logical and nonlogical mechanisms must generally contend with the nonsymmetry of solution versus nosolution; if we can obtain a solution (e.g., by guessing), and demonstrate or prove it, we have solved our problem; but if we cannot find an answer, we can almost never be sure that a solution does not exist.

Finally, an interesting and important question is, "What does it mean to know something?" The scientific viewpoint, grounded in the concept of operationalism, is that to know or understand something is to be able to predict its behavior. We usually express our knowledge of things by building mechanical or symbolic models, and relating the behavior of the model to the situation we wish to understand. It may be obvious that some very complex things (e.g., the universe) may not be understandable by any system less complex than the thing itself (or even have a description of lower complexity). However, it is not intuitively obvious that the specific way we attempt to express a problem, or the way we choose to describe the answer, should radically affect the difficulty of finding a solution. This assumes that we have not altered the competence of the system to deal with the problem, or the amount of information available to the system, but that we merely select a logically equivalent but different "phrasing." A dramatic example of this situation was presented in Box 2-4, in which a change in the way we are permitted to present (represent) the answer to the "parity problem" changes it from an unsolved problem to a trivial one. Finding effective representations appears to be at the heart of intelligent behavior; this is an issue we come back to repeatedly in the remainder of this book.

Appendixes

2-1

The Nerve Cell and Nervous System Organization

Plants do not have specialized cells (nerve cells) to transmit sensory and control information. While some very simple organisms[12] have specialized structures[13] that respond to external stimuli and coordinate movement of cell structures such as cilia, the specialized nerve cell is one of the main distinguishing attributes of members of the animal kingdom. All major groups of multicellular animals except the sponges have definite nerve cells (the sponges employ chemical means for internal coordination).

The nerve net, the most primitive system of organization of nerve cells, is found in the hydra (Fig. 2-15b). When any part of the hydra is stimulated, activity spreads out along the nerve net in all possible directions, eventually involving the entire organism. In addition to the more highly organized "nervous systems" based on one or more nerve cords and nerve cell concentrations called "ganglia," nerve nets are found in the blood vessels and intestinal walls of all vertebrates (including man).

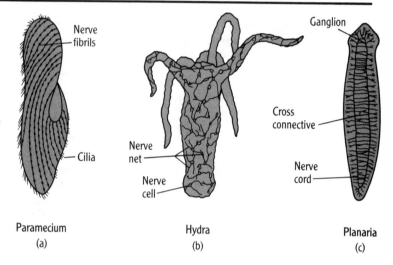

Paramecium
(a)

Hydra
(b)

Planaria
(c)

FIGURE 2-15   Nervous Systems of Various Primitive Organisms.

(a) Paramecium. (b) Hydra. (c) Planaria. (From *Biological Science: Molecules to Man*, BSCS Blue Version, 2nd edition, Houghton Mifflin, Boston, 1968, with permission.)

The planarian is one of the simplest organisms with a nervous system in addition to a nerve net (see Fig. 2-15c). A separate nerve cord runs along each side of its body terminating in a ganglion at the head end of the organism. It is quite possible that the nervous systems found in all higher organisms are merely size and complexity elaborations of the basic structure of the nervous system of the planarian.

The Nerve Cell

A nervous system is an organized network of nerve cells or neurons. Between seven and 100 different classes of neurons[14] have been identified in the human nervous system, three of which are shown in Fig. 2-16. Some of these cells are as long

---

[12]For example, the single cell Paramecium (kingdom Protista).

[13]For example, nerve fibrils as shown in Fig. 2-15a.

[14]Different definitions, based on somewhat arbitrary criteria, have been employed for classifying neurons.

59

APPENDIX 2-1

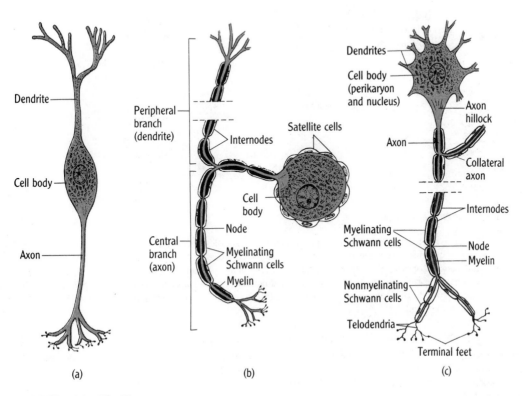

FIGURE 2-16   The Neuron.

Three different types of neurons. Myelin sheaths are shown in black. (a) Bipolar neuron (as found in the retina of the eye). (b) Pseudo-unipolar neuron (myelinated sensory neuron). (c) Multipolar neuron (myelinated somatic motor neuron). (From E.L. Weinreb. *Anatomy and Physiology*. Addison-Wesley, Reading, Mass., 1984, p. 135, with permission.)

as 3 meters, and depending on cell characteristics, nerve impulses travel at rates varying from 10 to 120 meters per second. As shown in Figure 2-16a, the typical nerve cell consists of three parts, the dendrites, the cell body, and the axon (also called the nerve fiber). The dendrites carry nerve signals toward the cell body, while the axon carries signals away. The nucleus of the neuron, located in the cell body, varies in form in different animals, and even within different parts of the

nervous system of the same animal.

Nerve structures are formed from bundles of neurons, arranged with the end branches of the axon of one neuron lying close to the dendrites of another neuron (Fig. 2-17). Each nerve cell can directly interact with up to 200,000 other neurons, although a more typical number of interacting neurons is somewhere between 1000 and 10,000. The point of contact between the components of two neurons is called a synapse. A small

microscopic gap between the two cells exists at the synapse, and it is known that the ease of nerve signal transmission across the synapse is altered by activity in the nervous system—a possible mechanism for learning.

If the end of a nerve fiber is sufficiently stimulated (i.e., there is a "threshold" below which the nerve cell does not respond) , the stimulus starts chemical and electrical changes that travel over the length of the fiber. These changes are

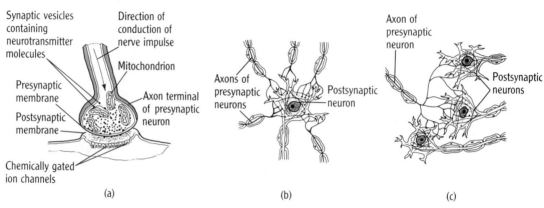

FIGURE 2-17   Nerve Structures.

(a) A chemical synapse. When a nerve impulse arrives at an axon terminal, chemical neurotransmitter molecules are released. The molecules diffuse across the synaptic cleft and attach to receptors on the membrane of the postsynaptic neuron. This attachment alters the three-dimensional shapes of the receptors and initiates a series of events that influence the activity of the postsynaptic neuron. (b) Many neuronal processes converge on a single cell. (c) Neuronal processes of a single cell diverge to a number of other cells. (From A. P. Spence and E. B. Mason. *Human Anatomy and Physiology*, Benjamin Cummings Publishing Co., Menlo Park, California, 1983, with permission.)

called the nerve impulse. After the impulse passes a segment of the nerve fiber, the segment recovers to its original state and is then ready for a new impulse.

Information Coding

One of the primary purposes of the neuron is to convey information. However, the brain uses stereotyped electrical signals for this purpose. These signals are virtually identical in all the nerve cells of all animals; i.e., they are symbols that do not in any way resemble the objects or concepts they represent. Thus, the origins and destinations of the nerve fibers must determine much of the content of the information they transmit. For example, signals reaching the brain from the optic nerve are known to contain visual as opposed to auditory information. In addition to the implicit source information, it is generally assumed that the only other piece of information a neuron can transmit is the equivalent of a single number (e.g., a magnitude representing the strength of a stimulus). Since the neuron nominally has an all-or-none response, it cannot use signal amplitude to encode magnitude information, but instead must use rate of firing or frequency. Neurons have a maximum firing rate of 1000 pulses per second.

Computation

It is generally assumed that the role the neuron plays in the brain's reasoning processes is equivalent to that of a logical switching element in a digital computer. While this is almost certainly too simple an analogy, we note that the neuron can compute a class of logical functions, called "threshold functions," since it has a sensitivity threshold, adjustable (adaptive) signal attenuation at each synapse, and an internal structure which allows the energy of incoming nerve signals to be integrated over both space and time. Thus, signals coming into different synapses at the same time, or even into the same synapse at different times, are "weighted" by the synapses and the resulting quantities summed. If this sum exceeds the sensitivity threshold, the neuron fires. The threshold functions include all the logical functions needed to construct a general purpose digital computer.

Further discussions can be found in Kuffler [Kuffler 76].

2-2

The Digital Computer

The first mechanical calculating devices were developed at least as early as the second century B.C. In more recent times, Pascal built a calculating machine in the seventeenth century. In the early 1800s, Joseph Marie Jacquard of France developed the idea of using a punched hole in a card to represent a number and control the operation of a loom. Charles Babbage used the Jacquard concept for his analytical engine in 1833, a machine he worked on until his death in 1871. This machine was quite close in concept to the ideas of the Harvard Mark I, developed almost a century later. Babbage's engine consists of two parts, a "store" to hold all the variables to be operated upon and for preserving previous results, and a "mill" into which the quantities to be operated upon are brought. Two sets of cards are used, one to direct the operations, and the other to hold the values of the variables that are to be operated upon. Augusta Ada Byron, the mathematically trained daughter of Lord Byron, wrote about the analytical engine: "We may say most aptly that the analytical engine weaves algebraic patterns just as the Jacquard loom weaves flowers and leaves." The mechanical complexities of the device and lack of financial support prevented Babbage from completing his engine.

Toward the end of the century (1886) Herman Hollerith realized that punched holes could be sensed by a machine to sort and manipulate the numbers represented by the holes. Hollerith cards and the associated machines were used for tabulation and statistical analysis by the U.S. Census Bureau. The first digital computer was the Harvard Mark I (automatic sequence controlled calculator, 1939). The operation of the machine was controlled by a plugboard that was wired to obtain a desired computation sequence; the arithmetic operations were carried out using relays. By 1946, the ENIAC, an all-electronic computer using vacuum tubes, replaced the electromechanical computer. It was a thousand times faster than the electromechanical devices, but still used a plugboard for control.

An important conceptual advance came at about the same time, when John von Neumann, Arthur Burks, and Herman Goldstine wrote an influential report, "Preliminary Discussion of an Electronic Computing Instrument." The report proposed a "stored program" concept to replace plugboards and programming switches. The control of the machine was to be carried out by means of a sequence of instruction codes stored as numerals in the memory of the computer. This so-called von Neumann architecture is the basis for the modern computer.

As discussed earlier, a computing device must have some way of storing its instructions and data, a means of manipulating the data, and some way of communicating with the user or the outside world. The memory of the computer stores the data and the instructions (the program) prepared by the user. The arithmetic operations (e.g., addition or subtraction) or logic operations (compare two quantities) are carried out in the arithmetic/logic unit. Communication with the outside world is carried out using an input device, such as a keyboard or a visual sensor, and the output can be printed, displayed on a screen, or used to activate a mechanical effector. The operation of the computer is "orchestrated" by the control portion of the system.

A binary coding scheme is often used to represent numbers and symbols in the computer. The reason for this representation is that there are electrical and magnetic circuits and devices that can be reliably switched into one of two stable states. Thus, a decimal number such as seven, represented in binary notation as 111, would appear in the computer as a sequence of three storage devices in the "1" or "on" state. The arithmetic unit is designed so that when it is given two numbers in binary form, it will carry out the required arithmetic operation and return the result in binary form.

It should be kept in mind that the term "memory" as used in the computer is not meant to indicate the type of capabilities possessed by the human memory. The computer memory can be thought of as consisting of ordered slots, each with an "address" in which data are stored. Data is retrieved by accessing the contents of the memory at a particular memory address, not by automatically linking data items by meaning. The programmer must devise specific accessing schemes to attain some desired form of data association. Much of the effort in artificial intelligence consists of devising representations that can overcome the address-based organization of the computer memory.

The operation of the computer is controlled by a "program," a set of instructions stored in the computer memory. The program specifies the data to be used and the operations to be carried out on the data. Conceptually, the program will eventually be converted into a set of instructions in which (for each instruction) one or more operands are extracted from computer memory, some simple arithmetic or logical operation performed, and the result returned to some new location in memory. All of the final program specifications are given in the form of binary operation codes that can be interpreted by the machine. Some of the instructions are "conditional " in nature, i.e., the next step to be carried out depends on the results of the computation. For example, a conditional instruction might be: "If the result of the current operation is positive, go to step 31, otherwise go to step 240." (This instruction is, of course, binary-coded and not in English.) The use of conditional instructions gives the programmer the ability to write programs that can react to the intermediate results of the computation; otherwise a program would merely carry out the same fixed sequence of operations regardless of the nature of the data.

The control unit examines the next instruction of the program, determines which of the other computer units will be needed, and sends the necessary control codes to each such unit. The timing of the computer operations is accomplished through the use of a "clock," a circuit that produces a continual sequence of timing pulses that synchronize the operation of the various computer elements.

Because it is very tedious to write programs using the primitive binary code required by the computer, programming languages (e.g., BASIC, Pascal, LISP) have been developed that allow the user to specify the desired operations at a higher conceptual level. These high-level language operations are converted by a "compiler" program into more primitive instructions, and then further translated into the low-level binary code required by the computer using an "assembler" program.[15]

For example, a high-level command such as *Add A to B and assign the result to C* will be converted to operations such as *Assign memory locations to numerical quantities A, B, and C. Retrieve A from memory and place it in register 1, retrieve B from memory and place it in register 2, add register 1 to register 2 and place the results in register 3. then store the contents of register 3 in memory location C.* These detailed instructions are finally converted to the computer's binary code.

---

[15]The compiler can be independent of the specific computer on which the program is to be run, but the assembler is usually specific to a particular type of computer. The compiler and assembler are often combined into a single program for more efficient operation.

3

The Representation of Knowledge

Intelligent behavior depends on being able to use stored knowledge about objects, processes, goals, causality, time, and action. Some of the questions that arise when trying to understand the nature and the representation of knowledge are:

- What is knowledge?
- Aside from the actual content, is the specific form in which knowledge is encoded an important factor in achieving intelligent behavior?
- How can knowledge be represented in the memory of a computer?
- Are there types of knowledge that cannot be described or discussed?

One of the remarkable attributes of human intelligence is the ability to convert a problem into a familiar form or *representation* that can be operated on using previously known techniques. In a simplified sense, this book puts forth the thesis that intelligence is largely the ability to create and manipulate descriptions. We are thus concerned with the nature of descriptions, what they are, their characteristics, and what their relation is to the things they describe.

This chapter will examine the concept of representation, and will discuss a variety of representations for different problem domains. We are particularly interested in representations that can be formally defined, and are thus suitable for computer mechanization.

REPRESENTATION: CONCEPTS

Two people view a basketball game. One person sees ten players moving around in a random manner, and notices that a ball and two hoops seem to be the focuses of action. The other person knows the rules of the game, has followed the teams, and therefore sees the strategy being used by each team. Two people listen to the crash of thunder. One person interprets it as the gods expressing anger at the people's sins, and the other interprets the thunder in terms of electrical discharge from the clouds. Two people are discussing the economic recession. One feels that it is a worldwide situation caused by the oil crisis, while the other person views it as a natural result of poor tax policies.

In all of these cases, we have an observed phenomenon that is interpreted in accordance with a stored framework (model, metaphor, representation) that is used by the person to deal with the outside world. Different areas of human intellectual and emotional activities access different representations of the world with different attributes—they construct different "realities." For example, science uses representations that will only accommodate things that can be measured or observed.[16] Thus Newton's laws of motion deal with force, mass, and acceleration of objects, all of which can be measured by instruments. Religion, on the other hand, uses representations that deals with things that are not observable, such as *heaven, hell, angels*, as well as attributes that are not measurable, such as *goodness, evil*, and *holiness*. These different fields thus

---

[16]To be accurate, we note that many physical quantities cannot be measured directly, but must be inferred from other measurements.

impose distinct requirements on their representations. For example, physics will require that a representation or model be able to predict the behavior of objects. Religion may expect the models or representations to affect the behavior and the mental state of its adherents.

A discussion of the role of representation in human thinking is given below. Later we will be mainly concerned with representations suitable for machine reasoning, i.e., representations that are formal or "rule-like." A general concern is how a machine might be given models or representations that would enable it to operate in the real world.

Form vs. Content of Knowledge

Knowledge can be defined as the stored information or the models used by a person or machine to interpret, predict, and appropriately respond to the outside world. It is important to distinguish between the *form* and the *content* of knowledge. For example, addition of numbers can be performed by storing a *look-up table* containing the sums of all acceptable input pairs of integers. Alternatively, an electronic counter can be used which can successively be incremented by the two integers to obtain their sum. From a functional or content standpoint, the two approaches will produce identical answers, but from a representational standpoint, there are significant differences that influence how efficiently we can perform the given task. The look-up table would be very fast, but would require a very large memory store if we had to deal with large integers. The electronic counter would be much more efficient in its hardware requirements, but would be much slower in

REPRESENTATION: CONCEPTS

producing the required answers. Thus, the specific structures by which knowledge is characterized, and its encoded form, can have a significant effect on its use in solving problems. Further, since no single representation or model can capture all aspects of a real object, an intelligent entity must employ a wide spectrum of representations to deal with the world.

Representing Knowledge

A representation of a situation (or object, or problem) is a translation of the situation into a system consisting of a vocabulary that names things and relations, operations that can be performed on these things, and facts and constraints about these things. The primary distinguishing characteristics of a representation are (a) what information is made explicit, and (b) how the information is physically encoded. The purpose of a representation is to simplify the problem of answering a restricted class of questions about the given situation, and thus the selection of the representation must be goal-directed. At least two distinct representations are required to match the competence of some given computing mechanism to the requirements of solving a real world problem: the first representation provides efficient symbolic apparatus for answering questions about the given situation, and the second translates the solution techniques of the first into the operations and storage structures inherent in the machine.

The "15 game" is a good example of converting a problem to an alternative representation, using the new formulation to aid in solving the problem, and finally translating the result back into the origi-

nal problem domain. In this game, two people take turns selecting numbers from 1 to 9. Once a number has been selected by one person, it is unavailable to the other. The person who first has exactly three numbers in his collection that add up to 15 wins the game. A sample game for two people, A and B, might be:

A 5 ; B 3 (A selects 5; B selects 3)
A 5,9; B 3,1 (A selects 9; B chooses 1 to prevent A from achieving 15 on his next move)
A 5,9,4; B 3,1,2 (A selects 4; B chooses 2 to block A)
A 5,9,4,6 win!! (A selects 6 and wins with 4+5+6 = 15)

Now suppose we analyze this game using the representation,

2	9	4
7	5	3
6	1	8

Choosing a number in the 15 game corresponds to putting a marker in the tick-tack-toe board shown above. Thus, A choosing 5 is equivalent to putting A's marker in the center of the tick-tack-toe board; the game sequence can be shown in the new representation as:

```
- - -    - A -    B A A    B A A
- A B    - A B    - A B    - A B
- - -    - B -    - B -    A B -
                                (win for A)
  1        2        3        4
```

Note that in the third step A forced the win, since a move was chosen that provided A with two possibilities for three in a row, and B could only block one of these two possibilities. The tick-tack-toe representation and strategy were used to play the 15 game in an expert manner; we make our moves in the tick-tack-toe domain, and report back with the number corresponding to the tick-tack-toe location chosen.

The Relation Between a Representation and Things Represented

As noted above, in its most general form a representation consists of a language for describing things in the world and a data structure or formalism for physically encoding the descriptions. A "model" is a specific description.

A natural language such as English or French is a representation in which the vocabulary (lexicon) has semantic content (meaning)—the words denote things in the world. In addition to the lexicon, the language includes constraints on what constitutes an acceptable structuring of words in a sentence, and rules for transforming words and sentences to account for singular, plural, tense, and sentence forms dealing with questions, commands, or statements. The written and spoken forms of a language are the data structures of the representation. Thus, a natural language is a representation with a "built-in" semantic content. The *meaning* of a description is fixed by the conventions of the language.

Logical and mathematical systems are also representations, but in such "formal languages" the vocabulary has no semantic content. To the extent that meaning can be ascribed to a logical expression, such meaning is not inherent in the expression but is an interpretation imposed on the expression by some outside agent.

The same logical expression can be assigned completely different meanings by different agents.

Most of the representations we describe in this chapter have very simple vocabularies with no semantic content—they are largely data structures that can be used by a computer to store and transform information in a manner specified by a set of rules or algorithmic procedures. This lack of *inherent* meaning in the representations employed by a computer leads to the obvious question of whether it is possible for a computer to "understand" anything in a way a person might.

In his 1985 presidential address to the American Philosophical Association, Dretske asserts [Dretske 85]:

> . . . . all cognitive operations (whether by artifacts or natural biological systems) will necessarily be realized in some electrical, chemical, or mechanical operation over physical structures. . . . This fact alone doesn't tell us anything about the cognitive nature of the operation being performed—whether, for instance, it is an inference, a thought, or taking a square root. For what makes these operations into thoughts, inferences, or arithmetical calculations is, among other things, the meaning of, or the semantics of, those structures over which they are performed. . . . Unless the symbols have what we might call an intrinsic meaning, a meaning they possess which is independent of our communicative intentions and purposes, then this meaning must be irrelevant to assessing what the machine is doing when it manipulates them. The machine is processing meaningful (to us) symbols, but the way it processes them is quite independent of what they mean— hence, nothing the machine does is explicable in terms of the meaning of the

symbols it manipulates or indeed, of their even having a meaning. . . . In order, therefore to approximate something of genuine cognitive significance, to give a machine something that bears a mark, if not all the marks, of the mental, the symbols a machine manipulates must be given a meaning of their own, a meaning that is independent of the user's purposes and intentions. Only by doing this will it become possible to make the meaning of these symbols relevant to what the machine does with them, possible in other words, to make the machine do something because of what the symbols mean, possible, therefore, to make these symbols mean something to the machine itself.

It should be noted that the arbitrary (even though fixed) conventions of a natural language are not enough to provide *intrinsic* meaning to a description of some aspect of the real world. This issue is further discussed later in this chapter and in Chapter 6.

ROLE OF REPRESENTATION

In the case of the 15 game, an appropriately chosen representation served the purpose of converting a given problem into another problem that has a known solution. Some other roles of representation are:

- *Interpretation.* Sensory information can be interpreted by using internal representations (models) of real-world objects. For example, visual information can be interpreted by comparing the sensed visual data with stored descriptions of objects.
- *Organizing function.* A representation may allow us to organize information so

that similarities and differences between objects and events are more readily identified. Plotting two sets of data on the same graph will visually show similarities and differences.
- *Questioning function.* Internal models lead us to ask questions about events. Why is a certain event occurring when our model predicts otherwise? We are thus guided to revisions in our models, the generation of a set of alternative models, or further attempts at data gathering from our surroundings.
- *Predictive function.* An internal model allows us to predict events that will result from actions. For example, a mathematical model of a rocket enables us to predict the motion of the rocket.
- *Deductive function.* Certain representations can be used to make new knowledge explicit by allowing deductions to be performed on the original knowledge. For example, given *All pit dogs are dangerous. This dog is a pit dog*, we can deduce *This dog is dangerous.*

REPRESENTATIONS EMPLOYED IN HUMAN THINKING

The concept of representation as a way of selectively, and even creatively modeling the world, has proved to be one of the key ideas underlying our understanding of both human and machine intelligence. In this subsection we briefly describe the representations used by people to solve real-world problems. Our exposition here will be general and descriptive, in contrast to the more detailed and technical discussion of the rest of this chapter which deals with the formal representations suitable for use in computers.

The Use of Models and Representations

Most people are unaware of their use of models in problem solving and in the way they view the world. As Robert North has stated [North 76]:

> Each of us carries around in his or her head a model of the world, of society, of the local community, of the family—even of oneself, and none of us can deal with any of these entities, even superficially, without reference to the appropriate mental construct or model. It is the only way we have of relating to other people and to our larger surroundings. We draw upon these models whenever we discuss affairs, whenever we vote, and whenever we plan for the future in any way.

George Kelly [Kelly 55] focuses on the psychology of personal constructs, the creative capacity of living things to represent the environment, not merely to respond to it. The point of view that dominates this work is "constructive alternativism," the creation of alternative constructions to explain things in the universe. Some key ideas are:

- *Reality is subjective.* "Each person personally contemplates the stream of events upon which he or she is so swiftly borne," and builds a personal model of reality.
- *People as scientists.* Every person, in his or her own particular way, is a "scientist" whose ultimate aim is to predict and control. There are differences between the personal viewpoints of different people just as there can be differences between the theoretical points of view of different scientists.

- *Representing the universe.* Life in one part of the universe, the living creature, is able to represent another part, the environment. Because man can represent the environment, he can place alternative constructions on it. Man views the world using patterns or templates that he creates, and then attempts to "fit" these templates to the realities of which the world is composed. The fit is not always very good. Man creates his own way of seeing the world in which he lives, the world does not provide this for him. The same events can often be viewed in the light of two or more systems, yet the events do not belong to any system. A construct (specific pattern or model for interpreting some aspect of reality) is used to forecast events and is tested in terms of its predictive efficiency. In general, people improve their internal constructs by increasing the repertoire of constructs, by altering the existing ones to obtain an improved "match" with the world, or by combining constructs. Interpretations of the universe will never be perfect, and thus are always subject to revision or replacement.
- *Psychological relevance.* "Man, to the extent that he is able to construe his circumstances, can find freedom from their domination. The person who orders his life in terms of many special convictions makes himself a victim of circumstances. Every little prior conviction not open to review is a hostage he gives to fortune; it determines whether the events of tomorrow will bring happiness or misery. The person whose prior convictions encompass a broad perspective, and has cast these in terms of

principles rather than rules, has a much better chance of discovering regularities in 'world events' than someone with a limited and inflexible set of models."

The Use of "Visual" Representations

There are many interesting examples of visual representations used by people to solve problems. For example, Koestler [Koestler 69] quotes Friedrich Kekule, the chemist who discovered the structure of the benzene ring in a dream:

> I turned my chair to the fire and dozed. Again the atoms were gamboling before my eyes. This time the smaller groups kept modestly in the background. My mental eye, rendered more acute by repeated visions of this kind, could now distinguish larger structures, of manifold conformation; long rows; all twining and twisting in snakelike motion. But look! What was that? One of the snakes had seized hold of its own tail, and the form whirled mockingly before my eyes. As if by a flash of lightning, I awoke.

The result of the dream was Kekule's insight that organic compounds such as benzene were closed rings rather than open structures.

The Nobel Prize–winning physicist Richard Feynman used a visual approach to the solution of particle physics problems which has become known as "Feynman diagrams." As described by Dyson [Dyson 79] this form of visual thinking was difficult to communicate to others:

> The reason Dick's physics was so hard for ordinary people to grasp is that he did not use equations. The usual way theoretical physics was done since the time of

Newton was to begin by writing down some equations and then to work hard calculating solutions to the equations. . . . Dick just wrote down the solutions out of his head without ever writing down the equations. He had a physical picture of the way things happen, and the picture gave him the solutions, directly and with a minimum of calculations. It was no wonder that people who had spent their lives solving equations were baffled by him. Their minds were analytical; his was pictorial. My own training since the far-off days when I struggled with Piaggio's differential equations had been analytical. But as I listened to Dick and stared at the strange diagrams that he drew on the blackboard, I gradually absorbed some of his pictorial imagination and began to feel at home in his version of the universe.

The scientific literature has many additional examples of visual representations used to solve problems. The choice and application of such representations is very much a mystery. In our attempts to build intelligent machines we are currently limited to the formal representations described in the following sections.

EFFECTIVENESS OF A REPRESENTATION

A good representation should allow all situations of interest to be easily described, and it should be stable, i.e., if the original situation changes slightly, its new representation should not be significantly different from the original representation. There should be little effect on the final form and content of the represented information even if there is a major change irrelevant to the class of questions that are of interest. The representation should also identify redundant information to allow compact storage in a physical (computer, brain) memory system.

The operations and data structures provided by the representation should result in simple computational procedures for answering questions relevant to the given situation. For example, in the matchstick puzzle of Chapter 1, the representation organized the information so as to reduce the size of the combinatorial search space. In the example of the 15 game, the representation converted a difficult game into a familiar one.

A representation should highlight the important information and thus simplify the relevance problem, as in the following "31 dominoes" problem. A domino is a rectangle with dimensions exactly equal to two adjacent grid squares (see Fig. 3-1).

Given an 8 × 8 grid (Fig. 3-1a), it is obvious that it is possible to find many arrangements in which 31 dominoes can be placed on the grid so as to cover 62 of the grid squares; Fig. 3-1(b) shows one such arrangement.

Are there always arrangements of the 31 dominoes that will leave any two selected squares uncovered? In particular, is there at least one such an arrangement that will leave two diagonally opposite squares uncovered, as shown in Fig. 3-1(c)? Try to solve this problem before looking at the answer we present below.

It is difficult for most people to prove the solution, namely, that the required configuration of dominoes cannot be found. However, if we color the grid with alternating black and white squares, as would be found on a checkerboard, we observe that the two diagonally opposite squares have the same color. Now we further observe that each domino covers exactly one black and one white square when placed on the board in a *legal* position. Thus, any possible legal covering with the 31 dominoes must leave one black and one white square uncovered. This condition is violated for the diagonally opposite squares. This simple solution to the posed problem was possible only after we changed the representation

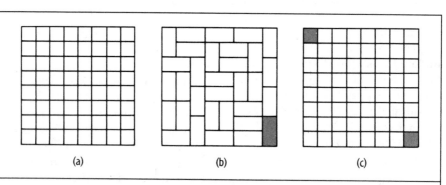

(a)   (b)   (c)

FIGURE 3-1   The 31 Dominoes Problem.

(a) An 8 × 8 grid. (b) One arrangement of 31 dominoes on 8 × 8 grid. (c) Desired coverage of 8 × 8 grid. Shaded areas on (b) and (c) are uncovered squares.

(by coloring the grid squares) to one that made explicit the critical constraint on any possible solution.

In addition to all the previous considerations, the utility of a representation often depends on its generality: there should be a number of reasonably distinct problem domains to which it can be applied.

REPRESENTATIONS EMPLOYED IN ARTIFICIAL INTELLIGENCE

A significant portion of AI research is concerned with creating and studying the properties of symbolic representations, since such representations lie at the heart of planning, reasoning, and problem solving. It is surprising that there are only about ten distinct representational systems of broad generality currently employed in AI research. We will explore some of these in more detail in subsequent chapters. The major representations are indicated below, and several of particular interest to this book are discussed in following subsections.

Feature space (or decision space). A feature space is formed by assigning a problem-related measurement to each axis of a multidimensional space. Figure 3-2 shows a two-dimensional feature space with one axis representing weight and the other height. One of the points shown represents an individual 6 feet tall and 200 pounds in weight. Points that are close together in this representation represent persons or objects that have similar height-weight measurements.

Relational graph/semantic net. A tree or graph structure is typically used to de-

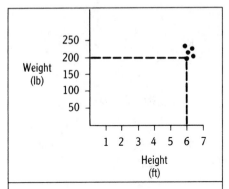

FIGURE 3-2

A Two-Dimensional Feature Space.

Point represents an individual who is 6 ft tall and weighs 200 lb. Cluster of points represents persons or objects with similar measurements.

scribe relationships between objects (e.g., objects in a story), often for the purpose of general question answering. The net shown in Fig. 3-3 represents the facts: John is a man, John likes Mary, John sees $object_1$, and $object_1$ is a book. Using this net, it is possible to answer questions such as "Who does John like?," and "Does John see a book?" Note that to answer the second question it is necessary to trace through both the path "John sees $object_1$" and "$object_1$ is a book."

Decision (or game) tree. In a typical tree structure, each node, representing a state, is connected to one or more successor states. The goal is to traverse the tree from an initial state to a desired final state. In the example shown in Fig. 3-4 we begin with two sets, one with the two elements + + and the other with the single element $. Two players take turns, and at each turn a player can choose any number of elements from one of the two

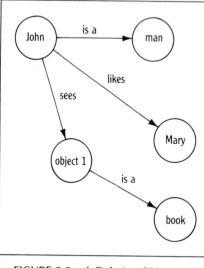

FIGURE 3-3   A Relational Net.

sets. The person taking the last element loses. The tree shows that the first player has three choices +, + +, or $, and shows the configuration that results after each choice. Subsequent lines show the choices remaining to the second player, and then the first player, until no further alternatives are available for either. The exhaustive tree for this game shows that the first player should take both + + elements on the first move.

State transition graph (or sequential machine).   This representation uses nodes and labeled links. The traversal of any particular link requires that the input conditions specified by its label are satisfied. This compact representation can be used to represent any algorithmic procedure, as discussed extensively in Chapter 2. The state diagram shown in Fig. 3-5 shows a "parity machine" that receives as input a string of 1's or 0's, and determines whether the number of 1's in the string is odd or even.

The machine goes into the ODD state when an odd number of 1's has been input, and into the EVEN state for an even number of 1's. The machine must be initialized to start in the EVEN state. The arrows indicate the transition to the same or the other state, and the 0 or 1 indicates the input symbol that causes the transition.

Frames.   A frame is a way of representing knowledge about the objects and events common to a particular situation. The elements of a given situation are stored as entries in the "slots" of the frame (see Chapter 6). In Fig. 3-6 we show an open frame for DOG, and a filled-in

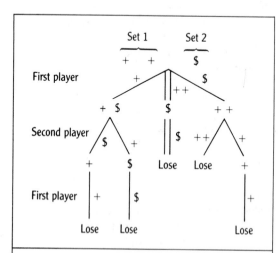

FIGURE 3-4   A Typical Game Tree.

Double lines mark the only path by which the first player can force a win.

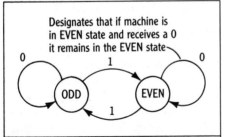

FIGURE 3-5
State Transition Graph for a Parity Machine.

object is a dog, then that object is an animal.

$$(ALL\ X)[DOG(X) \rightarrow (ANIMAL(X))\ ]$$

Mathematics. Mathematical representations are pervasive in all areas of AI; e.g., representations such as power series, Fourier transforms, the matrix form, and spatial coordinate systems play an important role in many areas of machine perception. The mathematical expression below specifies the relationship between R, x, y, and A.

$$R = x\cos A + y\sin A$$

Procedural representations. Knowledge about the world can be formulated in terms of procedures that allow specific tasks to be performed, as in

PROCEDURE: BOIL WATER
1-Obtain pot, and put water in it
2-Put pot over range burner, and turn on burner
3-Turn off burner when steam rises

This is an example of knowing by "knowing how." Thus, given the procedure we might know how to boil water;

frame for a specific dog, DOG-1. Note that there are slots that have default values, i.e., values that will apply unless otherwise specified. If we are told that DOG-1 is a three-legged, white and black-spotted Dalmatian named Penny , we can record this information in the DOG-1 frame on the right.

Logic. The propositional and predicate calculus are formalizations of the process of inferring new information from existing facts (see Chapter 4). The notation given below indicates that for all objects, if the

```
(?                            (DOG-1
  A DOG                         A DOG
    WITH [BREED = ?]              WITH [BREED = DALMATIAN]
         [FEET    = 4]default          [FEET    = 3]
         [EARS    = 2]default          [EARS    = 2] (default value)
         [NAME  = ?]                   [NAME  = PENNY]
         [SIZE    = ?]                 [SIZE    = ?]
         [COLOR = ?])                  [COLOR = WHITE WITH BLACK SPOTS])
```

FIGURE 3-6   A Frame for the Concept "A Dog."

(a) Concept of a dog using frame representation. (b) Instantiation of the frame for a specific dog.

however, we might not understand the concept "boiling water."

Production systems.   Production systems use rules of the form, IF *condition A* is satisfied THEN *consequence B* follows. The production rule approach is discussed in Chapter 7.

Isomorphic/iconic/analogical representations.   These are representations for which there is a direct structural relation to some of the properties of the domain being represented (see below and Chapter 9). In Fig. 3-7, we show that a house plan is an isomorphic representation of the actual physical house.

Feature Space (or Decision Space)

As indicated in the previous subsection, a feature space is formed by assigning a problem-related measurement to each axis of a multidimensional space. This representation can be used for many purposes, but is especially relevant for decision making and classification tasks. For example, consider the problem of classifying a person into the category *man* or *woman* given the person's height and weight measurements. In Fig. 3-8 we again show a two-dimensional feature space that uses height as one dimension and weight as the other. A (*height, weight*) measurement set, such as (5'10", 175 lb) is then repre-

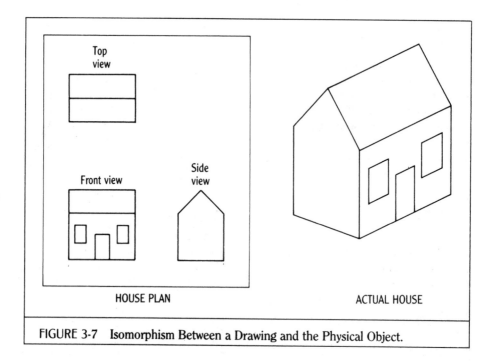

HOUSE PLAN   ACTUAL HOUSE

FIGURE 3-7   Isomorphism Between a Drawing and the Physical Object.

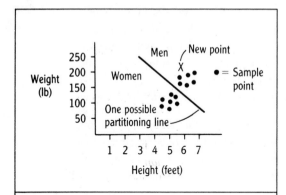

FIGURE 3-8

Example of Partitioning a Two-Dimensional Feature Space as the Basis for Making Classification Decisions.

and nonlinear programming. Basically, a *cost* of making a classification error is defined and is used to determine boundaries producing *expected-least-cost* classifications. For example, in the one-dimensional case shown in Fig. 3-9, we plot a height distribution for the classes men and women. We can select a decision line for separating the two classes, and if it is more "expensive" to make the mistake of classifying a man incorrectly as a woman, we will position the line toward the lower height values.

Decision Tree/Game Tree

We noted that a decision tree is often used to describe exhaustively all the consequences that can arise from some initial situation (state), assuming each state can

sented as a point in the feature space. It is possible to partition the space so that points that are typical examples of their class lie in a particular partition. In Fig. 3-8 the space has been partitioned into the classes *men* and *women*, based on a set of typical members of each class. Note that a new point, (6', 225 lb) falls in the male class. If the measurements are good indicators of the classes being represented, then the data for each class "cluster" into a compact region, and regions for distinct classes are well separated.

A well-chosen feature space can be partitioned into regions such that the points in each region belong to a single class of objects or events. One problem is to partition the feature space, based on a given set of labeled samples, called the *training set*. The partitioning boundaries can be generated using techniques from statistical decision theory, and linear

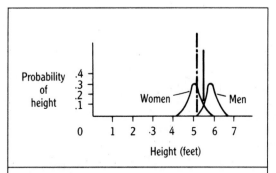

FIGURE 3-9

One-Dimensional Classification: Distinguishing Men from Women on the Basis of Height.

The decision line on the left (interrupted) is selected if classifying a man incorrectly is more "expensive" than misclassifying a woman. The solid line on the right should be used if both types of misclassification errors are equally costly.

only give rise to a specified number of successor states as a result of the application of a given set of operations or actions. For example, a tree could provide an explicit representation of all possible moves in a game of checkers. Many techniques are available to make an efficient traversal of the tree, and to limit the number of paths that must be examined.

One problem that often arises in the decision tree/graph representation is finding the shortest or longest path between two nodes in the graph, or, alternatively, determining which paths have a high "payoff" with respect to achieving some given goal. This type of problem is often handled using *relaxation*, and an example is shown in Fig. 3-10. Suppose we want to go from an origin node to a destination node taking the shortest path. In Fig. 3-10(a), we show the basic computation employed. In this example there are

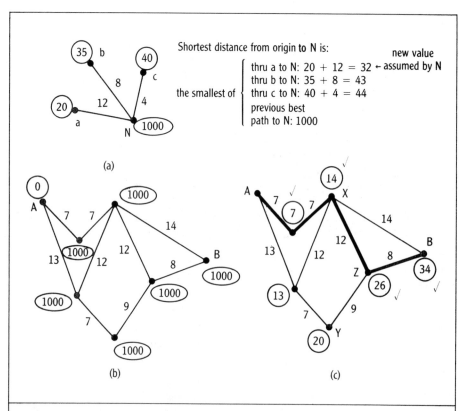

FIGURE 3-10   Finding the Minimum Path in a Graph using Relaxation.

(a) Basic approach. (b) Road network example. (c) Shortest path shown by thick line; e.g., shortest way from Z back to origin is: via $X = 14 + 12 = 26$, since via $Y = 20 + 9 = 29$.

paths to node N coming from nodes a,b, and c. Attached to each node is a circled number specifying the shortest distance from the origin node (not shown) to a,b, and c respectively. The shortest distance from the origin to N is then obtained as follows: For each node a, b, and c, form the sum of its circled number and the distance from that node to N. Select the smallest sum or the current value as the shortest distance from the origin to N. In Fig. 3-10(b) we show a graph, and in Fig. 3-10(c) the final results of the computation. A is the origin node and B is the destination node. The circled values in Fig. 3-10(b) are used to initialize the computation; the value 1000 could have been replaced by any number larger than any reasonable final answer. The computation described in Figure 3-10(a) can be performed at any node in any order. When the computation can no longer produce a change, (i.e., a reduction of an existing circled value, anywhere in the network), the circled value at the destination is the desired shortest path length. Note that, in general, we may have to perform the "update" computation of Fig. 3-10(a) many times at each node before no further change is possible. When we have completed the computation, we trace back through the circled nodes that led to this lowest number. This is shown by the check marks in Fig. 3-10(c).

Another approach to this problem uses various *pruning* techniques that ignore unpromising paths. One of the best known pruning techniques, the *alpha-beta heuristic* shown in Box 3-1, reduces the number of branches that must be analyzed by ignoring obvious *loser* branches.

Since the decision tree and other graph structure representations require an explicit description of the complete problem domain, they do not seem capable of dealing with the potentially infinite problems that are the core problems of AI. For example, the decision tree appears to require an exhaustive listing of all alternatives. However, there are three methods for removing this difficulty. (It should be noted that these methods do not guarantee that the "best solution" will always be found.) First, we can provide a single number estimate, an *heuristic evaluation function*, that indicates the value of exploring the (potentially infinite) remainder of the tree extending beyond some given node. Second, we can throw away information that does not appear to be important in finding a best solution, based on the assumption that only a few aspects of the problem need be considered to obtain an acceptable answer *most of the time*. Finally, if a mechanism exists for generating portions of the tree as needed, then only those parts of a tree that we wish to examine need to be generated; typically, only a finite portion of a potentially infinite tree need be searched to find a desired solution.

Isomorphic/Iconic/Analogical Representations

We usually do not appreciate the remarkable "isomorphic" representation known as a road map (Fig. 3-11). The road map can be used to answer an unbounded set of very complex questions. For a current location on the map, we might ask, What is the nearest major town, and how far away is it? What is the closest highway intersection where at least three roads come together? Note the complexity of trying to answer such questions by using tabular data, or other similar symbolic representations. For the first question, one would have to store the locations of all towns and be able to determine the road distance to each town from every road point. The second question would require that we either prestore or compute the intersection of all roads, and be able to determine the road distance of these intersections for all locations in the map. One can see some of the problems of storing the map information in a symbolic format that is still capable of providing the answer to any question that could have been answered by looking at the map itself.

The term "isomorphic", "iconic", or "analogical" representation is used to denote representations for which there is a direct structural and metric relation to some of the properties of the domain being represented. Technically, this type of a relationship is called an *isomorphism*, and we can say that an isomorphic representation is able to represent implicitly those properties of the domain preserved by the isomorphism. An interesting example of an isomorphic representation is the

---

 ## BOX 3-1 Game Trees and the Alpha-beta Heuristic

A game can be represented as a tree, where alternating levels indicate the moves available to each opponent. In the tree below, we show the value of the game situation to the first player as the lowest level of the tree:

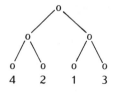

moves available to 1st player

moves available to 2nd player

value of each game situation to the first player

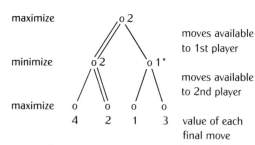

maximize

minimize

maximize

moves available to 1st player

moves available to 2nd player

value of each final move

The first player tries to select a move that will result in the best game situation, i.e., the highest value after the second player has made his selection, while the second tries to minimize this value. Using a mini-max analysis, we can project values up to all nodes of the tree. In the example below, if we look at the bottom row, we know that the minimizing player will choose the branch corresponding to a value of 2, rather than the branch corresponding to 4. Similarly, given the choice of a 1 or a 3 on the bottom row, the minimizing player will choose the 1. The maximizing player, given the choice of 2 or 1 on the second row will choose the 2. Thus, the best that the first player can achieve is the value 2, obtained by selecting the left-hand branch.

Complete evaluation of a game tree is usually impractical, and is indeed unnecessary. In the above tree, if the analysis is carried out from left to right, the maximizing player would eliminate the choice marked with * as soon as the value of 1 is projected up from the lowest level, since this is less than the other node (whose value, 2, is assumed to have already been determined). Thus, it is not necessary to evaluate the lowest level node whose value is 3.

The alpha-beta heuristic is a tree-pruning algorithm that formalizes the following concept: Whenever we project a value to a parent node from a lower node that is better than the existing value of the parent node, check how that parent node now compares with other nodes on its level. It may be that no further exploration is needed below that parent node.

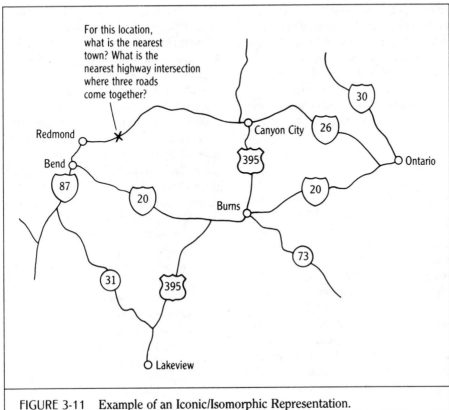

For this location, what is the nearest town? What is the nearest highway intersection where three roads come together?

FIGURE 3-11   Example of an Iconic/Isomorphic Representation.

string model for determining the shortest path in a graph (see Box 2-8). Consider the problem of finding the shortest route from city A to city B over some given network of roads. Construct a "map" made out of pieces of string to represent the roads connecting the cities. Let the length of each piece of string be proportional to the length of the road segment it represents, and knot together the strings at places where the roads intersect. Now with both hands, grasp the points in the string map corresponding to cities A and B and pull these points in opposite directions. The shortest path will correspond to the road segments represented by the

strings supporting the rest of the dangling road network.

Solving a problem using an isomorphic representation is often similar to performing a physical experiment on a "real-world" situation, as opposed to obtaining the solution by an algorithmic technique applied to a symbolic description. A physical experiment, unlike a symbolic solution, can proceed without complete specification or understanding of the problem domain. Thus, at least in part, the power of an isomorphic representation resides in the fact that there is no need to make explicit the problem domain constraints and relationships, since they are captured by the structure of the representation. Even if understood, attempting to make such knowledge explicit is often impractical because of the enormous amount of detail needed to capture the many aspects of the natural world. Isomorphic (iconic) representations are discussed in Chapter 9.

DISCUSSION

It is generally acknowledged that most elements comprising an AI system cannot function without knowledge of the application environment. For a computer system, this knowledge must be represented in some formal notation that can be manipulated for the purposes of storage, retrieval, and inference making. A basic philosophical question concerns the extent to which the complexities of the world can be reduced to a manageable set of symbolic relations susceptible to logical analysis (see [Nilsson 83]). There are those who feel that many subtle concepts cannot be captured using a formal representation [Pentland 83]. Some examples of things that are not readily represented by a symbolic description are a person's face, a taste, the sound of a musical instrument, and a smell.

The assumption that we can capture people's knowledge, actions, and experiences in a computer program by using formal representations has also been challenged by the phenomenologists.[17]

Martin Heidegger, a leading phenomenologist, believes that our implicit beliefs and assumptions cannot be made explicit. As Winograd [Winograd 86] says, "Heidegger rejects both the simple objective stance (the objective physical world is the primary reality) and the simple subjective stance (my thoughts and feelings are the primary reality), arguing instead that it is impossible for one to exist without the other. The interpreted and the interpreter do not exist independently: existence is interpretation and interpretation is existence"[p.31]. If the phenomenologists are correct, we can never capture the subtleties of interpretation required to function in the world until we find some way of capturing in the machine the interactive nature of interpretation.

We sidestepped a basic problem in representation: Suppose an intelligent entity has a wide spectrum of representations available. How can it determine which representation or model of the world is applicable for a given situation? People seem to select appropriate representations for real-world problems without difficulty. This problem of knowing which representation to use at any given time arises in many contexts, e.g., in the frame selection problem discussed in Chapter 6.

Finally, a question that still plagues our attempts to achieve machine intelligence: If a suitable model is not currently available, how can one systematically obtain a new and efficient model for the given situation? People are very adept at developing new representations when their existing ones are inadequate, but we have no idea how this is accomplished.

---

[17]Phenomenology is a philosophical examination of the foundations of experience and action.

Part Two

Cognition

4. Reasoning and Problem Solving
5. Learning
6. Language and Communication
7. Expert/Knowledge-based Systems

In this part of the book we deal with the general symbolic machinery that provides a basis for reasoning, planning, and communication. A main theme is the need for "representing" a problem in a form that permits its effective solution, and the difficulty of obtaining such representations automatically.

4

Reasoning and Problem Solving

In its most basic sense, reasoning is the ability to solve problems. However, simply because a device can solve a problem does not mean that it is capable of reasoning. For example, a pocket calculator can "solve" a variety of mathematical problems, but certainly such problem solving ability is not an example of reasoning. What are some of the necessary conditions that distinguish reasoning from "mechanical" behavior?

First, we require that a reasoning system be capable of expressing and solving a broad range of problems and problem types—including problem formulations that do not correspond to rigid templates anticipated by the system designer. (The pocket calculator, for example, fails this test.) Thus, our first requirement implies that a reasoning system be based on a set of representations that has broad expressive power.

Second, the system must be able to make *explicit* the *implicit* information that is known to it, i.e., for any information possessed by the system it can systematically obtain all equivalent representations of this information.[1] For example, from the information (1) all tigers are dangerous, and (2) this animal is a tiger, the system should be able to obtain the explicit statement (3) this animal is dangerous.

---

[1] This is meant in a conceptual sense; in practice, obtaining all equivalent representations could take an impractical amount of time.

Note that (3) was implicit in statements (1) and (2). Thus, we require a set of operations or transformations that produce other "valid" representations when applied to the representations of information possessed by the system. The system must be able to translate a problem situation expressed in some external representation into its own (internal)representation as well as being able to "syntactically" transform information already expressed in its own formalism. For example, a translation may be made from natural language to a logic formalism, and expressions in the logic formalism may then undergo additional transformations during the course of constructing a proof.

Third, we require that the system have a control structure that determines which transformations to apply, when a solution has been obtained, or when further effort is futile.

Finally, we require that all the above be accomplished with a reasonable degree of computational efficiency.

In the remainder of this chapter, we will consider a number of distinct formalisms for reasoning, and describe how these formalisms are applied to problem solving. Some of the issues addressed include:

- What is reasoning, and what is its role in intelligent behavior?
- How can a reasoning system use a formal language to represent things and their relationships in the world, and how can it solve problems using such a representation?
- What are the conceptual and practical limits of problem solving systems employing formal representations?
- How can a reasoning system deal with imprecisely formulated problems?
- How can a reasoning system select the best representation for a given problem?
- How can a reasoning system know which facts in its database are relevant to solving a given problem?
- How can a machine formulate a plan of action to achieve a desired goal?

HUMAN REASONING

Until the twentieth century, logic and the psychology of thought were considered to be one and the same. In Chapter 1 we quoted Boole's statement as to the purpose of his book on logic: *to investigate the fundamental operations of the mind by which reasoning is performed.* Thus, it is not surprising that often formal logic or probability theory is taken as the ideal, and human reasoning is found to deviate from this ideal. This point of view is in contrast to investigations in visual perception and language, where the biological system is taken as the exemplar and an attempt is made to attain similar performance by machine.

As discussed in Chapter 2, almost nothing is known about the physical machinery used by the brain to carry out its reasoning activity. Attempts to gain insight into the functional aspects, if not the actual brain mechanisms involved in human reasoning have motivated a large body of psychological research. However, unlike experiments in which the speed or accuracy of a perceptual or motor action can be objectively measured, experiments in reasoning are subject to contextual conditions and variables that are difficult to control, and that can only be quantified using subjective judgment. For example, since subjects come to such experiments with a lifelong experience of cooperativeness in conversation, they expect to encounter a cooperative experimenter who will provide them with information useful for solving the posed problem. Thus, although the experimenter may have provided redundant or misleading information, subjects will attempt to use this material to find a solution. There is also the problem of experiments that are foreign to the natural reasoning processes used by people, resulting in misleading conclusions. Scribner [Scribner 77] describes some of the fascinating cultural influences on logical processes.[2] Finally, the experiments often require that human subjects describe their reasoning activities as they solve a problem; the recorded protocols are then analyzed. Such protocol analysis suffers from the fact that people typically do not have access to the reasoning mechanisms that they are *really* using.

Much of the research on human judgment and reasoning is based on the study of "errors." This approach is similar to the study of optical illusions to understand the principles of visual perception or the study of forgetting to learn about memory. Research on systematic errors and inferential biases in reasoning can sometimes reveal the psychological processes that govern judgment and inference. Such research can also indicate which principles of logic and statistics are nonintuitive or counterintuitive. However, given the large body of work investigating human problem solving, there have been surprisingly few results concrete enough to be suitable for transfer to machine-based formalisms.

Human Logical Reasoning

Some of the rules of formal logic are quite intuitive for people, but many others are not. Experiments [Rips 77] have shown that people readily use forms of inference such as "From (P implies Q) and P you can deduce Q." For example, "If John is good, he will be rewarded. John is good. Therefore, John will be rewarded." However, the valid deduction "From (P implies Q) and (not Q) you can deduce (not P)" is mistrusted by people untrained in formal logic. For example, "If John is good, he will be rewarded. John will not be rewarded. Therefore, John is not good." The difficulty with this form may be due to the fact that people are not used to reasoning about what is not true. In addition, people tend not to seek negative information when carrying out reasoning processes.

People have difficulty with many deduction forms, "syllogisms," that deal with "all" and "some." For example, the invalid syllogism "Some A's are B's; some B's are C's implies that some A's are C's" is considered correct by most people. Figure 4-1 shows that there are situations for which this syllogism is false. The valid syllogism "Some B's are A's; No C's are B's; therefore some A's are not C's" was considered as invalid by 60% of tested subjects [Anderson 80].

---

[2]For example, suppose a subject is presented with the statements, *All women in Biranga are married. Mary lives in Biranga,* and is asked "Is Mary married?" In some cultures, subjects might reply that they cannot answer because they do not know Mary. Others will not accept the initial premise because they know that there are unmarried women in Biranga.

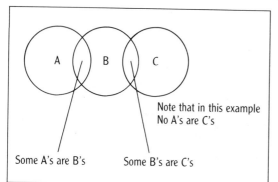

Note that in this example No A's are C's

Some A's are B's   Some B's are C's

FIGURE 4-1
The Use of a Venn Diagram to Test a Syllogism.

Testing the syllogism "Some A's are B's; some B's are C's; therefore some A's are C's." The diagram gives an instance in which the syllogism is false.

Johnson-Laird and Wason summarize the situation as follows [Johnson-Laird 77]: "There is not much of a consensus about the psychological mechanisms underlying deduction or even about so fundamental a matter as to whether or not human beings are basically capable of rational inference. . . . [p.76]." In later work, described by Gardner [Gardner 83, pp. 363–367], Johnson-Laird offers the theory that people reason by sequentially integrating the premises and conclusion of an argument into one or more "mental models" which are then searched for inconsistencies (i.e., any interpretation in which the premises lead to a denial of the conclusion). If no such inconsistencies can be found, the conclusion is accepted as valid; while formal logic provides systematic methods for searching for counterexamples, ordinary human reasoning employs no such methods.

Human Probabilistic Reasoning

There are major differences between human and formal probabilistic reasoning [Tversky 74]. When dealing with questions concerning the probability that object A belongs to class B, or the probability that event A originates from process B, a person generally evaluates the degree to which A is representative or resembles B, while ignoring prior probabilities, the effects of sample size, and a statistical principle known as "regression to the mean."[3]

In a typical experiment, subjects were shown brief personality descriptions of several individuals, allegedly sampled at random from a group of 100 persons—engineers and lawyers. For each description, the subjects were asked to assess the probability that it belonged to an engineer rather than to a lawyer. One set of subjects were told that there were 30 engineers and 70 lawyers, and the other group of subjects were told that there were 70 engineers and 30 lawyers. Ignoring the prior probabilities, the two sets of subjects came up with essentially the same probability judgments.

Other experiments have shown that people expect that a sequence of events generated by a random process will represent the essential characteristics of that process even when the sequence is short. For example, in tossing a fair coin, people regard the sequence H-T-H-T-T-H to be more likely than the sequence H-H-H-T-T-T [Tversky 74]. Thus, people expect that the essential characteristics of

---

[3]This is the phenomenon that exceptional performance is more often than not followed by disappointing performance and failures by improvement.

the process will be represented, not only globally in the entire sequence, but also locally in each of its parts.

Another heuristic used by people is assessing the probability of an event based on the ease with which instances or occurrences can be brought to mind. For example, one may assess the risk of heart attack among middle-aged people by recalling such occurrences among one's acquaintances. Concering this "availability" heuristic, Tversky and Kahneman have pointed out [Tversky 74]:

> Lifelong experience has taught us that, in general, instances of large classes are recalled better and faster than instances of less frequent classes; that likely instances are easier to imagine than unlikely ones; and that the associative connections between events are strengthened when the events frequently co-occur. As a result, man has at his disposal a procedure, the availability heuristic, for estimating the size of a class, the likelihood of an event, or the frequency of co-occurrences, by the ease with which the relevant mental operations of retrieval, construction, or association can be performed. However, this valuable estimation procedure results in systematic errors.

In both the logical and statistical domains, it appears that the human reasoning process is context-dependent, so that different operations or inferential rules are required in different contexts [Hayes 77]. Consequently, human reasoning cannot be adequately described in terms of context-independent formal rules. Furthermore, performance is dramatically improved when an experimental task is related more clearly to the subject's experiences. The difficulty in solving a posed problem is often not intrinsic to the logical structure of the task, but rather to the mode of presentation (e.g., [Johnson-Laird 77]).

FORMAL REASONING AND PROBLEM SOLVING

Requirements for a Problem Solver

A problem exists when there are conditions that certain objects must satisfy, given some set of constraints or facts. A solution is a way of satisfying the conditions. Thus, given the problem of getting from home to the airport, the database of facts should contain information concerning the transportation available, the time available, the distance to be traversed, etc. The condition to be satisfied is your presence at the airport, and the solution, the "plan," is the sequence of operations that you use in satisfying the condition consistent with the given (or implied) constraints.

An obvious first step in solving a problem is to recognize that a problem exists. However, prompt recognition that a problem exists may not be simple. For example, novice chess players may not notice that they are being drawn into a losing position until it is too late. A child may not realize that the bicycle is going too fast until it goes out of control. One might drive for a considerable distance before recognizing that one is lost.

Once the problem is recognized, the problem solver must represent it in a suitable formalism and then plan a course of action using this representation and a knowledge of the effects of proposed actions. As indicated in Chapter 3, the heart of the problem-solving process consists of choosing the right representation, and being able to set up the appropriate correspondence between the problem and the representation.

In carrying out a plan, the problem solver must know when the information at hand is inadequate and should be supplemented or supplanted. If the environment changes, the problem solver must change the plan accordingly. For example, in the airport problem, we may plan to take Bayshore Highway but find that construction has slowed traffic too much, requiring us to take First Street instead.

Any proposed solution must satisfy the conditions of the problem. However, in real-world problems we find that some of the most important conditions are not stated. In the airport problem, the important condition—"I want to get to the airport in a reasonable amount of time"—may not be stated. The solution "walk there" may satisfy the stated conditions but not the implicit ones.

Categories of Reasoning

There are many different systems of reasoning that can be used to solve problems. We divide these systems into the three major categories presented below; however, we will encounter some reasoning techniques that span more than one category.

Deductive Reasoning. In deductive reasoning, we attempt to find a "deductive chain" of "valid" assertions leading from statements which are assumed to be true, to some given assertion whose validity we wish to establish. The power of the deduc-

tive approach lies in the fact that the rules of deductive inference obtain new true statements from existing ones. Deductive arguments are characterized by their logical necessity; the conclusion is "entailed" by (implicit in) the premises.

Deduction is meaningful only in the context of a formal system in which symbols are combined and transformed under a given fixed set of rules. The essence of a deductive system is the maintenance of validity or consistency: a statement and its contradiction cannot both be derived. We are therefore guaranteed validity of derived results. However, to insure this property, deductive systems are often extremely awkward in expressing certain types of information. Thus, deductive logic systems have no practical way of dealing directly with probabilistic assertions, or with information implied by quantitative assertions requiring numerical computation; mathematical systems have no practical way of dealing directly with conflicting or probabilistic assertions, or with qualitative statements (e.g., "Bill looks quite a bit like John"); probabilistic systems, to the extent that they can be considered to be deductive, have no practical way of expressing relational information (e.g., "Bill is twice as tall as John"), and no effective way of manipulating assertions that are strictly either true or false.

Inductive Reasoning. In inductive reasoning (nondemonstrative inference), a form of reasoning basic to scientific inquiry, we attempt to find some generalization or abstraction that describes or categorizes a set of data. A major distinction between deduction and induction is that in induction we have a set of constraints to satisfy, rather than an explicit (given) assertion to establish. Further, inductive problems are less likely to be as precisely formulated as deductive ones.

For example, given the problem of finding the next number in the sequence <1,2,4,8,16>, most people will give the answer "32" without requiring any additional problem specification. It is typical of problems in induction that there is more than one acceptable answer to the problem (any answer could be justified in the above example). Such problems often require extrapolation, and generally do not permit a definitive way to check the "correctness" of a final answer. Premises support, but do not logically entail the derived solution. The rules of inductive inference do not provide an assured means for deriving new true statements from existing ones.

One of the most important distinctions between deductive and inductive reasoning is the amount of "evidence" that must be invoked to derive a new assertion (or verify some hypothesis). Because of assured consistency and computational considerations, deductive systems generally use long reasoning chains consisting of small steps; in each step, only a very small subset of the total set of "facts" known to the system is explicitly invoked. Deductive systems make "local" syntactic transformations—they cannot take a "global" perspective in solving a problem. On the other hand, because of the possibility of erroneous information, inductive systems use short reasoning chains consisting of big steps. Inductive systems generally attempt to explicitly use as much of their available information as

possible in every step since they depend on consensus to insure "correct" conclusions. Thus, inductive systems must work at a global level in solving a problem.

Analogical Reasoning. In analogical reasoning, we set up a correspondence between the elements and operations of two distinct systems. Typically, one of the systems is well understood, and the other is the one we wish to ask questions about; we answer the questions by posing them in the system we understand. An example of analogical reasoning is the solution to the 15 game by the known procedure for playing tick-tack-toe, as described in Chapter 3. Another example is using our knowledge and intuitions about fluid flow to reason about the flow of electrical current.

The major problem in reasoning by analogy is to find the correspondence between the known and unknown systems. For example, if we have an analogy, "An electric battery is like a reservoir," it is not the size, shape, color, or substance of a battery that is relevant, but rather that both store potential energy and release energy to provide power. Thus, only relationships dealing with the storage and release of energy would be meaningful in this analogy. The insight used by a person to recognize that a previously encountered situation is analogous to another situation eludes mechanization.

Common-sense reasoning, discussed later in this chapter, combines analogical and inductive techniques to solve everyday problems about the behavior of physical objects in the world. Analogical reasoning also plays an important role in learning, as will be shown in Chapter 5.

The following sections describe a number of different reasoning formalisms. No matter which formalism is employed, a major part of the reasoning process is the conversion of some given problem into that formalism. This conversion or translation step is actually a problem in analogical reasoning for which we have no adequate solution at present; i.e., we still consider the translation step to be a creative process.

THE DEDUCTIVE LOGIC FORMALISM

In this section we will discuss a special kind of reasoning called "logical deduction," in which true conclusions result when "rules of inference" are applied to true statements. Thus, we are interested in consistent systems in which one proposition may be inferred or deduced from other propositions. A deductive system with a consistent set of premises will be consistent in assigning truth-values to conclusions: such a system cannot prove both that B is true and that B is false. Although the words "true" and "false" are used in the continuing discussion, these words do not necessarily mean true or false in the real world. One should think of "true" and "false" as labels or values (truth-values) that have been assigned to statements, regardless of their relationship to the real world.

Below, we will describe how real-world situations are expressed in the notation of formal logic and how to deduce new facts from a given set of premises. We first describe the propositional calculus that allows us to deal with given

propositions (sentences), and compositions of such sentences, which must be either true or false. Then we will treat the predicate calculus that allows us to compose true or false sentences from more primitive elements than complete sentences. These two logic systems have been thoroughly investigated and are well understood, but they correspond to a very small part of the reasoning used by people. However, they form the basis of many AI reasoning programs, and are also part of the machinery underlying "logic programming," as typified by the language PROLOG, discussed in Appendix 4-1.

Propositional Calculus

The calculus of propositions deals with statements or sentences of the type "Water boils at 212 degrees Fahrenheit," "The number 3 is an even number," where the first sentence has an associated truth-value designated by T for true and the second one F for false. Sentences will be denoted by capital letters such as P, Q, R. The following "connectives" are used to combine or modify sentences.

Negation. Negation is indicated by a minus sign, e.g. $-P$, and designates "it is NOT the case that P." If P is true, then $-P$ is false; if P is false then $-P$ is true.

Conjunction. The conjunction of two sentences P, Q is true if both P and Q are true. Conjunction is designated by P&Q, read as P and Q, e.g. (the block is made of wood)&(the block is red).

Disjunction. The disjunction of two sentences P, Q is true if at least one of P,

Q is true. Disjunction is designated by PvQ, read P or Q, e.g. (Tom is a man)v(Tom is poor). PvQ allows us to express that at least one of the statements is true without saying which one is true.

Implication. Implication, designated as P→Q, asserts "if P then Q," where P is known as the antecedent and Q the consequent. The sentence is false only if the antecedent is true and the consequent is false; otherwise it is true. Note that, unlike the ordinary use of if-then, e.g., "If taxes rise then the market will drop," no causality is inherent in a logical if-then sentence.

A truth-table is a way of specifying the results of assigning all possible combinations of truth-values to a proposition. For the conjunction operation, the truth table is of the form:

P	Q	P&Q
F	F	F
F	T	F
T	F	F
T	T	T

Thus, P&Q is true only if both P and Q are both true. Two expressions are equivalent if (and only if) their truth-tables are identical. For example, to show that P→Q is equivalent to −PvQ, we develop the following truth-tables:

P	Q	P→Q	−PvQ
F	F	T	T
F	T	T	T
T	F	F	F
T	T	T	T

Since the columns P→Q and −PvQ are identical, P→Q is equivalent to −PvQ.

Proof by truth-table comparison is generally not practical because if n different propositional variables occur in the premises, then a table with 2^n rows must be filled out. A more efficient approach is to use an inference rule such as:

P	the block is heavy
P→Q	if the block is heavy, then the block is hard to move

Q	the block is hard to move

which can be informally expressed as: "if P is true, and if the statement P→Q is true, then we can infer that Q is true. This deductive rule ("modus ponens"), which can be proved by means of a truth-table, can be used to establish proofs without resorting to the truth-table.

The study of logic involves the study of various inference procedures and the technique of applying these procedures. Until the work of Hao Wang [Wang 60] in 1960, the use of such procedures required intuition, and thus these methods were unsuited for computer implementation. A more recent approach to computer mechanization of logic, called "resolution" [Robinson 65], will be described below.

Propositional Resolution

One can verify by truth-table comparison that the theorem QvS can be proved from the premises PvQ and −PvS. From an operational point of view, we can say that the P and −P terms in the two premises have been eliminated (resolved), leaving a single expression that is the disjunction (logical sum) of the remaining terms. Any proposition can be put in the form (P1)&(P2)&(P3). . ., where P1, P2, and P3 are expressions consisting of disjunctions of variables or negated variables. This transformation can be performed using the propositional equivalences shown in Box 4-1. P1, P2, and P3 are called "clauses," and clauses can be resolved to eliminate variables. For example, the expression (−PvQ)&(P) consists of the clause −PvQ and the clause P. P and −P in these clauses can be resolved to obtain the result Q. Clauses preceded by a negation sign must be transformed to remove the negation sign. A clause such as −(PvQ) must be converted to −P&−Q using De Morgan's theorem given in Box 4-1.

An important approach to theorem proving assumes that the theorem to be proved is false; i.e., its negation is true. Then one shows that this assumption, taken together with the premises, leads to the impossible situation of some variable and its negation both being true (a "contradiction"). Thus, if the negation of the theorem is inconsistent with the premises, the unnegated theorem must be consist-

ent with the premises and therefore true. Arriving at a contradiction is a useful termination condition for an automatic theorem-proving process. An example of a resolution proof is given below.

Given the premise (−PvQ)&(−QvR) &(−RvS)&(−Uv−S), we want to prove the theorem (−Pv−U). Note that this would require a truth-table of 2^6 rows for a truth-table proof. To prove the theorem by contradiction, we take the negation of the theorem, −(−Pv−U), which by De Morgan's theorem in the equivalence table of Box 4-1 is P&U. We place the clauses P, U in the set of clauses (we have placed each in a position that allows the reader to see how the resolution process is carried out):

P −PvQ −QvR −RvS −Uv−S U
            | | \ /
           Q\ | −S
              \ |
                \ |
                 R\ |
                   \ |
                     \ |
                       S

BOX 4-1 Equivalences in Logic

The following equivalences can be used to convert logic expressions to a standard normal form:

Propositional Calculus

$$P \& Q = Q \& P$$
$$P \vee Q = Q \vee P$$

$--P = P$ Double negation
$-(P \vee Q) = -P \& -Q$ De Morgan's theorem
$-(P \& Q) = -P \vee -Q$ De Morgan's theorem
$$P \& (Q \vee R) = P\&Q \vee P\&R$$

Predicate Calculus

$-(x)P(x) = (Ex)[-P(x)]$ P does not hold for all x = there exists an x for which P does not hold.

$$(x)[P(x) \rightarrow (y)[Q(y)]] = (x)(y)[P(x) \rightarrow Q(y)]$$

Since we obtain a contradiction, S and $-$S, for the negation of the proposition, the original proposition $-Pv-U$ must be true, i.e., deducible from the given premises.

Predicates

The propositional calculus is limited in its expressive power; sentences cannot be composed of primitives standing for individual objects and their properties or relationships, but must be composed of primitive elements that are capable of being assigned a truth-value. For example, there is no way of representing an individual such as "John" without making some explicit assertion about him, such as "John is a student." Also, the fact that certain relationships hold for some, or for all individuals, cannot be expressed without being explicit and exhaustive.

In order to provide additional expressive power, the propositional calculus is expanded to the predicate calculus by introducing terms, functions, predicates, and quantifiers, as follows:

Terms or individual variables serve the grammatical function of pronouns and common nouns. They are the things talked about, e.g., "car," "John," or unspecified things such as x, y, or z.

A "predicate" denotes a relationship between objects. A unary relation specifies a property of an object. Red(x), a unary relation, is a predicate expression that asserts that x is red. Father(John,Tom) asserts that John is the father of Tom. A predicate can take on a value of true or false when its variables have assumed specific values (converting them to terms).

Quantifiers

The universal quantifier, shown by parentheses around the variable,[4] e.g., (x), is the notation that indicates "for all x." Thus, "all men are animals" is expressed as $(x)[\text{Man}(x) \rightarrow \text{Animal}(x)]$. A second quantifier, "there exists," is designated by an E. "There is at least one x such that x is greater than zero" can be represented by $(Ex)(x > 0)$. "A red object is on top of a green one" can be represented by $(Ex)\ (Ey)[\text{Red}(x)\&\text{Green}(y)\&\text{ontop}(x,y)]$.

Universal and existential quantifiers can be combined in the same expression. Thus, "Everyone has a mother" can be expressed as $(x)(Ey)[(\text{Human}(x) \rightarrow \text{Mother}(x,y)]$.

Note that $(Ex)Q(x)$ allows us to express the fact that something has a certain property without saying which thing has that property, and $(x)[P(x) \rightarrow Q(x)]$ expresses the fact that everything in a certain class has a certain property without saying what everything in that class is.

Semantics

Even though we may use symbols that form English words, it must be kept in mind that to an automatic theorem proving system these are merely symbols that are to be manipulated. The system sees no difference between P(x) and Red(x); the meaning or semantics must be provided by the user mapping the variables and functions to things in the problem domain. The specification of a domain and the associations between logical sym-

---

[4]The confusion between parentheses denoting the universal quantifier and those used to denote the variables in a function is easily resolved by context.

bols and the problem domain constitute an *interpretation* or a *model* of the logical system.

Computational Issues

Mechanized inference techniques in the predicate calculus first convert the expressions into a normal form, consisting of propositional-type expressions; the various connectives and quantifiers are removed using the steps shown in Box 4-2. (In logic programming languages such as PROLOG [see Appendix 4-1], the expressions are written directly in a "clause" form, eliminating the need for this conversion.)

In the early 1930s, Herbrand

BOX 4-2 Converting Predicate Calculus Expressions to Clause Form

The following sequence of operations is used to convert a predicate calculus expression to clause form:

1. **Removing implications.** Occurrences of P→Q are replaced by −PvQ. Thus, $(x)[Man(x) \rightarrow Human(x)]$ is replaced by $(x)[−Man(x)vHuman(x)]$.

2. **Moving negation inwards.** We replace −[Human(Caesar)&Living(Caesar)] by −Human(Caesar)v−Living(Caesar). The quantifier "all" preceded by a negation is transformed as in the example −(y)[Person(y)] to (Ey)[−Person(y)]. That is, if not all things satisfy a predicate, then there must be at least one thing that does not satisfy it.

3. **Removing the existential quantifiers.** The removal of existential quantifiers, known as "skolemizing," is done by introducing new constant symbols. Instead of saying that there exists an object with a certain set of properties, one creates a name for one such object and simply says that it has the properties. Thus, for (Ex)[Female(x) &Motherof$(x,$Eve$)$], we say Female(G1)& Motherof(G1,Eve). When there are universal quantifiers in a formula, skolemization is not quite so simple. If we skolemized (x)[Human(x)→(Ey)(Motherof(x,y))], "every human has a mother" to (x)[Human(x)→ Motherof$(x,$G1$)$], we would be saying "every human has the same mother." Thus, we have to use a function, such as G2 in the expression, (x)[Human(x)→Motherof$(x,$G2(x))], to indicate the dependence of the y on the particular x selected.

4. **Moving universal quantifiers outward.** We can move universal quantifiers outward without affecting meaning. Thus, (x)[Man(x)→(y)[Woman(y)→ Likes(x,y)]] can be transformed to $(x)(y)$[Man(x)→ (Woman(y)→Likes(x,y))].

5. **Conjunctive normal form.** The expression is now transformed so that conjunctions no longer appear inside disjunctions, i.e., we obtain the form (P)&(Q) ..., where P, Q ... do not contain &. This normal form is used in propositional resolution.

6. **Clause form.** The formula we now have is made up of a collection of &'s relating things which are either literals or composed of literals connected by v's. If we have something like (A&B)&(C&(D&E)), where A,B,C,D,E represent (possibly complex) propositions that have no &'s in them, then we can ignore the parentheses and write A&B&C&D&E, and we can consider this a collection of clauses A,B,C, . . .

Proof procedures such as resolution can now be invoked in a manner similar to that described for the propositional calculus; the main distinction is due to the possible existence of variables in the predicate clauses which then requires the use of unification to achieve the necessary matching.

[Herbrand 30] proved that if a set of clauses containing variables is contradictory, then there will exist a finite set of variable-free instances of these clauses that can be shown to be contradictory by propositional methods. An efficient procedure for finding such a contradiction was developed in 1965 by J. A. Robinson [Robinson 65]. This procedure makes inferences by the use of "unification" and propositional resolution. Thus, once we have the expression in clause form, we can carry out these procedures to obtain a proof.

Propositional resolution requires that two clauses to be resolved have a common element (literal), negated in one clause and unnegated in the other. Sometimes a constant, another variable, or a function (not containing the variable) must be substituted for some given variable in order to satisfy the above condition. The process of finding substitutions that make two clauses resolvable is called *unification*. An important feature of the resolution method is that it does not require that the clauses being resolved contain only constants, but allows the most general possible form of the variables to be retained consistent with the resolution condition. For example, we can resolve the two clauses $P(c,x)\lor F$ and $-P(c,y)\lor G$ by making the substitution $x=y$; we need not assign a specific value to x or y.

Resolution proof procedures are hopelessly inefficient if they have no mechanisms to specify which of the many possible sequences of resolutions to select. Many different techniques have been developed to deal with this problem. For example, the "set of support" strategy takes the first clause to be resolved from the negation of the statement to be proved (because such a step will eventually be required to complete the proof). It further dictates that at least one resolvent in every resolution must be descended from the negation of the statement to be proved, because only such resolutions are relevant. The "linear format" strategy attempts to keep the sequence of resolutions relevant by requiring that each new resolution make use of the results of the previous one.

A good discussion of the "art" of setting up the proof strategy is discussed in Wos [Wos 84]:

> The use of an automatic reasoning program is an art, even though the program employs unambiguous and exacting notation for representing information, precise inference rules for drawing conclusions, and carefully delineated strategies to control those inference rules. . . . In using an automated reasoning program, one makes good choices for the representation, for inference rules, and for strategies. . . . Without strategy, an automated reasoning program will drown in new information. With strategy, a reasoning program can sometimes perform as a brilliant assistant or colleague.

Nonstandard Logics

In the first order predicate calculus it is not possible to represent relationships among predicates, temporal relationships, hypothetical assertions, beliefs, assertions of possibility, and vague asssertions based on incomplete information. In addition, there is no mechanism for deleting statements from the database. There is a growing literature devoted to the creation and exploration of alternative logics and associated inference mechanisms. Some of these systems are extensions designed to supplement standard logic, while others are alternatives to standard logic. These systems, being explored for use in AI, are described briefly below; a detailed treatment is given in Turner [Turner 85].

Modal logic is concerned with concepts of necessity and possibility. It extends standard logic by using the operators "it is necessary that" and "it is possible that." This type of logic can be used to deal with the concept of "belief," an important consideration in the planning of actions. A modal logic suitable for representing knowledge and action has been developed by Moore [Moore 85].

Temporal logic deals with the representation of time, important in automatic planning and in diagnosis. Concepts such as *is true, was true, will be true,* and *has always been true* must be expressed, as well as time-interval relationships such as *during, before,* and *overlaps in time.*

Higher order logic can represent properties of predicates or even properties of properties of predicates. For example, in the second order predicate calculus, equality can be defined as

$$(P)(x)(y)\ [x = y] \rightarrow [P(x) \rightarrow P(y)],$$

i.e., if x and y are equal, then for all predicates, the predicate of x equals the predicate of y. This quantification over predicates is not permissible in the first order predicate calculus.

In higher order logic, care must be taken to avoid contradictions of the sort discovered by Russell and treated by the theory of types in Russell and Whitehead's *Principia Mathematica.* Higher order logic has not as yet seen much use in AI.

Multivalued logics. While classical logic employs two truth-values, a multivalued logic can represent intermediate values. Multivalued logics are useful for situations in which one cannot always make a commitment to either true or false, and yet one wants a deductive system that is consistent.

Fuzzy logic. In fuzzy logic, predicates such as "red" and "tall" are considered as vague predicates, and an element is considered to have a "grade of membership" in any given set. Truth-values are also considered to lie on a scale between true and false. "A is small; A and B are approximately equal; therefore, B is more or less small" is an example of a fuzzy inference.

Nonmonotonic logic. In classical logic, the system increases its stock of truths as knowledge is added and as inferences are made. There is no mechanism for discarding information or revising beliefs. This aspect of classical logic is termed "monotonic." In nonmonotonic systems, inferences can be made on the basis of available data, but these inferences can be rejected and new ones made when new data become available.

INDUCTIVE REASONING

In inductive reasoning we form generalizations that characterize a class of data from the characteristics of a set of samples of the class. These generalizations, and the inferences based on them, are inductive because it is always possible that our initial conclusions will be invalidated by new evidence, acquired by observing a larger sample, or even a single new sample. Despite this risk, induction is an indispensable mode of reasoning, used continually in everyday life as well as in the development of scientific theory.

In this section we describe the Bayesian and Shafer-Dempster probabilistic formalisms; these formalisms are important tools used in inductive reasoning. While the deductive systems described previously cannot deal with conflicts in evidence because such conflicts lead to logical contradictions, probabilistic techniques are able to make predictions in the presence of conflicting evidence. These predictions will not always be true, but they are good guesses that make effective use of the given information.

Just as there are various forms of deductive reasoning, various forms of probabilistic reasoning are possible. The different forms depend on the nature of the belief measures used and how they are manipulated. Philosophers have identified at least four distinct versions of the concept of probability:

1. The measured frequency of occurrence of events.

2. The disposition of events (or a single event) to occur, e.g., "Everyone who looks at this car agrees that there is a low probability that it will be able to make the trip from New York to Los Angeles"

3. The subjective belief a person has about the likelihood of occurrences of different events

4. The logical relationship between evidence and relevant hypotheses, e.g., "If the patient has a fever and his glypus test is positive, then it is probable that he has Hendrix syndrome"

Probabilistic reasoning first requires the construction of a problem representation. This step, called "sample space construction," or developing the "frame of discernment," formulates the vocabulary and statements that will be used to describe the given problem. Next, a belief "value" is provided for each statement, either by ranking the statements, assigning a belief number to each, or assigning a lower and upper belief number (bound) to each. Finally, the known belief values are combined or pooled, and propagated to modify the belief numbers of other statements, and especially that of the target hypothesis. As in most AI problems, the representation step is crucial. It depends on the designer's understanding of the relevant events in the world, and the availability of evidence that relates to these events. Representation as an issue in probabilistic reasoning is discussed later.

Measures of Belief

There are various characteristics that a belief measure might have. A set of intuitively satisfying characteristics was proposed by Cox [Cox 46] and discussed in detail in Horvitz and Heckerman [Horvitz 86]:

1. Clarity. The propositions must be defined precisely enough so that one can tell when a proposition is true or false.

2. **Completeness.** It must be possible to assign a degree of belief to any proposition.
3. **Scalar continuity.** Measures of degree of belief should vary continuously between certain truth and certain falsehood.
4. **Context dependency.** The degree of belief in a particular proposition should depend on knowledge about the truth of other propositions.
5. **Consistency.** If two propositions are logically equivalent, the degree of belief in one proposition given certain evidence should equal the degree of belief in the other.
6. **Hypothetical conditioning.** The belief in the proposition A&B should be a function of the belief in A and the belief in B given that A is true.
7. **Complementarity.** The belief in the negation of A should be determined by the belief in A itself.

Cox showed that these seven properties are logically equivalent to the axioms of classical probability theory; alternative belief formalisms change one or more of these properties. Below we first describe belief revision in classical probability theory, and then discuss the Shafer-Dempster (S/D) theory that rejects several of the above properties.

Bayesian Reasoning

Bayesian reasoning is the classical mechanism used to revise belief, given new evidence [Feller 50, Parzen 60]. We begin with a probability distribution that completely describes our degrees of belief in a set of·hypotheses before obtaining new evidence. If a probability P is assigned to an event A, then $(1-P)$ is assigned to $-A$, the nonoccurrence of A. New evidence results in modifying or "conditioning" P based on computations relating evidence to the hypotheses.

In Bayesian reasoning, the logical form of the implication "if E then H," is replaced by "if E then H with a probability P." This "conditional probability" assertion is written $P(H|E)$, and is read "the probability of hypothesis H given that the evidence E is true." Probabilities are updated according to Bayes's theorem:

$$P(H|E) = P(E|H) \, P(H)/P(E).$$

This equation, derived in Box 4-3, states that we can update the probability of hypothesis H, P(H), given that new evidence E, assumed to be true, has been received. Bayesian calculus for complicated situations requires knowledge of the *a priori* probability of some events, e.g. P(H) and P(E), and depends on the sequential use of known conditional probabilities, $P(E|H)$, to evaluate the corresponding values for implied propositions. If the required *a priori* and conditional probability values are known, an evaluation path can be found to allow the computation of the likelihood of some target event. However, the determination of all these necessary *a priori* and conditional values is often impossible or impractical, and one is then forced to heuristic or approximation techniques to compute the unknown values.

When the relationship between events is unknown, a basic technique used is to assume their independence. We can then compute, rather than guess, the *a priori* values of joint events, such as

BOX 4-3 Conditional Probability and the Bayes Theorem

A conditional probability P(H|E) is the probability of an event or hypothesis, H, given that we know that some other event or hypothesis, E, is true. The relationships are readily derived using simple sets. Suppose we have N things, some of them with property H, some of them with property E, and some with both properties E and H as shown in the Venn diagram in Fig. 4-2.

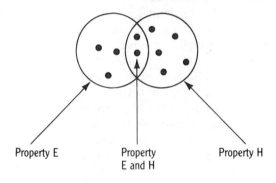

Property E   Property   Property H
                   E and H

FIGURE 4-2

Example of Conditional Probability Calculation Using the Venn Diagram Representation.

P(H|E)=N(E and H)/N(E)
N(E)=5
N(E and H)=2
P(H|E)=2/5

The conditional probability P(H|E) = N(E and H)/N(E), where N(E and H) is the number of elements that have both properties E and H, and N(E) is the number of elements with property E. If we divide the top and bottom of the right-hand side by N, the total number of elements, we get

$$P(H|E) = \frac{\dfrac{N(E \text{ and } H)}{N}}{\dfrac{N(E)}{N}} = \frac{P(E \text{ and } H)}{P(E)} . \qquad (4.1)$$

Using a similar argument, we can obtain the expression for P(E|H), the probability of the event E, given that event H is true:

$$P(E|H) = P(H \text{ and } E)/P(H). \qquad (4.2)$$

Since P(H and E) is the same as P(E and H), we can solve for P(H and E) in Eq. (4.2), P(H and E) = P(E|H)P(H), and substitute in Eq. (4.1) to obtain Bayes's theorem,

$$P(H|E) = P(E|H)P(H)/P(E). \qquad (4.3)$$

This says that if we have an initial (*a priori*) probability of event or hypothesis H, P(H), and we know that event E is true, then we can get an updated probability, P(H|E), assuming that we also know both the probability of event E, P(E), and the conditional probability of E given that H is true, P(E|H).

P(A,B). Thus if A and B are independent P(B|A)=P(B), so that P(A,B)=P(A)P(B|A) =P(A)P(B). Obviously, we get incorrect answers if we assume independence when it is not appropriate.

A second technique is to employ the *principle of insufficient reason*. This principle states that if there is no reason to believe x to be more or less likely than y, then assume that the probability of x equals that of y. Thus, in the absence of

any additional information, the probability assigned to any one hypothesis becomes a function of the number of hypothetical alternatives. This is an undesirable property since a particular hypothesis can always be broken down into several sub-hypotheses, thus altering the a priori probabilities assigned to other hypotheses. For example, given that an apple has disappeared in a locked room containing two men and a woman, we might assign to each of two competing hypotheses a probability of 1/2:

P1: A man ate the apple.
P2: A woman ate the apple.

However, we also could have formulated our hypotheses as:

Q1: Bill ate the apple.
Q2: Bob ate the apple.
Q3: Mary ate the apple.

Under the principle of insufficient reason, we assign Q1, Q2, and Q3 each a probability of 1/3. P2 and Q3 are identical assertions which are assigned different probabilities under the principle of insufficient reason simply because of the way we chose to express the remaining alternatives. Even if we could improve the value assignment process for the priors, we might still want to profess ignorance. However, Bayesian probability offers no mechanism to permit this option.

Belief Functions

The Shafer-Dempster belief function formalism [Shafer 76, Garvey 81] rejects the completeness assumption that asserts that a degree of belief can be assigned to any proposition. This approach also rejects the principle of insufficent reason or any probability assignment that provides a value to a proposition when not enough is known about the proposition. In addition, separate measures are assigned to a proposition and its negation, rejecting the complementarity assumption.

In the Shafer-Dempster formalism, the evidence received by a knowledge source results in its apportioning a "unit of belief" among a set of propositions.

The amount of belief (called "mass") committed to a proposition represents a judgment as to the strength of the evidence that specifically favors that proposition. It is not required that belief not committed to a given proposition should be given to the negation of the proposition. This is in contrast to the Bayesian approach in which a unit of probability must be apportioned between the two sides of every question.

The Shafer-Dempster formalism makes lack of information concerning probabilities explicit by expressing the belief in a proposition as a subinterval [support(a), plausibility(a)] in the unit interval [0,1]. Using this notation, a proposition would be written A[.25,.85] to indicate that the probability of A is between .25 and .85. The lower value represents the support for a proposition A, and sets a minimum value for its likelihood. The upper value denotes the plausibility of A and establishes a maximum likelihood. The support may be interpreted as the total positive effect a body of evidence has on a proposition, while plausibility represents the total extent to which a body of evidence fails to refute a proposition. The degree of uncertainty about the probability value for a proposition corresponds to the width of its interval. Table 4-1 presents some additional examples of belief assignment employing the Shafer-Dempster representation.

To use belief functions, one partitions evidence into relatively simple components, makes probability judgments separately with respect to each of these components, and then combines these judgments to obtain a final judgment that represents the total evidence.

TABLE 4-1 ■ Examples of Belief Assignment in the Shafer-Dempster Approach

[0,1]	no knowledge about the proposition
[0,0]	proposition is false
[1,1]	proposition is true
[.25,1]	evidence provides partial support for proposition
[0,.85]	evidence provides partial refutation of proposition
[.25,.85]	evidence is conflicting, providing both evidence for and against the proposition

The Shafer-Dempster formalism has the desirable property that the intervals become points when precise probability information is available, and under certain independence assumptions, the corresponding computations produce results consistent with Bayesian probability theory. If the only events that can occur are known to be either true or false, then the results of the Shafer-Dempster computations are consistent with those of deductive logic. The Shafer-Dempster formalism also provides a way of dealing with conflicting information, but now the resulting likelihoods can no longer be interpreted in the same way as Bayesian probabilities, and in particular, they no longer have a simple frequency of occurrence interpretation.

The underlying representation for the Shafer-Dempster formalism consists of an exhaustive list (L) of mutually exclusive event possibilities with each subset (A of L) interpreted as the "proposition" that the true state of the world is one of the elements of L contained within A. L is called a "frame of discernment," to emphasize that each possibility in L can always be split into more specific possibilities, i.e., the resolution with which we view the world can be increased, thus increasing the number of propositions that L discerns.

Single Belief Functions in the S/D Formalism. A "knowledge source" distributes a unit of belief across a set of propositions for which it has direct evidence in proportion to the weight of that evidence as it bears on each proposition. For example, if there are five possible events, a knowledge source KS1 might distribute belief as $<.13, .22, .35, 0, 0>$ for the events A, $-A$, B, C, D. Once mass has been assigned to a set of propositions, the evidential intervals can be determined directly. Support for a proposition A is the total mass ascribed to A or to its subsets; the plausibility of A is one minus the sum of the mass assigned to $-A$ or to the subsets of $-A$; the ignorance about A is equal to the mass remaining. For example, the evidential interval for the event A given by KS1 is [.13, .78], since the mass of $-A$ is .22.

Intuitively, mass is attributed to the most precise propositions a body of evidence supports. If a portion of mass is attributed to a proposition, it represents a minimal commitment to that proposition and all of the propositions it implies.

Composition of Individual Beliefs. There is a formal rule for combining belief functions, known as "Dempster's rule." Dempster's rule combines a belief function (constructed on the basis of one item of evidence) with a second belief function (constructed on the basis of another, *assumed independent* item of evidence), so as to obtain a belief function representing the combined body of evidence. An example of this procedure is given in Box 4-4. Dempster's rule makes explicit the fact that the S/D formalism has not escaped a critical weakness of all inductive methods, i.e., the need (for

---

 BOX 4-4 Combining Two Sets of Evidence Using Dempster's Rule

Dempster's rule for combining two different sets of evidence can best be understood by example. Suppose there has been a hit and run accident, and there are two witnesses. The witnesses are willing to assign belief as to the culprit as follows:

Witness #1: I'd say it was a Ford with belief .3
 I'd say it was a Chevy with belief .5
 I don't know how to distribute .2 of my belief.

Witness #2: I'd say it was a Chevy or a Toyota with belief .7
 I don't know how to distribute the remaining .3 of my belief.

We illustrate Dempster's rule using the following tableau:

Witness #1:

		Chevy or Toyota 0.14	Undistributed 0.06
Undistributed belief	.2	Chevy or Toyota 0.14	Undistributed 0.06
Ford	.3	null 0.21	Ford 0.09
Chevy	.5	Chevy 0.35	Chevy 0.15
		Chevy or Toyota 0.7	Undistributed 0.3

Witness #2

The belief distribution for witness #1 is shown on the left of the array, and for witness #2 at the bottom of the array. We multiply the row and column weights to obtain the values assigned to each element of the array. For example, the value of the upper left array element

is 0.2 * 0.7 = .14 . Whenever the evidence is incompatible, e.g., the belief of witness #1 that it was a Ford is incompatible with the belief of witness #2 that it was a Chevy or Toyota, we assign that product to the null set. When there is undistributed belief of one witness, we assign that cell the value of the other witness, e.g., undistributed belief for witness #1 causes the upper left cell to be assigned the Chevy or Toyota classification of witness #2.

When we add up all the areas, we obtain:

Pooled Ford values = 0.09

Pooled Chevy or Toyota = .14

Pooled Chevy = .35 + .15 = .50

Pooled uncertain = .06

Conflict (null set) = .21

Since there is 0.21 unit of conflicting mass, we normalize the mutually consistent pooled values so that they sum to 1.0 by dividing each by (1 - 0.21), to obtain:

Ford pooled belief = .11

Chevy or Toyota pooled belief = 0.18

Chevy pooled belief = 0.63

Uncertainty = 0.08

The evidential interval for Chevy is [.63, .89], indicating an uncertainty interval of .26.

These final results agree with our intuition. We would expect that the belief about the Ford would be decreased since witness #2 mentioned nothing about a Ford. The belief for a Chevy has been increased somewhat above the .5 belief of witness #1, since both witnesses have some degree of belief in the Chevy.

either practical or theoretical reasons) to *assume* independence of observations and/or events.

Representing a Problem in a Probabilistic Formalism

As in the case of logical reasoning, choosing an appropriate representation for a given problem is the creative step in probabilistic reasoning. We will illustrate the nature of the representation problem by an example, first describing the problem formulation and then showing the computations. Our example is inspired by the work of Shafer and Tversky [Shafer 85].

Suppose we have an election prediction service and wish to estimate the probability of candidate Jones being elected. There are many facets of election politics that might be considered, including the amount of campaigning effort, the effect of the world situation, the condition of the economy, etc. Suppose our election experts decide that "campaigning effort" is the most crucial determinant. They might set up the alternative strategies for a candidate: (1) maintain current level of campaigning, (2) slightly increase current level of campaigning, (3) greatly increase level of campaigning, and (4) decrease current level. Notice that the experts must supply an estimate of the probability of each event and of the effect that the event will have on winning the election.

Suppose it was felt that the other leading contender, Smith, should be taken into account in making the estimate. We might believe that candidate Smith's campaigning effort could be described by using three levels of activity. Now the interaction of Jones's and Smith's cam-

paign must somehow be computed. Estimates must be made of the probability of activity for Smith and the conditional probabilities of Jones winning, given various levels of activity for both Jones and Smith. At this point an important (and perhaps unrealistic) assumption must be made if we are to avoid estimating how Jones and Smith will respond to each other's strategies. We must assume that the campaign level of each candidate is independent of the activity of the other. A Bayesian computation for this situation is shown in Box 4-5, and an evidential reasoning approach is shown in Box 4-6.

After examining the results of the analysis, the analysts might make other partitions of the problem, using more or fewer levels of campaign activity, or introducing other campaign factors. For each of these it would be necessary to supply the required probability or belief measures.

Comments Concerning the Probabilistic Formalism

Our nominal view of the world embodies the concept that there is a unique course of events that can be characterized by observed or measured physical quantities. Our understanding of the world is, in turn, characterized by our ability to predict the values of these "observables." Physical theories (models, paradigms) can be ranked in terms of how accurately they perform the prediction task. Reality provides an exact and explicit basis for evaluation of proposed theories.

On the above grounds, we might consider probabilistic models as descriptions of processes and events that we

BOX 4-5   An Example of Bayesian Analysis

A four-level breakdown of campaign activity for Jones and a three-level breakdown of campaign activity for his opponent, candidate Smith, is shown in the table. Experts have assigned probabilities to each of Smith's activity levels. Entries in the table specify conditional probabilities that Jones will win, given the activity of Jones and the activity of Smith. Thus, a conditional probability of 0.3 in the upper left element of the table indicates that if Jones maintains his campaign and Smith increases his campaign, then there is a 0.3 chance of Jones winning. A conditional probability of 1 indicates a sure win for Jones, while a 0 indicates a sure loss. The table indicates that a candidate who decreases his campaign activity is going to be in trouble unless his opponent also does so.

	Probability of activity level				
	.85	Maintain	.3	.5	1.0
	.03	Increase slightly	.5	.6	1.0
Jones	.07	Increase much	.7	1.0	1.0
	.05	Decrease	0	0	.5
Probability of activity level →			.1	.7	.2
Political activity level →			Increase	Same	Decrease
				Smith	

The probability of Jones winning is the sum of the probabilities of his winning for each of the twelve situations described by the above table. The computation is known as a total evidence design since the final probability is the sum of the probabilities of all the possible situations. The probability for each pair of activity levels is determined by using the formula,

Prob(Jones wins|condition A and condition B)*Prob(A and B),
    where P(A and B) = Prob(A|B)*Prob(B).
The independence assumption allows us to say that P(A|B) = P(A).
Thus, Prob(Jones wins) = (.3)(.85)(.1)+(.5)(.85)(.7) + . . . + (.5)(.05)(.2).
    Prob(Jones winning) = .586

---

resort to when deterministic models are not available; they are necessarily cruder, but should be capable of being ranked in terms of accuracy on the same scale as the deterministic models.

Given two probabilistic descriptions of the same situation, such as provided by the Bayesian and Shafer-Dempster formalisms, we might expect to be able to compare their relative performance and choose one or the other as being more accurate. Thus, in the case of the election examples, presented in Box 4-5 and Box

4-6, the Bayesian formulation tells us that candidate Jones has a .586 probability of winning the election, while the Shafer-Dempster formulation tells us that the likelihood of candidate Jones winning is between .239 and .96 (both predictions were based on the same evidence). All this seems quite straightforward, except that the numbers produced by the two formalisms do not really mean the same thing, nor can they be directly compared or evaluated. Suppose, for example, that Jones wins the election. This fact cannot be used to favor either the Bayesian or the S/D approach since neither estimate has a clear meaning that is decisively verified by the real-world result.

Then what do the probabilities really mean? The Bayesian formalism assumes an underlying random process such that, if the election were held often enough under the same conditions, Jones would win 58.6 percent of the time. The Shafer-Dempster formalism provides a way of combining evidence which satisfies our intuition in regard to the ordering of possible outcomes (even when the evidence sources conflict), but does not always have a simple interpretation in terms of the relative frequencies of the outcomes of a random process. Thus, the Bayesian and Shafer-Dempster formalisms provide different underlying models of reality—they are not directly comparable, nor is there generally any way to choose

---

BOX 4-6 An Example of Belief Function Analysis

Referring to the Bayesian analysis of the two-candidate problem (Box 4-5), we choose to interpret the *a priori* probabilities for different levels of campaign activity as degrees of belief. Thus the degrees of belief for the four hypotheses concerning candidate Jones are (.85, .03, .07, .05). For candidate Smith we have (.1,.7, .2) as the degrees of belief for the three hypotheses concerned with his campaign activity. From Box 4-5 we see that Jones will win when the table entry has the value 1.0. We convert these 1 entries to the proposition "Jones will win" denoted by "Win" in the table on the right. The 0 entries are replaced by the proposition "Jones will lose" denoted by "Lose," and everything else by the proposition "We can't assign a win or lose judgment" denoted by "?"

We now combine these beliefs by Dempster's rule, again assuming independence. The use of Dempster's rule is similar to that shown for the Ford/Chevy/Toyota example of Box 4-4. We add up the products of compatible beliefs. For example, in the upper right-hand element, we have beliefs for Jones and Smith that both agree on the event "Win." We therefore get a contribution of .85*.2 toward that event. Adding up the areas pertaining to a win for Jones we get .85(.2) + .03(.2) + .07[(.7) + (.2)] = .239 .

Adding up the areas that support the proposition "Jones loses" we get (.05)(.1 + .7) = .04 .

	Degrees of belief	Political activity level			
Jones	.85	Maintain	?	?	Win
	.03	Slight increase	?	?	Win
	.07	Large increase	?	Win	Win
	.05	Decrease	Lose	Lose	?
	Degrees of belief →		.1	.7	.2
	Political activity →		Increase	Same	Decrease

Smith

This results in an evidential interval for Jones of [.239, .96], indicating a small support, a small refutation of the event "Jones will win," and a very large degree of uncertainty remaining. Thus, we are unable to choose a likely winner in this election.

These conclusions are weaker than the conclusion of the Bayesian analysis, since we are not claiming to have evidence about what will happen in the cases where our descriptions of Smith's and Jones's behavior do not determine the outcome of the election.

between them in unconstrained real-world situations.

ADDITIONAL FORMALISMS FOR REASONING

There are some forms of reasoning that involve combinations of the deductive/inductive/analogical paradigms. Below, we describe some of these: mathematics, programming systems, "production systems," and common-sense reasoning.

Algebraic/Mathematical Systems

In the algebraic/mathematical approach to reasoning, we start with a set of mathematically described (physical) relationships relevant to some (real-world) situation; the problem information is then phrased in terms of these known relations to provide a set of equations; the equations are solved using the standard techniques of mathematics.

Thus, solving a problem such as "If one person can do a job in 3 hours and another can do the same job in 5 hours, how long will it take for them to do the job together?" requires the following steps:

- We must know that the appropriate basic relationship is "rate of doing work times the time worked equals the amount of work done."
- We must assume that working together does not change the individual rates of work.
- We must reason that if a person can do a job in N hours, he does 1/N of the job in 1 hour. Thus, in the given problem, the first person works at a rate of 1/3 of

the job per hour, and the second at a rate of 1/5 of the job per hour.
- Time is represented by the variable t. We finally can write the equation $(1/3)t + (1/5)t = 1$
- The equation can now be solved for t using algebra.

Note that the difficult aspect of this type of reasoning consists of (a) knowing that the pertinent relationship is "rate times time equals work done," (b) that people are assumed by convention to work at a constant rate in this problem context, and then (c) translating the problem statement into these algebraic relations. These steps are quite difficult to automate in a general problem-solving context. However, if we know beforehand the types of problems that will be encountered, if the problem language is simple enough, and if no superfluous information has been provided, then we can write a program that solves such word problems by looking for "key words" (see Box 4-7).

Heuristic Search

One form of reasoning is to search through all possible alternatives for a solution to a problem. We often use this approach in our daily lives. For example, we misplace an object and search from location to location in an attempt to find it. Note that we do not blindly explore everywhere, rather we only search in the most probable locations for it. Problems are often amenable to solution by search, provided that there is some organized way of ruling out alternatives that have little probability of being a successful solution. Many AI techniques are based on heuris-

BOX 4-7   Solving Algebraic Word Problems by Computer

The STUDENT program, developed by Bobrow in the late 1960s [Bobrow 68], solves algebraic word problems phrased in natural language. STUDENT sweeps through the input statements several times, carrying out a different transformation on each pass until suitable algebraic equations are obtained. The equations are then solved.

The words and phrases of the problem are considered to be in one of three classes:

Variables. Words that name objects. One important problem that has to be dealt with is how to determine when two different strings refer to the same variable (e.g., at one point the problem might state "...John's money" while at another point the problem might ask "...how much is Tom's money and how much is John's.")

Substituters. These are words and phrases that are replaced to obtain a more standard representation, e.g., "twice" is replaced by "2 times."

Operators. These are words or linguistic forms that represent functions. One simple operator is "plus" which indicates that the two variables surrounding it are to be added.

An appreciation for the procedures used can best be gained from a printout of the various passes made by the program on a typical problem:

The original problem to be solved is:
(THE SUM OF LOIS' SHARE OF SOME MONEY AND BOB'S SHARE IS $4.50.
LOIS' SHARE IS TWICE BOB'S. FIND BOB'S AND LOIS' SHARE.)

After substitutions the problem becomes:
(SUM LOIS' SHARE OF SOME MONEY AND BOB'S SHARE IS 4.50 DOLLARS. LOIS' SHARE IS 2 TIMES BOB'S. FIND BOB'S AND LOIS' SHARE.)

After words have been tagged by function, the problem is:
((SUM/OP) LOIS' SHARE (OF/OP) SOME MONEY AND BOB'S SHARE IS 4.5 DOLLARS (PERIOD/ DELIMITER) LOIS' SHARE IS 2 (TIMES/OP 1) BOB'S (PERIOD/DELIMITER) (FIND/QUESTIONWORD) BOB'S AND LOIS' SHARE (PERIOD/DELIMITER)

Converted to simple sentences:
((SUM/OP) LOIS' SHARE (OF/OP) SOME MONEY AND BOB'S SHARE IS 4.5 DOLLARS (PERIOD/ DELIMITER)
(LOIS' SHARE IS 2 (TIMES/OP 1) BOB'S (PERIOD/ DELIMITER)
((FIND/QUESTION WORD) BOB'S AND LOIS' SHARE (PERIOD/DELIMITER)

Converted to equation form:
(EQUAL (LOIS' SHARE) (TIMES 2 (BOB'S)))
(EQUAL (PLUS (LOIS' SHARE OF SOME MONEY) (BOB'S SHARE)) 4.5 DOLLARS)

However, these equations were insufficient to find a solution. The program then assumes:
((BOB'S) IS EQUAL TO (BOB'S SHARE))
((LOIS' SHARE) IS EQUAL TO (LOIS' SHARE OF SOME MONEY))

A solution can then be obtained:
(BOB'S IS 1.5 DOLLARS)
(LOIS' SHARE IS 3 DOLLARS)

Note that since the system could only make a partial match on the name of the variables, it assumed that a partial match, e.g., BOB's to BOB's SHARE, was equivalent to a complete match. This allowed a solution to be obtained.

Thus, STUDENT is a system for dealing with a restricted class of problems, but it is very effective in this limited domain.

tic search procedures, rule-of-thumb techniques that direct the search process to the more attractive candidates for solution. Procedures that search for valid proof sequences, discussed in various parts of this chapter, are typically controlled by heuristic rules.[5]

Programming Systems that Facilitate Reasoning and Problem Solving

Conventional programming languages require the user to specify procedures that are to be carried out on the data. The flow of control, and the tests to be performed must be explicitly described. However, programming systems have also been designed to accept nonprocedural "programs," i.e., there are systems that permit the user to state his goal or intent, and the built-in mechanisms of the system attempt to devise procedures to attain these goals. Such systems are often written in programming languages that facilitate writing programs whose purpose is to reason and solve problems.

A formal algorithm for carrying out a reasoning procedure could be implemented in any one of the many programming languages that provide symbol storage, matching, combining of strings or lists, and some type of conditional branching operation. AI problem solving programs are more concerned with manipulating strings of symbols, e.g., rearranging symbols or substituting one symbol for another, than with numerical computation, e.g., multiplying two numbers together. Special languages designed

for AI programming have therefore been developed—the most popular being LISP and its dialects. A brief description of LISP is given in Appendix 4-1. In addition, many AI problems have the characteristic that after a certain amount of progress is made toward a solution, a dead end is reached, and the program must "backtrack," returning certain variables to their original state. This requires much bookkeeping activity that is extraneous to the "logic flow" of the solution for the given problem. The logic-based language PROLOG, described in Appendix 4-1, provides deductive procedures and automatic backtracking.

In a typical program, even one written in LISP or PROLOG, the flow of control and the utilization of data are specified by the program's code, but in "pattern-directed inference systems" (PDIS), the processing modules are activated by patterns in the input data or in the "working storage." A module is inactive until a certain data pattern or situation exists, at which point a response is made. The module's activity typically consists of adding or deleting data in the working store. Such a system is "data driven" rather than "program driven," and "programming" in such a system consists of specifying the pattern to be matched by each module and the corresponding action to be taken.

The system is controlled by software that handles the tasks of pattern matching, monitoring database changes, and carrying out the actions specified by the active modules. Typically, the control structure of the system is given, and the investigator supplies the specifications of the modules.

An important type of PDIS is the

---

[5]The subject of heuristic search techniques is discussed extensively in Nilsson [Nilsson 71] and in Pearl [Pearl 84].

"rule-based" or "production" system, discussed further in Chapter 7, in which each module is a rule that has a left-hand side containing the pattern templates that must be satisfied, and a right-hand side that specifies the actions to be carried out. Because the rules are kept separate from the control structures, it is possible to modify rules without requiring any programming changes to the rest of the system. The OPS-5 production language presented in Appendix 4-1 is an example of a rule-based system. A typical rule is of the form [(A AND B)→C], which specifies that if both A and B appear in the input or working storage, then C will be entered into the working storage. Entering a new fact or assertion by satisfaction of the left-hand side of a rule is called "forward chaining" or "antecedent driven" reasoning. It is also possible to interpret the same rule as "if we want to establish C, then it is first necessary to establish both A and B." This is known as "backward chaining" or "consequent driven" reasoning. Backward chaining is often used to set up a goal tree that directs the search for needed data items.

Practical production systems consist of many rules, typically several hundred to a few thousand, and have been applied to a variety of applications, most notably in the form of "expert systems" (see Chapter 7). Systems such as OPS-5 depart from the "pure" PDIS by providing features that permit the programmer to exercise a considerable degree of control over the processing.

Common-Sense Reasoning

The reasoning techniques that we have dealt with in this chapter use representa-tions of numerical quantities and prop-ositions, i.e., formalisms based on the concept of number and on the algebra of sets. However, we have not yet discussed another type of reasoning used by people; their impressive ability to reason using common-sense theories of the world— their everyday beliefs about what the world is like. Such reasoning appears to be qualitative in nature. For example, consider the reasoning used in answering the following question: "What happens if we turn on the water tap in the bathtub, with the plug in the tub?" We reason as follows. For some time the level of the water will rise, until it reaches the top of the tub. The water then flows over the sides of the tub, and covers the bathroom floor. After the bathroom floor is covered to some level, the water will flow to other rooms and will leak into the floor, drop-ping onto any room below. If some of the water finally escapes from the house, and it is cold enough outside, the water may freeze, possibly into icicle-shaped forms.

Devising a qualitative theory of liquid behavior, and developing an associated reasoning formalism is extremely difficult, since one must first deal with a coherent body of water, then, as it overflows, some of the water separates from the main body, forming a new body of water on the floor, followed by the conversion to indi-vidual drops as it falls into the room be-low. Somehow the formalism has to deal with the creation of new objects from old, the qualitative physics of water flow, and the interaction of water with gravity forces, physical surfaces, temperature of the environment, etc.

Some of the issues that arise in trying to represent and reason about common-sense knowledge are as follows:

Representing common-sense knowledge.
In order for an intelligent entity to
deal with everyday things, it must
have a database consisting of descriptions of these things. The database
would have to include descriptions of
general spatial properties, the behavior of materials and liquids, and have
a "naive" understanding of topics
such as physics, botany, zoology,
ecology, etc. For example, the database would have to capture the properties of water, including properties
when it is still, slowly moving, or en-
ergetically moving. The behavior in
each of these activity states depends
on whether the water is flowing on a
surface, contained, or unsupported.
In addition, the formulation must
consider whether the water is in bulk
form or divided (as in a mist), and the
time-history of the situation.

A collection of papers describing
efforts to formalize common-sense
knowledge is contained in Hobbs
[Hobbs 85].

Qualitative reasoning. A special type of
reasoning seems to be involved in
dealing with everyday objects. Although the real world is continuous
to our senses, a person does not have
to possess continuous representations, such as those typically provided
by mathematics and physics, to deal
with this world. It seems that people
deal with the world by treating it
qualitatively using only a few values
for any of the variables, e.g., very big,
big, medium-sized, small, very small.
Similar quantizations may be employed for nearness, strength of

forces, weights, etc. Reasoning based
on this type of vague quantization
seems to be adequate for solving
everyday problems, for being able to
tell how something works, or using
something in a way for which it was
not intended, e.g., using a fallen tree
as a seat. Formalisms for qualitative
physics and common-sense reasoning
about causality are described in
De Kleer [De Kleer 84] and Kuipers
[Kuipers 84].

Relevance. Given a real-world situation,
how can a reasoning system determine which other objects will have a
significant interaction with the current object of interest? We are (again)
faced with the relevance problem in
trying to determine what aspects of
what objects, in the whole universe,
should enter the reasoning process.[6]

PROBLEM SOLVING AND THEOREM PROVING

Previous sections described a variety of
reasoning techniques; this section will
discuss how these techniques can be used
to solve problems. Basically, the approach
is to:

(a) Represent the concepts, relationships, and constraints of the task
environment in the formalism required by the problem solver.

(b) Apply the solution techniques mechanically by operating on the representations; the "meaning" of the

---

[6]The problem of relevance is a vital part of the
gestalt psychologist view of problem solving as
originally formulated by Max Wertheimer
[Wertheimer 61].

expressions is neither required nor used by the problem solver.

The power of any general problem solving approach is that a large number of interesting problems can be cast into some common form. However, converting the problem to this form is often the main step in obtaining a solution. Once the problem is in the required form, the role of the computer can generally be viewed as equivalent to searching a decision (or game) tree to find a required node or best path.

At the present time there are many classes of problems that (for practical reasons) cannot be put into the form required by existing machine-based general problem solvers. Some examples are: scene analysis problems, in which the machine must describe or understand a real-world scene; language understanding problems; and problems for which all the relevant conditions cannot be specified, e.g., artistic creation.

Representing the Problem

To illustrate the nature of the representation issue for the various general problem solving approaches, we will use a classic example, the monkey/bananas problem (the M/B problem):

"A monkey and a box are in a room, and some bananas are hanging from the ceiling, just out of reach of the monkey. What should he do to get the bananas?"

Given just this statement of the problem, a person readily identifies the pertinent operators concerned with moving the monkey, pushing the box, standing on the box, and finally, reaching for the bananas.

A person ignores other possible operations such as the monkey throwing the box, kicking the wall, scratching himself, etc. Thus, when we present a mechanical problem solver with only the "relevant" operations, we are greatly simplifying the problem solving effort required. How, then, might the problem be presented to a general problem solving program? The initial conditions are clear:

The bananas are at location L. The monkey is at location X. The box is at location Y.

The basic operations available could be indicated as follows without giving away the solution:

The monkey can walk from location x to location y.

If the monkey and the box are at location x, the monkey can push the box from location x to location y, or he can climb the box.

If the monkey can reach the bananas, he can grab them.

The crucial question that now arises is: how can we specify reachability of the bananas? In a neutral way we might say:

The bananas are 6 feet off the floor. The reach of the monkey is 5 feet. The box is 2 feet high. If the monkey stands on the box his reach will be extended by the height of the box.

An alternative formulation, and one that gives the problem away is:

If the monkey stands on the box his reach is within the height of the bananas.

An even more blatant form is:

If the box is under the bananas and the monkey stands on the box, then he can reach the bananas.

We will show how the problem can be represented for the most blatant form of the problem statement using the predicate calculus, the PROLOG logic programming language, OPS-5 (a production rule system), and the general problem solver (GPS) formalism. The intent is to illustrate the nature of these formalisms in a simple problem situation. Each of the approaches must deal with the frame problem, i.e., the problem of knowing what things in the world change as a result of an action. For example, if the monkey was at location b and moves to location c, a reasoning system must determine what objects have changed their location (e.g., the monkey's pants, but not necessarily the box he was standing on).

The Predicate Calculus Representation for the Monkey/Bananas (M/B) Problem

The representation for a predicate calculus approach to the monkey/bananas problem is given in Appendix 4-2, as described in Nilsson [Nilsson 71b]. For his exposition, Nilsson simplifies the problem by ignoring the need for the monkey to go to and remain with the box, and we will follow his example.

The frame problem is handled by using the concept of *state*, e.g., the box is considered to be at a certain location, b, in a particular state, s,: AT(box, b,s). "States" and "objects" are represented by state variables and object variables, respectively. Relations between objects, and properties of states and actions are indicated using "situational fluents" which are functions that include states among their arguments, and whose result is also a state. An operation carried out on an object can be viewed as changing it from one state to another. For example, if the monkey climbs the box, we can consider it to be in a new state of "on-boxness." Given a time sequence of operations carried out on an object, we can say that the various operators caused the object to transition from state to state. The proof procedure must find the sequence of operators that will convert the initial state in which the monkey does not have the bananas to the state in which he does. This final state is given in terms of the sequence of states that produced it, thus indicating the sequence of operations that must be used to obtain the end result. A good proof procedure will avoid blind alleys and explore only paths that seem promising.

The initial state is described by -ONBOX(s0), the monkey is not on the box at the initial state s0. The bananas are at location C. The question now posed is "does there exist a state such that the monkey has the bananas?," or formally, (EXISTS s)HAS__BANANAS(s). The predicate calculus solution using resolution, is given [Nilsson 71b] as

HAS__BANANAS[GRASP(CLIMB__BOX(PUSH__BOX(C,s0)))].

Note the role of the state variable in describing the sequence of operators:

1. Pushing the box to C starting in initial state, s0, causes the new state

PUSH__BOX(C,s0), and we can call the new state s1.
2. The CLIMB__BOX operator then causes a new state, CLIMB__BOX(s1), which we call s2.
3. GRASP(s2) results in a new state s3.
4. Finally, HAS__BANANAS(s3) is the desired solution.

The predicate calculus expression that describes the effect of GRASP provides most of the solution, since the problem solver is specifically told that the monkey should be on the box and the box should be at the location of the bananas in order for the monkey to grasp the bananas. The "solution" is the sequence of operations that will satisfy the needed conditions for GRASP.

PROLOG Representation of the M/B Problem

The PROLOG representation of the monkey/bananas problem is given in Appendix 4-2. The frame problem is handled by retracting old and asserting new database items, e.g., at(monkey,b) is retracted when the monkey moves to c, and at(monkey,c) is asserted. The order of statements in the program is unimportant, except when two rules deal with the same goal (then, the first one encountered will be used). However, the order of terms within statements is crucial, since the analysis of the right-hand side proceeds from left to right. Thus, if we set up the overall goal in the following manner,

> hasbananas :- at(bananas,X),
> move(box,X), move(monkey,X),
> onbox (X).

we are stating that wherever the bananas happen to be located, that should also

be the location of the box. The system will first instantiate the value of X for at(bananas,X). It will then have the ideal goal when it attempts to process the next clause, at(box,X), since it will force the location of the box to be at the same location as the bananas. If we were to reverse the terms,

> hasbananas:-
> move(box,X), at(bananas,X), etc.,

the move(box,X) goal will cause a non-productive and semi-infinite search as the system tries all possible values of X.

Notice also, that in the hasbananas top-level goal, the use of the same variable forces the onbox operation to be carried out only under the bananas. This prevents the monkey from getting on the box every time his location was the same as the box. Many such subtle "cheats" are scattered throughout the program.

Production Rule (OPS-5) Representation for the M/B Problem

A production rule representation of the monkey/bananas problem, using OPS-5, is given in Appendix 4-2. The frame problem is handled by the "remove" and the "make" operations. A set of production rules is used for GO, PUSH, CLIMBON, and GRAB, that cause the monkey to move, push the box, climb on the box, and grab the bananas, respectively. Note that the set of rules for PUSH forces the monkey to move the box to where the bananas are. The rule says that if the monkey and the box are at location 1 and the bananas are at location 2, then make location 2 the location of the monkey and the box. The GO and PUSH rules occur before the CLIMBON rule, and therefore set things up so that although CLIMBON is satisfied, these other rules take priority until the monkey and the box are under the bananas. CLIMBON is thus prevented from firing before the appropriate situation is obtained, avoiding the embarrassing outcome of a monkey trapped on the box, but not under the bananas, with no operator to remove him. The careful arrangement of the rules can be thought of as a way of implicitly programming the desired state sequence. Because the behavior of the system can be quite sensitive to the order of the rules, the designer may have to program the system by entering special conditions to keep certain rules from firing at the "wrong" time. For a complete (70 pages) exposition of how the M/B problem can be handled in OPS-5, see Brownston [Brownston 85].

General Problem Solver Representation for the M/B problem

The general problem solver (GPS) [Ernst 69] was a system developed in the 1960s in which problem solving is carried out by reducing the differences between the current state and a goal state, an approach known as "means-ends analysis." To use GPS on a problem, it is necessary to specify the objects and the operators for transforming the objects. An initial state and a goal state are also specified. The specificiations must include how the differences between states are to be measured, and how the procedures to be used relate to state differences. "Programming" in GPS consists of providing these specifications.

The representation for the GPS approach to the monkey/bananas problem is

given in Appendix 4-2. This formulation was originally presented by Ernst and Newell [Ernst 69]. The task environment includes the operators to be used (CLIMB, WALK, MOVE_BOX, and GET_BANANAS), the "pretest" conditions for their actuation, and the effects of the operators. The "differences" that must be considered between the present state of the world and what one would like it to be are given, along with the difficulty of reducing each difference. Finally, the specific task is given, including the ultimate goal and the initial state.

Probably the most significant information given is the quantification of the difficulty of reducing each difference. This is the implicit control information that enables the system to solve the problem. Since the difference between the goal state and contents of the monkey's hand is indicated as the most difficult problem, GPS tries to eliminate that difference, and it must create a subgoal to accomplish this. Since the next most difficult difference is associated with the location of the box, it attempts to satisfy this subgoal. Notice that the box being under the bananas is a specific pretest for getting the bananas into the monkey's hand. The box location goal is satisfied by causing the monkey to move the box to the desired location. The monkey's place pretest indicates that the monkey must be on the box in order for the monkey to get the bananas. This then causes the monkey to climb onto the box. Note that without the given difference ordering, the monkey would climb the box whenever he was at the box. If a way of climbing down was provided, then the monkey would cycle at this point.

Formalisms or Reasoning Systems?

In the above examples, we have illustrated that the M/B problem can be solved in each of the major deductive formalisms previously discussed. It was also noted that a valid solution would not be obtained if there were slight alterations in how the problem was presented, or in how the operators were defined and ordered. It is clear that these deductive formalisms are not "reasoning systems" in the full sense of this term, (see the definition of reasoning in the introduction to this chapter), but rather a framework for problem solving in which human understanding and intervention is still a necessary ingredient. The human must "bias" the mapping of the problem into the selected formalism so that the "syntactic" transforms invoked by the formalism operate in a highly constrained search space known to contain the desired answer. The pigeon and the banana problem, an amusing analog to the monkey/bananas problem taken from the field of psychological experimentation, is presented in Box 4-8.

Relating Reasoning Formalisms to the Real World

Formal systems for reasoning are constructed to achieve specific goals such as completeness and consistency. Because of the means used to achieve these goals, there will often be a mismatch between the formal system and the type of expressions and reasoning used by people. For example, a formal system will assign "true" to the implication "If the moon is made of Swiss cheese, then France is a country," since this is of the logical form "false implies true." However, most people expect there to be a relationship between the two parts of the implication, and would consider this example inane. Even the conjunction AND does not

---

 ### BOX 4-8   The Pigeon and The Banana Problem

We have indicated the various ways in which the designers had to give away the solution to allow their programs to solve the monkey/bananas problem. The following study concerning problem solving by pigeons (*Nature*, March 1, 1984), shows that what we had been calling the monkey/bananas problem was actually the *pigeon and the banana problem*.

The researchers first trained four pigeons to push a box toward a green spot at the base of a cage wall. The birds did not push when the spot was removed. Next, the animals were trained to climb onto a box and peck at a banana placed overhead. Each bird was occasionally placed alone with the banana until the bird neither flew nor jumped toward it. The pigeons were able to solve the feeding problem; they pushed a box placed at the edge of the cage until they could climb onto it and peck at the banana.

Several other pigeons were trained to peck at the banana but were not taught to climb onto the box; to climb and peck but not push the box; and to climb, peck, and push the box, but not toward a target. These birds also learned not to jump or fly toward the banana. But none of them could solve the feeding problem.

The successful birds had to be given all the explicit steps needed to solve the problem; they were only required to put together the correct sequence.

translate directly to the logical form; e.g., in the sentence "John AND Mary are a happy couple," "couple" cannot apply to John or Mary individually. (We cannot conclude that John is happy AND Mary is happy.)

There are many real-world concepts about causality, imagined or fictitious events, verb tenses, imperative forms, and modal forms, to name only a few, that are readily expressed in natural language and are reasoned about by people, but are difficult to capture in any of our existing formalisms.

DISCUSSION

We have described the nature of "problems," and formalisms for reasoning about problems. The difficulty of converting even well-posed problems into a suitable formalism has been indicated; the difficulties of converting ill-posed problems are even more overwhelming. Indeed, one might consider intelligent behavior as the ability to strip away nonessential elements from a problem to allow application of a suitable problem-solving approach.

This chapter has concentrated on the problem-solving machinery once the problem representation process has been carried out. In a way, this is like looking under the lamppost for an object that has been lost at night somewhere else. Unfortunately, we are forced into this stance because most of the AI work in mechanized reasoning has dealt with the formal (proof) machinery, and not with the automatic problem conversion process.

There is still much controversy concerning the role of logic and deductive inference in common-sense reasoning.

One view is that logic can be used for analysis of knowledge, but not for reasoning by intelligent agents. The other view claims that logic is the only approach that offers: (1) an assured procedure for deriving new facts from known or assumed truths, (2) the ability to say that an existentially quantified proposition is true without knowing exactly what object makes it true, and (3) the ability to reason by cases.

It was shown that the logic representation can be thought of as providing a language for making assertions about the world; various deductive formalisms can then operate on this representation to answer questions, devise plans, and solve problems. However, the computational feasibility of the deductive process is strongly dependent on the way that the assertions are expressed, and the nature of the external guidance that has been provided. Combinatorial explosion must be avoided, since all of the formalisms have a worst case computational cost that increases exponentially with the number of initial assertions.

Although there are various strategies incorporated into theorem provers to improve the efficiency of the proof-finding process, there are no effective purely syntactic mechanisms that can direct an automatic proof system to select only those statements that are relevant, but still adequate, to obtain the desired proof. If we have a large database, many unproductive paths are typically pursued, and an enormous number of inappropriate deductions carried out.

In a very important sense, deductive systems have to be "programmed" if they are to avoid the necessity for the equivalent of exhaustive search: the user must understand, and supply to the system, some approximation to the solution of the problem to be solved. There is thus an equivalence between what has been called the "automatic programming problem," and automatic problem solving by deductive systems. Since very little progress has been made in finding a general solution to the automatic programming problem, we should not expect currently available deductive systems to be capable of functioning autonomously as general problem solvers.

Appendixes

4-1

AI Programming Languages

The LISP Programming Language

In programming computers for artificial intelligence applications, one is often required to represent arbitrary objects and the relationships among them. This is in contrast to other computer applications where numerical computation is the main theme. The LISP language, designed in 1958 by John McCarthy of Stanford University, has become the primary language used in AI. (Some of the present-day variants include INTERLISP, FRANZLISP, MACLISP, COMMONLISP, and ZETALISP.) Simple lists, such as (object1 object2 object3), and more complicated structures, such as

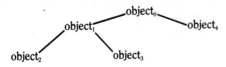

can be uniformly represented. LISP commands permit the programmer to extract elements from lists, to combine lists in various ways, and to carry out mathematical and logical operations. A conditional branching function and facilities for extensive data structure manipulation are also provided.

One characteristic of LISP that is often puzzling to the novice is that procedural knowledge is expressed as a composition of nested functions. Rather than having a program consisting of a series of sequential steps, as in most conventional languages, in LISP the desired operations are expressed in the form of a single complex function that is composed of simpler functions. Also, much use is made of recursion in which the function calls itself. This is illustrated in the following LISP program for factorial.

```
(Define                              ;define a function
      (factorial (Lambda (N)         ;factorial is the name of the
                                     ;function, and the argument is N
      (cond ((zerop N) 1)            ;if N = 0, then result = 1 and return
      (T (times N (factorial (sub1 N)) ;otherwise, N*factorial(N-1)
 ]                                   ;close with required number of
                                     ;right parentheses
```

A more complex problem programmed in LISP is given on the following page.

There are many reasons for the success of LISP: it was the first available programming language having the needed flexibility for AI problems, and it became the language of choice in university AI centers. However, a more important reason is that excellent programming environments were developed for the language, consisting of powerful sets of highly integrated editing and debugging tools. An important feature of these environments was that LISP code was interpreted and the programmer could see the results of executing a portion of such code immediately, without having to go through a tedious compilation process. Thus, LISP provided an interactive environment in which all data and functions could be inspected or modified by the programmer. An error in a function or data object could be corrected, and the correction tested, without the need to recompile the program. It is LISP's interactive environment that allows massive programs to be developed one "layer" at a time.

Another useful feature is the dynamic allocation of storage: intermediate results from subsidiary functions are passed on to the calling function, but are not retained after they are used. Thus, the system can automatically recover the memory storage that was used in obtaining the intermediate results, freeing programmers from the responsibility for detailed memory management.

Finally, the LISP language syntax is quite simple: a LISP program is a binary tree. This uniformity of syntax and functions permits a LISP program to examine other LISP programs, and to produce additional LISP programs that can be executed.

A recent contribution to the popularity of LISP is the development of personal work stations based on this language. These "LISP machines" have good graphics,

powerful computational capabilities, and can be networked to other machines so that results and programs can be shared.

The Tower of Hanoi Problem in LISP. The Tower of Hanoi problem is a good example of the use of recursion and of the type of thinking that goes into representing a problem in the LISP language. We are given three pegs, LEFT, MIDDLE, and RIGHT and N disks of decreasing size on the LEFT peg.

LEFT   MIDDLE   RIGHT

The problem is to move the disks one at a time from the LEFT peg to the RIGHT peg without putting a larger disk on a smaller disk. The MIDDLE peg can be used as an intermediate storage location when required. The basic approach is to assume that we can get the top N-1 disks to an intermediate peg. We now can place the remaining large disk on the RIGHT peg. The problem is then to move the N-1 disks to the RIGHT peg. This can be accomplished by repeating the original procedure, i.e., using a recursive approach.

The LISP solution uses a function HANOI(N, SOURCE, DESTINATION, OTHER), where N is the number of disks, SOURCE (where a disk is to be taken from), DESTINATION (where the disks removed from SOURCE are to be placed), and OTHER (the current intermediate storage location). SOURCE, DESTINATION, and OTHER take on the values LEFT, RIGHT, and MIDDLE, in any order. For example, HANOI(1, MIDDLE, LEFT, RIGHT) indicates that a disk is to be removed from MIDDLE and placed on LEFT.

Note 1 says that if we can somehow move N-1 disks from SOURCE to some intermediate peg, OTHER, then (Note 2) the remaining disk, the Nth disk, can be moved

The actual LISP program is:

```
(HANOI
    [LAMBDA (N SOURCE DESTINATION OTHER)
        (COND
            ((EQP N 1)                          ;if N = 1
                (PRIN1 "MOVE THE DISK ON")      ;message to user to move
                (PRIN1 SOURCE)                  ;disk from the current
                (PRIN1 "TO")                    ;value of SOURCE to the
                (PRIN1 DESTINATION)             ;current value of DESTINATION
            )
            (T (HANOI (SUB1 N) SOURCE OTHER DESTINATION) ;Note 1
                (HANOI 1 SOURCE DESTINATION OTHER)        ;Note 2
                (HANOI (SUB1 N) OTHER DESTINATION SOURCE) ;Note 3
            )
        ))
    ])
```

from SOURCE to DESTINATION. Then (Note 3) we now transfer the N-1 disks from OTHER to DESTINATION using the original SOURCE peg for intermediate storage.

The sequence of operations of the program for the case of 3 disks is shown in Fig. 4-3. The reader is encouraged to work through the LISP program to see how the recursion "unwinds."

The PROLOG Programming Language

Although one can express a problem in predicate calculus and then remove the resulting quantifiers using techniques shown previously, an attractive alternative is to express the logical expressions directly in a quantifier-free clausal form. This is the approach adopted for the programming logic language PROLOG [Clocksin 81]. The motivation for such "logic programming" is that programs will be easier to write (and to read) than programs in a procedural language, since they do not require an explicit statement about how things are to be done, but are more like a specification of what the program should achieve.

The PROLOG clausal form is a restricted subset of the standard form, having the advantage that simple and efficient theorem provers have been developed for it. For some sentences the standard form allows a more economical and natural expression than the PROLOG form. See Kowalski [Kowalski 79] for a comparison.

PROLOG programs consist of (1) declarations of facts about objects and their relationships, (2) rules that define objects and their relationships, and (3) questions about objects and their relationships. A period follows

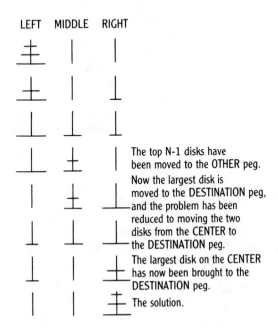

The top N-1 disks have been moved to the OTHER peg.

Now the largest disk is moved to the DESTINATION peg, and the problem has been reduced to moving the two disks from the CENTER to the DESTINATION peg.

The largest disk on the CENTER has now been brought to the DESTINATION peg.

The solution.

FIGURE 4-3
Solution of the Tower of Hanoi Problem.

every statement in PROLOG. Some examples of PRO-LOG expressions are given below.

Facts: Some examples of facts in PROLOG are: likes(mary,john).; valuable(gold).; owns(john,gold).; and father(john,mary). Any number of arguments can be used in a fact. To the system, a fact is of the form a(b,c,d, . . .); the mnemonics are merely an aid to the programmer. The programmer must decide what any of the fact expressions mean, e.g., valuable(gold) could mean that a specific piece of gold is valuable, or that in general the mineral gold is valuable.

Questions: Once we have some facts, we can ask questions about them. Thus, the question ?- owns(mary,book). causes PROLOG to look in the database of facts for that fact. If owns(mary,book) is in the database, the system answers "yes," otherwise it responds "no."

Variables: If we want to ask "Who does John like," we express this using a variable, e.g. ?-likes(john,X). If the database contains likes(john,flowers)., PROLOG will respond with X = flowers. The variable X is now "instantiated" to have the value "flowers."

Conjunctions: We can ask "Is there anything that both John and Mary like" by using the expression "?-likes(mary,X),likes(john,X)., where the comma between the facts stands for the conjunction AND. PROLOG first finds an entry of the form likes(mary,something)., and instantiates X to "something." The system then tries to find an entry in the database: likes(john,something). If no such entry is found, then the system backtracks and tries to find another fact that satisfies "likes(mary,X)." If it finds one, then a new value of X is instantiated and the system tries to find "likes(john,X)" for the new value of X. All of this backtracking is performed automatically by the system.

Rules: Rules have the form "(consequence) IF (conditions)," meaning that a certain consequence follows if the conditions hold. For example "likes(john,X) IF likes(X,wine)" indicates that John likes any X, IF X likes wine. Using the PROLOG notation B:- A for B IF A, the relationship "sisterof(X,Y)" can be defined as:

sisterof(X,Y) :- female(X),parents(X,m,f),parents(Y,m,f).

which says that X is the sister of Y if X is female and if X and Y have the same parents.

Built-in predicates: PROLOG has a set of built-in predicates that provide the programmer a way of expressing control information about how the proof is to be carried out. This is necessary because without such mechanisms PROLOG would spend unacceptable amounts of time trying to carry out proof procedures that are not fruitful. (For example, the "cut" symbol written "!", that allows the programmer to indicate to the system which previous choices it need not consider again when it backtracks through the chain of satisfied goals.)

A simple PROLOG program is given below, along with a target question and a trace of how the program carried out the deduction. Note that each rule can read both in a declarative way and a procedural way. Thus the user can make declarative statements that the system can use in a procedural manner. Both the declarative and procedural interpretations are given only for the first of the two rules.

```
                         % Rule 1
descendant (B,C) :-  % declarative: C is a descendant of B
                     % if C is an offspring of B.
     offspring(B,C)  % procedural: To determine that C
                     % is a descendant of B
                     % determine that C is an offspring of B


                         % Rule 2
descendant(B,C) :-   % To determine that C is a descen-
                     % dant of B,
     offspring(D,C), % determine both that C is an off-
                     % spring of D
     descendant(B,D).% AND that D is a descendant of B
```

offspring(abraham,ishmael). % This is the database
offspring(abraham,isaac).   % of offspring data
offspring(isaac,esau).
offspring(isaac,jacob).

The following trace shows how the question "is esau a descendant of abraham?" is processed. "Call" indicates a rule is to be invoked in an attempt to answer a question or achieve a subgoal. The return is either a "failure," or a successful "exit" with the instantiated variable indicated. The numbered lines indicate the "depth" of the portion of the proof being worked on. For example, line (4) is examining whether isaac is a descendant of abraham, and this then requires that the proof of isaac being an offspring of abraham (5) first be established. The control of the system is goal driven, i.e., the system proceeds from rule to rule as needed to satisfy subgoals. When there is a failure, the system automatically backtracks or tries an additional rule related to the current goal.

```
    | ?- descendant(abraham,esau).
            We are asking if esau is
            a descendant of abraham
(1) Call : descendant(abraham,esau) ?
(2) Call : offspring(abraham,esau) ?
(2) Fail : offspring(abraham,esau)
                Can't be established by first rule,
                so now try 2nd rule, 1st part
(3) Call : offspring(__119,esau) ?
                119 is an i.d. number that PROLOG
                has used to designate a variable.
(3) Exit : offspring(isaac,esau)
                Finds that esau is offspring of isaac
(4) Call : descendant(abraham,isaac) ?
                Now work on 2nd part of 2nd rule
(5) Call : offspring(abraham,isaac) ?
                Determine if isaac was offspring of abraham
(5) Exit : offspring(abraham,isaac)
                From database, he was
(4) Exit : descendant(abraham,isaac)
                From first rule, isaac is a descendant
                of abraham
(1) Exit : descendant(abraham,esau)
                Since both conditions of 2nd rule are
                satisfied, esau is a descendant of abraham
yes
                Therefore answer is "yes"
```

OPS-5: A Programming Language for Production Systems

OPS-5 [Forgy 77] is a language for writing production systems programs. If the goal (condition) portion of a rule is satisfied, then the "action" portion causes some change to occur in working memory. One can store items in working memory using the "make" command. "Remove" is used to remove items, and "modify" to change items. Thus the fact that a block named block1 has the color "red" is added to working memory by

```
            (make block
                    name block1
                    color red)
```

A typical production rule would be written:

```
(p find-colored-block          ;p denotes production
    (goal                      ;if there is a goal which
            status active      ;is active to find
            object block       ;a block
            color  <z>)        ;of a certain color
    (block                     ;and there is a block
            color  <z>         ;of that color
            name <block>)      ;with a certain name


            ———————→


    (make result pointer<block>)
                    ;then enter a pointer in
                    ;working storage that
                    ;indicates the name of the
                    ;block that satisfies the goal.
    (modify status satisfied)
                    ;and change the goal marking
                    ;to satisfied
)
```

This says that

IF in the working memory there is an item known as a goal, and if that goal is to find a block of a certain color, and if there is also an item in working memory describing a block of that color.

THEN make an item called a "result" that points to the block and change the goal item to indicate that it is now satisfied. (The pointer result can then be used by any other rules requiring a block of that color.)

An OPS-5 program consists of a set of such production rules and stored items. The system is activated when new items appear in working memory that cause certain rules to be activated. The activated rules add, delete, and modify items in the memory to cause further activity. Production rule programming requires a different way of thinking than conventional procedural programming.

4-2

The Monkey/Bananas Problem

The Predicate Calculus Formulation

The following predicates and operators are given as part of the predicate calculus formulation of the M/B problem [Nilsson 71a]:

Predicates

ONBOX(s), monkey is on the box in state s
AT(box,b,s), box is at location b in state s,
HAS__BANANAS(s), monkey has bananas in state s

Operators

(It is important to remember that each operator returns a new state value)

GRASP(s), the state attained when grasping bananas in state s,
CLIMB__BOX(s), the state attained when the monkey climbs box in state s,
PUSH__BOX(x,s), the state attained when the monkey pushes box to location x starting in state s.

The preconditions and effects of operators are expressed in the predicate calculus notation:

(It is assumed that the monkey and the box are never separated.)

PUSH__BOX(x,s): If the monkey isn't on the box, in the state s, then the box and the monkey will be at location x in the new state attained by applying PUSH__BOX to state s.

$$(ALL\ x\ ALL\ s)[-ONBOX(s) \rightarrow AT(box,\ x,\ PUSH\_\ BOX(x,s))]$$

CLIMB__BOX: The monkey will be on the box in the state attained by applying the operator CLIMB__BOX to the state s. Note that the argument of ONBOX is a new state, CLIMB__BOX(s).

$$(ALL\ s)[ONBOX(CLIMB\_BOX(s))]$$

GRASP: If the monkey is on the box and the box is at C (the location of the bananas) in state s, then the monkey will get the bananas in the state attained by applying GRASP to state s.

$$(ALL\ s)[(ONBOX(s)\ AND\ AT(box,c,s) \rightarrow HAS\_BANANAS(GRASP(s))]$$

In addition, it must be stated explicitly that the position of the box does not change when the monkey climbs on the box.

$$(ALL\ x\ ALL\ s)[AT(box,x,s) \rightarrow AT(box,x,CLIMB\_BOX(s))]$$

As described in the text, the predicate calculus solution using the above formulation is:

$$HAS\_BANANAS[GRASP(CLIMB\_BOX(PUSH\_\ BOX(C,S0)))].$$

This solution, and its conversion to a plan that could be used by the monkey to obtain the bananas is described in Nilsson [Nilsson 71a].

APPENDIX 4-2

The Monkey/Bananas Problem in PROLOG

The PROLOG formulation for the monkey/bananas problem is shown below; see text for additional comments. The initial conditions are shown first, followed by the rules.

```
offbox.                        %these are the given initial conditions.
at(bananas,c).                 %lower case characters are constants.
at(monkey,a).                  %thus, a,b,c are constants that represent
at(box,b).                     %fixed locations of the monkey, the box, and the bananas.

hasbananas :-                  %this is the top level goal. It states
    at(bananas,B),             %that the monkey has the bananas when
    move(box,B),               %the box and the monkey have been moved
    move(monkey,B),            %to the same location as the bananas,
    onbox(B).                  %and the monkey is on the box.

move(monkey,B) :-              %to achieve the goal of moving the monkey
    ( at(monkey,B);           %to B, either the monkey is already at B, or
    at(monkey,C),              %the monkey is at C and we should establish
        goto(C,B) ).           %goto(C,B) that moves him from C to B.

move(box,B) :-                 %to achieve the goal of the box at B
    ( at(box,B);              %either the box is already at B or
    at(box,C),                 %the box is at C, and we should establish
        pushbox(C,B) ).        %pushbox to move the box from C to B.

goto(B,C) :-                   %to get the monkey from B to C, either
    ( at(monkey(C));          %he is already at C, or he is off the box,
    offbox,
    retract(at(monkey,B)),     %and we then retract his former location
    assert(at(monkey,C)) ).    %and assert his new one.

pushbox(B,C) :-                %to push the box from B to C,
    offbox,                    %the monkey must be off the box,
    at(box,B),                 %the box must be at B
    move(monkey,B),            %the monkey must be at B,
    retract(at(monkey,B)),     %and we then retract the previous
    retract(at(box,B)),        %locations of the box and the monkey,
    assert(at(monkey,C)),      %and assert the new ones.
    assert(at(box,C)).

climbbox(B) :-                 %to establish climbbox,
    offbox,                    %establish that the monkey is off the box,
    move(box,B),               %move the box to B,
    at(monkey,B),              %establish that the monkey is at B
    retract(offbox).           % retract offbox.
```

REASONING AND PROBLEM SOLVING

```
onbox(B) :-          %this merely says that if we establish
    climbbox(B).     %climbbox, we establish onbox. This
                     %statement could be eliminated by replacing
                     %onbox by climbbox in all the other statements.
```

A trace of the operations that occur when we ask to establish hasbananas is given below. The numbers shown on the left refer to depth levels of search, and the numbers such as __85 represent the labels of temporary variables used by the system:

```
| ?- hasbananas.                            top goal
    (1) 0 Call : hasbananas ?
    (2) 1 Call : at(bananas,__85) ?
    (2) 1 Exit : at(bananas,c)              at(bananas,c) established
    (3) 1 Call : move(box,c) ?             trying to move the box to c
    (4) 2 Call : at(box,c) ?
    (4) 2 Fail : at(box,c)
    (5) 2 Call : at(box,__102) ?
    (5) 2 Exit : at(box,b)
    (6) 2 Call : pushbox(b,c) ?            pushbox(b,c) needed to
                                          satisfy move(box,b)
    (7) 3 Call : offbox ?                 trying to satisfy pushbox
    (7) 3 Exit : offbox
    (8) 3 Call : at(box,b) ?
    (8) 3 Exit : at(box,b)
    (9) 3 Call : move(monkey,b) ?         has to move the monkey to b
    (10) 4 Call : at(monkey,b) ?
    (10) 4 Fail : at(monkey,b)
    (11) 4 Call : at(monkey,__143) ?
    (11) 4 Exit : at(monkey,a)
    (12) 4 Call : goto(a,b) ?             using goto to move the monkey
    (13) 5 Call : at(monkey(b)) ?
    (13) 5 Fail : at(monkey(b))
    (14) 5 Call : offbox ?
    (14) 5 Exit : offbox                  establishes that offbox is true
    (15) 5 Call : retract(at(monkey,a)) ?
    (15) 5 Exit : retract(at(monkey,a))
    (16) 5 Call : assert(at(monkey,b)) ?
    (16) 5 Exit : assert(at(monkey,b))
    (12) 4 Exit : goto(a,b)
    (9) 3 Exit : move(monkey,b)           monkey moved to box at b
    (17) 3 Call : retract(at(monkey,b)) ?
    (17) 3 Exit : retract(at(monkey,b))
    (18) 3 Call : retract(at(box,b)) ?
    (18) 3 Exit : retract(at(box,b))
    (19) 3 Call : assert(at(monkey,c)) ?
    (19) 3 Exit : assert(at(monkey,c))
    (20) 3 Call : assert(at(box,c)) ?
```

---

(20) 3 Exit : assert(at(box,c))
(6) 2 Exit : pushbox(b,c)
(3) 1 Exit : move(box,c)   box moved to c
(21) 1 Call : move(monkey,c) ?
(22) 2 Call : at(monkey,c) ?
(22) 2 Exit : at(monkey,c)
(21) 1 Exit : move(monkey,c)
(23) 1 Call : onbox(c) ?   establishing onbox
(24) 2 Call : climbbox(c) ?   establishing climbbox
(25) 3 Call : offbox ?   verifying that monkey is off box
(25) 3 Exit : offbox   verified monkey off box
(26) 3 Call : move(box,c) ?
(27) 4 Call : at(box,c) ?   verifying that box is at c
(27) 4 Exit : at(box,c)
(26) 3 Exit : move(box,c)
(28) 3 Call : at(monkey,c) ?   verifying that monkey is at c
(28) 3 Exit : at(monkey,c)
(29) 3 Call : retract(offbox) ?
(29) 3 Exit : retract(offbox)
(24) 2 Exit : climbbox(c)   monkey can climbbox
(23) 1 Exit : onbox(c)
(1) 0 Exit : hasbananas   monkey has bananas
yes

The Production Rule Formulation

In the OPS-5 production rule formalism, a set of productions is used, each of which specifies the items that can appear in working storage, and the actions that will result when these items actually do appear. If more than one production is satisfied by items in working storage, then the production highest on the list will be activated. Thus, the ordering of the productions is important.

In the production rule approach to the monkey/bananas problem, the initial contents of working storage are:

Initial: goal working, at monkey r, at box b, at banana s, on monkey floor

This says that a goal is being worked on, the monkey is at r, the box is at b, the bananas are at s, and the monkey is on the floor.

The set of productions are:

```
go
((goal working)                  ;if we are still working on a goal,
 (at monkey <loc1>)              ;goal, and the monkey is in loc1,
 (at box (<loc2> <> <loc1>))     ;and the box is at loc2 not equal to loc1,
 (on monkey floor)               ;and the monkey is on the floor
 ───────────>
 (remove 2)                      ;remove from working storage the
 (make at monkey <loc2>))        ;fact that monkey is at loc1, and replace monkey location with loc2
```

```
push
((goal working)
   (at monkey <loc1>)              ;if monkey is at loc1 and the box
   (at box <loc1>)                 ;is at the same location
   (at banana (<loc2> <> <loc1>))  ;and the banana is not at loc1
   (on monkey floor)               ;and the monkey is on the floor
   ———————→
   (remove 2)                      ;remove ws entry for monkey location
   (remove 3)                      ;remove ws entry for box location
   (make at monkey <loc2>)         ;enter into ws that monkey is at loc2
   (make at box <loc2>))           ;and so is the box

climbon
((goal working)
   (at monkey <loc1>)              ;if the monkey is at loc1,
   (at box <loc1>)                 ;and the box is at loc1
   (on monkey floor)               ;and the monkey is on the floor
   ———————→
   (remove 4)                      ;delete fact that monkey is on
   (make on monkey box))           ;floor, and add to ws the fact that monkey
                                   ;is now on box

grab
((goal working)
   (at banana <loc1>)              ;if the banana is at loc1
   (at box <loc1>)                 ;and so is the box,
   (at monkey <loc1>)              ;and so is the monkey,
   (on monkey box)                 ;and the monkey is on the floor
   ———————→
   (remove 1)                      ;goal has been satisfied
   (remove 2)                      ;banana has been removed
   (make monkey has banana))       ;enter result in ws
```

The sequence of working memory states is:

after go: goal working, at monkey b, at box b, at banana s, on monkey floor

after push: goal working, at monkey s, at box s, at banana s, on monkey floor

after climbon: goal working, at monkey s, at box s, at banana s, on monkey box

after grab: at monkey s, at box s, on monkey box, has monkey banana

APPENDIX 4-2

General Problem Solver Representation

In the GPS approach to the monkey/bananas problem, we are given a task environment that specifies the set of places, the operators, the "differences," the difference ordering, and the task. These are as follows:

I. Task Environment
   A. Miscellaneous: the set of places on the floor = (place1, place2, under the bananas)

   B. Operators
      1. CLIMB
         Pretest: The monkey's place is the same as that of the box
         Result: The monkey's place becomes on the box.
      2. WALK
         Variable: x is in the set of places
         Result: the monkey's place becomes x.
      3. MOVE__BOX
         Variable: x is the set of places
         Pretests: the monkey's place is in the set of places
                   the monkey's place is the box's place
         Results: The monkey's place becomes x
                   The box's place becomes x

(Note: the difference ordering discussed below keeps the monkey from being on the box at this point. Thus, one can omit the test for the monkey being on the floor to move the box.)

      4. GET__BANANAS
         Pretests: The box's place is under the bananas
                    The monkey's place is on the box
         Results: The contents of the monkey's hand is "bananas"

   C. Differences (this indicates the kinds of difference that one can have between what is and what should be. For example, the monkey's place may be different than the desired monkey's place.)

      D1 is the monkey's place
      D2 is the box's place
      D3 is the contents of the monkey's hand

   D. Difference ordering (this indicates the order of difficulty in reducing a difference)

      D3 is more difficult to reduce than is D2 which is more difficult to reduce than D1 (Thus, it is more difficult to take care of the difference of the monkey's hand being empty, than it is to change the difference involved with the monkey's location.)

II. Specific Task
   A. TOP GOAL: Transform the Initial OBJ into the Desired OBJ
            (i.e. take the situation described by Initial OBJ and somehow attain the Desired OBJ)

REASONING AND PROBLEM SOLVING

B. Objects
   1. Initial OBJ
      a. The monkey's place is place1
      b. The box's place is place2
      c. The contents of the monkey's hand is "empty"

   2. Desired OBJ
      The contents of the monkey's hand is "bananas"

GPS will first note that there is a difference to be reduced with respect to the contents of the monkey's hand when the Initial OBJ is compared to the Desired OBJ. There is no way of achieving this reduction directly, since the pretests for GET_BANANAS are not satisfied. In trying to satisfy these preconditions, GPS will find differences between what is and what should be, and guided by the difference ordering, GPS will choose the next difference to eliminate. The program tries to eliminate the more difficult differences before trying the simpler ones. The various WALK, MOVE_BOX, and CLIMB operators will have to be exercised before the GET_BANANAS operator can be invoked.

5

Learning

Learning can be defined as any deliberate or directed change in the knowledge structure of a system that allows it to perform better on later repetitions of some given type of task. Learning is an essential component of intelligent behavior—any organism that lives in a complex and changing environment cannot be designed to explicitly anticipate all possible situations, but must be capable of effective self-modification. There are several basic ways to learn, i.e., to add to one's ability to perform or to know about things in the world:

1. **Genetically-endowed abilities.**
   Knowledge can be stored in the genes of men or animals, or in the circuits of machines.

2. **Supplied information.**
   Someone can demonstrate how to perform an action or can describe or provide facts about an object or situation.

3. **Outside evaluation.** Someone can tell you when you are proceeding correctly, or when you have obtained the correct information.

4. **Experience or observation.** One can learn by feedback from his environment; the evaluation is usually done by the learner measuring his approach to some explicit goal.

5. **Analogy.** New facts or skills can be acquired by transforming and augmenting existing knowledge that bears a strong similarity in some

respect to the desired new concept or skill.

In computers, the first two types of learning correspond to providing the machine with a predesigned set of procedures, or adding information to a database. If the supplied information is in the form of advice, rather than a complete procedure, then converting advice to an operational form is a problem in the domain of reasoning rather than learning. Types 3, 4, and 5 in the above list involve "learning on your own," or autonomous learning, and present some of the most challenging problems in our understanding of intelligent behavior. These types of learning are the subject of this chapter.

Autonomous learning largely depends on recognizing when a new problem situation is sufficiently *similar* to a previous one, so that either a single generalized solution approach can be formulated, or a previous solution can be applied. However, the recognition of similarity is a very complex issue, often involving the perception of *analogy* between objects or situations. We will first discuss some aspects of animal and human learning, and then representations and techniques for discovering and quantifying similarity (including methods for recognizing known patterns). Finally, techniques for automatic machine learning will be described. We will address the following questions:

- How do animals and people learn?
- How can we quantify the concept of similarity?
- How can we identify a particular situation as being similar to or an instance of an already-learned concept?
- How much do you have to know in order to be able to learn more?

- What are the different modes of learning, and how can such ability be embedded in a computer?

HUMAN AND ANIMAL LEARNING

Complicated behavior patterns can be found in all higher animals. When these behavior patterns are rigid and stereotyped, they are known as *instincts*. Instincts are sometimes alterable by experience, but only within narrow limits. In higher vertebrates, especially the mammals, behavior becomes increasingly modifiable by learning even though rigid instinctive behavior is still present.

It is now recognized that inheritance and learning are both fundamental in determining the behavior of higher animals, and the contributions of these two elements are inextricably intertwined in most behavior patterns. Inheritance can be regarded as determining the limits within which a particular behavior pattern can be modified, while learning determines, within these limits, the precise character of the behavior pattern. In some cases the limits imposed by inheritance leave little room for modification, while in other cases the inherited limits may be so wide that learning plays the major role in determining behavior.

Experiments conducted by W. H. Thorpe of Cambridge University [Thorpe 65] show some instances of the interaction between inheritance and learning. He raised chaffinches in isolation and found that such birds were unable to sing a normal chaffinch song. Thorpe then demonstrated that young chaffinches raised in isolation and permitted to hear a recording of a chaffinch song when about six months old would quickly learn to sing properly. However, young chaffinches permitted to hear recordings of songs of other species that sing similar songs did not ordinarily learn to sing these other songs. Apparently chaffinches learn to sing only by hearing other chaffinches; they inherit an ability to recognize and respond only to the songs of their own species.

When chaffinch songs are played backward to the young birds, they respond to these, even though to our ears such a recording does not sound like a chaffinch song.

Thus a chaffinch song is neither entirely inherited or wholly learned; it is both inherited and learned. Chaffinches inherit the neural and muscular mechanisms responsible for chaffinch song, they inherit the ability to recognize chaffinch song when they hear it, and they inherit severe limits on the type of song they can learn. The experience of hearing another chaffinch sing is necessary to activate, and perhaps somewhat adjust, their inherited singing abilities, and in this sense their song is learned.

Types of Animal Learning

It is possible to classify the many types of animal learning according to the conditions which appear to induce the observed behavior modifications:

Habituation and sensitization. Habituation is the waning of a response as a result of repeated continuous stimulation not associated with any kind of reward or reinforcement. An animal drops those responses that experience indicates are of no value to its goals. Sensitization is an enhancement of an organism's responsiveness to a (typically harmful) stimulus. Instances of both habituation and sensitization can be found in the simplest organisms.

Associative learning. Associating a response with a stimulus with which it was not previously associated. An example of classical conditioning, or associative learning, is Pavlov's experiment in which a dog learned to associate the sound of a bell with food after repeated trials in which the bell always rang just before the food was provided. Another form of conditioned learning, called *operant conditioning*, or instrumental learning, is illustrated by the *Skinner box*. A hungry rat is given the opportunity to discover that a pellet of food will be given every time he presses on a bar when a signal light is lit, but no food will be provided when the light is off. The rat quickly learns to press on the bar only when the light is lit. The distinction between classical and operant conditioning is that in classical conditioning the conditioned stimulus (e.g., bell) is always followed by the unconditioned stimulus (e.g., food), regardless of the animal's response; in operant conditioning, *reinforcement* (e.g., food) is only provided when the animal responds to the conditioning stimulus (e.g., light is lit) in some desired way (e.g., pressing on the bar).

Trial-and-error learning. An association is established between an arbitrary action and the corresponding outcome. Various actions are tried, and future activity profits from the resulting reward or punishment. This type of learning can often be classified as a form of operant conditioning as described above.

Latent learning. Learning that takes place in the absence of a reward. For example, rats that run through a maze unrewarded will learn the maze faster and with fewer errors when finally rewarded (compared to other rats that never encountered the maze before, but received rewards from the start of the learning sessions).

Imprinting. The animal learns to make a strong association with another organism or sometimes an object. The sensitive phase in which learning is possible lasts for a short time at a specific point in the animal's maturation, say a day or two after birth, and once this phase has passed, the animal cannot be imprinted with any other object. For example, it was found that a duckling will learn to follow a large colored box with a ticking clock inside if the box is the first thing it observes after hatching. The duckling preferred the box to its mother!

Imitation. Behavior that is learned by observing the actions of others.

Insight. This type of learning is the ability to respond correctly to a situation significantly different from any previously encountered. The new stimuli may be qualitatively and quantitatively different from previous ones. An example would be (1) a monkey obtaining a bunch of bananas above his reach by moving a box under the bananas and standing on the box, (assuming that he had never seen this procedure used before), and (2) subsequently using the box as a tool to obtain objects out of his normal reach. The first part of the monkey's activities involve problem solving, the second involves learning. We note here the difference between learning and problem solving: problem solving involves obtaining a solution to a *specific* problem, while learning provides an approach to solving a *class* of problems.

The evolution of anatomical complexity among animals has paralleled a steady advance in learning capability from simple habituation to associative learning, which appears first as classical conditioning and then as trial-and-error learning. It is as if evolutionary progress in the powers of behavioral adjustment consists of elaborating and coordinating new types of responses that are built upon and act with the simple ones of more primitive animals.

Some remarkable examples of animal learning are presented in Box 5-1.

Piaget's Theory of Human Intellectual Development

A study of the intellectual development of a child can provide insight into learning mechanisms. Based on an extensive series of experiments and informal observations, Piaget [Flavell 63] has formulated a theory of human intellectual development. Piaget views the child as someone who is trying to make sense of the world by discovering the nature of physical objects and their interaction, and the behavior of

BOX 5-1   Examples of Animal Learning

Visual Learning

Pigeons have been trained to respond to the presence or absence of human images in photographs. The pictures are so varied that simple stimulus characterization seems impossible. The results suggest remarkable powers of conceptualization by pigeons as to what is human.

Monkeys have been trained to select the pictures of three different insects from among pictures of leaves, fruit, and branches of similar size and color.

Counting

A raven learned to open a box that had the same number of spots on its lid as were on a key card. Eventually, the bird was trained to lift only the lid that had the same number of spots on it as the number of objects in front of the box.

Pigeons have been trained to eat only a specific number of grains out of a larger number offered. They have also learned to eat only a specific number N of peas dropped into a cup (one at a time at random intervals ranging from 1 to 30 seconds); the pigeon never sees more than one pea in the cup at a time, but only eats the first N.

A jackdaw learned to open black lids on boxes until it had secured two baits, green lids until it had three, red lids until it had four, and white lids until it had secured five.

A parrot after being shown four, six, or seven light flashes is able to take four, six, or seven pieces of irregularly distributed food out of trays. Numerous random changes in the time sequence of visual stimuli did not affect the percentage of correct solutions. After the bird learned this task, the signal of several light flashes was replaced by notes on a flute. The parrot was able to transfer immediately to these new stimuli without further training.

Learning Visual Landmarks

The female digger wasp can efficiently and consistently locate her nest when she returns from hunting. It has been shown that she locates the nest by noting both distant and adjacent landmarks.

When a beehive is moved to a new location, the worker bees coming out on foraging flights will pause and circle in increasing arcs around the new site for a few moments before flying off. The insect learns the relative positions of new landmarks in this manner, so as to be able to find its way back.

The goby can jump from pool to pool at low tide without being stranded on dry land, even though they cannot see the neighboring pools before leaping. The gobies apparently swim over rock depressions at high tide and thereby learn the general features and topography of the limited area around the home pool. They then use this information in making their jumps at low tide.

---

people and their motivations. Thus, Piaget views the child as developing increasingly well-articulated and interrelated representations that are used to interpret the world. Interaction with the world is crucial because when there is sufficient mismatch between the representations and reality, the representations are modified or transformed. Piaget thinks of the child's intellectual development as having four discrete stages:[7]

1. **Sensorimotor stage** (years 0–2).
   By discovery through trial-and-error

---

[7]There has been some controversy as to whether the development occurs in discontinuous jumps or as a single continuous process that can be partitioned into discrete stages. Cunningham [Cunningham 72], in an attempt to formalize intelligence, describes these stages in terms of data structures and operations on these structures.

---

manipulation experiments, children develop a simple cause-and-effect understanding of how they can physically interact with their immediate environment. In particular, they develop an ability to predict the effects on the environment of specific motor actions on their part; for example, they learn to correctly judge spatial relations, identify and pick up objects, learn that objects have permanence (even when they are no longer visible), and learn to move about. They also develop an ability to use signs and facial expressions to communicate.

2. **Symbolic-operational or preoperational stage** (years 2–7).   Children start to develop a symbolic understanding of their environment. They develop an ability to communicate via natural language, to read and write, and form internal representations of the external world; they can now perform mental experiments to predict what will happen in new situations. However, their thinking is still dominated by visual impressions and direct experience; their generalization ability is poor. For example, if 5-year-old children are shown a row of black checkers directly opposite a row containing an equal number of red checkers, they will say that there are an equal number of each. If the red checkers are now spaced closer together, but none are removed, the children say there are more black than red checkers. Their visual comparison of the lengths of the two rows dominates the more abstract notion of numerical equality. The ability of preoperational children to form or to

recognize class distinctions is also poor—they tend to categorize objects by single salient features, and assume that if two objects are alike in one important attribute, they must be alike in other (or all) attributes.

3. **Concrete-operational stage** (years 7–11).   Children acquire some of the concepts and general principles which govern cause-and-effect relationships in their direct interaction with the environment. In particular, they develop an understanding of such concepts as invariance, reversibility, and conservation; e.g., they can correctly judge that a volume of water remains constant regardless of the shape of the container into which it is poured. Five-year-old children can follow a known route (e.g., getting home from school), but cannot give adequate directions to someone else, or draw a map. They do not get lost because they know that they must turn at certain recognized locations. The 8-year-old is able to form a conceptual picture of the overall route and can readily produce a corresponding map. Until children reach the age of 11 or 12 years, their method of discovery is generally based on trial-and-error experimentation. They do not formulate and systematically evaluate alternative hypotheses.

4. **Formal-operational stage** (years 11+).   The young adult develops a full ability for symbolic reasoning, and the ability to conceive of possibilities beyond what is present in reality.

Recently, many of the Piaget experiments have been interpreted in terms of information-processing metaphors, seeking explanations as to why children perform better on intellectual tasks as they get older. Basically, the questions are (1) do children think better (because they can hold more information in working memory, can retrieve information faster, and can reason faster), or (2) do they know more (have more knowledge, enabling them to perform tasks more efficiently)? Anderson [Anderson 85] discusses experiments that indicate that both effects are present.

One basic aspect of Piaget's theory is that children develop an understanding of their physical environment by manipulation of objects within it; he believed that language played a much less important role. A challenge to his work is based on the idea that the child's performance in some of his experiments was less a matter of competence, than of learning the correct meaning of certain verbal expressions such as "same amount," or "more than."

While Piaget's theory attempts to describe the changes in, and characteristics of, human learning ability, it provides very little insight into the specific mechanisms that underlie such learning ability. Thus it provides very little guidance with respect to the question of how to build machines capable of learning. As Margeret Boden has written [Boden 81]:

> One of the weaknesses of Piagetian theory . . . is its lack of specification of detailed procedural mechanisms competent to generate the behavior it describes . . . Even Piaget's careful description of behaviors . . . is related to uncomfortably vague remarks about the progression of stages, without it being made clear just

how one stage (or set of conceptual structures) comes to follow another. . . .

SIMILARITY

Assigning names or labels to objects, events, and situations is one of the most important and recurring themes in the study of intelligent behavior. This *pattern-matching problem* typically involves measuring the degree of similarity between data describing the given *state of the world*, and previously stored models. Basically, a common representation for the objects under consideration must be found, and then a metric must be defined relative to this representation quantifying the degree of similarity between any of the objects and models.

The pattern-matching problem arises in many situations: For example, the < IF (condition) THEN (action)> template is a basic method of encoding knowledge within the computer paradigm, and is used in a variety of applications ranging from computer programming to the way rules are structured in expert systems (see Chapter 7). Determining when an existing situation matches the IF condition of a template is a pattern-matching problem. Another example of the pattern matching problem is trying to find similar symbolic patterns in two logical or algebraic expressions so that they can be combined or simplified. (The *unification problem* in the predicate calculus, discussed in Chapter 4, is an example of a sophisticated matching problem.) Finally, a significant portion of vision and perception is concerned with *recognizing* a known sensory pattern (i.e., the pattern recognition problem).

Some similarity problems can require that we find an exact match, while others are satisfied with finding an approximate match. This critical distinction separates the methods based on the symbolic approaches typically employed in the *cognitive* areas of AI, from those based on measurement (feature) spaces and statistical decision theory that are often employed in the perceptual areas of AI. In both cases, the objects being compared are usually first transformed into some canonical (standard) form to allow the computational procedures to deal with a practical number of primitive elements and relationships.

Note that there is the question of level of generality to be used in similarity evaluation, even after conversion to a canonical form. For example, if we are comparing two concepts, one of which contains the trigonometric term *sine* and the other *cosine*, then we have to move to the more general term *trigonometric function* in order to obtain a match. Knowing the level of generality to use in a matching operation is often crucial in performing similarity analysis.

Similarity Based on Exact Match

The exact match problem usually arises in a precise world, such as the *game world*; e.g., when we try to match a chessboard configuration against a stored set of configurations. Sometimes partial exact matches are sufficient, while at other times a match of the entire description is required.

A representation often used for exact matching is the graph with labeled arcs

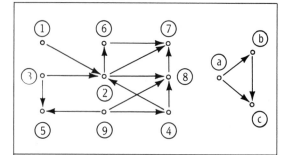

FIGURE 5-1

Graph Representation and the Partial Match Problem.

The problem is to find instances of the subgraph in the graph (e.g., 9,4,8 corresponds to a,b,c).

and nodes, as shown in Fig. 5-1. Mathematically, in the complete match problem one tries to find a mapping (isomorphism) between two graphs so that when a pair of connected nodes in one graph maps to a pair in the other graph, the edge connecting the first pair will map to the edge connecting the second pair. The partial match problem of finding isomorphisms between a graph and a subgraph is computationally more difficult because there are many more combinations to be tested.

Another common matching problem involves strings of symbols, as shown below:

Find the string "SED" in the string:

"A REPRESENTATION OFTEN USED FOR MATCHING"

As in the graph case, the complete match of two strings is less difficult than trying to match a substring against a string.

Similarity Based on Approximate Match

Approximate match problems arise in attempting to deal with the physical world. For example, in visual perception the sensed object can differ from the reference object due to *noisy* measurements, i.e., measurements degraded due to the effects of perspective, illumination, etc. Because many of these differences are at too low a level of resolution to be meaningful, or are irrelevant to our ultimate purpose, we must define a metric for goodness-of-match, rather than expecting to find an exact match. Using this approach, two objects are given the same label if their match score is high enough. In Appendix 9-1 we describe matching of two shapes using a "rubber sheet" representation. We imagine one of the figures to be drawn on a transparent rubber sheet and superimposed on the other; we match the figures by stretching the rubber sheet as required. The measure of goodness of match is based both on the quality of match between individual components of the objects being compared, and the required stretching of the rubber sheet to attain a match between components of the figures.

LEARNING

Unsupervised (unmonitored and undirected) learning is really a paradox: How can the learner determine progress if he does not know what he is supposed to learn from his environment? This situation presents severe problems in attempting to devise programs that can learn. If the designer introduces very specific criteria for success, then the learning program is given too much focus; in fact, an explicit statement of how to evaluate success can provide the machine with just those concepts that were supposed to be learned. Unfortunately, if criteria for success are not provided, then learning is minimal.

We take the view that a system learns to deal with its environment by instantiating given models or by devising new ones. It will be convenient to divide autonomous learning techniques into the following model-based approaches:

- **Parameter learning.** The learner has been supplied with one or more models of the world, each with parameters of shape, size, etc., and it is the purpose of the learner to select an appropriate model from the given set, and to derive the correct parameters for the chosen model. A model can be as simple as the description of a straight line, and in this case the parameters can be the slope of the line and its distance from some given point in space. Another model could be a decision making device with weighted inputs, and the parameters to be found are the weights.

- **Description learning.** Here the learner has been given a vocabulary of names and relationships, and from these he must create a description which forms the desired model.

- **Concept learning.** This is the most difficult form of learning because the available primitives are no longer adequate. New vocabulary terms must be invented that allow efficient representation of the relevant concepts.

Two basic problems in autonomous learning are (1) the credit assignment problem: how to reward or punish each system component that contributes to an end result, and (2) local evaluation of progress: how to tell when a change is actually progress toward the desired end goal.

Model Instantiation: Parameter Learning

Almost all AI systems with *learning ability* are limited to learning within a given model or representation. That is, current AI systems do not significantly modify their basic vocabulary (representations). Typically, learning consists of adjusting the parameters of the given model based on statistical techniques, or inserting and deleting connections in a given graphical representation.

Parameter Learning Using an Implicit Model. In the implicit form of parameter learning, the model is not given directly, and may, in fact, never be known. Two examples of this type of learning are described below.

The Threshold Network. Early computer scientists thought of the brain as a loosely organized, randomly interconnected network of relatively simple devices. They felt that many simple elements, suitably connected, could yield interesting complex behavior, and could form a *self-organizing system*. The system could learn because the random connections were designed to become selectively strengthened or weakened as the system interacted with its environment. A form of implicit model

would thus be formed. In the 1960s, the threshold device was studied intensively as the basic element in such a self-organizing system. The name "perceptron" was often used to designate the basic device in which weighted inputs are summed and compared to a threshold. In a typical implementation for visual pattern recognition, a two-dimensional retina is set up so that local regions of the retina can be analyzed by feature detectors, as shown in Fig. 5-2.

Sets or vectors of k retinal values, $X = [x_1, x_2, \ldots x_k]$, are passed to N feature detectors, each of which determines a score $f_i(x)$ representing the degree of presence or absence of some specific feature or object in the image. These feature scores[8] are then combined in a weighted vote:

$$SUM = w_1{}^*f_1 + w_2{}^*f_2 + w_3{}^*f_3 + \ldots w_N{}^*f_N.$$

SUM is compared to a threshold, T, and if SUM is greater than T, we say that the system responds positively. We want the system to respond positively for one class of objects and negatively for objects not in this class, e.g., positively when it is presented with the character "B," and negatively when presented with "A."

An algorithm for adjustment of the weights (i.e., the *training*) of such a system is described in Appendix 5-1. Although such training capability is attractive, this type of device has serious innate limitations; if it must make a global decision about a pattern by examining local features, then there are certain attributes

---

[8]The N feature detectors are typically threshold devices that produce an $f(x)$ equal to $+1$ if the feature is present, or a -1 if it is absent.

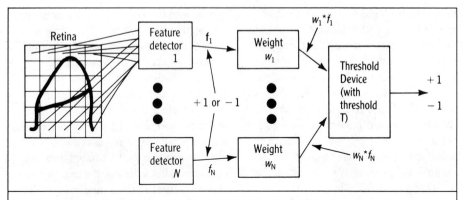

FIGURE 5-2   A Threshold Device Used as a Pattern Classifier

Patterns are assigned to one of two categories, labeled $+1$ or -1.

of the pattern that it cannot deduce. For example, connectivity of patterns as shown in the examples of Fig. 5-3 cannot be determined by local measurements (see Minsky [Minsky 67]). Intuitively, one can see the difficulty: different pieces of each pattern are critical for keeping the pattern connected, and there is no single weighting arrangement that can capture the connectivity concept.

There has recently been renewed interest in threshold networks because of the development of new techniques for obtaining the network parameters (learning algorithms). The techniques are based on "simulated annealing," a statistical mechanics method for solving complex optimization problems. (The name comes from the fact that the procedure is analogous to the use of successively reduced

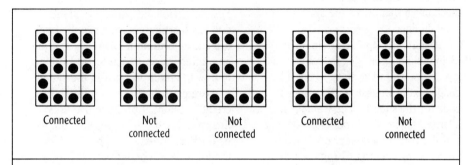

FIGURE 5-3
The Connectedness Problem Cannot be Solved by a Single Threshold Device.

temperature stages in the annealing of metals.) These techniques can be used to find the weights in a multilevel threshold network by considering the weight determination problem to be a minimization problem in many variables. This approach avoids being trapped in local minima by the use of two mechanisms: (1) the adjustments are made randomly, and (2) an adjustable "temperature" parameter, T, controls the probability of acceptance of any change in a variable.

To minimize a function $E(x_i)$ of the many variables, (x_i), the minimum E is found by starting with a random set of x_i and introducing small random perturbations into these x_i. If a perturbation decreases E, it is accepted. If a perturbation increases E it is accepted with a probability that is a function of the change in E and the parameter T: the probability decreases with the size of the change in E and increases with increasing T. By beginning with a high T there is a high probability of acceptance of a change in x_i. T is decreased as the process proceeds, thus decreasing the probability of the acceptance of a bad perturbation. The random acceptance of "bad" perturbations as a function of the change in E and T is the mechanism that drives the system out of local minima.

Using this approach Sejnowski [Sejnowski 85] was able to train a multi-layer network to transform natural language text in English to the phonetic code for the sounds. The training set was a large sample of natural language text and the corresponding phonetic codes prepared by linguists. Using the training set, the network weights were adjusted using simulated annealing so that the phonetic codes developed by the network agreed with the codes in the training set prepared by the linguists. The spoken form of the text was obtained by feeding the phonetic code developed by the threshold network into a sound synthesizer. It is rather dramatic to hear the effects of the training process: the output of the network is first a babble of sounds, and then becomes more and more human-sounding as the training process proceeds. After training, the network is able to synthesize the sounds of text not in the training set.

It should be recognized, however, that adjustment of weights to correctly recognize the members of a training set is not the critical issue in building a learning system. What we require is that the corresponding recognition rule generalizes distinctions represented by the training set so as to be applicable to new members of the class. Since the weight-adjustment learning algorithms do not address this question, even successful generalization on a few selected problems provides very little assurance that this type of approach can be successful on a wide range of real problems.

The "Bucket Brigade" Production System.   Holland [Holland 83] introduced a learning mechanism (the bucket brigade algorithm or BBA) which offers an interesting approach to the problem of how to credit portions of the system that are contributing to a solution, the credit assignment problem. He uses the production rule representation, to be further discussed in Chapter 7, of the form, IF < condition > THEN < action >.

In a *production system*, all the productions interact with a global list (GL), or working storage, which stores information representing the current state of the world; when the <condition> part of a production is satisfied, the <action> portion of the rule is executed. Typically, the internal action taken is to alter or add to the information stored in GL; there might also be some external action (such as sending a message) which does not concern us here. Pure production systems are completely data driven, and thus do not require an explicit control or sequencing mechanism. The only control function required of the system is to determine which productions are satisfied by the information stored in GL, and to carry out the actions of these satisfied productions. A collection of rules of this type can be considered to be an implicit model of the domain to which these rules apply.

In the BBA approach, when the <condition> portion of a production is satisfied it does not automatically activate the <action> portion. Rather, the production is allowed to make a bid based on an associated utility parameter (which measures its past effectiveness and its current relevance); only the highest bidding productions are allowed to fire. As shown in Fig. 5-4, the BBA treats each production rule as a middleman in an economic system, and its utility parameter is a measure of its ability to make a profit. Whenever a production fires, it makes a payment by giving part of the value of its utility parameter to its suppliers. (The suppliers of a production P are those other productions that posted data on GL that allowed P's condition portion to be satisfied.) In a similar way, a production receives a payment from its consumers when it helps them satisfy the condition part of their rules.

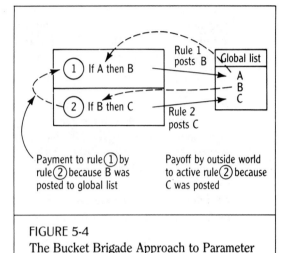

FIGURE 5-4
The Bucket Brigade Approach to Parameter Learning.

If a production receives more from its consumers than it pays out to its suppliers, then it has made a profit and its capital (utility parameter) increases. Certain actions produce payoffs from the external environment, and all productions active at such a time share this payoff. The profitability of a production thus depends on its being part of a chain of transactions that ultimately obtains a payoff from the environment, and such that this payoff exceeds the incurred expenses. In this way, a production can receive due credit even though it is far removed from the successful action to which it contributed.

Parameter Learning Using an Explicit Model. In parameter learning for an explicit model, a pattern or situation is expressed as a list of attribute measurements corresponding to the arguments of the model. The model itself also contains *free* parameters which may be adjusted to improve performance. Learning consists of changing the free parameters (which can be measurement weights as in the case of an implicit model) based on observed performance. An example of learning using an explicit model is an adaptive control system. Here, the system, e.g., an aircraft, is modeled using equations that describe its dynamic response. Algorithms are provided that adjust the parameters of the dynamic model, based on the measured in-flight performance of the aircraft.

One of the earliest and most effective parameter learning programs for an explicit model is Samuel's checker-playing program [Samuel 67], described in Box 5-2.

Most game-playing programs (including Samuel's) use a *game tree* representation in which branches at alternate *levels* of the tree represent successive moves by the player and his opponent, and the nodes represent the resulting game (or board) configuration. Typically, the complete tree is too large to be explicitly represented or evaluated. Instead, a value is assigned to nodes a few levels beyond the current position using an *evaluation function* that guides the program in the selection of desirable moves to be made. This evaluation function is not guaranteed to provide a correct ranking of potential moves; it usually takes into account the number, nature, and location of the pieces, and other attributes that the designer feels characterize the position.

 BOX 5-2   Checkers: Parameter Learning Using a Problem-Specific Model

Samuel's checker-playing program is a successful example of parameter learning using a problem-specific model; this program is able to beat all but a few of the best checker players in the world. A game tree representation is used in which each node corresponds to the board configuration after a possible move, and the move to be made is determined after assigning values to the nodes and choosing a legal move leading to the node with the highest score. Since a full exploration of all possible moves requires the evaluation of about 10^{40} moves, the approach is to evaluate only a few moves by applying a heuristic evaluation function that assigns scores to the nodes being considered. To improve the performance of the checker player,

one can allow it to search farther into the game tree, or one can improve the heuristic evaluation function to obtain a more accurate estimate of the value of each position.

Samuel improved the look-ahead capability of his system by saving every board position encountered during play, along with its most extensive evaluation. To take up little computer storage space, and to retrieve the results rapidly, required the use of clever indexing techniques and taking advantage of board symmetries. When a previously considered board position is encountered in a later game its evaluation score is retrieved from memory rather than recomputed. Improved look-ahead capability

comes about as follows: If we look ahead only three levels to a board position P, but P has a previously stored evaluation value that represents a look-ahead of three levels, then we have performed the equivalent of a look-ahead of six levels.

The evaluation function depends on (1) measures of various aspects of the game situation, such as "mobility," (2) the function to be used to combine these measures, and finally (3) the specific weightings that should be used for each measure in the evaluation function. The designer supplies the measurement algorithms and the form of the function to be used, while the weightings are obtained by a "learning" procedure. The system *learns* to play better by adjusting weights

The problems in designing a good evaluation function are (1) the choice of the components of the evaluation function, (2) the method of combining these components into a composite evaluation function, and (3) how to modify the components and the composite functions as experience is gained in playing the game. (The credit assignment problem arises here: how to assign credit or blame due to something that happened early in the game, since the good or bad results do not show up until much later.)

The third factor is the one that typically constitutes the machine learning to play the game. Note, however, that this learning is crucially dependent on the cleverness of the human designer in solving the first two problems.

Model Construction: Description Models

Programs capable of forming their own description models take an initial set of data as their input, and form a theory or a set of rival theories with respect to the given data. The theories are descriptions or transformations that satisfy the initial data. The program then attempts to generalize these theories to cover additional data. This typically results in a number of admissible theories. Finally, the program chooses the strongest theory from these,

---

BOX 5-2 (*continued*)

which determine how much each parameter contributes to the evaluation function. Samuel investigated two forms of the evaluation function:

1. A function of the form
   MOVE__VALUE = SUM(w_i*f_i),
   where f_i is the numerical value of the ith board feature, and w_i is the corresponding weight assigned to that feature. Since each feature independently contributes to the overall score, the weight can be considered as a measure of the importance of that feature. Thus, features with low weights can be discarded.
2. An evaluation function in which features were grouped together to obtain a score by using a look-up table that says *If board feature A has a value of X, and board feature B has a value of Y, . . . , then that group of features has a score of Z*. The values assigned to the grouped features in the look-up tables correspond to the weights in the first evaluation function; these are modified by a learning procedure.

The detailed record of games played by experts, *book games*, were used for training the system, the checker program taking the part of one of the experts. If the program makes the move that the expert made for a particular game situation, the evaluation function was assumed to be correct, since it caused the correct path in the game tree to be taken. If the wrong move was made, then the evaluation function was modified. Various *ad hoc* weight modification schemes were incorporated into the program. Samuel found that the second evaluation function was far more effective than the first.

The approach of relating specific board positions and corresponding expert responses has an important advantage. Reward and punishment training (learning) procedures can be based on the local situation, rather than on winning or losing the game (because the expert has a global view in mind when making his move). This local indication of ultimate success or failure is not usually available in non-game playing situations.

i.e., one that best explains the data encountered to date.

Learning analogical relationships. An early investigation of this class of problems by T.G. Evans [Evans 68] still stands as a remarkably insightful work on

analogy and the learning process (see Box 5-3). Evans dealt with the machine solution of so-called geometric-analogy intelligence test questions. Each member of this class of problems consists of a set of line drawings labeled Figures A, B, C, C_1, C_2,

---

BOX 5-3   Solving Geometric Analogy Problems

In 1963, Tom Evans [Evans 68] devised a computer program, ANALOGY, which could successfully answer questions of a type found on IQ tests: *Figure A is to figure B, as figure C is to which of the following figures?* The operation of this geometric analogy program can best be illustrated by a *toy* example. Suppose we have the patterns shown in Fig. 5-5. In describing figure A, the program would first assign names to each pattern. Thus,

$$(A1 = +), \quad (A2 = -),$$
$$\text{and} \quad (A3 = o).$$

Similarly, in figure B,

$$(B1 = -), \quad (B2 = +),$$
$$\text{and} \quad (B3 = o).$$

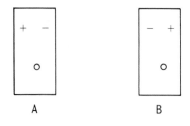

A   B

FIGURE 5-5
Geometric Analogy Example.

In figure A, analysis would reveal that A2 is to the right of A1, A3 is below A1, and A3 is below A2. Analysis of figure B would show that B2 is to the right of B1, B3 is below B1, and B3 is below B2.

Comparing the descriptions of the two figures, the program would find that A1 = B2, that A2 = B1, and A3 = B3. From this it would deduce that the transformation rule is: interchange A1 and A2 to obtain figure B from figure A.

Suppose we have the patterns shown in Fig. 5-6.

We want the program to answer the question: figure A is to figure B as figure C is to which figure (C1, C2, or C3)? Again, the program has to find the correspondences between subfigures in figure C and the subfigures in figures C1, C2, and C3.

After determining these correspondences, the program can apply the transformation found between figures A and B, and will find that both figures C2 and C3 are possible answers. It finally determines that figure C3 is not acceptable because the Z pattern has also been transformed (from bottom to top). Thus, it is sometimes necessary to specify

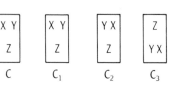

C C_1 C_2 C_3

FIGURE 5-6
Analogy Test Patterns.

which things remain constant, as well as which things change, in specifying the transformation rule. For example, in the transformation rule relating figures A and B, it is necessary to assert that the bottom pattern does not change its location with respect to the two other patterns. Given this extended transformation rule, figure C2 is selected as the desired solution.

ANALOGY uses a fixed model provided by the designer (the set of transformation operators), and finds, by exhaustive search, the proper transformation parameters for the various pairs of figures. The approach depends on having a small number of patterns in each figure, otherwise the combinatorial growth of the pattern relationship lists would become excessive.

... The task to be performed can be described by the question, *Figure A is related to Figure B, as Figure C is related to which of the following figures?* To solve the problem the program must find transformations that convert Figure A into Figure B and also convert Figure C into one of the answer figures. The sequence of steps in the solution is as follows:

- Overlapping subfigures must be identified in line drawings, e.g., two overlapping circles must be recognized as such.
- The relationships between the subfigures in a main figure must be determined, e.g., the dot is inside the square.
- The transformations between subfigures in going from Figure A to Figure B must be found, e.g., the triangle in Figure A corresponds to the small square in Figure B, or the dot inside the square in Figure A is outside the square in Figure B.
- The subfigures in Figure C that are analogous to the subfigures in Figure A must be recognized.
- The program must analyze what figure results when the transformations are applied to Figure C.
- The transformed Figure C must then be compared to the candidate figures.

A description of Evans' ANALOGY program is given in Box 5-3.

Learning descriptions. A study by Winston [Winston 75] deals with developing descriptions of classes of blocks-world objects (see Box 5-4). Given a set of objects identified as to class, known as a training set, the program is to produce (learn) a description of the class. The program is given a set of description primitives and develops a description of the

object class as training objects are presented one at a time. The program notes the commonalities between positive instances, and differences between negative instances and the current description. Each example leads to a modified description that ultimately characterizes that class of objects. When a training example is presented that is incompatible with the present description, the program backtracks to a previous description and attempts to modify it so as to be compatible with the new instance.

The final description produced by Winston's system is dependent on the vocabulary provided and on the sequence of examples shown. In addition, the program must assume that the class labeling of the examples is correct, since the modification of the description depends on the class assignments given. Furthermore, some of the examples that are not of the class must differ only to a small extent from those that are in the class; otherwise, the program will not be able to discover the fine distinctions between membership and nonmembership in the class. (For example, in learning what an "arch" is, the program is given the example of a non-arch whose support posts touch, but is otherwise a valid arch. This allows the program to detect this important difference between a non-arch and an arch.)

Learning generalizations of descriptions and procedures. It is possible to consider the problem of generalizing a description (or a procedure) as a search problem in which the space of all possible descriptions is examined to find (learn) the most general description that satisfies a set of training examples. This approach is used in LEX [Mitchell 83], a program

BOX 5-4   Learning Descriptions Based on (Given) Descriptive Primitives

In 1970, Patrick Winston [Winston 75] devised a learning program which was able to produce descriptions of classes of simple block constructions presented to the program in the form of line drawings. (A specialized subprogram converted these line drawings into a semantic network description.)

The semantic net in Fig. 5-7 indicates that an arch, such as is shown in the figure, consists of three pieces, a, b, and c. Training

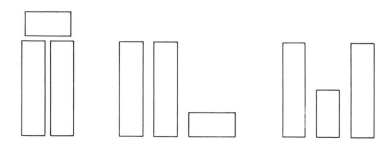

FIGURE 5-8

Block Structures That Do Not Form an "Arch."

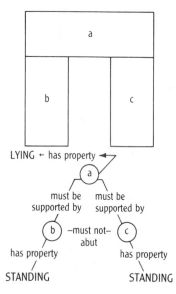

FIGURE 5-7

Semantic Net for the Concept "Arch."

instances cause the various links to be inserted, e.g., that piece a has the property of being supported by pieces b and c; pieces b and c must not abut; and piece a must be lying down while pieces b and c are standing.

The *must not abut* description is deduced by the system only after showing it a non-arch example consisting of a set of blocks in which the supports do abut, as shown in Fig. 5-8. An implicit requirement is that examples of a non-arch should not have characteristics that differ from the existing arches and are not important in defining the arch class. If the top block in an example is curved, and the supports touch, then the program will not know which of the two deviations is causing the blocks to be an instance of a non-arch. Thus, each non-arch used

for training must be a *near-miss* to an actual arch.

If examples are shown to the system in which the top piece is always a rectangular solid, then the program will assume that this is a requirement for an arch. Only after the system is shown an arch consisting of a triangular top piece will the description be broadened to include both rectangular and triangular top pieces.

An approach such as Winston's that tries to find a description that is consistent with all of the training instances will be strongly affected by erroneous data, i.e., data in which a false-positive or false-negative instance has been given. A false-positive causes the description to be more general than it should be, and a false-negative causes the description to be overspecialized.

that learns "rules of thumb," known more formally as *heuristics*, for solving problems in integral calculus. Basically, a rule indicates that if a certain form of mathematical expression is found, then a specific transformation should be applied to the expression. Sometimes these procedures involve looking up the integration form in a table, while at other times they may involve carrying out operations on the expression to convert it to a more manageable form. The program begins with about 50 operators (procedures) for solving problems in the integral calculus, and it learns a set of successively more general heuristics which constitute a strategy for using these operators (Box 5-5).

The *generalization language* made available to LEX is crucial since it determines the range of concepts that LEX can describe, and thus learn. For example, the designer has provided a generalization hierarchy that asserts that *sin* and *cos* are specific instances of a *trigonometric function*, and that a trigonometric function is a specific instance of a *transcendental function*. LEX uses four modules:

1. The *problem solver* utilizes whatever operators and heuristics are currently available to solve a given practice problem.
2. The *critic* analyzes the solution tree generated by the problem solver to produce a set of positive and negative training instances from which heuristics will be inferred. Positive instances correspond to steps along the best solution path, and negative instances correspond to steps leading away from this solution path.
3. The *generalizer* proposes and refines heuristics to produce more effective problem solving behavior on subsequent problems. It formulates heuristics by generalizing from the training instances provided by the critic.
4. The *problem generator* generates practice problems that will be informative (i.e., they will lead to training data useful for proposing and refining heuristics), yet easy enough to be solved using existing heuristics.

These modules work together to propose and incrementally refine heuristics from training instances collected over several propose-solve-criticize-generalize learning cycles.

Unlike most systems that retain only a single description at any given time, LEX describes each partially learned heuristic using a representation (called *version space*) that provides a way of characterizing all currently plausible descriptions (versions) of the heuristic. The basic ordering relationship used in the version space representation of rules is that of *more-specific-than*. For example, the precondition (large red circle) is more specific than (large ? circle), which is more specific than (? ? circle), where ? indicates that this condition need not be satisfied. More formally stated, a rule G_1 is more-specific-than a rule G_2, if and only if the preconditions of G_1 match a proper subset of the instances that G_2 matches, and provided that the two heuristics make the same recommendation.

LEX stores in version space only the maximally specific and maximally general descriptions that satisfy the training data. Thus the more-specific-than relation (provided as part of LEX's originally given, hierarchically ordered vocabulary) partially orders the space of possible heuristics, provides the basis for their efficient representation, and a prescription for their generalization.

Concept Learning

In concept learning, the learning system must develop appropriate concepts (descriptive primitives) for dealing with its environment. Because of its difficulty, little progress of a general nature has been made in this problem area. One of the few significant efforts that both addresses the issue of concept learning, and has achieved some computational success, is AM. The AM program [Lenat 77] runs experiments in number theory and analyzes the results to develop new concepts or theorems in the subject.

The program begins with 115 incomplete data structures, each corresponding to an elementary set-theoretic concept

---

BOX 5-5 Version Space: A Representation for Descriptions

The LEX program [Mitchell 83b] deals with the problem of learning rules of thumb to solve calculus integration problems. Each heuristic rule suggests an integration procedure (operator) to apply when the given expression satisfies a corresponding functional form. LEX uses a representation called *version space* to keep track of the rules that it is learning. Stored information is kept to a reasonable size by including only the most specific and the most general descriptions of the rules that satisfy the training examples.

The program is given a set of operators for solving calculus problems. A typical operator,

OP1: INTEGRAL (u dv) →
uv - INTEGRAL (v du),

indicates how the INTEGRAL of an expression can be solved, and often the solution is recursive, i.e., it requires solution of an additional INTEGRAL.

An example of a version space rule is shown in Fig. 5-9(1). The most specific heuristic is marked S and indicates that if a specific expression, {3x cos(x) dx}, is encountered, then operator 1 should be used, with the variables u and dv in this operator replaced by the specific values shown.

The most general rule, denoted by G, indicates the substitutions that should be made in operator 1 for the more general expressions f1(x) and f2(x). Thus while many additional heuristics are implied, S and G completely delimit the range of alternatives in a predefined general-to-specific ordering.

Assume that a new training instance involving {INTEGRAL 3x sin(x)} is encountered, and the program discovers the solution

INTEGRAL 3x sin(x) dx →
Apply OP1 with u = 3x and
dv = sin(x)dx.

Given the generalization hierar-

chy supplied by the designer,

$$sin(x), cos(x) \rightarrow trig(x) \rightarrow transc(x) \rightarrow f(x)$$

$$kx \rightarrow monom(x) \rightarrow poly(x) \rightarrow f(x),$$

LEX determines that the most specific version of the heuristic of Fig. 5-9(1) could be generalized to include both cos(x) and sin(x), by using *trig(x)* in place of cos(x). This generalization is shown in the revised version space representation of the heuristic rule, Fig. 5-9(2).

However, an example in the form {INTEGRAL sin(x) 3x} provides evidence that the most general form of the heuristic rule, as specified in Fig. 5-9(1), can fail unless it is further restricted. Specifically, the original generalization proposed is: Apply OP1 with u = f1(x) and dv = f2(x) dx, but the *sin(x)*3x training example shows that this assignment of u and v can result in a more complicated expression that OP1 cannot integrate, and that an interchange of f1(x) and f2(x) may be

(such as *union* or *equality*). Each data structure has 25 different *facets* or slots such as *examples, definitions, generalizations, analogies, interestingness*, etc., to be filled out. Very interesting slots can be granted full concept module status. This is the space that AM begins to explore guided by a large body of heuristic rules.

AM operates under the guidance of 250 heuristic rules which indirectly control the system through an *agenda mecha-* *nism*, a global list of tasks for the system to perform, together with reasons why each task is desirable. A task directive might cause AM to define a new concept, or to explore some facet of an existing concept, or to examine some empirical data for regularities, etc.,The program selects from the agenda that task that has the best supporting reasons, and then executes it. The heuristic rules suggest which facet of which concept to enlarge

BOX 5-5 *(continued)*

(1)	VERSION SPACE REPRESENTATION OF A HEURISTIC
S: INTEGRAL 3x cos(x) dx→Apply OP1 with u=3x and dv= cos(x) dx
G: INTEGRAL f1(x) f2(x) dx→Apply OP1 with u=f1(x) and dv=f2(x) dx

(2)	REVISED VERSION SPACE REPRESENTATION OF THE HEURISTIC
S: INTEGRAL 3x trig(x)→Apply OP1 with u=3x and dv=trig(x) dx
G: g1: INTEGRAL poly(x) f2(x) dx→Apply OP1 with u=poly(x), and dv=f2(x) dx
g2: INTEGRAL transc(x) f1(x) dx→Apply OP1 with u=f1(x), and dv=transc(x) dx

GENERALIZATION HIERARCHY SUPPLIED BY DESIGNER

$$sin(x), cos(x) \rightarrow trig(x) \rightarrow transc(x) \rightarrow f(x)$$
$$kx \rightarrow monom(x) \rightarrow poly(x) \rightarrow f(x),$$

FIGURE 5-9
Version Space Representations of Various Forms of a Heuristic Rule for Symbolic Integration.

necessary depending on the specific functional form of f1 and f2. The description of the heuristic in version space is revised to take this new information into account by breaking the most general form of the heuristic into two statements. In addition,the generalization hierarchy is used to replace f1(x) in one generalization by its more specific name *polynomial*, and in the other expression to replace f2(x) by its more specific name *transc(x)*. The revised form of the heuristic of Fig. 5-9(1), after the two training examples just discussed, is shown in Fig. 5-9(2).

We note that the learning process described here always involves the *narrowing* of a description represented in version space. This narrowing occurs in discrete steps, based on the predefined hierarchically ordered vocabulary for the given problem domain.

next, and how and when to create new concepts. Lenat provided the system with a specific algorithm for rank-ordering concepts in terms of how interesting they are. The primary goal of AM is to maximize the *interestingness* level of the concept space it is enlarging.

Many heuristics used in AM embody the belief that mathematics is an empirical inquiry—the approach to discovery is to perform experiments, observe the results, gather statistically significant amounts of data, induce from that data some new conjectures or new concepts worth isolating, and then repeat this whole process again. An example of a heuristic dealing with this type of experimentation is *After trying in vain to find some non-examples of X, if many examples of X exist, consider the conjecture that X is universal, always-true. Consider specializing X.*

Another large set of heuristics deals with *focus of attention*: when should AM keep on the same track, and when not. A final set of rules deal with assigning interestingness scores based on symmetry, coincidence, appropriateness, usefulness, etc., For example, *Concept C is interesting if C is closely related to the very interesting concept X.*

Experimental evidence indicates that AM's heuristics are powerful enough to take it a few levels away from the kind of knowledge it began with, but only a few levels. As evaluated by Lenat, of the 200 new concepts AM defined, about 130 were acceptable and about 25 were significant; 60 to 70 of the concepts were very poor.

Although AM is described as "exploring the space of mathematical concepts," in essence AM was an automatic programming system, whose primitive actions produced modifications to pieces of LISP code, which represent the characteristic functions of various mathematical concepts. For example, given a LISP program that detects when two lists are equal, it is possible to make a "mutation" in the code that now causes it to compare the length of two lists, and another mutation might cause it to test whether the first items on two lists are the same. Thus, because such mutations often result in meaningful mathematical concepts, AM was able to exploit the natural tie between LISP and mathematics, and was benefiting from the density of worthwhile mathematical concepts embedded in LISP. The main limitation of AM was its inability to synthesize effective new heuristics based on the new concepts it discovered. It first appeared that the same machinery used to discover new mathematical concepts could also be used to discover new heuristics, but this was not the case. The reason is that the deep relationship between LISP and mathematics does not exist between LISP and heuristics. When AM applied its mutation operators to viable and useful heuristics, the almost inevitable result was useless new heuristic rules.

In evaluating the accomplishments of AM, there is also the question of the extent to which the designer implicitly supplied the limited set of mathematical concepts that were (or could be) generated by the system, by supplying the particular initial set of heuristics, frame *slots*, and the definitions and procedures that determine how these slots get instantiated. An extensive criticism of AM, and a later related program called EURISKO, was offered by Richie and Hanna [Richie 84]. In their response [Lenat 84], Lenat and Brown compare the AM/EURISKO approach to that of the perceptron, a device described earlier in this chapter:

> The paradigm underlying AM and EURISKO may be thought of as the new generation of perceptrons, perceptrons based on collections or societies of evolving, self-organizing, symbolic knowledge structures. In classical perceptrons, all knowledge had to be encoded as topological networks of linked neurons, with weights on the links. The representation scheme used in EURISKO provides much more powerful linkages, taking the form of heuristics about concepts, including heuristics for how to use and evolve heuristics. Both types of perceptrons rely on the law of large numbers, on a kind of local-global property of achieving adequate performance through the interactions of many relatively simple parts.

DISCUSSION

There are several key issues that have arisen in our exposition of the learning process:

Representation. As is the case in other areas of AI, having an appropriate representation is crucial for learning—it is often necessary to be able to modify an existing representation, or create a new one, in dealing with a given problem domain. However, the learning programs reviewed had relatively fixed representations, provided by the designer, which bounded the learning process. For example, the problem of telling when a situation, object, or event is similar to another lies at the heart of the learning process; a related problem is determining when something is a more general or specific instance of something else, i.e., determining the generalization hierarchy. Most of the systems examined use a generalization hierarchy provided by the designer, and methods for measuring similarity almost invariably depend on comparing predefined attribute vectors, or graph matching based on a predefined vocabulary. Thus, existing learning systems are inherently limited to instantiating a predefined model; their ability to really discover something new, or to exhibit continuing growth is virtually nonexistent.

Problem generation. A system should be able to generate its own problems so that it can refine its learned strategies. This type of problem generation is seen in a child learning to use building blocks. Various structures are tried so that the *physics* of block building can be learned. LEX, and to some extent AM, were the only machine learning programs discussed that had the ability to effectively select problems. In all the others it is up to the human operator (or trial and error) to choose appropriate problems to promote learning.

Focus of attention. A learning system should be able to alter its focus of attention, so that problem solutions can be effectively found. Many of the programs that we examined used a fixed approach to problem solving, and did not have the ability to focus on a problem bottleneck. Capability in this area is related to self-monitoring, i.e., if one knows how well he is doing, then critical problem areas can be identified, and priorities can be altered accordingly.

Limits on learning ability. How is new learning related to the knowledge structures already possessed by a system? To take an extreme example, no matter how many ants we test, or how hard they try, it is inconceivable that an ant could devise the equivalent of Einstein's theory of relativity. On what grounds is this intuition based? It certainly appears to be the case that any system with a capacity for self modification, or learning, has limits on what it can reasonably hope to achieve. At present, we do not even have a glimmering of a theory that quantifies such limits. The amount of knowledge current machine learning systems start off with is invariably based on practicality and other *ad hoc* criteria.

Human learning. There appears to be almost nothing in the physiological or psychological literature concerning human learning that can aid us in the design of a machine that learns. The mechanisms used by the human to learn autonomously when immersed in a complex environment remains a mystery. In particular, the ability of the human to form new concepts when required is not understood.

Perhaps the most interesting open question is whether it is possible for a mechanical process to create new concepts and representations using an approach more powerful than trial and error. At present, no such procedure is known.

Appendix

5-1

Parameter Learning for an Implicit Model

As was shown in Fig. 5-2, a threshold device accepts a set of binary inputs, e.g., TRUE or FALSE, 0 or 1, −1 or +1, and outputs a binary result. Each input is multiplied by a weight, w_i, and if the sum of the weighted inputs exceeds a threshold value, T, then the output is one value, otherwise it is the other. The threshold device can be used for general computing purposes, since appropriate weight settings will cause it to behave like the AND, OR, and NOT functions mentioned in Chapter 4. However, this device (function) has special significance for classification-type (pattern recognition) computations.

Much of the work on threshold devices has dealt with the question of how different classes of objects could be recognized by automatic adjustment of the weights, w_i. Suppose we have two classes A and B and for objects in class B we want the sum of the weighted inputs, $SUM = w_1 f_1 + w_2 f_2 + \ldots$, to be greater than a threshold, T. We know intuitively that if in the training mode we obtain a SUM less than T for a test pattern in class B, then the weights corresponding to positive input terms should be increased and those corresponding to negative input terms and the value of the threshold should be decreased. (The converse action should be taken if SUM is incorrectly greater than T for test patterns in class A.)

It is possible to prove a surprisingly powerful theorem which says that if a single threshold device is capable of recognizing a class of objects, then it can learn to recognize the class by using the following weight adjustment procedure:

1. Start with any set of weights.
2. Present the device with a pattern (described by a vector of −1, +1 valued features) of class C, or not of class C.
3. If the pattern is classified correctly (SUM > T for a pattern

in C; SUM $=<$ T for a pattern not in C) then go to step 2.

4. If SUM $=<$ T for a pattern, X, in C, replace each w_i by $(w_i + f(x))$ and T by $(T-1)$; If SUM $>$ T for a pattern, X, not in C, replace each w_i by $(w_i - f(x))$ and T by $(T+1)$.

5. Go to step 2.

After a finite number of iterations, in which correctly labeled members of the input population are used in the weight adjustment procedure, the device will correctly recognize these patterns. The order in which the input patterns are presented is not important; it is only required that the number of appearances of each pattern is proportional to the length of the *training* sequence (i.e., to the total number of patterns actually presented). Note

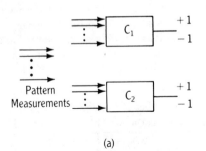

Class	C_1	C_2
1	-1	-1
2	-1	$+1$
3	$+1$	-1
4	$+1$	$+1$

(a)   (b)

FIGURE 5-10

Classifying a Pattern as Belonging to One of Four Classes.

(a) Threshold network. (b) Encoding of class designation with respect to the two output devices of the threshold network.

that the theorem only assures us that members in the training sequences will be correctly identified. Correct classification of new patterns will occur only if the training examples are truly representative of class C and its complement, and the features are well chosen. For example, if a feature such as color does not distinguish one class from an-

	Feature Detectors		
Input Patterns	**FD1 Enclosures** If <2 Enclosures $\rightarrow -1$ If $\geqslant 2$ Enclosures $\rightarrow +1$	**FD2 Verticals** If <2 Verticals $\rightarrow -1$ If $\geqslant 2$ Verticals $\rightarrow +1$	**FD3 Horizontals** If <3 Horizontals $\rightarrow -1$ If $\geqslant 3$ Horizontals $\rightarrow +1$
1 A	-1	1	-1
2 B	1	-1	1
3 B	1	1	-1
4 A	-1	-1	-1
5 B	1	-1	-1
6 A	-1	1	1
7 B	-1	-1	1
8 B	1	1	1

TABLE 5-1 ■ Outputs of Three Feature Detectors for a Set of Patterns

other, then measurements of this feature cannot contribute to the classification process.

Although we have discussed classification using two classes, the approach can be extended to many classes (see Fig. 5-10). The figure shows how the binary output of two classifiers can be used to classify a pattern into one of four classes.

An example of threshold device parameter learning is presented in Tables 5-1 and 5-2. The problem is to tell whether a set of measurements derived from a pattern on a

TABLE 5-2 ■ Learning to Recognize a Set of Patterns by Adjustment of Weights in a Threshold Network (The training sequence is the set of input patterns 1–7 of Table 5-1)

Input Pattern	Class	FD1	FD2	FD3	Weighted Sum	New T	New W1	New W2	New W3	
0	—	—	—	—	—	0	0	0	0	
1	−1	−1	1	−1	0	0	0	0	0	
2	1	1	−1	1	0	−1	1	−1	1	←change
3	1	1	1	−1	−1	−2	2	0	0	←change
4	−1	−1	−1	−1	−2	−2	2	0	0	
5	1	1	−1	−1	2	−2	2	0	0	
6	−1	−1	1	1	−2	−2	2	0	0	
7	1	−1	−1	1	−2	−3	1	−1	1	←change
1	−1	−1	1	−1	−3	−3	1	−1	1	
2	1	1	−1	1	3	−3	1	−1	1	
3	1	1	1	−1	−1	−3	1	−1	1	
4	−1	−1	−1	−1	−1	−2	2	0	2	←change
5	1	1	−1	−1	0	−2	2	0	2	
6	−1	−1	1	1	0	−1	3	−1	1	←change
7	1	−1	−1	1	−1	−2	2	−2	2	←change
1	−1	−1	1	−1	−6	−2	2	−2	2	
2	1	1	−1	1	6	−2	2	−2	2	
3	1	1	1	−1	−2	−3	3	−1	1	←change
4	−1	−1	−1	−1	−3	−3	3	−1	1	
5	1	1	−1	−1	3	−3	3	−1	1	
6	−1	−1	1	1	−3	−3	3	−1	1	
7	1	−1	−1	1	−1	−3	3	−1	1	
8	1	1	1	1	3	−3	3	−1	1	←This pattern, not in the training set, is correctly identified by the "learned" set of weights

APPENDIX 5-2

retina depicts the presence of the character A or the character B. The threshold device outputs -1 to indicate the character A and $+1$ to indicate the character B. Three feature detectors make measurements on the pattern values in the retina to determine three different characteristics or features of the pattern.

Table 5-1 shows the responses of the three feature detectors for a set of eight patterns. Note that the output of a feature detector is $+1$ or -1.

Table 5-2 shows the sequence of trial weights obtained using the weight adjustment procedure described previously. The three weights are initially zero, and are modified whenever the input pattern is misclassified. For example, input pattern 2 has a weighted sum that does not exceed the threshold. This is incorrect, since pattern 2 is in the $+1$ class. Therefore the weight modification procedure is used.

The procedure continues until all of the patterns are correctly classified. Once the correct set of weights has been obtained, the device can classify a pattern that it was not trained on, as shown in the response to pattern 8.

6

Language and Communication

The notion of a shared model is inherent in the word "communicate," which is derived from the Latin *communicare*, to make common. People 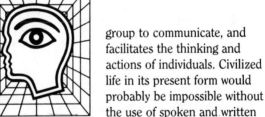 communicate to command, question, inform, promise, threaten, amuse, arouse, and convince other people. Thus a person has an intended idea, request, or command to communicate with another. The idea, request, or command encoded into their shared language is communicated to the recipient, who derives the meaning of the message using a "model" of the person communicating the message, the context of the communication, the appropriate "world knowledge," and knowledge of the language.

A language is a set of vocal or written signs and symbols that permits a social group to communicate, and facilitates the thinking and actions of individuals. Civilized life in its present form would probably be impossible without the use of spoken and written language. Language, in the full sense of the term, is species-specific to man. Members of the animal kingdom have the ability to communicate through vocal signs, facial expressions, and by other means, but the most important single feature characterizing human language is that people are essentially unrestricted in what they can talk about.[9] As will be described later, animal communication

---

[9] We say "essentially unrestricted" because, while poetry and creative writing make an attempt, there is no adequate way to describe sounds, smells, taste, and other experiences in a written or spoken languages.

systems are, by contrast, very tightly circumscribed.

Human thought and language are closely linked; as a matter of fact, some believe that the language we speak critically influences both the way we think and the way in which we perceive reality (the Sapir-Whorf hypothesis).

This chapter describes the nature of communication using language, how language encodes meaning, and work in computational linguistics that attempts to provide a basis for computer *understanding* of natural language. We will find that building computer systems for effective interaction with people requires that language be considered in the context of a communication situation. In this larger context, the relationship between participants in a conversation, and their states of mind, are as important to the interpretation of an utterance as the linguistic components from which the utterance is formed. We will discuss a number of questions that are still being actively, and sometimes heatedly, debated:

- Can animals, particularly chimps and gorillas, acquire and creatively use natural language?
- Must children be trained to acquire language, e.g., by their parents, or do children have an innate capability to form a "theory" of language on their own?
- Does the language one speaks determine the way one perceives the world, or are people's world views independent of the language they speak?
- What is the purpose of communication, and to what extent is communication possible without language?
- How is the human brain organized to provide linguistic competence?

- Are there things you can express in language that cannot be expressed in any other form of communication?
- What is the relationship of language to reasoning and intelligence? Can a person be intelligent without some form of language (e.g., spoken, written, or sign language)?
- What are the limits of a computer's ability to employ natural language—are there linguistic expressions whose meanings cannot be derived by a machine, and if so, what is their general nature?
- Is it possible for a machine to truly understand natural language, or is the machine, at best, merely manipulating tokens so that it only appears that understanding is taking place?

The first part of this chapter concerns human and animal communication, and the second part, machine communication.

LANGUAGE IN ANIMALS AND MAN

If we define language broadly enough, then it can be said that both animals and humans are capable of communicating with other members of their species via language. However, in animal communication the language is very limited, restricted to a number of sounds associated with signaling danger, establishing territory, indicating anger, etc., without the *creative* aspect of human language in which a set of basic sounds is used to express indefinitely many thoughts, and respond appropriately to an indefinite range of new situations.

LANGUAGE IN ANIMALS AND MAN

Brain Structures Associated with Language Production and Understanding

What little is known about the role of the brain in communication has been derived by studying the relation of brain damage to performance [Geschwind 79]. Figure 6-1 shows the regions of the human brain that have been identified as being relevant to linguistic activity.

Broca's area is named after Paul Broca, who in the 1860s noted that damage to a particular region of the cortex on the side of the frontal lobes gives rise to speech disorder (aphasia). He showed that damage to this area on the left side of the brain causes aphasia, but damage to the corresponding area on the right side leaves speech intact. In 1874, Karl Wernicke identified an area on the temporal lobe of the left hemisphere that plays a crucial role in communication. By relating defects in the Broca and Wernicke areas to loss of performance, Wernicke formulated a model of language production.

In this model, the underlying "structure" of an utterance arises in Wernicke's area and is transmitted to Broca's area through a bundle of nerve fibers called the *arcuate fasciculus*. Broca's area develops a "program" for vocalization that is then passed to the face area of the motor cortex, to activate the appropriate muscles of the mouth, lips, tongue, and larynx. When a word is heard, the sound is received by the auditory cortex and then passed to Wernicke's area where it is "understood." When a word is read,

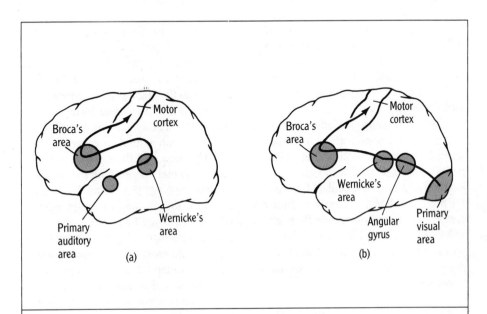

FIGURE 6-1   Brain Signal Flow for Language Production and Understanding.

(a) Speaking a heard word. (b) Speaking a written word. (After N. Geschwind. *Sci Am* 243:180-199, 1979.)

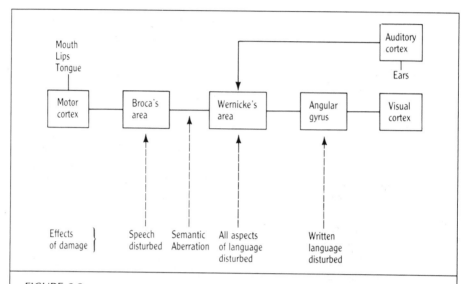

FIGURE 6-2
Schematic of the Structures Involved in Language Production and Understanding, Showing Effects of Brain Damage.

the information from the visual cortex is transmitted to the *angular gyrus* where it appears to be transformed so as to be compatible with the "auditory form" of the word; it is then transmitted to Wernicke's area.[10]

Figure 6-2 shows the effect of damage to each of the components of the brain's linguistic communication system: When Broca's area is damaged, speech is no longer fluent or well articulated. When the path from Wernicke's area to Broca's area is damaged, semantically aberrant speech is produced, but if Wernicke's area is intact there will be normal comprehension of spoken and written communication.

Damage to Wernicke's area disrupts all aspects of the use of language, as can be seen from the central role that it plays in the system shown in Fig. 6-2. Finally, damage to the angular gyrus disrupts the signals from the visual cortex to Wernicke's area and causes difficulties in dealing with written language.

This view, that there are discrete cerebral centers performing specific aspects of language processing, has been called the *localizationist-connectionist* view. As discussed by Springer and Deutsch [Springer 85], present-day investigators with more holistic views of brain function contend that the situation is more dynamic than implied by localization theories, involving simultaneous interactions of many areas for each brain function.

Even to the extent that specific re-

---

[10]It is difficult to understand what evolutionary mechanism could have prepared the angular gyrus for this role! Some relevant ideas can be found in Box 2-3.

gions of the brain are identified as being associated with various communication functions, it is important to note that these functions can be assumed by other brain regions. For example, a considerable degree of recovery can occur when Broca's area is injured since the surrounding regions share its specialization in latent form.

Human Acquisition of Language

Normal children are born with the ability and the drive to acquire the languages to which they are predominantly exposed from infancy. By late childhood the basic vocabulary of the "native" language has been acquired, together with its phonological and grammatical structure. The time-table of language acquisition derived from Lenneberg [Lenneberg 67] is shown in Table 6-1.

The behaviorist vs. innateness controversy. For a long time, scholars considered language acquisition to be carried out largely by analogy from observed patterns of sentences occurring in utterances heard and understood by the child. For example, Skinner [Skinner 57] incorporates the major aspects of linguistic behavior within a "behaviorist" framework, relating verbal behavior to variables such as *stimulus, reinforcement,* and *deprivation,* as used in animal experimentation. Subsequently, a number of lin-

---

TABLE 6-1 ■ Timetable of Language Development in the Child

3 months. When talked to, and nodded at, smiles, followed by voicelike gurgling sounds (cooing)

4 months. Responds to human sounds more definitely, turns head, eyes search for speaker, occasional chuckling sounds

5 months. Vowel-like cooing interspersed with consonantal sounds

6 months. Cooing changing into babbling, resembling one-syllable utterance

8 months. Distinct intonation patterns: utterances signal emphasis and emotions

10 months. Appears to wish to imitate sounds, but imitations are never quite successful

12 months. Definite signs of understanding some words and simple commands, sound sequence replicated

18 months. Definite repertoire of words, three to 50, much babbling, intricate intonation pattern, understanding progressing rapidly

24 months. Vocabulary of more than 50 items, two-word phrases, increased interest in language

30 months. Fastest increase in vocabulary, no babbling, utterances of at least 2 words, intelligibility not very good, but good understanding

3 years. 1000-word vocabulary: 80% of utterances are intelligible

4 years. Language well established

The timing of language development shown on this table is meant to be indicative; some children will progress faster and others slower than these milestones. (After E. H. Lenneberg. *Biological Foundations of Language.* Wiley, New York, 1967.)

guists led by Chomsky [Chomsky 75] have stressed the inherent grammar-building disposition and competence of the human brain, which is activated by exposure to language during childhood. In this point of view, no formal language instruction is necessary. One merely immerses the child in an environment in which the language is spoken, and the innate ability of the human brain to derive the appropriate grammatical structures and rules will automatically provide the child with linguistic competence.[11]

In examining the development of a child's language, one can find evidence supporting each of these views. The naming of objects with which the child is familiar and the association of *no* with disapproved behavior are examples of classical conditioning. Marshall [Marshall 80] discusses the body of evidence showing that the speech addressed to young children, termed "motherese," is typically different from that addressed to older children and adults:

> In the heyday of the "nativist" accounts of language acquisition [the early 1960s] it was widely assumed that the speech heard by children was a haphazard collection of sentence fragments, mistakes, backtrackings, throat clearings, and other kinds of unintelligible gibberish. There is now a considerable body of evidence showing that the speech addressed to young children is typically very different from that addressed to older children and adults.[p.115]

He cites recent work showing that

some aspects of motherese are causally related to and can facilitate the rate of language acquisition.

Advocates of the Chomsky view point out that the *telegraphic speech* used by children is not a simple repetition of the adult's sentences. Thus, a parent will say "He is going out." but the child will convert this to "He go out." In general, parents do not seem to pay attention to such bad syntax; they do not even seem to be aware of it [Brown 77]. Study of complex sentences produced by children indicates that children apply their own grammatical rules (which are not direct imitations of adult grammar) in a systematic manner, and seem to acquire the conventional rules only through time and experience.

Recent experiments with infants young enough to be unaffected by their linguistic environment further support Chomsky's view that inborn knowledge and capacities underlie the use of language. Studies of speech perception in infants show that children have an innate perceptual mechanism adapted to the characteristics of human language [Eimas 75]. The research is based on the study of phonemes, the smallest units of speech that affect meaning. Phonemes are the auditory units that are analogous to the consonants and vowels of written language. We perceive speech "categorically," i.e., we are aware of the discrete phonemic categories, rather than of the continuous variation in the acoustic properties of sound.

Experiments with infants as young as one month can be carried out by measuring the rate that the infant sucks on a pacifier while being exposed to acoustic

---

[11]Note that this ability to learn by "immersion" disappears after approximately the first decade of life.

information. Increased sucking rate indicates the child's increased interest in a phenomenon. Another approach is to hold the child's attention with a toy, while a loudspeaker in another part of the room plays an acoustic signal. When a sound of interest occurs, the child turns in the direction of the loudspeaker.

It has been found that infants respond to phoneme categories rather than to the continuous gradations in acoustic properties of the signal. In one experiment, one group of infants was exposed to a phoneme sequence, another to an acoustic sequence, and a control group was exposed to no acoustic stimulus. In all of the groups, the sucking rate decreases at about the same rate. However after five minutes, a change in phoneme or acoustic signal is made. In the case of the group with the changed phonemic signal, the sucking rate increases to the original high value, while for the group with the changed acoustic signal the sucking rate continues to decrease.

Studies further show that all infants have the same inborn linguistic mechanism, but that the infant's linguistic environment causes the child to retain and improve perceptual capacities corresponding to phonemic distinctions in the parent language, while losing the ability to detect distinctions that do not occur in the native language. For example, English-background infants of six to eight months respond to Hindi consonantal contrasts, but lose this ability by age 10 to 12 months. Interestingly, the inactive perceptual mechanisms do not disappear completely, e.g., adult speakers of Japanese can, with enough experience, learn to distinguish the phonemes /r/ and /l/.[12]

"Carving up the world" into conceptual categories. People do not perceive the world as a continuum without any intrinsic boundaries. Rather, we partition the world into objects and categorize these objects as belonging to named classes. This classification allows us to relate new objects and events to classes of similar things with known properties.

Although such categorization seems to come quite naturally to us, we might be hard put to explain why we called the object in front of us a "bush." Do we have an image of a prototype bush stored in our mind to which we compared the object? On reflection, what might a prototype bush be? Do we have a list of bushlike properties, concerned with size of the object and shape of the branches and of the leaves? How do we asign the bush to the more general class or category of "vegetation?"

Though they cannot name the categories and relationships, very young children, 12 to 24 months old, have the ability to group and order objects on the basis of the various physical and functional relationships that hold among objects [Nelson 73]. Children of that age

---

[12]Categorical perception of speech sounds is not species-specific to the human. Other mammals, such as the chinchilla also have this ability, as do macaque monkeys [Flavell 85]. Aslin [Aslin 83] conjectures that since other mammals possess auditory categorical perception, this ability may have been acquired quite early in evolutionary history, before the capability for human oral speech. Thus, it is conceivable that human speech sounds are the way they are partly because our mammalian auditory system is constructed to readily discriminate and categorize these sounds.

group are first shown ten toy objects belonging to the same conceptual category, e.g., furniture. When they are shown a new pair of objects, a chair and an apple, they pay more attention to the apple than to the chair, since the chair is recognized as being a member of the category recently observed. The apple is attended to because of its novelty [Ross 80]. Even more remarkable is the fact that two-year-olds have been shown to possess scene schemas for how places look, e.g., what is to be expected in a kitchen scene [Mandler 83].

Flavell has written [Flavell 85]:

> Young children probably have representations of class-inclusion relations that are, in most important respects, not qualitatively different from those of older people. . . . However, they . . . are less able to talk and reason about class hierarchies and class-inclusion relations than older people are.

Subjects with damage to the posterior regions of the brain sometimes suffer from *nominal* or *anomic aphasia* in which they lose the ability to name and categorize objects. It has been suggested that this impairment is a result of disruption of associations involving different sensory modalities that are part of the naming act. Brown [Brown 80], relates the range of speech disorders ranging from phonological (production of speech) to semantic (meaning of the utterance) to the "triune" brain organization described in Chapter 2.

Animal Acquisition of Language

In the late 1960s, the Gardners of the University of Nevada published results indicating that a chimpanzee named Washoe was able to learn American Sign Language (ASL) [Gardner 69]. ASL was chosen to overcome the vocal limitations of the chimp. Washoe learned signs for hundreds of different objects and occasionally put together creative combinations of signs. (For example, the Gardners report that Washoe labeled a duck as a water bird.)

Herbert Terrace and his group at Columbia University attempted to duplicate this work by training a baby male chimp. After four years of work, they found that the chimp could indeed learn the American Sign Language (ASL) names of objects, but they claim that he could not reliably combine signs into grammatically correct sentences [Terrace 81]. They conclude that chimps cannot generally combine symbols to create new meanings. They also claim that analysis of videotapes made by their group, and by other groups, reveals that chimps often imitate signs made by humans, and this accounted for many of the "sentences."

Psychologist Francine Patterson at Stanford [Patterson 78] has reported that the achievements of Washoe have now been surpassed by Koko, a female gorilla trained since 1972.

A fierce controversy still rages between the animal language advocates and those who believe that any results indicating sophisticated language use or understanding by animals are due to unconscious clues given by the trainer.[13]

---

[13]This is called the "clever Hans" effect after a horse that was supposedly performing arithmetic computation, but was actually picking up very subtle cues from the trainer (apparently unbeknownst to the trainer).

Skeptics might be convinced of the possibility of animal language if the acquisition of a language enabled the animal to accomplish a nonlanguage-related task that it could not do before, e.g., if an animal with language skills could solve a problem while those without such skills would fail. To date, no one has attempted to demonstrate this. An anthology of important articles on both sides of the controversy is given in Seboek [Sebeok 80].

LANGUAGE AND THOUGHT

A study of American Indian languages led some scholars to speculate on the relationship between language, culture, and thought patterns. It was hypothesized that the world as mirrored in each language might have a strong effect on the perception and thought of the individual. Along these lines the linguist Edward Sapir has said: "We see and hear and otherwise experience very largely as we do because the language habits of our community predispose certain choices of interpretation."

This idea was further developed by Benjamin Lee Whorf, and is now known as the Whorfian hypothesis [Whorf 56]. It is also known as the linguistic-relativity hypothesis because it proposes that thought is relative to the language in which it is conducted [Carroll 56].

> When Semitic, Chinese, Tibetan, or African languages are contrasted with our own, the divergence in analysis of the world becomes more apparent; and, when we bring in the native languages of the Americas, where speech communities for many millenniums have gone their way

independently of each other and of the Old World, the fact that languages dissect nature in many different ways becomes apparent. The relativity of all conceptual systems, ours included, and their dependence upon language stand revealed.

Using the differences between Standard Average European (SAE) languages and the Hopi language, Whorf investigated the question, *Are our own concepts of 'time,' 'space,' and 'matter' given in substantially the same form by experience to all men, or are they in part conditioned by the structure of particular languages?* For example, the Hopi do not say "I stayed five days," but rather "I left on the fifth day," because the word day can have no plural. Whorf's conclusions [Carroll 56] are as follows:

> Concepts of "time". . . are not given in substantially the same form but depend upon the nature of the language or languages through the use of which they have been developed. . . . Our own "time" differs markedly from Hopi "duration." . . . Certain ideas born of our time-concept, such as absolute simultaneity, would be either very difficult to express or impossible and devoid of meaning under the Hopi conception.

Whorf found that there is a considerable difference between SAE concepts of 'matter' compared to Hopi, but that there was no great difference in the concept of 'space.'

In a later study [Carroll 56], researchers tested two groups of Navajo children, one group that spoke only English and the other only Navajo. In the Navajo language certain verbs of handling require special forms depending on the shape of the object being handled. The experiment compared the two groups with respect to how often they used shape, form, or material rather than color as a basis for sorting objects. It was found that the Navajo-speaking children tended to sort objects on the basis of form at significantly earlier ages than did the English-speaking children. The fact that the Navajo language required attention to shapes and forms seem to make the Navajo-speaking children pay more attention to this aspect of their environment.

The Whorfian hypothesis is still a subject of debate: Alford [Alford 78] has surveyed criticisms of the hypothesis, and Malotki [Malotki 83] has recently carried out a deep analysis of Hopi that disagrees with Whorf's conclusions concerning the temporal concepts.

A widely held view is that there is indeed a correspondence between language and the ways of conceiving the world, but that language differences are caused by the experiences or needs of a particular people, rather than by the dictates of some arbitrarily defined linguistic system—i.e., it is ultimately the physical environment rather than the arbitrary choice of language that structures our thought processes. Thus, because it is important for Eskimos to be able to describe the different types of snow and ice, they will create different words for these.

As indicated by Rosch [Rosch 77], our categorization of the world is not arbitrary; it depends on information in the natural world to which we as a species are geared to respond (see Box 6-1). In this view, language, for the most part, follows upon discriminations made by individuals rather than playing a controlling role in how one classifies the world.

 BOX 6-1   Natural Categories and Natural Kinds

The Sapir-Whorf hypothesis and related investigations imply that the language we use critically affects our view of the world and how we are able to think about things in the world. It is therefore important to determine the extent to which differences between languages are arbitrary, and the extent to which similarities are accidental. In particular, how and why does a language "carve up the world" in a particular way?

There had been a long standing belief that (1) the common objects of the world can be classified into distinct groups; (2) these groups can be defined by specific criterial attributes which are relatively independent; and (3) people speaking different languages made different distinctions, i.e., formed different categorizations suited to their particular needs. Thus, it was noted that while the color spectrum is continuous, every human culture has a somewhat different way of breaking it up into named color categories; some cultures employ only two or three named colors. A person growing up within a culture learns the color names that have been arbitrarily chosen by that culture.

In the 1970s Eleanor Rosch performed experiments which demonstrated that members of different cultures remember and make color similarity judgments that are indistinguishable from each other in spite of significant language differences (see Chapter 12 of Gardner [Gardner 85]). Based on these experiments and other observations Rosch concluded that:

1. Naming practices of cultures are relatively unimportant compared to the innate organization of the human nervous system in making category judgments.

COMMUNICATION

The Mechanics of Communication

To communicate with a person or machine, the receiver must know that you are communicating with it, must be willing to listen, be able to understand your language, and possess a similar social and conceptual "frame of reference." To be most effective, the receiver must have some way of signaling success in understanding your message, and you must be able to tell after a while whether or not the receiver understands what you are trying to say. Most of these requirements are fulfilled automatically when we speak to another person. We attract the other person's attention, we note by physical cues whether or not the person is listening, and the person signals understanding by nodding or by responding with a communication. We can tell whether the listener understands by analyzing the responses. When people realize their messages are not being properly understood, they modify or terminate their conversation.

There are also cultural assumptions. Once we realize that a person speaks our language and shares our cultural framework, we can make a point using an expression such as *A rose by any other name smells as sweet,* and assume that the person understands that we are trying to indicate that the intrinsic properties of an object are not altered by the name we assign to it. If not given the requisite knowledge and reasoning ability, a machine might treat this as an ordinary sentence and place in its database some statement such as *The odor of a rose*

BOX 6-1 *(continued)*

2. There is considerable redundancy in the appearance of members of natural categories (e.g. birds, trees, flowers)—their defining features are not independent; our recognition mechanisms exploit these redundancies.
3. Human categorization is more closely linked to similarity to an exemplar or prototype of a class than to the presence of a fixed set of features.
4. Categories in the real world are not sharply defined, but blend into one another.

Other attacks on the classical views of concept and category came from Wittgenstein [Wittgenstein 68] who felt that concepts are neither mental constructs in the head nor abstract ideas in the world, but rather are community-developed tools for accomplishing things. Putnam [Putnam 75] believed that the world is not a perceptual jumble that can be arbitrarily partitioned, but rather that there are inherent structures, "natural kinds," that allow us to form stable generalizations and then reason about things in the world.

Objections to the classical view of language and category can be summarized as follows: To deal effectively with their environment, people form linguistic categories for things that appear similar or behave in similar ways; such categorizations reflect the perceptual structure of the perceiver and are not arbitrary. Nevertheless, people also form categories far removed from direct perceptual observation, e.g., the categories of odd and even numbers. Such categorizations, essential to human cognition, more closely follow the classical view.

*is not affected by the name assigned
to it.*

People use various methods of communicating commands, questions, anger, information, promises, threats, belief, and desires to other people. They communicate not only by written and spoken language, but also by *body language*, nonverbal communication involving body posture, facial expression, seated position, and other body signs. Such nonverbal communication, though very subtle, can be interpreted with great accuracy.

Often the same words can mean different things depending on the social setting, or the tone and intonation used. For example, the question, *Are you going to get the book?* can be used as a question, as a threat, or as a command.

Vocabulary of Communication

The vocabulary used by people is much smaller than one might expect. The following tables are for English, but they are about the same for French, Russian, and many other "natural languages,"especially those employing phonetic alphabets. Table 6-2 shows that only a small portion of the words in an abridged dictionary are commonly known; an average adult's

TABLE 6-2 ■ Size of Vocabulary Employed by Various Sources	
Source	No. of Words
Child	3,600
14-year-old	9,000
Adult	12,000–14,000
Abridged dictionary	150,000
Dante's *Divine Comedy*	5,900
Homer's poems	9,000
Shakespeare's works	15,000–25,000

After A. Kondratov. *Sounds and Signs*. MIR Publishers, Moscow, 1969.

vocabulary consists of about 10% of all dictionary words.

From Table 6-3 we see that with a 3000-word vocabulary we can expect to recognize 90% of the words on a page of general text. A 1000-word spoken vocabulary will allow the same recognition of spoken words. Computer understanding of language would be simple if language understanding was merely a matter of looking up word meanings, since the required vocabulary is not large in terms of computer memory. The next section will point out the reasons why understanding is far more than the stringing together of individual word meanings.

TABLE 6-3 ■ Frequency of Use of Spoken and Written Language Words		
Spoken Language Vocabulary	Written Language Vocabulary	Probability of Appearance of Words in Speech or Text
750	—	75.0%
—	1000	80.5%
—	2000	86.0%
1000	3000	90.0%
2000	5000	93.5%

After A. Kondratov. *Sounds and Signs*. MIR Publishers, Moscow, 1969.

Understanding Language

As indicated above, language understanding is a form of reasoning in which the intended communication of the source is deduced from the combination of the spoken or written message, the recipient's intuitions as to the "state of mind" of the source, the context, knowledge of the language, and knowledge about the world. When one examines the problems involved in understanding a natural language expression, one wonders how people are able to learn language as children, and how the thought encoding and understanding process comes so effortlessly. For example, consider the following two sentences:

1. I have a headache tonight.
2. I will have a headache tonight.

The surface meaning of the first sentence is that the speaker is feeling ill, but the deeper meaning can be a refusal to be sociable or romantic. The second sentence, because prediction of illness is usually not possible, would be considered an insulting refusal.

Many of the sentences that are used by people are ambiguous in some way, but people are so facile at decoding the meanings that the ambiguities often go unnoticed. For example, the sentence *Time flies.* would not be considered to be ambiguous since most people would see only the statement *Time passes quickly.* and not the command *Determine the flight speed of a set of insects!* In addition, people are unaware of how much general knowledge is often required to understand even simple sentences in natural language. In the following sentences supplying the word or idea referred to by *It* requires knowledge about a variety of objects in the world:

The car ran over the toy in the driveway.

> *It* shouldn't have been there.
>
> *It* was scratched and had to go to the garage.
>
> *It* was scratched and had to be repaved.
>
> *It* was too bad.

Notice that each of the *Its* refers to a different aspect of the original sentence. The first *It* refers to the toy, because we know that cars belong in driveways whereas toys do not. The next *It* refers to the car, because we know that scratched cars can be fixed in a garage. The next *It* refers to the driveway, because driveways are repaved. Finally, the last *It* refers to the whole incident. A remarkably broad knowledge database is required to supply the proper referent for each of the *It* terms.

An even more sophisticated level of reasoning is needed to understand sentences such as: "Mary wondered why everyone was driving under 55, and then she saw.". . . "The man handed the teller a note and she pressed the silent alarm." The first sentence requires the knowledge that the number refers to 55 miles per hour, that the speed limit is 55 miles per hour, that if one exceeds this limit one can get a speeding ticket that costs time and money, and that therefore drivers heed this limit when a police car is close by. The second sentence requires the knowledge that the teller is a bank teller, that bank robbers often hand a note demanding money to the teller, and that help can be summoned by pressing the silent alarm.

Spoken Language. Spoken language has an additional problem that must be overcome to understand an utterance. When people speak, they run their words together so that, for example, someone who does not speak English might hear "Didja sayuwer goin?" instead of "Did you say you were going?" Thus, a person who does not speak English would not be able to understand what was said by listening to that sentence, writing down the words, and then looking them up in a dictionary. "Didja" and "sayuwer" are not in the dictionary. The separating of words, called "segmentation," requires an understanding of the language. Therefore, a computer designed to understand spoken language must be provided with rules that indicate how to segment the words (plus all of the other knowledge that it takes to interpret the utterance).

Sign Language as Language. Language extends beyond the obvious spoken and written forms. We immediately think of sign languages such as American Sign Language ("Ameslan" or ASL), British Sign Language, etc. that are, in the words of Oliver Sacks [Sacks 86],

> . . . . complete in a 'Chomskian' way. Their syntax and grammar are complete, but have a different character from that of any spoken language. Thus it is not possible to transliterate a spoken tongue into Sign, word by word or phrase by phrase—their structures are essentially different. It is often imagined, vaguely, that sign language is simply [an alternate version of the user's native tongue such as] English or French: it is nothing of the sort; it is itself, Sign. . . . Sign language enables its users to discuss any topic,

concrete or abstract, as economically and effectively as speech.[14]

Speaking is an ability that must be taught to the deaf, and it takes many years. On the other hand, the deaf show an immediate and powerful disposition to sign. Deaf children whose deaf parents use sign language make their first signs when they are about six months old and have considerable sign fluency by the age of 15 months. As Sacks says, "This is intriguingly earlier than the 'normal' acquisition of speech, suggesting that our linguistic development is, so to speak, retarded by speech, by the complexity of neuromuscular control required. If we are to communicate with babies, we may find that the way to do so is by Sign."

A child can become fluent in signing by the age of three years, and then can acquire reading and writing, and even speech. There is no evidence that signing inhibits the acquisition of speech, and the reverse is probably true.

David Wright [Wright 69], who became deaf at the age of seven years, provides an interesting insight into the role of spoken language in the development of childrens' world knowledge. He comments on a congenitally deaf schoolmate, "She was far from stupid; but having been born deaf her slowly and painfully acquired vocabulary was still too small to allow her to read for amusement or pleasure. As a consequence there were almost no means by which she could pick up the fund of miscellaneous and temporarily useless information other children unconsciously acquire from conversation or random

---

[14]Prior to 1750 there was no hope of literacy or education for most of those born deaf. The Abbé de l'Épée founded the first school for the deaf in 1755.

reading. Almost everything she knew she had been taught or made to learn."

MACHINE UNDERSTANDING OF LANGUAGE

The goal of computational linguistics is to develop theories and techniques that would allow a computer to derive *meaning* from natural language expressions, and produce written or spoken natural language. Determining the intent of a message, rather than only its literal content, requires a combination of language-specific and general common-sense reasoning mechanisms. In the most sophisticated applications, a language understanding program must model the beliefs and knowledge of the agents participating in the communication and be able to deal with incomplete and sometimes inconsistent information.

Faking Understanding

If the responses from a computer seem reasonable, people will tend to ascribe more understanding to the computer than actually exists. A classic example of this is Weizenbaum's ELIZA program [Weizenbaum 66], which takes the role of a nondirective psychoanalytic therapist. The role is relatively easy to imitate because this type of psychoanalysis elicits the patient's responses by reflecting his statements back to him. ELIZA uses a set of stored word patterns, such as:

    INPUT: I am _____.
    OUTPUT: Why are you _____?

ELIZA merely uses the words that appear in the _____ portion of the input to construct the output. Thus, an input of *I am very sad* will result in an output of *Why are you very sad?*. If the words "mother," "father," "brother," or "sister" appear in the input, an ELIZA canned response might be *Tell me more about your family*. When ELIZA cannot find a word pattern that matches, it responds with ambiguous phrases designed to elicit further responses from the user, such as: *Tell me more. In what way? Can you think of a specific example?* It is simple to include features so that "canned" phrases are not repeated during a session, and to provide phrases in random order so that no fixed pattern of response is detected by the user.

A typical ELIZA dialogue is:
    All men are alike.
IN WHAT WAY?
    They are always bugging us about something or another.
CAN YOU THINK OF SPECIFIC EXAMPLES?
    Well, my boyfriend made me come here.
YOUR BOYFRIEND MADE YOU COME HERE?

ELIZA was so effective that people used the program to seek advice, even when they were told of its internal structure and that it lacked *any* mechanism for understanding. This ready acceptance of ELIZA as a real therapist motivated Weizenbaum to warn of the dangers of applying the computer to areas requiring human judgment [Weizenbaum 76].

What Does it Mean for a Computer to Understand?

It is very clear that, given its simple template-matching design, the ELIZA program does not in any sense understand its input or output. However, as we devise more sophisticated computer programs for dealing with natural language, we are faced with a deep philosophical question: What kind of ability to manipulate the written or spoken symbols of a language amounts to a *true understanding* of that language? A thought experiment, "the Chinese room," by the philosopher John Searle [Searle 84] vividly captures the problem of computer understanding. Searle states that he understands no Chinese at all and can't even distinguish Chinese symbols from some other kinds of symbols. He imagines that he is locked in a room with a number of cardboard boxes full of Chinese symbols, and is given a book of rules in English that instruct him how to match these Chinese symbols with each other. The rules tell him that a certain sign is to be followed by a certain other sign. The people outside the room pass in more Chinese symbols and, following the instructions in the book, he passes Chinese symbols back to them. Unknown to him the people who pass him the symbols call them *questions* and the book of instructions that he works from they call *the program*; the symbols he gives back to them they call *the answers to the questions* and they call him *the computer*.

> Suppose that after a while the programmers get so good at writing the programs and I get so good at manipulating the symbols that my answers are indistinguishable from those of native Chinese speakers. I can pass the Turing test for understanding Chinese. But all the same I still don't understand a word of Chinese and neither does any other digital computer because all the computer has is what I have: a formal program that attaches no meaning, interpretation, or

content to any of the symbols. . . . What this simple argument shows is that no formal program by itself is sufficient for understanding, because it would always be possible in principle for an agent to go through the steps in the program and still not have the relevant understanding.

Hofstadter [Hofstadter 83] answers as follows:

> Our response to this is basically the 'systems response,' that it is a mistake to try to impute understanding to the (incidently) animate simulator; rather it belongs to the system as a whole, which includes what Searle characterizes as a 'few slips of paper.'

To the "system" advocates, Searle suggests that the person in the room should simply memorize or incorporate all the material in the few slips of paper. The systems people retort that a key part of Searle's argument is in glossing over questions of order of magnitude and that nearly all of the understanding must lie in the billions of symbols on paper.

Others say that "understanding" is achieved by an entity when (a) it has adequately modeled some situation of interest, and (b) this restricted model is strongly linked to the "world model" of the entity, i.e., many, or most of the relevant associations have been explicitly established. In the Chinese room example, condition (b) has not been satisfied, and indeed, to the extent that a "computer entity" consists of a disconnected set of models, performance does not imply understanding. However, if the computer has a sufficiently rich integrated world model, then any reasonable *operational definition* of the term "to understand" will be satisfied. Note that this view disagrees with Hofstadter—the critical factor is not the complexity of some restricted model of interest, but rather the connections of the restricted model to a comprehensive world model.

A related but distinct point of view (see Box 6-2) holds that words and sentences are not ultimately definable in terms of an objective world, but that every reading or hearing of a text constitutes an act of giving meaning to it through interpretation. Interpretation depends on a person's tradition or preunderstanding and as people experience the world their understanding changes as does the meaning they derive. Thus meaning is not a linkage between text and reality, but rather a dynamic coupling between users of a common language.

And so the discussion rages back and forth. The question of what constitutes "real understanding" will become increasingly pertinent as machines become more competent and assume a greater decision making role in human affairs.

The Study of Language

Language can be examined from many different points of view, including the study of language universals, language acquisition and use, and philosophy of language, to name only a few. We will be concerned here with the following aspects of language because of their relevance to computer understanding: (1) syntax, the study of sentence structure; (2) semantics, the study of meaning; and (3) pragmatics, the study of the uses to which language is put and how speaker's goals are achieved by uttering sentences in context. While this partition is useful for discussion purposes, it should be kept in mind that there is not always a clear line separating these topic areas. Winograd [Winograd 74] uses the analogy of a jigsaw puzzle to explain the role of syntax, semantics, and pragmatics.

The shape of the jigsaw pieces might correspond to the syntax of language—

BOX 6-2   A Philosophy of Understanding

Research in understanding of language assumes that meaning is derived from a string of words and their context. This assumption of a unique meaning is challenged by the philosopher Hans-Georg Gedamer [Gedamer 76] who insists that interpretation depends on a person's tradition or pre-understanding; as people experience the world their understanding changes and the meaning they derive changes. Winograd [Winograd 86] indicates the relevance to AI of hermeneutics, the

science and methodology of interpretation,

In a way, frame-based computational systems approach meaning from a hermeneutic direction. They concentrate not on the question, 'How does the program come to accurately reflect the situation?' but rather 'How does the system's preknowledge (its collection of frames) affect its interpretation of the situation?' The meaning

of a sentence or a scene lies in the interaction between its structure and the preexisting structures of the machine.

Unlike a person who can modify existing mental frames or incorporate new ones based on experience, at the present time the computer program must rely on its designer for these modifications. Without this ability to change, the machine will not be able to make increasingly mature interpretations.

UNDERSTANDING LANGUAGE →

message — SYNTAX — SEMANTICS — PRAGMATICS — intended meaning

← GENERATING LANGUAGE

FIGURE 6-3
The Approach to Computer Understanding and Generation of Language.

there are rules for how the different shapes fit together and some pieces can be assembled without regard to what appears on them. . . . We might view things like color and texture as a kind of simple picture semantics which indicates what sorts of elements can fit with others. . . . Finally, there is a more sophisticated pragmatics or reasoning based on knowledge of pictures. If a picture of an elephant is emerging, it might be useful to look for something with the color and texture of an elephant tail, and then use its further color and shape information to guide the process.[p. 46]

The role of syntax, semantics, and pragmatics in understanding and generating language is shown in Fig. 6-3. In the understanding-language direction, the structure of the message, derived by syntactic analysis, is processed semantically to extract the literal meaning of the sentence. A pragmatics analysis derives the "intended meaning" by using world knowledge, knowledge of the context, and a model of the sender. The process operates in reverse in language generation. We show the connections as dashed lines to avoid giving the impression that the process is necessarily a sequential one. There are some approaches that blur the distinction between syntactic and semantic analysis, and some that deal with syntax,

semantics, and pragmatics in parallel, moving back and forth from one to the other as the analysis proceeds.

Natural language offers a remarkable palette that enables people to communicate information about objects, actions, beliefs, intents, and desires that occur over time and space. The nuances of meaning must be captured by the computer if it is to have the linguistic power possessed by people. However, for a computer to deal with the "meaning" of natural language expressions, it must convert the things portrayed by natural language to a form that is amenable to computer manipulation under the guidance of a formal set of rules. Ideally, the transformation from natural language to a computer representation would provide a means for the computer to reason about the information, deal with questions, take requested actions, and make appropriate responses. The present state of the art is far from "ideal" since we do not know how to represent in a computer the full scope of meaning that is indicated above. Instead, the available representations are limited to the modeling of meaning in specialized domains such as storage and retrieval of information in an application-specific database, interacting with people in constrained situations, and answering questions about, or paraphrasing, a given segment of focused text.

Syntax. No speech community has ever been identified where communication is restricted to single-word discourse. Instead, words are concatenated (strung together), and we know of no language where words are strung together randomly. It is generally assumed that there must be a finite set of rules that defines all grammatical operations for any given language. Any native speaker will generate sentences that conform to these grammatical rules, and any speaker of the speech community will recognize such sentences as grammatical.

The study of syntax is a fascinating one in its own right, having widespread implications that range from ideas on language universals to conjectures about language acquisition by children. For our purposes, we will take a more limited point of view and consider that the purpose of syntax is to provide a structural representation that will be useful in the understanding process.

Computational linguistics attempts to develop formal rules that assign structural descriptions to sentences in an explicit and well-defined manner. To indicate the nature of a formal approach, consider a simple *phrase structure grammar* using rules of the type,

$$\text{Sentence} \rightarrow \text{NP} + \text{VP},$$

where $\rightarrow$ stands for "is made up of," + stands for "followed by," and the capitalized letters stand for category symbols such as "sentence," "noun phrase," or "verb phrase." Thus, the rule says *a sentence is made up of a noun phrase (NP)*

followed by a verb phrase (VP).

The primitive set of "rewrite rules" given below is indicative of the machinery of a phrase structure grammar:

1. Sentence→NP + VP
2. NP→T + N
3. VP→Verb + NP
4. T→the
5. N→(man, ball . . .)
6. Verb→(hit, took, . . .)

Note that a rule such as rule 2 can be interpreted either descriptively (declaratively), *A sentence is a noun phrase followed by a verb phrase*, or as a procedure that says *If you want to find a noun phrase, look for "the" followed by a noun*.

The rules can be used to analyze the phrase structure of a sentence, as shown in Fig. 6-4.

The procedure of Fig. 6-4 is called *bottom-up parsing*. The part of speech of every word is found in a lexicon or dictionary, and then the rules are used

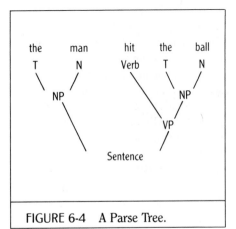

FIGURE 6-4   A Parse Tree.

to join the parts of speech together into phrases. In the bottom-up approach, much time could be spent examining combinations that are not legal. An alternative approach, known as *top-down parsing*, attempts to find instances of given rules in the text. Thus, one would look for verb followed by noun phrase because we know that this forms a verb phrase. In this approach, one searches for what is expected or wanted in the way of structure. Sophisticated parsers use a combination of top-down and bottom-up strategies.

A major problem in parsing is caused by the fact that many words have multiple part-of-speech assignments. The multiple assignments lead to many possible structures since, as the analysis of the sentence proceeds from left to right, many potential phrases must be retained until further words are encountered that show that a particular phrase structure is or is not possible. For example, in parsing the sentence "The table covers were soiled," it is necessary to consider "covers" as both a noun and a verb, so that after scanning the leftmost three words we would have both (the table)(covers) and (the table covers) as structural partitions. Only when the word "were" is encountered can we drop the first parsing.

The structural analysis of a typical sentence is far more complex than our example might imply, as shown in the parse tree of Fig. 6-5. Note that many more word and phrase classes are used in comparison to the simple example presented in Fig. 6-4. This additional structure is necessary to represent the more complex relationships among words and phrases found in most natural language

expressions. However, because of its limited expressive power, the rewrite-rule formulation is not suited to describing procedures needed for sophisticated parsing. For example, it is difficult to express the constraints that must be satisfied among various parts of speech, such as agreement between subject and verb. Further, rewrite rules are unable to express high-level guidance as to the strategies to be used in parsing a sentence. Therefore, other more general representations have been developed; Appendix 6-1 describes two such representations.

In addition to trying to represent the complexities of the parsing process, it is important to be able to describe efficient parsing techniques. The approaches shown in Appendix 6-1 are known as "nondeterministic parsers" because the parser makes a best guess at any particular stage, but may have to back up if the guess turns out to be wrong. The chart parser representation described in Appendix 6-1 is especially suited for describing efficient backtracking procedures. Another approach is that of Marcus [Marcus 80, Thompson 84] who believes that much of the effort expended by ordinary parsers is due to the multiple parsings resulting from local structural ambiguity, rather than the ambiguity of the full sentence. He feels that people use a single local parsing that follows from the partial structure and the next four or five words, rather than developing all possible local parsings and then choosing the most applicable one. Using this approach, his "deterministic parser" stores fragments of the syntax tree in several temporary buffers, and uses a set of rules to determine the most likely local parse.

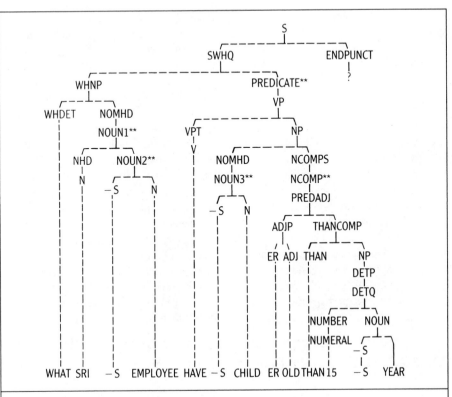

FIGURE 6-5   Output from DIALOGIC, a Sophisticated Parser.

Parse tree for "What SRI employees have children older than 15 years?" WHNP = interrogative noun phrase; WHODET = interrogative determiner; NHD = pronoun modifier head; SWHQ = what question; VP = verb phrase; NP = noun phrase; NCOMPS = noun-phrase complement; PREDADJ = predicate adjective; DETQ = determiner/quantifier phrase.

Semantics.   The question of meaning is a deep philosophical one. For our purposes here we will consider the derivation of meaning as the problem of converting a sentence to a representation that can be related to real or imaginary objects in a possible world. Semantics will be used as the basis for expressing the literal meaning of an expression; the intended meaning will be derived using pragmatics.

There are two main approaches to the assignment of literal meaning to an expression. The first is "lexical" semantics that gives prime importance to *content* words. By assuming that such words have a direct relationship to "deeper" notions, the lexical semanticist hopes to show how words fit together. The representation of the semantics of a sentence is a paraphrase in which the content words of the original sentence have been rewritten and fitted together using their generic representations. The paraphrase is the program's "understanding" of the input.

In the "compositional" semantics approach, the meaning of a complex expression depends on the meaning of its subexpressions. Thus, the analysis of a phrase is its translation into formulas of an appropriate logical calculus. This is accomplished by using rules that describe how to bring together the formulas of subphrases of the phrase while taking into account the context of the phrase. Compositional semantics attempts to provide logical descriptions of how a phrase or word modifies another. The phrase, translated into a logical expression, is usable in a formal deduction system and forms the basis for any next step in the meaning derivation process, perhaps involving the pragmatics of the situation.

Lexical Semantics. Conceptual dependency (CD) theory is an example of a nonformal lexical semantics approach based on a set of elementary concepts (semantic primitives) that are used to express the meaning of an utterance. Schank and his colleagues [Schank 81] maintain that an extremely small set of primitive actions will account for what must be represented in the physical world. The CD representations should be identical for different sentences that describe the same event in quite different linguistic constructions. Some primitive actions such as *transfer*, *propel*, and *ingest* are shown in Box 6-3, and cover many simple physical events and human interactions.

In the CD approach, meaning is considered to be the primary issue, and the study of syntax is guided by the de-

---

 BOX 6-3   The Conceptual Dependency (CD) Approach

The conceptual dependency approach uses a very small number of primitives to represent the actions of the physical world. Some of the key conceptual dependency primitives are presented below, using simple sentences as examples:

| John went to New York. |

actor: john
action: PTRANS (physical transfer of location)
object: John
direction TO: New York
　　　FROM: unknown

| The rock hit the boy. |

actor: unknown

action: PROPEL
　　└→ CAUSED { state:　contact
　　　　　　　　object1: rock
object: rock
direction: TO: boy
　　　　object2: boy
　　　FROM: unknown

| John drank a glass of milk. |

actor: John
action: INGEST
object: milk
direction: TO: mouth of John
　　　FROM: glass

instrument used (level I)

　actor: John
　action: PTRANS (physical tranfer)
　object: glass containing milk

direction: TO: mouth of John
　　　　　FROM: table

instrument used (level II)

　actor: John
　action: MOVE (movement of part of body)
　object: hand of John
　direction: TO: glass
　　　　　FROM: unknown

instrument used (level III)

　actor: John
　action: GRASP
　object: glass of milk
　direction: TO: hand of John

mands of the theory of understanding. Originally there was not to be an independent syntactic pass. Over the years this restriction has been relaxed, but semantics still tends to be the main focus. Every "content word" is considered to have an associated set of "slots," variables whose values are to be established, such as *actor*, an *action* performed by that actor, an *object* that the action is performed on, and a *direction* in which the action is oriented. This form forces the system to postulate actors, objects, etc. that may have not been explicitly mentioned in a sentence describing an event, but which nevertheless must exist. When converting a sentence into CD form, one of the prime motivators of the system is *slot-filling*, i.e., instantiating the actor, object, . . . slots by the words of the text.

The CD approach would translate the sentence "John went to New York" to a representation that indicated that the content word "went" is a primitive action known as PTRANS (for physical transfer of location). The "actor" John carried out PTRANS, the "object transferred" was John, the "direction-to" was New York and the "direction-from" is unknown. The word 'went' motivates the search in the sentence for the actor, object, and direction to fill the "slots" in the PTRANS semantic primitive structure.

Scripts were developed by Schank's group as additional methods for representing the context of a discourse. The script, a description of an event such as going to a restaurant, serves to organize the knowledge that people must have to understand some coherent segment of

---

BOX 6-3   (*continued*)

Here we see the potentially unbounded expansion of instruments. The analysis reads "John drank the milk by getting the milk to his mouth by moving his hand to the milk and grasping the glass."

The CD work has been applied to SAM [Schank 81], a program that answers questions about stories. Given the input "John went to a restaurant. He sat down. He got mad. He left," the program produces:

John was hungry. He decided to go to a restaurant. He went to one. He sat down in a chair. A waiter did not go to the table. John became upset. He decided he was going to leave the restaurant. He left it.

Note that John could have gotten mad for various reasons, but the script used to help interpret the above text only provided one reason for getting mad, namely that the waiter did not come.

Another CD work is PAM [Schank 81], a program that reasons about people's intentions. Given the story,

John loved Mary but she didn't want to marry him. One day, a dragon stole Mary from the castle. John got on top of his horse and killed the dragon. Mary agreed to marry him. They lived happily ever after,

PAM produces,

John was in love with Mary. She did not want to marry him. A

dragon took her from the castle. He learned that that dragon had taken her from the castle. He mounted a horse. It took him to her. He killed the dragon. She was indebted to him. She told him that she was going to marry him. He married her. He and she were happy thereafter.

Other CD efforts described by Schank and Riesback [Schank 81] are TALE-SPIN, a program that writes simple stories, and POLITICS, a program that simulates human ideological understanding of international political events. In all of these, natural language sentences are converted to CD form, and the various scripts and plans are used to direct the slot-filling operation.

human experience. In addition, scripts point out what behavior is appropriate for a particular situation. For example, a subway script would specify the participants (riders, cashier, conductor), the objects (turnstile, train, seat), and the episodes (getting a subway token, going through the turnstile). Understanding a story first requires the determination of what script is referred to in the story, i.e., setting up a correspondence between the vocabulary of the script and the story. (Note that this brings us face to face again with the problem of relevance, "how does a system know which script to choose?") Next, that script is used to identify and fill in the important details in the causal chain being built.

Compositional Semantics. The term "compositional semantics" is used to indicate a system in which the meaning of a complex expression depends only on its subexpressions. This permits every well-formed subexpression to be used as the basis for meaning-dependent processing. The computational linguistics approach to compositional semantics has been to derive a logical form from natural language expressions, and to use this form as the basis for deriving the meaning of the expressions. When a sentence is ambiguous the analysis must furnish distinct logical form representations for the different readings. The logical form is used as the intermediate step between the original sentence and the final expression that captures the meaning.

The essential problem for a theory of logical form is to represent in a logical formalism specific concepts of natural language such as events, actions, and

processes; time and space; collective entities and substances; and propositional attitudes ("believe") and modalities ("should"). The theory is concerned with the question of what particular predicates, functions, operators, and the like are needed to represent the content of natural language expressions. Moore [Moore 81] surveys key problems that arise in representing the content of English expressions. Two typical examples of the type of problem that Moore discusses are:

- How can one reconcile statements that refer to points in time with those that refer to intervals? ("The company earned $5 million in March" does not mean that at every point in time during March the company earned $5 million.)
- How can one deal with collections? ("Newell and Simon wrote *Human Problem Solving*" does not mean that they each did it simultaneously.)

DIALOGIC [Grosz 82], is an example of a system that translates English sentences into logical form representations. Given the question, "What SRI employees have children older than 15 years?," the parser first produces the tree shown in Fig. 6-5. The system then converts the tree to a logic formalism after assigning additional attributes to nodes in the tree, identifying the quantifiers, heads of noun phrases, verb phrases, and adjectives. The final logical form is assembled by a procedure that determines the scope of the quantifiers and takes into account the characteristics of the database to be searched.

The final expression, shown in Fig. 6-6, can be paraphrased as, "Who is each employee such that the company of the

LOGICAL FORM	EXPLANATION
[QUERY	;Sentence is a query
(WH employee1	;Find someone in the ;database, say employee1
(AND (EMPLOYEE employee1)	;who satisfies the ;predicate EMPLOYEE
(EMPLOYEES-COMPANY-OF employee1 SRI))	;AND is employed by SRI
(SOME child2 (CHILD child2)	;There exists someone ;say child2 who satisfies ;the predicate CHILD
(AND	;AND also satisfies the ;predicate CHILD-OF for
(CHILD-OF employee1 child2) ((*MORE* OLD) child2 (YEAR 15))]	;the variable employee1 ;and child2 satisfies ;MORE OLD than 15

FIGURE 6-6   Logical Form Obtained by the DIALOGIC System.

employee is SRI and some child of the employee is older than 15 years?" This transformation of the original sentence is far from trivial, since the predicates relevant to the database such as EMPLOYEE, EMPLOYEE-COMPANY-OF, and CHILD must be identified with the words of the question, and the quantifier SOME and its scope has to be determined.

To obtain an answer to a question, the logical form of the question is considered to be a theorem to be proved, using the database (expressed in formal logic, also) as the set of axioms. Other natural language programs that interact with a retrieval database are described briefly in Box 6-4.

Comparing Lexical and Compositional Semantics.   As described in the discussion on representation (Chapter 3), there are three main components of a representational system: (1) the "vocabulary" of the representation,[15] (2) the models based on this vocabulary which describe the structures and relationships among the things in the world and can be used to predict behavior, and (3) the symbolic formalism and the physical encoding that is used in the computer.

The lexical semantics approach uses a vocabulary of about ten to twenty basic concepts, some of which are complex enough to be considered models. Additional models are provided to capture more complex activities in the world, such as going to a restaurant, taking a train,

---

[15]In the case of a formal representation for natural language, this vocabulary could include both natural language and logic terms.

BOX 6-4   Question-answering Systems

Much work has been carried out in relating queries, written in a limited subset of natural language, to a database of facts about some limited domain. To answer questions, the system uses the statements contained in the database to reach a conclusion that fits the question. This box provides brief descriptions of two natural language "front ends" for retrieval systems. Both convert a query to a logical expression for use in searching the database.

The LUNAR System

The LUNAR system [Woods 77] is an example of a question-answering system in which the parser provides a structural description of the question, and interpretation rules identify the logical connections among the linguistic elements that correspond to database entries. Retrieval operations are performed using the query expressions produced by the interpretation rules. Thus, LUNAR transforms the question, "Do any samples have greater than 13 percent aluminum oxide?" into the expression,

(TEST (FOR SOME X1 ((SEQ
   SAMPLES) CONTAIN X1
   (AL203)
   (GREATERTHAN 13 PCT))))

The LUNAR database contained chemical data on lunar rock and soil composition from the Apollo moon missions. A question such as "What is the average concentration of aluminum in high alkali rocks?" would first be parsed. The phrase "high alkali rocks" would be found to correspond to a set of entries in the database, and 'aluminum' would be identified as one of the attributes. The phrase "average concentration" would be recognized as a particular set of computations that the system knew about, the computation would be made, and the answer given to the

---

what to do if one needs money, etc. In compositional semantics, the vocabulary used is that of formal logic, plus certain of the words in the original sentence. To make the logical form refer to something in the actual world we must supply additional assertions about the actual world, i.e., we must supply a model of the world of interest. Thus, the same logical form could mean different things, depending on the world model being used.

Each of the approaches to semantics has its strengths and weaknesses. The lexical approach is not general, and therefore tends to have an unlimited growth of special situations. However, its use of frames as a focusing device is very effective computationally, and it is robust with respect to ungrammatical sentences. Some of the major problems in script-based parsing include (1) indexing diffi-

culties with a large database of scripts, (2) the problem of having multiple scripts activated simultaneously, (3) the difficulty of amending, generalizing, or creating scripts based on experience, and (4) general representation problems such as modeling physical objects, participant's point of view, and causal relationships. The compositional semantics approach is quite general, and has all the power of formal logic, but lacks the focusing mechanism provided by the frame structure. One way of obtaining this focusing mechanism is to couple the compositional semantics to an automatic planner, as is done in the KAMP system described in Box 6-5.

Pragmatics.   To use language with the competence of a native speaker requires more than the description of syntactic,

BOX 6-4   (continued)

user. LUNAR had an extensive grammar that covered a subset of English, and could handle some pronouns and definite determiners. Thus, it could establish a limited dialogue capability.

LIFER

The LIFER system [Hendrix 78] is a system for creating English language interfaces to other computer software, such as database management systems. The goal was to provide a systems designer who is not a linguist with the ability to tailor a natural language "front end" to an application. LIFER allows the systems designer to specify the nature of the processing to be carried out on the natural language inputs by writing pattern and response expressions. These can be thought of as more complex than, but similar to, the ELIZA patterns described previously. One of the useful features of LIFER is its ability to handle ellipsis. Thus in the series of questions "How old is John?" "How tall?" and "Mary?" the last two questions would be interpreted as "How tall is John?" and "How tall is Mary?"

When a given pattern is recognized by the parser, the associated expression is evaluated to produce the desired response. For example, a specification "HOW <ATTRIBUTE> IS <PERSON>" indicates that when an input sentence such as, "How old is John?" is entered, the system should identify "old" with <ATTRIBUTE> and "John" with <PERSON>. These "interpreted" words are then used in appropriate interactions with the application software. For example, a user can specify that the word "sum" as in "What is the sum of 3 and 4?" be used to call a summation function that uses 3 and 4 as arguments.

semantic, and discourse rules: human language behavior is part of a coherent plan of action directed toward satisfying a speaker's goals. Thus, pragmatics requires the use of reasoning and planning techniques, since the speaker must develop a plan of how to convert intent into a string of words, and conversely, the receiver must reason from the message to determine what that intent is.

The importance of considering the context of an utterance in deriving meaning is discussed by Searle in his classic book on speech acts [Searle 69]:

> The unit of linguistic communication is not, as has been generally been supposed, the symbol, word or sentence, . . . but rather the production or issuance of the symbol or word or sentence in the performance of the speech act. . . . More precisely, the production or issuance of a sentence token under certain conditions is a speech act, and speech acts . . . are the basic or minimal units of linguistic communication. A theory of language is part of a theory of action. . . .

Some of the problems that must be considered in pragmatics are how to deal with multiple sentences and extended discourse, and how to resolve references because such discourse analysis requires a model of what the participants know, believe, desire, and intend. (The referring problem was described in the "toy in the driveway" earlier in this chapter.)

Pragmatics in the CD Approach.   When a script cannot make sense of a new input, possibly due to the fact that some additional pragmatic knowledge is required, the CD approach turns to *plans*, a set of actions and subgoals for attaining a

BOX 6-5   KAMP, A Program that Plans Utterances

The knowledge and modalities planner (KAMP) [Appelt 85] uses formal logic to plan utterances. Rather than go through the rather technical formalism, we will indicate the planning and reasoning used by describing a typical utterance problem solved by KAMP. The example shows the complex intertwining of reasoning and discourse operations. Consider a computer program, Rob, capable of performing speech acts but no other actions. A person, John, is to carry out the physical actions of repairing an air compressor. Rob is the expert and knows how to assemble the compressor, what tools are needed, and where the tools are located. Suppose that Rob wants the pump to be removed from its support. Rob reasons as follows:

1. For John to remove the pump he must unfasten the bolts attaching the pump to the platform.
2. To accomplish this, John must know what the right tool is, must have this tool, and must be next to the pump.
3. Rob assumes that John knows that the pump is attached to the platform so that it will not be necessary to tell him from what the pump must be unbolted. Thus, Rob starts to form the utterance, "Remove the pump," without including "from the platform."
4. A *critic* routine within the Rob program now indicates that it

cannot be assumed that John knows the tool needed to carry out the removal. In addition, for John to have the wrench requires that he know where it is, and must go there and get it.
5. According to Rob's model of what John knows, John does not have this knowledge, so Rob must inform him of the need for the wrench and its location.
6. Rob now forms the complete utterance, "Remove the pump with the wrench in the toolbox."

It is difficult to imagine how people carry out these reasoning determinations so effortlessly and so rapidly!

---

goal. A knowledge of planning helps the program comprehend the motives of the actors. Once the plans and goals of a character in the text have been figured out, then guesses can be made concerning the intentions of an action in the unfolding story. From the CD point of view, to understand a narrative is to keep track of the goals of each of the characters in the text, and to interpret actions as a means of achieving these goals.

For example, consider the story, "John needed money for a down-payment on a house. He called his sister." To make sense of the story, we cannot expect to

find a *paying for a house* script, and even if one did exist, it is not clear that the *sister* relation would be included. Thus, the system must have knowledge about the goal of raising money and plans for how this can be achieved. One plan might be *contact friends or relatives*. Since the sister is a relative, the connection between the original two sentences can now be made.

In this approach, an extensive set of plans must be stored in the database, and some technique for locating relevant plans must be provided. Notice that, as an attempt is made to deal with "deeper" meaning, a more and more sophisticated model of human actions is required.

Pragmatics in the Compositional Semantics Approach. In a formal approach to the planning and "decoding" of an utterance, logic is used to model the linguistic components of the discourse. An example of this approach is the knowledge and modalities planner (KAMP) [Appelt 85], which takes a set of axioms about the state of the world, the preconditions and effects of actions, the beliefs of different agents, and a description of a given agent's high-level goal, and produces an utterance plan that takes into account the abilities and beliefs of the other agents. Pieces of the utterance are constructed to supply information that the planner thinks the intended listener requires to understand the message and to carry out its intent. The linguistic actions are refined until an English sentence is completely specified. Box 6-5 indicates how the planning operation causes a sentence to be constructed based on the speaker's knowledge of the "local world" and a model of the recipient's knowledge and beliefs.

DISCUSSION

Language provides both a basis for social cooperation and a tool for thought. While many animal species can communicate, and the higher primates even seem capable of elementary forms of symbolic encoding of information, the full power of language use appears to be a distinguishing characteristic of the human species— perhaps its only distinguishing characteristic. The essential element of linguistic competence is a (shared) representation that is general enough to allow almost any situation of relevance (to the intercommunicating group) to be easily expressed, and is extendible, to allow one to deal with new concepts and situations.

While we easily recognize the importance of language for communication, how vital a role does it really play in our thinking and reasoning processes? If symbolic language was our only internal knowledge representation, then we would have to agree with the Whorfian hypothesis (see Chapter 3, "The Representation of Knowledge"). However, there is strong evidence to suggest that we have access to additional internal representations (e.g., iconic representations, see Chapters 8 and 9), and thus the role and importance of language in our thinking remains an open issue.

Where do we stand in terms of developing a machine that can use natural language at a human level of performance? In a very shallow sense, we have already reached this goal as noted in the case of the ELIZA program. In the deepest sense, it has been argued that we can never reach this goal since machines can never fully share human experience, and thus their conversation will always be distinguishable from that of a member of our culture. From that point of view the computer will always be an "alien intelligence," i.e., possibly intelligent, but lacking the "first-hand" experience with our culture to deal with linguistic situations like a native. But given these qualifications, we might still ask how far we have come in allowing a machine to carry on an intelligent conversation (i.e., the essence of the Turing test).

We saw that when we attempt to

devise programs capable of what appears to be advanced language understanding, we are faced with the Chinese room problem of determining what understanding really means—this issue is obviously very far from resolution. It further appears that the issue of language ability cannot be separated from that of intelligence. To have a machine participate in sophisticated discourse, we encounter the same problems faced in other AI domains: attaining human-level performance in reasoning, planning, and problem solving. The mechanical aspects of language production and understanding are at one end of a continuous scale; creativity and intelligence progressively impinge on linguistic ability as we move along this scale.

Despite advances in the field that have led to useful applications, particularly those involving human interaction in natural language with a retrieval database, there is still a long way to go. Important first steps have been taken for dealing with utterance involving multiple agents, but the knowledge and beliefs, and the plans and goals of all participants must be known for the analysis to proceed. Finally, the subtleties of understanding a joke, composing a sophisticated poem or story, or paraphrasing a complex body of text still elude us.

Appendixes

6-1

Representing Parsing Algorithms

This appendix briefly describes two approaches for describing and constructing parsing algorithms, the augmented transition network (ATN) and the chart grammar representations.

The Augmented Transition Network

The ATN network representation is a variant of the state transition diagram discussed in Chapter 3. It provides a convenient notation for specifying the operation of a given parser. As shown in Fig. 6-7, the ATN is a network of nodes and arcs, with symbols attached to the arcs that indicate what constituents must be recognized to traverse the arc. The network in the figure uses the constituents AUX (auxiliary verb), NP (noun phrase), and V(verb). Simple constituents such as noun and verb are identified by looking up the words in a dictionary, but auxiliary ATNs are used to recognize more complex sentence constituents such as NP and VP. Symbols on arcs show what constituent must be recognized to traverse the arc. Numbers indicate tests that must be satisfied to traverse the arc and/or the action to be performed. "Agreement" is with respect to the previous arc. Registers are provided to store

APPENDIX 6-1

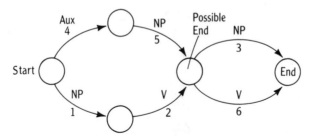

FIGURE 6-7   Example of an Augmented Transition Network.

Notes. Tests required to traverse arc and additional actions to be taken:

1 = Test: Constituent must be NP.
   Action: Label constituent as "subject;"
   Label sentence "declarative."

2 = Test: Constituent must be V that agrees
   with subject.
   Action: —

3 = Test: Previous constituent must be transitive verb; present constituent must
   be NP.
   Action: Label present constituent "object."

4 = Test: Constituent must be AUX.
   Action: Label constituent as V; label sentence
   as "question."

5 = Test: Constituent must be NP; constituent
   must agree with previous constituent V.
   Action: Label constituent as "subject."

6 = Test: Constituent must be V; constituent must
   agree with previous constituent (subject).
   Action: —

intermediate results. To parse a sentence we begin at the start node on the left and move through the network until we come to an end node. (There are several end nodes since a sentence could consist of NP + V, as in "The boy walked," or could have an additional NP as in, "The boy walked to school.")

The ATN of Fig. 6-7 can parse sentences such as "The boy walked home. Has the boy walked? The boy walked." For example, to parse "The boy walked home," we begin by determining from another ATN that "the boy" is a noun phrase (NP). Note 1 on that arc indicates that "the boy" should be labeled as "subject" and the sentence as "declarative." A dictionary then indicates that the next word "walked" is

a verb, and note 2 on that arc indicates that if it agrees with the subject "the boy" then the arc can be traversed. Finally, an ATN will find that "home" is a noun phrase (NP), and note 3 indicates that if the verb "walked" is transitive, then "home" can be labeled as "object" and the arc can be traversed, completing the parsing.

The ATN formalism can concisely express a complex parsing procedure in an elegant form suitable for computer implementation. The disadvantage of the ATN is that it is difficult to modify large networks without causing unforeseen side effects, and the ATN formalism cannot conveniently describe efficient ways of searching for the required syntactic components.

Chart Parsing

The chart parser representation [Earley 70, Kay 73] is able to describe efficient ways of searching for relevant syntactic components. The chart uses edges in a graph to represent terminal symbols (words) and nonterminal symbols (such as NP). A sentence is parsed by constructing edges that span increasingly large sections of the original graph of terminal symbols (words). The computation is organized so that when a successful grouping of constituents is found (such as an article and a noun forming a noun phrase), these are retained for possible use when backtracking is required, while unsuccessful groupings are discarded. Parsing the sentence "The

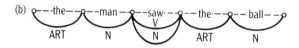

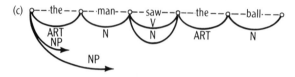

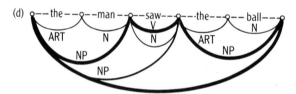

FIGURE 6-8   Example of Chart Parsing.

(a) Representing sentence using words as edges in a graph. (b) Assigning word classes.
(c) Forming edges that span more than a single node. (d) Completed parse.

man saw the ball" would be represented as the following sequence of operations. We begin with the words of the sentence as edges in a graph (see Fig. 6-8[a]). The parsing of the sentence will consist of spanning increasingly large portions of the graph.

The first step is to assign the syntactic class of the word. If a word has multiple syntactic classes, multiple edges are used, as shown for the word "saw"(Fig. 6-8[b]). The system now tries to determine edges that subsume more than one edge, e.g., to form NP to span ART and NOUN. While in the process of trying to complete this spanning, an edge is either "active" or "complete." The chart parser uses rules concerning active and complete edges to control the spanning operation. In Fig. 6-8(c), two active NP's are in progress, one that will be complete after "the man," and the other after "the man saw," which, unless the lexicon indicated otherwise, could be considered by the system as a type of saw, e.g., the same noun-noun form as a "wood saw," or a "metal saw."

Eventually, a set of edges will satisfy the requirements for the sentence, as shown in Fig. 6-8(d).

7

Expert/Knowledge-based Systems

Early workers in the field of AI hoped to construct an intelligent machine with a perception component that sensed and interpreted the world, a component that allowed the system to learn from its experiences, and a mechanism for solving general problems arising in interactions with the environment. The knowledge database would be provided initially by the human designer, and then develop autonomously as the system learned about the world.

Although research based on this paradigm is still being pursued, workers on systems that aspire to a human level of performance have considerably scaled down their original goals. Emphasis has moved from a general problem solving approach to a concentration on specialized problem domains. The basic assumption is that the main source of capability in problem solving resides in the knowledge database of the system, rather than in the power of the deductive apparatus used. There is no perceptually based autonomous learning component in these systems. Rather, all of the knowledge is entered by the human designer, or user, of the system; the emphasis is on better ways to express and use the specialized knowledge. *Expert systems* based on this philosophy have already been applied to diagnosis and design problems in many fields, and have turned out to be some of the most commercially

189

successful applications of artificial intelligence.

Even though the problem scope has been narrowed in going from general problem solving to nonlearning expert systems, many basic issues still remain. For example, there is the fundamental question as to whether the incremental acquisition of piecemeal knowledge can lead to global understanding of a subject. There is the issue of whether intelligent behavior can still be achieved if we partition off, and operate within, an isolated segment of human knowledge or experience. The issue of control also arises: there must be some method of determining which knowledge is pertinent to a given situation and how to guide the sequence of deductions or transformations without explicit programming. Thus, many of the problems that arise in the design of expert systems involve familiar AI issues, and especially the trade-offs between generality and effectiveness of operation.

This chapter will be primarily concerned with the "production system" approach. We will briefly describe its importance in the psychological modeling of intelligence, but we will focus particularly on its use in expert systems. We will also discuss general issues, such as the problem of knowledge acquisition, knowledge representation, and knowledge utilization. Some of the questions to be addressed are:

- What are the characteristics of a human expert?
- What is a production-rule expert system?
- What are the characteristics of a knowledge domain that make it suitable as an application for an expert system?
- How can a domain of knowledge be represented by data structures in the memory of the computer, and how can this knowledge database be used in problem solving?
- What are the basic AI issues that arise in the design of expert systems?

HUMAN EXPERTS

The dictionary defines an expert to be a person with a high degree of skill in, or knowledge of, a certain subject. The word comes from the Latin *experius*, past participle of *experiri*, to try. The word is apt, because an expert usually attains that status by investing a large amount of time in trying, in obtaining experience in the special domain.

The term *prodigy* is used when exceptional ability is shown at an early age. There have been prodigies in mathematics, chess, and music, but it is rare to find prodigies in acting, writing, drawing, and painting. It is interesting that while there are some notable exceptions, few mental prodigies meet early expectations, while most musical prodigies do go on to successful careers.

A remarkable memory ability characterizes many classes of experts; for example, chess masters are able to play many games simultaneously while blindfolded. To study visual memory in chess, subjects are typically exposed to a board position for a short time and are later asked to reproduce the board. Chess masters impressively outperform novices only when meaningful board positions are used. When the pieces are put down at random, then little difference exists. De Groot [De Groot 65], in his study of chess masters, used an introspective method where the expert described his inner thinking processes. Chess masters reported remembering the positions of "chunks" consisting of four or five pieces rather than individual pieces. The same type of results have been obtained in analyzing the abilities of computer programming experts [McKeithen 81]. Both experts and novices are shown programs for a brief time. Experts are quite good at reconstructing these programs. However, when presented with scrambled, meaningless programs, experts perform in a manner similar to the novice.

Thus, pattern retention and recognition play an important role in expert performance. Simon [Newell 72a] estimates that masters have acquired on the order of 50,000 different chess patterns that they quickly recognize. These stored patterns and their analysis free the expert to concentrate on deeper strategies. Studies of computer programming [Soloway 80] also indicate that experts in that field have a large supply of "templates" that are applied to programming problems.

Studies of expert-vs.-novice problem solving in physics [Larkin 81] have shown that the reasoning approach used by the novice differs from the expert. The novice uses a means-ends analysis, setting up and satisfying a sequence of subgoals. This requires the retention of many intermediate results. The expert seems to "know where he is going," and uses forward reasoning. The expert has the experience to know which of the possible forward reasoning alternatives are relevant to the solution.

Representation is a crucial issue. In some fields, such as mathematics, experts often convert problem statements into the terms of their specialty, and then use their expertise in that specialty to solve the problem. Experts may have a collection of models that they employ in solving problems, e.g., a specialist in internal medicine will use a model of the digestive system, of the blood circulation, etc., in order to develop hypotheses concerning an illness.

When attempting to devise machines that are expert in a specialty, it is desirable to emulate some of the key characteristics of the human expert:

- Use of appropriate models of the world and the ability to reason using these models
- A smooth falling off of competence as the problem departs from his area of expertise, and ability to deal with departures from a standard problem
- Knowledge of the limits of the expertise
- Ability to learn from experience
- Ability to explain what is being done and why it is being done

In the remainder of this chapter, we describe some mechanisms used to achieve expert behavior in a machine.

PRODUCTION SYSTEMS

The production system (PS) is a simple concept that has been used in a wide variety of applications, ranging from investigations of human intelligence to computer-based expert systems. In 1943, Emil Post, a mathematician at the City College of New York proposed an "if-then" rule-based system that indicated how strings of symbols could be converted to other symbols [Post 43]. Post used his productions to study computability. While he and Turing worked independently, it was later shown that the Post system is formally equivalent to the Turing machine.

In the 1960s Newell and Simon [Newell 72] embedded the generality of the if-then representation in a data-driven control structure to produce the present concept of a production rule system that views computation as the process of applying rules *in an order determined by the data*. This view is fundamentally different from the explicit sequencing of control found in conventional programs. A PS consists of three components:

1. **Working memory (WM).** The data representing the current state of the "world." The WM can be finite or "unlimited" in size. Various strategies can be used in the finite case when the WM fills up, e.g., drop the oldest data, keep only important data, etc.

2. **Production rules.** A set of rules of the form, If < condition in WM > THEN < action >, often designated using the notation $A \rightarrow B$. This indicates that "if pattern A matches a pattern in WM, take the action described in B." In expert diagnosis systems, rules are often of the form: IF < evidence e is present in the WM > THEN < add hypothesis h to the WM >. Rule-based systems permit representation of knowledge in a highly modular manner, and are relatively easy to modify, allowing knowledge to be added incrementally.

3. **Rule interpreter.** The control module that carries out the matching operation to determine the next rule to be activated. Some strategies used when the condition portion ("left

side") of more than one rule is satisfied are: rule execution, based on the ordering of rules on a rule-list; rule execution of more specific rules before general rules; and rule execution based on the length of time since a rule was previously invoked.

Thus, "Computation" in a PS is the action taken when the condition for a particular rule is satisfied by data in the WS, the repository of information about the current state of the world.

Control Structures Used in Production Systems

The strategy used by the rule interpreter is called the "control strategy." The control strategy can be employed in various ways: (1) the data-driven mode[16] that interprets rules to mean that if a specified condition is observed in the WM, then a corresponding action is taken; (2) the backward chaining mode[17] that interprets a rule to mean that if a certain action is desired, the system should try to establish the corresponding condition, and (3) a mixture of these.

Data-Driven Control. At first glance, the rules used in a production system (PS) seem very much like the well-known *if-then* conditional statements used in most high-level programming languages. However, although the form is the same, the way that the rules are used differs consid-

---

[16]Also called the antecedent, event driven, or forward chaining mode.
[17]Also called the consequent, goal driven, or hypothesis driven mode.

PRODUCTION SYSTEMS

erably. Unlike a conventional system in which the program performs the sequence of programming steps specified by the programmer, activity in a PS is controlled strictly by the content of the working storage. At every computation cycle of the system, the left-hand sides of the set of rules are examined to determine which rules are satisfied by the contents of the working storage. As indicated above, if more than one rule is activated, there must be a method of determining which rule should be allowed to act. A typical "recognize-act" computation cycle is:

- **Selection.** A determination is made as to which rule modules and working storage items are allowed to be considered for use during the next cycle.

- **Matching.** The active rules examine active working storage looking for a pattern match.

- **Scheduling.** A determination is made as to which of the satisfied rules should be allowed to *fire*.

- **Execution.** The rules perform their actions in the order determined by the scheduling operation.

By choosing the rule to be executed on the basis of the contents of the working storage, a complete re-evaluation of the state of the system must be performed every computation cycle. This is one of the key features of a PS: a PS is sensitive to any change in the entire environment (any new data in memory) and can react to such changes within a single cycle. The price of this responsiveness is the computation time required for the re-evaluation.

Because the working storage is accessible to every rule in the system, this database acts as a broadcast communications channel.

In a *pure* PS, the specified action (right-hand side) is a simple action and not a complex procedure. Also, one avoids rules that place private messages in the working storage (messages that enable only special rules to be activated). Practical expert systems often depart from the pure PS format. For example, it may be natural to use certain rules in various stages of problem solving, and to use different rules in other stages. The set of productions is therefore often tagged to indicate at which stage of the problem solving procedure they can be activated. The more we depart from *purity* of PS, the more we lose the advantage of modularity of the PS rules.

Goal-Driven Control. In goal-driven control, the rules are used in a *backward-chaining* mode, by examining the rules in the database to see if a desired goal can be found on the right-hand side of some rule. If such a rule is found, then the system determines the facts required to actuate the left-hand side. Further backward chaining may be required to accomplish this, and at any time several backward chains may be in progress. This type of control limits attention to the rules that can contribute to the goal. For example, suppose the goal is to establish D and we have the following rules:

$$A \rightarrow B \quad (1)$$
$$B \rightarrow C \quad (2)$$
$$C \rightarrow D \quad (3)$$

The system finds the goal, D, on the right-hand side of rule (3) and backward chains by looking at the left-hand side of (3) to find that the required subgoal is finding C in the working storage so that rule (3) can be activated. Working on this subgoal then leads to (2) which could place C in the working storage if there were a B in the working storage. B is the new subgoal, leading finally to (1) which tells the system to establish A, possibly by asking the user if A is true.

Note that if the user asks why the system wants to know A, it can delineate the backward chaining sequence as the explanation. Thus, it would state that knowing A would, by rule (1) establish B, which by rule (2) would establish C, which by rule (3) would establish our original goal of D. This type of explanation merely indicates the role that the data and the rules play in the computation and does not try to present a deeper explanation of the situation.

An example of backward chaining as used in an expert repair system is presented in Box 7-1.

Other Control Strategies. A combination of data-driven and goal-driven procedures is often used in a practical system. For example, information volunteered by

---

 BOX 7-1   Use of Backward Chaining in an Expert Repair System

Suppose we have the set of rules given below as part of the rules in an expert system for repairing automobile air conditioners.

- RULE 002: IF CAR DOES HAVE THERMAL LIMITER, AND THERMAL LIMITER DOES NOT HAVE POWER, THEN FAULTY FUSE.
- RULE 008: IF CLUTCH DOES NOT HAVE POWER, AND CAR DOES NOT HAVE THERMAL LIMITER, THEN FAULTY FUSE.
- RULE 017: IF TEST LIGHT CONNECTED TO CLUTCH WIRE, AND TEST LIGHT IS OFF, THEN CLUTCH DOES NOT HAVE POWER.
- RULE 021: IF TEST LIGHT CONNECTED TO THERMAL LIMITER WIRE, AND TEST LIGHT OFF, THEN THERMAL LIMITER DOES NOT HAVE POWER.

Suppose the expert system is trying to establish that the air conditioning system is not working because the fuse is faulty. It establishes FAULTY FUSE as a goal. The system backward chains, looking for rules that have a THEN part FAULTY FUSE. RULE 008 and RULE 002 are such rules. Since the system has no information that can satisfy the IF part of these rules, it must ask the user a question.

System: Does the car have a thermal limiter?
User: No.

From this answer, the system finds that RULE 002 does not apply, but RULE 008 does. However, the IF part of RULE 008 requires CLUTCH DOES NOT HAVE POWER. The system has a new goal, and looking at the THEN parts of the rules, it finds RULE 017. RULE 017 requires that a test be performed by the user, and the system informs the user:

System: Connect test light to clutch wire. What is status of test light.
User: Test light is off.

The system now notes that the IF part of RULE 017 has been satisfied and that CLUTCH DOES NOT HAVE POWER. Now the IF part of RULE 008 is satisfied, and system can report to the user: "The fuse is faulty."

the user can be used in a data-driven mode to determine a goal for the goal-driven phase. The PROSPECTOR geology expert system, described in Box 7-2, works in a goal-driven mode when it seems to be making progress, but returns to the user for help in goal selection when serious trouble is encountered.

The production system formalism is useful when the knowledge can be expressed as an independent set of *recognize-act* pairs, but may be inappropriate to represent other types of knowledge, such as set/element (taxonomic) relations among objects in the domain. The PROSPECTOR system addressed this problem by using a semantic network representation in a rule-based inference system. This representation retains the desirable modularity of a rule-based approach, while permitting an explicit, structured description of the semantics of the problem domain.

PRODUCTION SYSTEMS IN PSYCHOLOGICAL MODELING

Some investigators view human behavior in terms of an information processing system, consisting of a long-term memory (LTM), a short-term memory (STM), and an ability to carry out certain processes involving symbols. They hope to gain insight into the nature of human information processing by performing psychological experiments with human subjects involving symbol manipulation and memorization, and then developing a computer model that behaves the same way. Newell and Simon [Newell 72] state their interest in production systems (PS) as the compu-

tational tool for carrying out this investigation:

> We confess to a strong premonition that the actual organization of human programs closely resembles the production system organization. . . . We cannot yet prove the correctness of this judgement, and we suspect that the ultimate verification may depend on the PS proving relatively satisfactory in many different small ways, no one of them decisive.

The features of production systems that particularly interest these investigators can be summarized as follows:

1. A production system is a completely general programming methodology; in theory, it can be used to express any desired computation.
2. The rules of the PS provide a uniform encoding of the information that instructs the PS how to behave.
3. In a PS, each production is independent of the others.
4. The PS has a strong stimulus-response flavor.
5. The productions themselves seem to represent "meaningful components" of the problem solving process.
6. The dynamic working memory for a PS corresponds to human short-term memory, and the human long-term memory may correspond to the rule-base of the PS.

Newell's production-based approach [Newell 73] was used to test theories that attempt to explain the results of certain memory scanning tasks. The subject memorizes a set of digits and responds to a digit flashed on the screen by indicating whether or not it was in the original set. The response times of the subject are

BOX 7-2   Prospector, A Geology Expert

The PROSPECTOR system emulates the reasoning process of an experienced exploration geologist in assessing a given prospect site or region for its likelihood of containing an ore deposit of a certain type. The empirical knowledge contained in PROSPECTOR consists of a number of models that encode knowledge about certain classes of ore deposits. An ore deposit model is encoded as an inference network, a network of connections or relations between field evidence and important geological hypotheses. For example, PROSPECTOR includes a sulfide model, a carbonate lead/zinc model, a copper model, a nickel sulfide model, and a sandstone uranium model. These models are intended to represent the most authoritative and up-to-date information about each class of ore deposit.

Given a rule such as *Barite overlying sulfides suggests the possible presence of a massive sulfide deposit*, a semantic network is used for the antecedent, and a separate one for the consequent. The networks are represented using links and nodes; conceptually, the network for the antecedent of the barite rule would be:

> *There is some entity, E-3A, that participates in an overlying relationship, (PHY-REL-3A) with some other entity, E-3B. Furthermore, E-3A is composed*

of barite, and E-3B is composed of some material, V-3A, that is a member of sulphides.

The semantic network representation has the advantage that all parts of a consequent and a related antecedent do not have to match. Rules can be linked implicitly through set/element chains. For example, suppose that a sample composed of galena is observed. Since galena is an element of the lead sulfides which in turn is a subset of the sulfide minerals, this observation is relevant to a rule concerning sulfides, and can automatically activate such a rule.

In the interactive consultation mode, the geologist typically has promising field data and wants assistance in its evaluation. He or she provides the program with a list of names of rocks and minerals observed, and enters other observations expressed in simple English sentences. The program matches these data against its models, requests additional information of potential value for arriving at more definite conclusions, and provides a summary of the findings. The user can ask at any time for an elaboration of the intent of a question, or for the geological rationale for including a rule in the model, or for an ongoing trace of the effects of answers on PROSPECTOR's conclusions. The performance of PROS-

PECTOR depends on the number of models it contains, the types of deposits modeled, and the completeness of each model. Each model is encoded as a separate data structure, independent of the PROSPECTOR system *per se*. Thus PROSPECTOR is a general mechanism for using such models to deliver expert information about ore deposits to a user who can supply it with data about a prospect or region.

To deal with the uncertainty of user observations, PROSPECTOR uses an inference mechanism based primarily on subjective probability theory. A probability is associated with every statement in the knowledge base, measuring the degree to which the statement is believed to be true. When engaged in consultation about a particular propect, PROSPECTOR uses the specific geological evidence furnished by the user to update the values of its stored probabilities.

In developing the ore deposit models, a significant result has been the evolution of a methodology to acquire and encode models. This methodology involves interviewing techniques, principles for determining the overall structure of a model, tools for interactive construction, modification, and testing of models, and methods for evaluating and revising a model.

noted. The production system was refined to incorporate new hypotheses about how the symbols were brought into the subject's memory, and eventually a successful simulation was built around a small number of productions.

Some of Piaget's results have also been modeled by psychologists using the production rule representation. For example, for tasks involving the ordering of members of a set of objects based on length, weight, or size, Young [Young 76, Boden 81] shows how the behavior of any given stage in a child's development can be described by a specific production rule system.

PRODUCTION RULE–TYPE EXPERT SYSTEMS

An expert system is a program that uses large amounts of knowledge about a single domain to achieve a high level of competence in that domain. While most expert systems do not use the pure PS form, the PS framework can be found in most current applications. Some characteristics of such systems are discussed below.

It is not trivial to build up a database of rules in practical application domains, since human experts often have trouble in converting informal knowledge into formal rules. In addition, it is difficult to capture the ability of an expert to deal with uncertainty. While various Bayesian and ad hoc approaches to uncertainty have been incorporated into expert systems, experts often cannot make useful estimates of the required a priori probabilities or belief values.

As is typical of a PS, the expert systems are often highly reactive; i.e., the choice of actions to be performed next by the system depends primarily on significant features of the current situation, rather than on the type of fixed control structure that characterizes conventional software systems. Another difference from a conventional system is that theoretically the rules are modular in nature; rules can nominally be added and deleted without affecting other rules. In practice, though, there are often side effects, some of which can be quite subtle.

The expert system must be able to communicate with the user in a mode that is natural for the particular application. The systems are often interactive, using a graphics display and communicaiton via an approximation to a natural language (e.g., English) extended to include the jargon of the application domain. Furthermore, many expert systems can retrace the reasoning sequence employed and explain what was done at each step and why, often based on keeping a time-history of the rule firings or the backward chaining.

In addition to the use of production rules to represent domain knowledge, frame-based representations have been incorporated into many recent systems to provide significant help with the rule-management task by providing a means of organizing and indexing modular collections of production rules according to their intended usage [Fikes 85].

Applying Expert Systems Expert systems can only be used in applications where knowledge can be expressed by formal rules, such as medicine, engineering, and science, to aid users in design or diagnosis tasks. For example, the Dendral and Meta-Dendral systems [Buchanan 78] for analyzing mass spectrometer data were among the first successful applied systems; MYCIN is an expert system that acts as a consultant to the physician in the field of infectious disease, [Buchanan 84, Shortliffe 76]; R1 is an expert system for designing computer configurations, [McDermott 80, McDermott 81]; and PROSPECTOR is a consultant system for geological exploration, [Duda 79].

There are no expert systems to aid in the writing of poetry or novels, or in painting a picture, since these creative arts have not been expressed in formal rules (and may never be). Another requirement for an application is the existence of consensus among experts as to what is a proper procedure or what is valid knowledge. Lack of consensus often exists among experts in art, music, and literature. The problem of consensus even arises in technical fields when a lack of understanding exists, e.g., in medicine a disease that baffles the experts may result in differing opinions as to diagnosis and remedies. One may also have schools of thought in a particular field, such as exists in the various approaches to psychiatric problems and their treatment. Finally, for a field to be suitable for expert system application, there must be a certain degree of stability over time. The effort of constantly changing rules of an expert system and validating the results would make the system unattractive.

Two examples of expert systems for relatively stable domains are PROSPECTOR in the field of geology (see Box 7-2)

and MYCIN in the field of medicine (see Box 7-3).

Plausible Reasoning in Expert Systems

In some applications, such as engineering design, the rules are usually stated as certainties, e.g., "If conditions A and B exist, THEN perform some action." In diagnosis systems, such as the MYCIN medical system and the PROSPECTOR geology expert, the rules have a probabilistic flavor, "If there is evidence A and evidence B, THEN hypothesis C is true with certainty of 0.7." There also may be a measure of uncertainty attached to the evidence itself, e.g., the user may feel that the probability of evidence A being true is 0.8. Terms such as "probability" and "certainty" are not probabilities based on frequency as in the case of coin tossing or card games, but rather are subjective scores given by an expert to indicate the relevance of evidence to a hypothesis, or the believability that a certain piece of evidence is true. Such estimates are used in everyday life when we talk about the probability of a team winning the game.

If we have a database with a large number of rules containing subjective probability estimates, the expert system must be able to derive new scores for hypotheses as new evidence is presented to the system. Each rule in the database has an associated rule strength that measures the degree to which a change in the probability of the evidence changes the probability of the hypothesis. This change can be positive or negative, since evidence can be either favorable or unfavorable for a hypothesis. These rule

BOX 7-3   MYCIN, A Medical Expert System

The MYCIN system diagnoses blood and meningitis infections, and recommends drug treatment. MYCIN conducts its consultation with the user in English, and constructs lines of reasoning leading to a diagnosis and treatment plan. MYCIN's was the first major rule-based system, [Buchanan 84]. A typical MYCIN production is:

IF: (1) The site of the culture is blood, and (2) the gram stain of the organism is gramneg, and (3) the morphology of the organism is rod, and (4) the patient is a compromised host THEN: There is suggestive evidence (0.6) that the identity of the organism is *Pseudomonas aeruginosa*.

There are also productionlike rules concerning the use of other rules:

IF: (1) The patient is a compromised host, and (2) there are satisfied rules which mention in their premise *Pseudomonas*,

and (3) there are satisfied rules which mention in their premise *Klebsiella* THEN: There is suggestive evidence (0.4) that the actions associated with the former rules (2) should be executed before the latter (3).

Each rule supplied by an expert has associated with it a *degree of certainty* representing the expert's confidence in the validity of the rule (a number from 1 to 10). An *ad hoc* procedure is used to cumulate the degrees of certainty of the rules used in an inference chain.

An interesting feature of MYCIN is that it can expose its line of reasoning by offering explanations of various kinds. "Why" and "how" questions can be asked by the user during consultation. The user can ask the system, "Why do you want to know that?" and "How did you conclude that?" For example, if MYCIN asks the user "Is the patient's illness with ORGANISM-1 a hospital acquired infection?" and the user responds with WHY?, MYCIN answers:

MYCIN: (1.0) This will aid in determining the category of ORGANISM-1 since it has already been established that (1.1) the gram stain of ORGANISM-1 is gramneg, and (1.2) the morphology of ORGANISM-1 is rod, and (1.3) the aerobicity of ORGANISM-1 is facultative. Therefore, if (1.4) the infection with ORGANISM-1 was not acquired while the patient was hospitalized then there is strongly suggestive evidence (0.8) that the category of ORGANISM-1 is *Pseudomonas aeruginosa*.

Similarly, if the user asks HOW (1.3), the system will indicate the chain of reasoning that was used in establishing "aerobicity." Because of MYCIN's many useful features, such as interaction in English, explanatory power in answering WHY and HOW questions, and the careful construction of an expert database, it has become the model for many subsequent expert systems.

strengths are usually obtained by interviewing an authority; strengths that are expressed initially in verbal terms such as "encouraging," "very unlikely," etc., must be translated to a numerical scale. Changes in probability are then computed using some *ad hoc* or formal scheme (see the section on probabilitistic reasoning in Chapter 4 for further discussion of this topic).

An example of a formal approach to probability updating is PROSPECTOR's use of Bayes's theorem for modifying the probability of a hypothesis based on evidence E. This approach assumes that before any information has been obtained from the user, every rule S has been assigned some prior probability P(S) by the designer. As evidence is acquired from a user, an updated probability of S is computed. If E' denotes all the evidence accumulated up to some point in the consultation, then the probability $P(S|E')$ denotes the current probability of S given the evidence E'. The updating relationships and an actual PROSPECTOR computation are presented in Appendix 7-1. The simplest form of updating involves a hypothesis affected by a single piece of certain evidence. The next more complicated situation involves a hypothesis affected by a single piece of uncertain evidence, e.g., the user says, "I am 70 percent certain that evidence E is true." The most complicated case deals with updating a hypothesis using multiple rules, each with uncertain evidence. There are many subtleties that arise in the actual analysis, concerning uncertainty of evidence, independence of evidence, and the prevention of inconsistencies.

Basic AI Issues

At present, expert systems do not acquire their expertise through experience, but rather, they are given the needed information and the organization of this information by a *knowledge engineer*. An expert system can be considered as an *idiot savant* that can deal very effectively with a specialized field, but is incompetent to deal with topics not in this field. It is instructive to examine the reasons for the limitations of existing PS-based expert systems:

- **Lack of learning capability.** The designer of the system, and not the system, learns by experience as the system is used, and modifies the rule database accordingly. Because it is a nontrivial task to determine which rules need

modification when the system is not performing up to expert standards, the designer must consult with the human experts to determine how the rules have to be modified or augmented. The system itself has no way of determining why the end user may not be satisfied, and no way of automatically correcting the source of the difficulty.

- **Lack of ability to generalize.** There is no reason to expect that the addition of incremental amounts of knowledge will lead to global understanding. To be able to *understand*, the system must be able to generate *higher level* concepts by comparing and generalizing problem situations or groups of knowledge elements. No such ability has been provided in existing systems. As we have indicated previously in Chapter 5, this ability to make comparisons and to determine similarity is a crucial part of generalization and learning.

- **Explanation.** The explanation approach used in most expert systems is in terms of rules that have been satisfied or will be satisfied if certain information is provided. However, the user often desires a causal explanation based on physical reasoning. This type of explanation usually requires that there be a model of the process being discussed. Several recent medical expert systems use such models for this purpose.

- **Need for representing control knowledge.** Although a pure production system is conceptually attractive, the problem of control quickly arises in any practical system. Control must be exerted when more than one rule is activated by the working storage. The

BOX 7-4   **Shallow and Deep Reasoning in Expert Systems**

Most current expert systems can be said to use "shallow" reasoning, since there is no mechanism in the system for "understanding" the domain of expertise. An expert system based on deep reasoning uses a model of the domain to motivate the reasoning processes. For example, a shallow electronic troubleshooting system would contain rules supplied by an expert relating failure symptoms to possible circuit problems. A "deep" system would use models of electronic components and their role in circuits to reason about the symptoms and how they imply failures of components. The difference between these approaches is well stated by De Kleer [De Kleer 84a] who has developed a program that can reason about electronic circuits, determining the effects caused by components of the circuit, and their purpose (teleology) in the circuit:

If I were interested in building a performance pro-

gram, the temptation for including. . . . extra knowledge would be overwhelming. However, that would be short-sighted. To understand what causal reasoning, or teleological reasoning is, one must study it in isolation uncorrupted by other forms of reasoning. Otherwise one has merged two types of reasoning without ever identifying either one individually. In addition, little scientific progress is made and we are not much closer to the ultimate goal. . . . To achieve robust performance, the underlying theories must be identified. This methodology stands in sharp contradistinction with the popular expert-systems methodology. Expert systems are aimed at producing what performance is possible in the short term without consideration of the longer term. Typically this is achieved by recording as many of the heuristics and rules of thumb that experts actually use in practice, as possible. This is misguided.

The reasoning of experts is based on underlying theories that must be teased out. The expert systems approach can be caricatured as a stimulus-response model—good for some purposes, but ineffective in the long run.

De Kleer is correct in his assessment of what is required to attain a sophisticated expert system, but he dismisses too casually the importance of rule-based systems that use an extensive knowledge base. He is advocating a complete return to the philosophy of general reasoning in place of an extensive knowledge base. See *Artificial Intelligence*, December 1984, for an entire volume devoted to this point of view. The ideal approach is probably a system capable of both deep and shallow reasoning, together with the ability to perceive and learn. However, we should remember that it took nature 5 billion years to design such systems!

designer must provide some method for determining which rule is to change the state of the world first, and whether the other activated rules are to be allowed to fire. In addition, since the matching process is time-consuming, procedures must be preprogrammed to determine which rules should be examined, and this often depends on what phase of the problem the system is working on. This

latter difficulty is related to the frame selection problem, i.e., whenever a situation is encountered where a particular set of rules is most applicable, then attempts at matching should be restricted to the set of rules in a particular frame.
- **Reasoning.**   Qualitative or common-sense reasoning is not feasible since most current systems are based on

independent "chunks" of knowledge (rules), rather that on an integrated model. Thus, the system has no "overview" of its supposed field of expertise. Box 7-4 discusses some attempts to deal with this problem.

- **Fragility.** Most currrent systems are fragile. The term "fragility" is used to denote a system that suddenly loses competency when it strays somewhat from its intended domain. (This is in contrast to the performance of human experts which tends to degrade smoothly in a similar situation.) Since expert systems are designed to be narrowly focused, there may be no resolution to this problem.

DISCUSSION

In this chapter we showed how a rather simple concept, the production system, has been used in psychological modeling and in expert systems. The PS offers an interesting approach to control, one that allows the data to direct the processing. Another important feature is the modularity of the rule base, so that rules can be added and deleted without the need to modify the control structure.

Expert systems based on the PS concept have become one of the most successful and active areas of applied AI. Although often not "pure" PS, they usually retain the important features of data driven control, modularity of rules, and explanation ability. In spite of their advantages, the corresponding disadvantages of PS, described in the previous section, are severe enough to question their long-term potential. Without the ability to perceive, learn, and reason, these systems would seem to have a limited role to play in future intelligent systems.

Appendix

7-1

PROSPECTOR Procedure for Hypothesis Updating

This appendix illustrates how PROS-PECTOR propagates the effects of new evidence through its inference networks (chains of evidence and hypotheses). Interactions between separate chains are not treated here.

The "odds-likelihood" form of Bayesian updating was used in PROSPECTOR because it was felt that geology experts could make their estimates best in that form.

The procedure involves three quantities:

1. The prior odds for the hypothesis, $O(H)$, where $O(H) = P(H)/(1\text{-}P(H))$. Note that this odds relationship corresponds to the layman's use of odds, e.g., when $P=0.8$, the odds are $0.8/(1-0.8)=4$, or four to one.
2. The posterior odds for the hypothesis, given that evidence

E is observed to be present, $O(H|E) = p(H|E)/(1-p(H|E))$.

3. The likelihood ratio, $LS = P(E|H)/P(E|\tilde{H})$, a ratio of the probability of the appearance of evidence given that a hypothesis is true, to the probability of evidence if the hypothesis is not true.

The updating relationship involving these quantities is given by a form of Bayes's theorem:

$$O(H|E) = LS * O(H)$$

If LS is large, it means that the observation of E is encouraging for H. When LS is infinity, E establishes H.

A complementary set of equations describes the case in which E is known to be absent, i.e., when $\sim E$ is true:

$$O(H|\sim E) = LN*O(H) \text{ , where}$$
$$LN = P(\sim E|H)/P(\sim E|\sim H)$$

The quantity LN is called the necessity measure. If LN is much less than unity, the known absence of E transforms neutral prior odds on H into very small posterior odds in favor of H. If LN is large, then the absence of E is encouraging for H.

An inference rule, If E THEN (to degree LS, LN) H, states "The observed evidence E suggests (to some degree) the hypothesis H." To apply the rule, the expert must not only describe E and H, but must also supply numerical values for LS, LN, and O(H).

The updating formulas cannot be applied directly when the user is unable to state that the evidence E is either definitely present or definitely absent, but they can be extended to accommodate uncertainty in E, see [Duda 76] for details. In the example below [Duda 79], we will use a nonlinear function of the change in probability of E as a weighting factor to obtain the new odds.

The approach is to linearly interpolate between two known points on the plot of P(H|E) vs. P(E). One known point is P(H|E) when E is certain, and for the other

we use the priors for both P(H) and P(E). The corresponding values in the odds updating formula at these two points is that (1) when E is known to be true, the new odds equals (LS)*(old odds), and (2) the case where we have no new evidence, for which the new odds equals the old odds (the case of the priors).

PROSPECTOR Probability Update Computations. The relationships used in the updating computation given below are:

- Probability = odds/(1 + odds)
- Odds = probability/(1 − probability)
- New odds = old odds * likelihood ratio

The rules that will be used are given below. (Abbreviations will be used, e.g., SMIR for "suggested morphology of igneous rocks," to shorten the exposition; LS = likelihood ratio.)

- IF INTRUSIVE BRECCIAS THEN SUGGESTIVE MORPHOLOGY OF IGNEOUS ROCKS (SMIR) WITH LS = 20.
- IF SMIR THEN HYPABYSSAL REGIONAL ENVIRONMENT (HYPE) WITH LS = 300.
- IF HYPE THEN FAVORABLE LEVEL OF EROSION (FLE) WITH LS = 200.

The system begins with the following *a priori* probabilities: SMIR = 0.03, HYPE = 0.01, and FLE = 0.005. If the user indicates certainty for INTRUSIVE BRECCIAS, the following probability updating takes place:

1. SMIR odds = 0.03/(1 − 0.03)
   = 0.031
   Revised SMIR
   odds = 20*(0.031)
   = 0.62
   (The LS for the INTRUSIVE BRECCIAS multiplies the SMIR odds.)

   Revised SMIR
   prob. = 0.62/(1 + 0.62)
   = 0.38

2. HYPE odds = 0.01/(1 − 0.01)
   = 0.0101
   For a weighting factor of 0.36, the revised HYPE
   odds = 0.0101*300*0.36
   = 1.09

   (The HYPE odds have been increased by the LS of 300, weighted by a function of the degree to which SMIR has increased from its prior probability.)

   Revised HYPE
   prob. = 1.09/(1 + 1.09)
   = 0.52

3. FLE odds = 0.005/(1 − 0.005)
   = 0.005
   For a weighting factor of 0.515, the revised FLE
   odds = 0.005*200*0.515
   = 0.52

   Revised FLE
   prob. = 0.52/(1 + 0.52)
   = 0.34

Thus, the user indicating certainty for INTRUSIVE BRECCAS has increased the probability of SMIR from 0.03 to 0.38; of HYPE from 0.01 to 0.52; and of FLE from 0.005 to 0.34. The propagation of probability updates continues in this manner throughout the network.

Part Three

Perception
(Vision)

Intelligence is a natural phenomenon. It developed in response to the requirement of living systems to predict changes in their environment—both as a result of their own actions, as well as those due to external agents and natural processes.

In this book, we discuss intelligence from two perspectives: cognition and (visual) perception. Cognition, covered in the preceding portion of the book, includes the general symbolic machinery which provides a basis for reasoning, planning and communication.

Visual perception, directly concerned with modeling the environment based on sensory information, is discussed in the following two chapters.

It might appear that cognition and perception are two different aspects of the same set of processes: cognition concerned with the nature of the reasoning mechanisms, and perception concerned with their application to modeling and understanding the external world. Unfortunately, things are not quite this simple. The propositional representations and techniques we previously discussed do not appear to be adequate to deal with the major problems of perception. On the other hand, the "iconic/isomorphic" representations that appear necessary for modeling sensor-derived data do not provide a basis for the reasoning techniques we currently understand. The story we tell in this book is far from complete.

8

Vision

Our purpose in this chapter is to explore the concept that visual perception is a form of intelligent behavior, and to examine the way in which organic vision evolved and functions. In particular we will address the following questions:

1. What is the relation between vision and intelligence?
2. Is vision a mechanical or a creative act?
3. What does it mean to "see" something; do all sighted organisms see the same world?
4. What types of visual systems has nature designed, and what universal principles underlie these designs?
5. How is the information from the eye coded into neural terms, into the language of the brain—what is the nature of the brain's description of the visual world, and how is it obtained?
6. How do context, expectations, and scene details blend together to create a perceived image—why do we see illusions; how do we perceive patterns?

THE NATURE OF ORGANIC VISION

Human vision is so effortless, we tend to forget, or possibly not even realize, that there is a difficult problem to be solved. Most people assume that the eye furnishes the brain with a copy or model of the external world. This is not so. From a set of distorted two-dimensional images projected onto the retinas of our eyes, we must create a world. The eye is just a sensor; the visual cortex of the human brain is our primary organ of vision.

Any sensory organ is an information filter that extracts only part of the total information available to it. In addition, the sensory organ necessarily forms a *representation* or physical encoding of the received information that facilitates the answering of some questions about the environment, but makes it extremely difficult or impossible to answer others. For example, an examination of the encoded information produced by the human eye reveals that at any instant of time the eye has sensed only a small part of the electromagnetic spectrum, and has extracted an image of the scene from a particular viewpoint in space (parts of the scene will be occluded and not appear in the image). There has been no partitioning of the scene into meaningful elements, but the geometrical properties and relationships of objects have been retained in a somewhat accessible form.

At lower levels in the evolutionary scale, organic eyes act less like cameras, but rather more like a set of *goal-oriented* detectors. In the case of the frog's eye, a static scene results in very little information being recorded or transmitted. Only when the frog is looking at a moving object that might be something edible or an enemy, does the frog's eye transmit significant amounts of information to its brain.

Thus, an attempt to define vision on the basis of the structure of a particular type of receptor, i.e., the organic eye, will not address the important question of how the information acquired by the eye is transformed into an interpretation of the surrounding environment. Further, the quality (faithfulness), completeness, and even the encoding of the information provided by the eyes of different organisms vary considerably. It is more appropriate to consider vision to be the process of converting sensory information into knowledge of the shape, identity, or configuration of objects in the environment. This functional, rather than structural, definition concerns itself more directly with what we would intuitively say that vision is all about. We will find that:

- The main organ of vision is the component that does the interpretation, e.g., the brain in the human, rather than the human eye that does the sensing.
- Sensory organs other than the eye can be thought of as providing *visual* information to the interpretation organ. Examples of such sensory organs are the ear of the bat, the sense of touch of a blind person, and the heat detector of a pit viper.
- The memories of past visual experiences, and *wired-in* processing machinery may have a greater influence on how a scene is interpreted than the immediate information provided by the external sense organs.

In the following sections of this chapter, we will consider vision from both structural and functional viewpoints, and we will show that vision is a *creative* rather than a *mechanical* process.

THE EVOLUTION AND PHYSIOLOGY OF ORGANIC VISION

Our purpose in this section is to provide an understanding of the architecture of organic visual systems by examining the evolution and physiology of such systems. In particular, we would like to identify universal mechanisms devised by nature, that offer a solution to the problem of visual understanding of the world.

Seeing and the Evolution of Intelligence

When a camera, a human, an insect, and a frog look at the same scene they do not *see* the same image. In its simplest sense, we can define *seeing* as the physical recording of the pattern of light energy received from the world around us. *Perception*, the interpretation of what we see, is a much more complex process, and will be discussed in following sections.

Seeing, as defined above, consists of three operations: (1) the selective gathering-in of light emanating from the outside world, (2) the projection or focusing of this light on a light sensitive (photoreceptive) surface, and (3) the conversion of the light energy into a pattern of chemical change or electrical activity that is related in some specific way to the scene from which the light originated.

Most living organisms are in continual competition for the raw materials needed to sustain life, and thus they require knowledge of their surrounding environment. However, we cannot conclude that the more information an organism can gather, the better off it is, since the acquisition of information extracts a price in energy, organizational complexity, and the possibility of malfunction. Further, the nature of what is biologically useful information differs widely across the spectrum of living things. For example, the most important aspect of the light energy impinging on a plant, or on many one-celled animals, is the direction from which the light is coming. This detection task can be accomplished by comparing the amount of light energy received on the differently oriented external surfaces of the organism; there is no need to create an *image* of the surrounding environment.

Thus, in an evolutionary sense, the first simple eyes are light-sensitive cells on the body surfaces of organisms that respond only to light intensity, or to variations in intensity. As we proceed up the animal evolutionary scale, we find specially adapted light-sensitive cells appearing in various configurations on the skin of the organisms. Sometimes the cells appear in a randomly scattered arrangement, as in the case of the earthworm, but more commonly they form special arrangements, as in the lining of a depression or pit. The pit is more useful than a flat or convex surface arrangement of cells because the pit provides protection (especially if the opening of the pit can be narrowed in the presence of intense light or other dangerous conditions), more precise directional information, and is a better shadow detector (signaling the possible approach of a predator).

The evolution of the light-sensitive pit is thus justified as a non-imaging light detector with a simple function. However, as shown in Fig. 8-1, once light passes

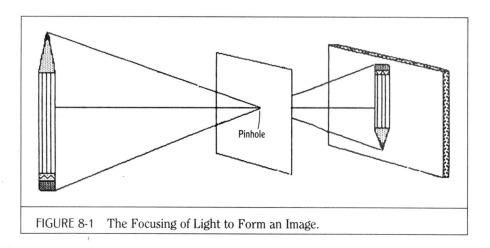

FIGURE 8-1　The Focusing of Light to Form an Image.

through a narrow opening, an image is formed. The existence of this more structured information about the environment could have provided a significant incentive for the incremental evolutionary development of a nervous system capable of interpreting and exploiting this information.[1] Thus, we see the possibility of a direct link between the evolution of vision and intelligence.

A simple organism generally cannot move very far or very fast, and is therefore primarily concerned with its local environment. The level of illumination and illumination gradient, touch, sound (vibration), smell, and taste (chemical analysis) provide all the information needed for adequate functioning. As the organism becomes physically more competent, the dimensions of the environment of its immediate concern expands. Things farther away become important, and sensors that provide such information, primarily vision in creatures that live on land and in the air, become essential. In particular, we note that vision at a distance is useful only in conjunction with a brain that is capable of planning some future course of action, as opposed to reflexive reaction to some local event. On the other hand, a highly competent brain would have little purpose in an organism with little information to process and no ability to use the results of such processing. Thus, it would appear that physical, perceptual, and intellectual competence are interdependent and must evolve as a coherent whole, rather than as independent entities.

[1]The inverted image, caused by a light-focusing eye or pit, could explain why the left brain hemisphere controls the right side of the vertebrate body, and vice versa. Assuming some primordial vertebrate had a single light-forming pit at its anterior end, the left side of this pit would receive signals from the visual field covering the right half of the organism's environment. Evolutionary pressures (as discussed in Chapter 2) would then cause the sensory processing machinery and motor control circuits for the right half of the body to develop in as close proximity as possible to the left light-sensitive portion of the pit. Subsequent evolutionary steps leading to the development of a more sophisticated brain apparently retained this initial structural plan.

Evolution and Physiology of the Organic Eye

We know that life first appeared on earth over 400 million years ago, since fossil records go back at least that far. Because of the similarities in the basic structural units of living things (e.g., all plant and animal forms are built using the same 20 amino acids linked into reasonably similar protein chains), it is likely that all life, as we now know it, had a common origin. Evolution, starting with the same raw material, has produced a small number of basic types of living things which have proved to be successful through the test of millions of years and billions of generations (see Box 2-1).

While there are probably on the order of 2 million distinct species,[2] there are probably less than a few hundred really distinct organizational plans on which these life forms are built. However, of all the varieties of life, only two basic types of imaging eyes have evolved and have come into widespread use. These two types are (1) the single lens, camera-like eye found mainly in the mollusks (especially the squid, cuttlefish, and octopus) and chordates (e.g., fish, amphibians, reptiles, birds, and mammals), and (2) the multilens compound eye found mainly in the arthropods (e.g., insects, lobsters, crabs, crayfish, spiders, centipedes).

The compound eye (Box 8-1) is functionally distinguished from the camera eye (Box 8-2) primarily with respect to achievable resolution, sensitivity, and geometric

fidelity. Even though the compound eye does not produce a single coherent image, the light tubes associated with each of the *ommatidia* dissect the image of nearby objects into a mosaic that is similar to the mosaic produced by an image on the cells of the retina of the camera eye. Thus the nerve fibers leaving the compound eye can carry image information very similar to that of the nerve fibers of the camera eye. However, the single lens of the camera eye can form a sharp retinal image of objects located almost anywhere in its field of view.

This ability to focus requires a sophisticated control mechanism that can identify something of interest in the prefocused image, and move or distort the lens to sharpen the boundary between the object of interest and the background. To take advantage of the sharp image, we need a very finely partitioned retina (each human retina has approximately 130 million light-sensitive cells, some with a diameter of one to two micrometers, which is on the order of a few wavelengths of visible light). We also need a computing capacity capable of dealing with this huge volume of data and making almost instantaneous decisions.

The less highly evolved nervous systems of the organisms employing the compound eye probably cannot use (and therefore do not need) the very high resolution required to provide precise shape information. The compound eye cannot be focused, and thus will produce a reasonable facsimile of a true image only for fairly close objects. The number of nerve cells carrying the mosaic information to the brain of the compound eye organism is typically a few thousand in contrast to

---

[2]Collections of living organisms similar in form and life history, and generally having the ability to interbreed.

the 1 million such fibers in the human optic nerve emanating from each eye.

By reasoning from structural properties of a sensing organ, it is possible to draw conclusions about what aspects of the visual information acquired by the organ are utilized. Because of the low quality of the image and lack of computing power to analyze it, the majority of the organisms possessing compound eyes probably do not rely primarily on vision in making final decisions about the identity of objects they must deal with; quite likely, such decisions are based on the chemical senses, which are highly developed in the arthropods.

Let us look at some other structural properties of organic image forming eyes, and see what they tell us about their owners. In addition to shape information, color is an important attribute for identifying or classifying objects. The mechanism by which organic eyes detect color differences is described in Appendix 8-1. The important point for our discussion is that a retinal cell that is sensitive to a particular color must of necessity ignore the light energy associated with other colors.

 BOX 8-1   Insect (Compound) Eyes

Insects have compound eyes, each eye composed of many facets (ommatidia). Each facet has its own separate lens, a small collection of nerve cells, and a single exiting nerve fiber. Each facet points in a slightly different direction resulting in a form of *mosaic vision*—each facet sees a slightly different portion of the visual field. It is not yet known how distinct or complete an image can be formed in the insect brain, but the faceted eye is well suited for perceiving rapid movement.

Typical values for the number of facets in each eye are 4000 for the housefly, 9000 for the water beetle, 3900 for the queen honeybee, 6300 for the worker honeybee, and 13,000 for the drone. Seemingly, the drone needs a large number of facets to find the queen

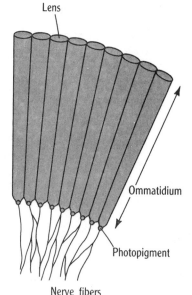

FIGURE 8-2   General Schematic of the Faceted Eye.

during the mating flight. It has also been observed that the size of the facets in the insect eye may vary significantly. For example, the dragonfly eye, which can discern moving objects several hundred feet away, shows a gradual reduction in facet size from top to bottom. This architecture, in which the upper part of the eye is used for distant vision, and the lower part for nearby vision (similar to bifocals), is designed to support its hunting pattern in which it first detects a distant flying insect, tracks, and finally captures it by scooping the prey up in a basket-shaped arrangement of its legs.

Figure 8-2 shows a general schematic of the faceted eye, indicating the interconnection of its nerve fibers. See also [Gregory 78, Hutchins 66].

Hence, the ability to see color means a loss of sensitivity in dim light, and the possibility of not detecting the movement of some object in the visual field because the moving object did not provide sufficient color contrast. The price that must be paid to see the world in color is too high for most organisms, and especially for those that use use their eyes primarily to detect, rather than identify, objects in their environment.

Most animals are color blind (e.g., the dog, cat, horse, cow, pig, sheep); of all the mammals, only man and some primates can see color.[3] Day-active birds, most reptiles, as well as all fishes that have been tested, can see color. Frogs and salamanders are color blind. Bees and a number of mollusks (squid and octopus) can see color.

The issue of sensitivity versus resolution occurs not only across species boundaries, but within the eyes of individual organisms. For example, in the human eye (as well as in many other vertebrates) there are two distinct visual systems based on two types of photoreceptor cells—*rod cells* and *cone cells*. The cone cells can extract color information, and are used for detailed vision; they are small in size, are most densely located near the center of each retina (especially in the area called the fovea), and in the foveal region they communicate with the brain through about as many ganglion cells as there are cone cells. The rod cells are two orders of magnitude more sensitive to light than the cone cells, their relative density is greatest in the peripheral regions of the retina, they are incapable of detecting color, and they work in groups which feed the brain through a much smaller number of shared ganglion cells. It appears that the main function of the rod cells is to detect anomalies (e.g., movement) in the visual field and then to allow the cone cells to do the detailed analysis via eye slewing and focusing. In very dim light, where the cone cells cannot function, the rod cells must also take over the responsibility for shape perception. Since the sensitive rod cells are most dense on the periphery of the retina, to identify an object at night, it is best not to look directly at it, but rather to look at the object out of the corner of your eye.

In regard to visual information, most insects and lower organisms are more concerned with detection than with classification. They have eyes that typically are designed for sensitivity and broad field of view, rather than precise resolution. These eyes either have large receptor cells, or rodlike networks feeding their brains through shared ganglion cells. The eyes of these insects do not focus nor are they independently movable; typically there are two compound eyes anchored to opposite sides of the head, where they monitor largely nonoverlapping fields of view.

Eye and Brain

How is the pattern of light energy projected onto the light-sensitive cells of the eye transformed into a model of the external world? Even for simple organisms, we know little of the structure of their neural machinery, and even less about the way the machinery actually functions. It would

---

While almost all mammals possess some degree of hue discrimination, this faculty plays a small role in their behavior, typically being completely dominated by the intensity component of the received light.

appear that much of the visual processing in lower organisms is carried out in neural networks located adjacent to the photoreceptive cells. As we ascend the evolutionary scale, more of this processing is shifted to the brain (a process called *encephalization* which occurs in other senses and muscular control functions as well). The human retina, for example, is an extension of the embryonic brain tis-

 BOX 8-2   The Human (Camera) Eye

The human (camera*) eye is a remarkable instrument with respect to both sensitivity and resolution. In clear air, a candle flame is just visible at a distance of ten miles; thus, 10^{-14} parts of the light produced by a single candle is sufficient to stimulate vision. The mechanical energy of a pea, falling from a height of one inch, would, if translated into luminous energy, be sufficient to give a faint impression of light to every person that ever lived [Pirenne 67]. Some of the parameters of the human visual system are:

- 120 million rod cells in each eye.
- 6 million cone cells in each eye.
- 2000 cone cells in each fovea in the region of maximum uniform density.

*Using a camera analogy to understand the operation of the human eye is an oversimplification in at least two important respects, (1) the measured performance of the eye is much better than its component specifications would permit if the eye really did behave as a camera, and (2) the eye has no shutter, and even though the scene information projected on the retina is in constant motion, our perception of the world is not blurred. The brain appears to extract information from the "optic flow" across the retina rather than by analyzing a static image.

- 1 million nerve fibers in the optic nerve exiting each eye.
- Diameter of cone cells in fovea: 1 to 3 micrometers.
- 250 million receptor cells in the two eyes vs. 250,000 independent elements in a TV picture.
- Distance from effective center of lens to fovea: 17 mm.
- Interpupillary distance: 50 to 70 mm.
- Visual angle subtended by fovea: 20 minutes of arc for region uniform maximum cone density, 1 to 2 degrees for rod-free area, 5 degrees for a 50 percent drop in visual resolution (with the arm extended, the raised thumb subtends an angle of 2 to 2.5 degrees; one minute of arc corresponds to a retinal image of five micrometers).
- Angle with respect to visual axis of eye at which rod density is maximum: 15 to 20 degrees.
- Rod cells are on the order of 500 times more sensitive to light than cone cells.
- Visible portion of the electromagnetic spectrum: 0.4 to 0.7 micrometers.
- Wavelength of maximum rod sensitivity: 0.51 micrometers (green).

- Wavelength of maximum cone sensitivity: 0.56 micrometers (orange).
- Intensity range: 10^{16} (160 decibels).
- Minimum visual angle at which points can be separately resolved: 0.5 to 2 seconds of arc for alignment of lines (0.04 to 0.16 micrometer, less than 10% of the diameter of the smallest foveal cell); 10 to 60 seconds for dots (range of values is due to disagreement across reference sources). If the pupil is 3 mm in diameter and a 0.55-micrometer light is used, the image of a point will produce a central circle of 3.7 micrometers on the retina. This would mean that the illumination from two points 25 to 30 seconds apart would overlap.
- Object distance from eye for stereoscopic depth perception: 10 inches to 1500 feet (1500 feet corresponds to a retinal disparity of approximately 30 seconds of arc).
- Involuntary eye movements: 10 to 15 seconds of arc for tremor; slow drifts of up to 5 minutes of arc.

Figure 8-3 shows the anatomy and nervous organization of the human eye.

sue, whereas the lens of the eye develops from embryonic skin tissue.

How then is the information from the eyes coded into neural terms—into the language of the brain—and then interpreted? When light strikes the retina, the decomposition (bleaching) of pigments in the rods and cones results in electrical activity, which is integrated in the bipolar and ganglion cells comprising the sixth and eighth levels of the ten-layer system of the retina (Fig. 8-3). As discussed in Chapter 2, the ganglion cells of the eye feed the brain with visual information coded into chains of electrical pulses. The rate of "firing" of the cells is proportional to the logarithm of the intensity of the original stimulation (Fechner's law). Other attributes of the illumination, such as color, are determined by which cells are firing. For example, as indicated in Appendix 8-1, the cone cells are differentially sensitive to the red, green, and blue components of the illumination because of differences in the chemical composition of their photosensitive pigments; these cells are intermixed in the fovea, and their relative excitation provides the brain with information about the color of the objects being viewed.

As depicted schematically in Fig. 8-4, the human retina is effectively divided vertically down the middle; the nerve fibers from the left half of each retina send information about the right half of the visual field to the *striate cortex* in the left occipital lobe of the brain. Similarly, the right half of each retina sends information about the left half of the visual field to the right striate cortex. The role played by the *lateral geniculate body* is not currently understood—it appears to simply relay the information it receives.

(However, there is some evidence that it is functionally involved in the processing of color information.)

The nerve fibers from the eye, reaching the striate cortex, preserve the topology and much of the geometry of the imaged scene information; a portion of the striate cortex, called the *visual projection area*, is in approximate one-to-one spatial correspondence with the retina. Stimulation of nerve cells in this projection area by a weak electric current causes the subject to *see* elementary visual events, such as colored spots or flashes of light, in the expected location of the visual field. Lesions in the projection area lead to *blind spots* in the visual field consistent with the retina-to-cortex mapping, although some pattern vision is left intact. For example, contours of perceived objects are completed over blind spots.

In the human, the region of the striate cortex immediately surrounding the visual projection area is called the *visual association area*. Electrical stimulation of cells in the association area give rise to complex recognizable visual hallucinations (images of known objects or even meaningful action sequences). Local lesions of this part of the occipital cortex neither reduce visual acuity nor lead to loss of any portion of the visual field; the essential symptom associated with such lesions is disturbance of the perception of complete visual complexes, the inability to combine individual impressions into complete patterns, and the inability to recognize complex objects or their pictorial representations. For example, some patients with visual association area lesions can describe individual parts of objects and can reproduce their outlines accu-

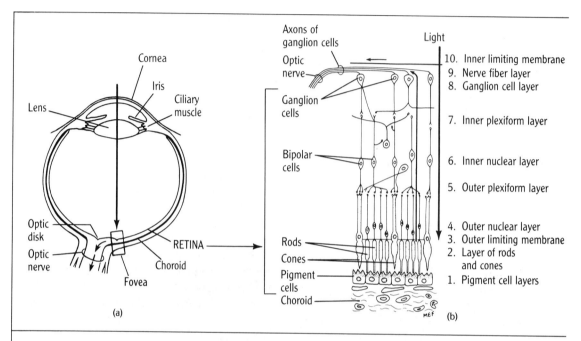

FIGURE 8-3

From Retina to Optic Nerve: the Conversion of Light Signals to Nerve Impulses.

(a) Anatomy of the human eye. The *optic disc* forms a blind spot where nerve fibers leave the eye to form the *optic nerve*. The *ciliary muscle* controls the focus of the *lens*. The pupil is the opening at the center of the *iris*. (b) Neural organization of the retina. The cellular arrangement in the retina appears to form ten layers, when viewed by light microscopy, numbered 1 through 10 from the innermost pigment layer to the outermost fiber layer. Light rays pass through the neural layer to reach the rod and cones. Nerve impulses are propagated in the opposite direction from the rods and cones to the optic nerve. [(a) and (b) from E. L. Weinreb. *Anatomy and Physiology*. Addison-Wesley, Reading, Mass., 1984, p. 246, with permission.] (c) Distribution of rod and cones in the human eye. (d) Diagrammatic representation of the photoreceptor cells showing the organelles as viewed by electron microscopy. (From E. L. Weinreb. *Anatomy and Physiology*. Addison-Wesley, Reading, Mass., 1984, p.247 with permission.) (e) The extrinsic muscles of the eye viewed from above. (From A. P. Spence and E. B. Mason. *Human Anatomy and Physiology*, 2nd edition. Benjamin Cummings, Menlo Park, Calif., 1983, p. 393 with permission.)

rately, yet are unable to recognize the objects as a whole; other patients are unable to see more than one object at a time in the visual field.

The integration of perception with the cognitive functions in the human is demonstrated in patients with lesions in the *parieto-occipital* regions of the brain (i.e., the regions physically located between the primary vision and speech centers). Such patients experience great difficulty in attempting to perform tasks involving spatial relationships. For example, even though they think they understand a task such as "Draw a triangle below a circle," they cannot appreciate

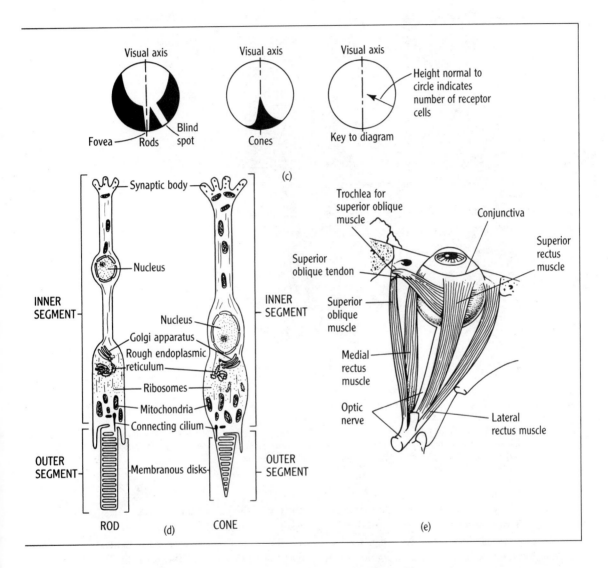

the difference between this task and that of drawing the circle below the triangle; they typically will draw the figures in the sequential order in which they are given in the instructions. The perception of embedded figures is affected by lesions almost anywhere in the cortex, although these effects are most pronounced when the lesions occur in the speech association areas (left temporal and parietal lobes). Injury to the parietal lobes can result in right-left reversals, copying problems, and in left visual field distortions. Right temporal lobe lesions appear to interfere with the understanding of complex pictorial material.

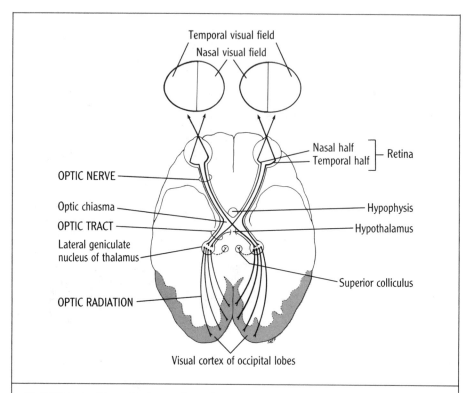

FIGURE 8-4   Nerve Pathways from the Retina to the Visual Cortex of the Brain.

Nerve fibers from the right side of each retina pass to the right side of the brain; nerve fibers from the left side of each retina pass to the left side of the brain. (From E. L. Weinreb. *Anatomy and Physiology*. Addison-Wesley, Reading, Mass., 1984, p. 254, with permission.)

Any defect of the human cortex leads to imperfect perception and reproduction of pictorial objects. On the other hand, the removal of the entire forebrain in fish or birds appears to have little effect on their visual discrimination. As in man, the destruction of the visual cortex in adult mammals leads to complete loss of pattern vision, but this is not true for young animals. For example, young cats in whom the striate cortex is completely destroyed show unimpaired performance on all visual tasks; obviously, some other portion of the cat's brain is capable of assuming the visual function.

In lower animals, subcortical centers play the major role in pattern vision. The *superior colliculus*, for instance, is the most important visual center in fish and amphibians. As we move up the evolutionary scale, the visual function is first concentrated almost completely in the striate cortex of the occipital lobe, as in the rat, and finally spreads out over the whole cortex of the brain when we reach the evolutionary level of the monkey.

How do the neural circuits of the brain produce its perceptions of the world? There is very little we can say about the relationship between brain architecture and the performance of high-level functions, but we know a little about how some of the more elementary neural processing is accomplished. In particular, there are a few processing tricks that nature has discovered that are so important that we find them employed in almost all eyes (or visual systems) of all species. One of these is *lateral inhibition* (or *center-surround inhibition*) for detecting when something different or unusual has occurred in the visual field; this technique is discussed in Box 8-3. At a less detailed level, we also have some insight into how

---

BOX 8-3 Lateral Inhibition and Adaptation—The Enhancement of Contract in Space and Time

Most of the biologically important information about the surrounding environment provided by our senses remains essentially constant from one instant to the next. It would be inefficient for our sensory systems to keep telling us things we already know, and indeed, this does not happen: animal nervous tissue is designed so that its response diminishes, and even stops, with repeated stimulation. This process, called adaptation, can be dramatically demonstrated by using a special apparatus to cause an image to be projected onto a fixed location on the retina (normally, even a static scene would move around on the retina due to the constant movement of the eye). When such "stabilized" images are produced, they quickly disappear from conscious perception. Sometimes, coherent meaningful segments of the visual field will reappear, only to fade out again. This proves that adaptation is occurring not only in the retinal tissue, but also at higher levels in the brain.

Most sensory tissue (retina of the eye, cochlea of the ear, pressure-sensitive nerves of the skin), and even portions of the brain (cerebellar and cerebral cortex), is organized so that stimulation of any given location produces inhibition in the surrounding nerve fibers. It is shown (next chapter) that the effect of this structural organization of nervous tissue, called *lateral inhibition*, is to (mathematically) differentiate the signals being processed. In the case of visual information, such (spatial) differentiation causes gradual changes in the contrast between an object and its background to become more abrupt, thus enhancing the ability of the visual system to detect objects of interest in the visual field. For example, if

FIGURE 8-5
Intensity Step Wedge Used to Demonstrate Lateral Inhibition.

you align two sheets of paper so that only a narrow slit is visible along the length of the intensity step wedge shown in Fig. 8-5, and count the number of regions which appear to have different intensities, this number will be less than that obtained when the full step wedge is visible. Lateral inhibition is an area effect, and peering through the narrow slit prevents it from operating; local contrast is insufficient to allow us to see all the intensity boundaries when lateral inhibition is suppressed.

In human perception, the contrast enhancing effect of lateral inhibition produces what are called *Mach bands*. If a sharp shadow is produced on a flat surface, a thin bright band will appear to parallel the shadow line on the illuminated side, and a corresponding dark band on the occluded side. These bands are not physically present, but are subjective phenomena—essentially "overshoot" and "undershoot" caused by our neural circuits mathematically differentiating the step discontinuity in illumination.

BOX 8-4 Feature Detection and the Frog's Eye

In Appendix 8-2 we note that neural circuits in the visual cortex of the human brain appear to detect generic image features, such as oriented line segments. In contrast, lower organisms tend to search directly for goal-specific features; the corresponding computation is often carried out by neural networks in the sensing organ. The frog's eye provides a good example.

In 1953, Barlow [Barlow 53] found that one particular type of ganglion cell in the frog's retina was excited when a black disk, subtending a degree or so of arc, was moved rapidly to and fro within the receptor field. This caused a vigorous discharge that could be maintained as long as the movement continued.

Barlow suggested that these retinal neurons were "bug detectors" and that the frog's feeding responses might partially originate in the retina.

A classic work on the physiological basis of information extraction from a visual image was by Lettvin et al [Lettvin 59]. They found that the frog eye uses four different types of neural structure to extract patterns of information from the visual signal: (1) edge detectors that respond strongly to the border between light and dark regions; (2) moving contrast detectors that respond when an edge moves; (3) dimming detectors that respond when the overall illumination is lowered; and (4) convex edge detec-

tors that react when a small dark, roughly circular object moves in the field of vision. The response of this detector increases as the object moves steadily closer to the frog.

The convex edge detector provides the visual information used by the frog to detect and catch flies. Note that this detector requires motion: a dead fly is of no interest to the frog.

Similar experiments were subsequently carried out with higher animals. However, by the 1970s it was realized that in higher organisms, visual perception is considerably more than a collection of specialized neural feature detectors.

---

stereoscopic vision works (Appendix 8-2) and how, at least in some animals, features or attributes of perceived objects are computed (Box 8-4).

THE PSYCHOLOGY OF VISION

Our purpose in this section is to explore the nature of the algorithmic techniques employed by organic visual systems through an examination of their successes and failures in interpreting both natural and contrived images.

Perceiving the Visual World: Recognizing Patterns

Humans and a few other organisms live in a world of shape and color. We perceive

ourselves as moving through a stationary environment, rather than ourselves being stationary and the surrounding environment as moving. We can recognize and actually perceive common objects as having an expected shape, even though we view them from different distances, orientations, and under unknown lighting conditions. Thus, if we look obliquely at a circle drawn on a flat surface, we see the expected circular shape, even though the image projected onto our retina is an ellipse, (Fig. 8-6). We can adjust to more than ten orders of magnitude of light intensity variation without conscious awareness, and are not bothered by shadows or partial occlusions. It is obvious that perception is not the inevitable result of a set of stimulus patterns, but rather a best interpretation of sensory data based on the past experience of both the organism and its ancestors. While the senses do not directly give us a faithful model of the world, they do, however, provide evidence for checking hypotheses about the nature of our surrounding environment. Perhaps the most concise way of summing up our visual capability is that, except in the case of physical injury, it appears to operate flawlessly, spontaneously, and without surprises (or indeed, we are both shocked and surprised).

Of the full range of perceptual skills needed to completely model the world, we will limit our discussion in this section to the problem of recognizing patterns, and of necessity, our discussion will be descriptive rather than explanatory.

At the highest levels of performance, shape recognition involves the ability to ignore variations in size, brightness, position, and orientation. It is known, for example, that if a person (or animal) learns to identify a shape using one part of his retina, he is able to identify the same shape when it is presented to other parts of the retina, or even the other eye. On the other hand, when the brightness of an object and its background are inverted, even humans are sometimes unable to recognize the object. Many species (e.g., human, rat) can recognize a shape from its outline, while others (e.g., octopus) have great difficulty in recognizing the outline if they have been trained to recognize the filled-in shape.

When a rat or octopus is trained to discriminate between a horizontally elongated rectangle, and a square with sides equal to the height of the rectangle, and is shown the rectangle rotated by 90 degrees, it treats the rotated rectangle as if it were the square. After being trained with a square and a triangle, an octopus responds to a diamond (45-degree rotation of the square) as if it were the triangle. Humans have great difficulty recognizing faces presented upside-down.

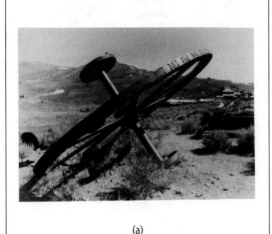

(a)

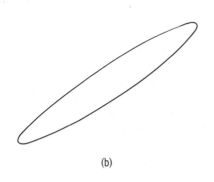

(b)

FIGURE 8-6
Shape Constancy—an Ellipse Seen as a Circle.

(a) Photograph of a wheel (photo courtesy of O. Firschein).
(b) Actual shape of wheel as it appears in the photograph.

The inability of some higher organisms to deal with such apparently simple variations as a 90- or 180-degree rotation, seems, at first, to be rather strange. After all, there are almost trivial mechanical procedures that could undo such a variation. One possibility is that while the human visual system can generally decompose (partition) the visual field into meaningful subunits (see below), most other organisms may not have this ability. If a visual system cannot extract and manipulate portions of an image, then the *normalization* operations needed for robust pattern vision become almost hopelessly complex, and impossible to implement.

We know that even simple organisms have the ability to recognize patterns. (The development of vision in infants is discussed in Box 8-5.) For example, bees and ants utilize visual landmarks in finding their way back to the nest. The wasp *Philanthus* locates the entrance to its nest by the arrangement of visual markings and objects around it; bees can recognize their hive by colored marks at the entrance, and can determine if the colors have the proper spatial arrangement when approaching the hive from an arbitrary direction. However, bees cannot distinguish among geometrical shapes (triangle, square, circle, ellipse), but appear in such cases to be able to respond only to some gross measure of the degree to which the figure is branchy (vs. solid) or divided up into parts (Fig. 8-7).

In discussing pattern vision, we have tended to talk about it as if it were a single integrated function in any given organism. This is an oversimplification—biologically important visual tasks are often handled by special mechanisms. For

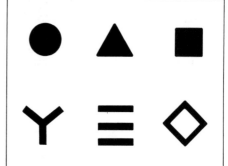

FIGURE 8-7
Perception of Shape by the Bee.

For the bee, figures of the upper row are indistinguishable from one another. The same applies to the lower row. But the bee readily distinguishes figures of the lower row from those of the upper row. (After V. B. Wigglesworth. *The Principles of Insect Physiology*, p. 207.)

example, in the human, visual pattern perception is not performed uniformly for all tasks. It appears that the human brain has distinct procedures for processing visual information about faces—a task of great biological importance.

In lower organisms, the ability to recognize hereditary prey, or a mate, appears to be carried out with a sophistication orders of magnitude beyond that exhibited for abstract patterns. For example, the *Pepsis* wasps hunt tarantulas as food for their larvae (their own food consists of flower nectar). Only the female hunts, and she is a specialist—each species of wasp hunts only one species of tarantula. She searches for her prey in desertlike terrain, even locating and entering the tarantula's underground tunnels or burrows. In order to achieve her purpose, she must force the tarantula (a very large and fierce hunter itself) over on its back and sting it in the soft membrane between the basal joints. The almost always successful wasp now digs a sloping foot-long tunnel of just the right size to hold the paralyzed tarantula, drags the tarantula into this burrow, cements her eggs to its abdomen, and then seals the

 BOX 8-5 Development of Vision in Infants

To study infant perception, the experimenter exposes the child to visual stimulation and notes the reaction such as eye movements, eye fixations, sucking, head turning, and reaching. Although the design of experiments using infant subjects has improved in recent years, there is still ambiguity in the results concerning inborn versus acquired capabilities and this leads to controversy among the various theories of early perception. Some of the difficulty lies in the fact that important parts of the visual system are not fully developed at birth. This includes the retina, the lateral geniculate nucleus, and the visual cortex. Many of the changes in early development therefore reflect maturation of the neural system, particularly the visual cortex. The other problem in carrying out experiments is that the infant cannot be kept in a controlled environment, and it is therefore difficult to isolate characteristics that are under investigation. A good review of the field is given in Banks and Salapatek [Banks 83] and in Flavell [Flavell 85]; some of the highlights are given below.

Newborn infants. Newborn acuity is very poor (about 20/600), as is contrast sensitivity, both improving considerably during the first 6 months. Infants prefer to fixate some patterns over others, and repetitive patterns over random ones, but there is no good theory as to why one is preferred over another. Faces are preferred over nonsense patterns of equal contour density, and familiar faces are preferred over unfamiliar ones [Salapatek 77]. Newborns do not scan a figure very extensively; their gaze gets captured by a single feature or part of a figure.

2–3 months. By 3 months of age, the scanning limitations are overcome. Infants can distinguish patterns on the basis of their shape and form. By 2 months of age infants can make some color discrimination, and by 3 months color vision is quite good, and there is some improvement in color discrimination after that. Three month old subjects can perceive touching objects as two objects rather than one. There is some suggestion that they react to "looming objects," objects that appear to move toward them suddenly [Yonas 81].

4–6 months. "Biological motion," caused by luminous spots placed on the hip, arm joints, and leg joints of a person running in place in a darkened room is preferred to random motion of the spots [Fox 82]. Biological motion right side up is preferred to upside down biological motion.

A "visual cliff" consists of a horizontal sheet of glass resting just above a patterned surface on one side and spanning a deep depression on the other side. Prelocomotive babies (younger than 7 months) when slowly lowered toward the glass put out their hands just prior to touchdown on the shallow side but not on the deep side [Svedja 79], showing that they perceive the depth.

Spelke [Spelke 82] showed that infants of 4 months perceive as one continuous object a reciprocating rod whose center is hidden by a block. This holds even if the two visible parts of the partially occluded object differ from one another in size, shape, color, texture, and alignment.

In the postinfancy period, the child develops the ability to attend selectively to wanted information in the sensed input, while tuning out or disregarding unwanted information [Flavell 85].

tunnel with soil and sand. The wasp grub feeds on the tarantula, and on the order of a year later emerges from the burrow as an adult wasp. The searching, fighting, and building activities described above appear to require perceptual abilities equal to almost any capability of the human visual system—except that such perceptual behavior in the wasp is not general; for most other visual tasks its behavior has the various limitations mentioned earlier.

Perceptual Organization

Everything we see, we see for the first time. While parts of a scene may correspond to objects we have some previous acquaintance with, we almost never see the same objects in the same configuration under the same lighting conditions from the same perspective in space. Unless we can decompose or partition a scene into coherent and independently recognizable entities, the complexity of natural scenes would seem to render human-type vision impossible.

How can we partition a scene into independent components without already knowing what might be present? If we were only searching for a few well-known objects, we might attempt to exhaustively determine if each of the objects were present at each possible location in the visual field. However, there are probably thousands of objects that can appear in an almost infinite variety of configurations and orientations that we can recognize; exhaustive matching against stored models is not a reasonable explanation of human perception.

It is largely agreed that there must be a set of generic criteria, applied independently of scene content, that underlies the procedures discovered by nature for partitioning the visual field. Discontinuities in scene properties (e.g., distance, material composition, motion) are the most likely clues as to where partitions should be inserted. A significant portion of the work in computational vision (next chapter) is devoted to the partitioning or perceptual organization problem, the critical issue being that of relating image intensity variations to physical discontinuities in the scene.

Psychologists have also attempted to discover the *laws* underlying the partitioning decisions made by the human visual system. One of the earliest and intuitively most acceptable collections of such laws was proposed by Wertheimer in 1923 and elaborated by Koffka in 1935. These *gestalt laws* include:

- **The Law of Proximity.** Stimulus elements that are close together tend to be perceived as a group (Fig. 8-8a).

- **The Law of Similarity.** Similar stimuli tend to be grouped; this tendency can even dominate grouping due to proximity (Fig. 8-8b).

- **The Law of Closure.** Stimuli tend to be grouped into complete figures (Fig. 8-8c).

- **The Law of Good Continuation.** Stimuli tend to be grouped so as to minimize change or discontinuity (Fig. 8-8d).

- **The Law of Symmetry.** Regions bounded by symmetrical boarders tend to be perceived as coherent figures (Fig. 8-8e).

- **The Law of Simplicity.** Ambiguous stimuli tend to be resolved in favor of the simplest alternative. For example, if

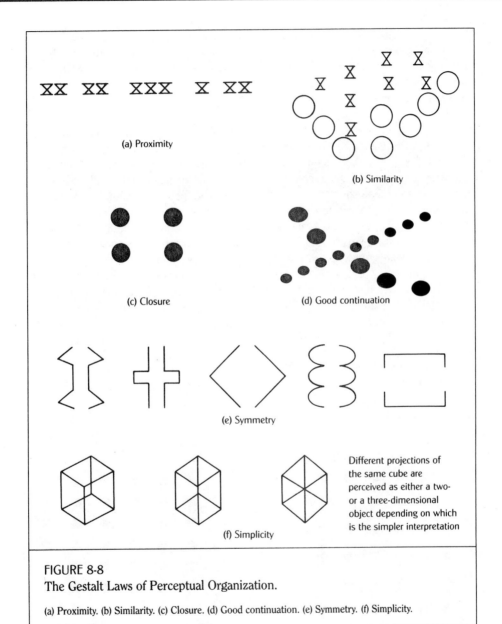

FIGURE 8-8
The Gestalt Laws of Perceptual Organization.

(a) Proximity. (b) Similarity. (c) Closure. (d) Good continuation. (e) Symmetry. (f) Simplicity.

fewer different angles and line lengths are required to describe a figure as three-dimensional, the observer will select this alternative over the two-dimensional interpretation (Fig. 8-8f).

• **The Law of Common Fate.** If a group of dots were moving with uniform velocity through a field of similar though stationary dots, the moving dots would be perceived as a coherent group.

None of these laws are as simple as they first appear. For example, proximity grouping seems to be based on measurements in perceived space (as opposed to proximity measured by retinal distance) and is influenced by prior experience as demonstrated in Fig. 8-9.

A major problem with the above set of gestalt laws is that there is no explanation as to the purpose they serve, or how the given criteria contribute toward achieving the intended purpose. It is possible to argue that all perceptual decisions are implied explanations of how sensed data relates to scene content. As an explanation, any partitioning decision must satisfy criterion for believability—i.e., completeness (explaining "all" the data), stability (consistency of explanation), and limited complexity (economy of explanation). This alternative viewpoint does not conflict with the gestalt laws, but rather provides a broader basis for understanding them. Additional ideas about the nature of perceptual organization, such as the existence of a primitive perceptual vocabulary and a "preattentive visual system" are discussed in Chapter 9.

Visual Illusions

To understand how something works, we often have to stress it, take it apart, or even break it. How can we discover the nature of the algorithms employed by organic (especially human) visual systems? Examining neurologic structure in an attempt to deduce function is a hopeless task for anything other than the simplest types of mechanical or reflex mechanisms. Introspection is unreliable, available only in the human, and even here, language is not always suitable for describing perception or intent. Further, the operations of many (if not most) visual functions are not accessible to introspection.

Observation of performance suffers from two defects—it is not always clear that the organism and the experimenter have the same task in mind (or that the

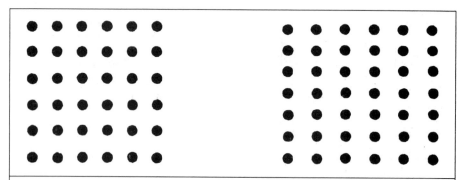

FIGURE 8-9   Proximity Grouping Can Be Altered by Recent Experience.

When first viewed, the grouping of the dots on the left is ambiguous. After looking at the array on the right for one or two minutes, however, the array on the left appears to be grouped into rows.

organism is seriously interested in performing the task). Furthermore, it takes a great deal of ingenuity to design a task in which performance will fully explain the underlying algorithms. Visual illusions have provided much of the information on which theories of the functioning of organic visual systems are based. What are visual illusions, and why are they so fascinating?

In a sense, everything we perceive is an illusion since we can never exactly recreate objective reality through our senses. The term "illusion" is reserved for those situations in which our perceptions differ markedly from what we know corresponds to the actual physical situation. Further, there must be no reason to believe that processing involved in the perception of an illusion is in any way unusual or unique; generally the causative factor should be some circumstance associated with the scene, or the context under which it is viewed. Illusions are fascinating because we expect our sense of vision to be infallible (seeing is believing). We are not surprised when our muscles fail to do exactly what we want, and we know that we can misinterpret the direction of a sound, or can confuse a very hot object with a cold one via our sense of touch, but we almost never question our visual decisions—in fact, we routinely trust our lives to them. How is it possible then, that we are so readily misled by visual illusions, even when we know what the true situation is?

The most remarkable aspect of human vision is not that it is subject to failure, but rather how accurate it is in spite of its limited and distorted inputs. The human eye is far from a perfect instru-

ment; it distorts the image that it projects onto the retina (even under the best conditions) because of its finite aperture, out-of-round lens and cornea, different index of refraction at different wavelengths, and imperfect focusing machinery. It is obvious that there are a number of relatively independent problems that the visual system must deal with, and it is not unreasonable to assume that illusions are due to a failure of one or more of the mechanisms set up to deal with these problems. It is very unlikely that a single mechanism underlies all illusions. In particular, the visual system is able to compensate for the various distortions introduced by the limitations of the imaging system of the eye.

- It can compensate for the change in appearance of objects due to the projective transformation inherent in even a perfect camera-type imaging system.
- It can resolve the ambiguity resulting from the projection of the three-dimensional world onto a two-dimensional retina.
- It can provide true information about surface reflectance and color under a wide variety of illumination conditions.
- It can provide a stable frame of reference and an unblurred image, even when the eye is constantly in motion.

Under normal circumstances, while any one of these compensating functions might fail, there appears to be enough redundancy to allow a very clever integrating system to detect and correct the error so that the final perception is faithful to the physical situation. Illusions are produced when we are presented with an impoverished visual environment that eliminates the normal redundancy, and overloads or deliberately misinforms a single functional system.

Thus, the Ponzo illusion (Fig. 8-10) appears to be due to the fact that we are interpreting what is really a two-dimensional picture as if it were a three-dimensional object. This implies that we have built-in machinery for automatically compensating for the shrinking of the image of an object with increasing distance: something that is perceived (via other processing channels in the visual system) to be located further away, but projects onto the retina with the same length as something nearby, is judged to be larger.

In the Necker cube (Fig. 8-11), two configurations—given face in front, given face in back—are reasonable interpretations of the imaged data, and there are no cues to cause one interpretation to dominate. Therefore, the perceptual system appears to formulate and offer us in turn these alternative hypotheses. This is an indication of a reasoning process carried

FIGURE 8-10
The Ponzo Illusion: Apparent Depth Alters Size Perception.

A feature that is near the narrowing end of the exterior lines gets expanded and looks longer than it would if placed below, where the lines widen. The perspective effect induced by the converging lines causes our visual system to make size corrections for the three-dimensional phenomenon of change in size with distance. (Photo courtesy of O. Firschein.)

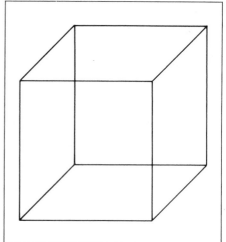

FIGURE 8-11
Perceptual Ambiguity (Multistable Perception).

This figure alternates in depth: a face of the cube sometimes appears as the *front*, and sometimes as the *back* face. We can think of these ways of seeing the figure as the result of alternative perceptual *hypotheses*. The visual system entertains alternative hypotheses, and will settle for one solution only when there are no obvious alternatives.

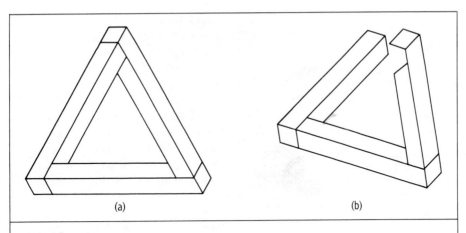

FIGURE 8-12
The "Impossible" Triangle.

(a) A seemingly impossible three-dimensional object. (b) The same three-dimensional "triangle" from a slightly different view, showing that it is possible after all.

out by the perceptual system at a level below our conscious awareness.

In the *impossible* triangle (Fig. 8-12) we have two separate phenomena. First, when certain visual cues are present, we assume we are viewing a coherent object in three-dimensional space. Once we have made this assumption, our visual system assumes that the object we are viewing is in *general position*; that is, a slight change in our viewing position should leave our basic perception of the object unchanged. This second assumption appears to be hard-wired into our processing—even when we know the assumption is invalid for a given situation, we cannot avoid invoking it. There are undoubtedly other such hard-wired assumptions that nature has decided are good bets to make in general, even if there are occasional exceptions to their validity.

Finally, in the case of the subjective contour (Fig. 8-13), we use circumstantial evidence (e.g., gaps in the black circles) to deduce the presence of an occluding object. Once this decision has been made, other "channels" in the visual system alter our perceived interpretation of intensities, distance, etc., to make the complete interpretation a consistent one. This again shows the existence of a system capable of deductive reasoning and consistency maintenance operating below the level of our conscious awareness. Vision is not the simple task our introspection tells us about.

Visual Thinking, Visual Memory, and Cultural Factors

We briefly discuss three phenomena related to vision; (1) visual thinking, the use of images to aid the reasoning process;

FIGURE 8-13   Subjective Contours.

The white square that appears to be occluding the black circles is an illusion—it is actually the same intensity as the background.

(2) visual memory, the use of visual images for remembering; and (3) pictorial perception and culture, the effect of our culture in teaching us how to understand pictures.

Visual Thinking.   Some people believe that all thinking is basically perceptual in nature, and that the ancient dichotomy between seeing and thinking, between perceiving and reasoning, is false and misleading. In fact, some feel that visual thinking is a skill that can be learned, and that it improves with practice (see [Arnheim 69]). In Chapter 3 we described the visual thinking used by the physicist Richard Feynman, and by Friedrich Kekule, the chemist who discovered the structure of the benzene ring in a dream.

Visual Memory.   It has been known since the time of the Greeks that a list of objects can be effectively memorized if they are set in the context of a vivid visual scene. The more vivid the scene, the better the objects are remembered. Typically, a reference set of images is used that is easy to remember, and that has a natural order. One such reference set using the numbers from one to ten is presented in Box 8-6. Another approach uses a mental traverse through a place known to the user, for example, a walk through one's house. Objects to be remembered are vividly associated with the reference images. Recall then consists of summoning up the reference images and remembering the object associated with each. The implication here is that we employ distinct mechanisms (and representations) for both symbolic and for iconic information, and that our storage and recall ability for iconic information is significantly better than that available for symbolic information.

Pictorial Perception and Culture.   A picture is a pattern of lines and shaded areas on a flat surface that depicts some aspect of the real world. The ability to recognize objects in pictures is so common in most cultures that it is often taken for granted that such recognition is universal in man. Experiments described by Deregowski [Deregowski 74] show that people of one culture perceive a picture differently from people of another, and that the perception of pictures calls for some form of learning.

Conventions for depicting spatial arrangements of three-dimensional objects in a flat plane can give rise to difficulties in perception. These conventions give the observer depth cues that tell him the objects are not all the same distance from him. Inability to interpret such cues is bound to lead to misunderstanding of the picture as a whole. For example, a typical cue is given when the larger of two known objects is drawn considerably smaller to indicate that it is farther away. Another cue is overlap, in which portions of nearer objects overlap and obscure portions of objects that are farther away. A third cue is perspective, the convergence of lines known to be parallel to suggest distance. In experiments carried out in many parts of Africa, it was found that both children and adults found it difficult to perceive depth in such pictorial material.

Some cultures use pictures that depict the essential characteristics of an object even if these characteristics cannot be seen from a single viewpoint. In such *split drawings*, an elephant appears in a top view with its four legs spread out, two on each side (Fig. 8-14). This split type of drawing to represent three-dimensional objects appears, and has been developed to a high artistic level, in various cultures. It is used by children in all cultures, even in those cultures where the style is considered manifestly wrong by adults.

 ## BOX 8-6 A Memory Technique based on Images

The task of memorizing a list of thirty digits printed on a piece of paper, after a few seconds of inspection, would probably be impossible for all but a very small number of people. On the other hand, an aerial picture of the Golden Gate Bridge could easily be memorized so that at some future time it could be distinguished from a variety of other scenes. It seems clear that the means by which we try to remember the information required for these two visual tasks is considerably different. In the case of the numerals, our memorization is primarily based on assigning a specific name, the name of the numeral, to each depicted object. In the case of the natural scene, our memory is primarily that of a picture. This box indicates how names of objects can be remembered by connecting them to a set of reference images.

A set of ten reference images for use in memorization and recall are contained in the following rhyme. The images are easy to remember because the name of each image rhymes with its corresponding number in the sequence:

One is a bun

Three is a tree

Two is a shoe

Four is a door

Five is a hive

Seven is heaven

Nine is wine

Six is a stick

Eight is a gate

Ten is a hen.

To remember a shopping list of (1) eggs, (2) milk, (3) meat, and (4) apples, we would make vivid associations with the first four reference images. The more vivid the association, the stronger the retention of the item will be: (1) the egg has been crushed by the bun and sticky egg yolk is flowing out of the bun; (2) milk has been poured into a shoe and is running out of the eyelets of the shoe; (3) meat is hanging from the branches of a tree. It smells bad and the flies are buzzing around it; and (4) apples have been thrown at the door. They have left a trail of apple slime on the door, and there is apple mush in front of the door.

This memory technique not only enhances our ability to memorize a list of items, but it also permits us direct access to the nth item on the list. For example, to remember the third term, "three is a tree," we simply recall the image associated with the tree.

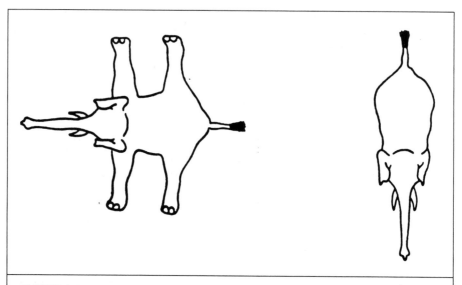

FIGURE 8-14
Conventions for the Two-Dimensional Representation of Three-Dimensional
Objects are Culture-Specific.

Split-elephant drawing (left) was generally preferred by African children and adults to the top view
perspective drawing (right). (From J. B. Deregowski, in: *Image, Object, and Illusion.* W. H. Freeman.
San Francisco, Calif., 1974, with permission.)

DISCUSSION

What distinguishes living from inanimate
objects? In one sense, inanimate objects
respond to the current state of the universe; that is, their behavior can be simply
described by reference to the *current*
values of some set of physical variables.
The behavior of living entities, on the
other hand, appears to be most readily
described in terms of the *future* values
of these variables. All living organisms
attempt to model and predict how their
environment will change with time—their
actions are based on these predictions;
certainly the model of reality that the
human invokes allows him to peer forward

and backward in time. Metaphorically
speaking, nervous tissue is a time machine
that somehow has managed to free itself
from moving in lock step with the clock
that drives the inanimate universe.

Since the universe is too complex
and interrelated for any practical model to
completely capture the details of even a
local environment, living organisms must
continually compare current and predicted values to physical reality and adjust
the relevant model parameters. The information to accomplish this task is provided
by the senses. Different species have different models that impose different information needs, and thus their sensors
measure different attributes of their

environment—in a sense, they live in different worlds.

No finite organism can completely model the infinite universe, but even more to the point, the senses can only provide a subset of the needed information; the organism must correct the measured values and guess at the needed missing ones. In most organisms these guesses are made automatically by algorithms embedded in their neural circuitry, and are the best bet the organism can make based on the past experience of its species. Even good bets occasionally fail, so it is likely that all organisms experience illusions. Indeed, even the best guesses can only be an approximation to reality—perception is a creative process.

In spite of the apparent diversity of organic life, nature has returned again and again to just a few solutions to the problems of perception. If we ignore minor differences in design, only two basic types of eyes have found widespread use, and the underlying neural components are almost identical in all animal life. We even find strong similarities in the circuits which do the initial processing of sensed data (e.g., the use of lateral inhibition). It is only in the later stages of neural processing that significant structural and functional differences can be found.

It would appear from neurological studies that most of the human brain is involved in visual perception, and we have earlier presented arguments to support the view that intelligence evolved to support the perceptual process. When a person says "I see" after solving a difficult mathematical or conceptual problem, he is voicing a piece of wisdom that we are just beginning to appreciate, that his perceptual machinery, diverted from its nominal tasks, probably played a substantial role in producing the solution.

Appendixes

8-1

Color Vision and Light

At any instant of time, the light incident on a surface, or received by the human eye, can be characterized by its intensity (energy) and color (frequency). The spectral peak of ambient light incident on the surface of the earth changes throughout the course of the day (see Fig. 8-15). During most of the day[4] the sun provides the main source of illumination and the ambient peak hovers around 550 nanometers. However, during the twilight period, when the sun's rays in their longer path through the earth's atmosphere are

---

[4]During moonlit evenings, the spectral peak is similar to that of broad daylight since the moon reflects the sun's light rather uniformly over the visible spectrum. The other main source of illumination at night is the airglow that results from oxygen activation in the earth's atmosphere; this source has a sharp "green" spectral peak at 558 nm. Starlight provides a faint source of illumination with a spectral peak shifted somewhat toward the red end of the spectrum.

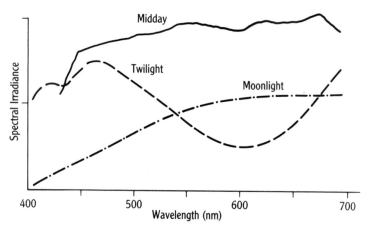

FIGURE 8-15

Spectral Irradiance During Midday, Twilight, and Moonlight.

(After J. N. Lythgoe. *The Ecology of Vision.* Clarendon Press, Oxford, 1979, p. 95.)

ancestors, and such species would be unlikely to find a use for color vision which, as we previously noted, requires high light levels. However, it has been argued [Lythgoe 79] that a visual system with two sets of detectors, one tuned to that of the spectral peak of the ambient light, and the other set of detectors with their spectral peak offset somewhat, can provide a more effective means for detecting a bright target against a dark background than a singly tuned set of detectors. Thus, even though not evolved for this purpose, such a two-spectral response system would provide the sensory information required for the subsequent evolution of color vision.

more scattered by small airborne particles, the ambient light peak shifts toward the blue end of the spectrum (the Purkinje shift). For day-active animals, especially those that need to move about at twilight, the sensitive rod system, with a spectral peak shifted toward the blue frequencies and a high-resolution cone system tuned to operate in direct sunlight, is an excellent adaption to environmental conditions (Fig. 8-16).

There are many considerations relevant to the evolutionary appearance of color vision in a species. For example, many mammals are nocturnal, or evolved from nocturnal

FIGURE 8-16

Spectral Sensitivity of the Human Eye.

Only the nominal shape of the sensitivity curve is shown here. Precise values can be found in G. Wald. *Science* 101; 653-658, 1945.

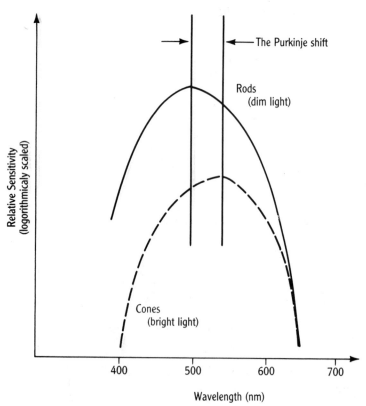

Given the appropriate environmental conditions, color enhances an organism's ability to identify visible objects, determine their physical properties (e.g., ripe compared to immature fruit), and can play an important role in visual communication. For example, sexual displays and body markings are typically based on color cues in organisms with color vision.

How does the eye measure the spectral attributes of light energy impinging on it, how is this information represented internally, and how is it transformed into the subjective impression we call color?

The Young-Helmholtz theory, formulated in the early part of the nineteenth century, asserts that there are three color-sensitive types of receptors in the eye which correspond respectively to red, green, and blue, and that all color perception is the result of the relative strength of the signals received from these three receptor systems. This theory, while possibly valid for simple patches of light, is not sufficient to explain human color perception in complex natural scenes. Edwin Land [Land 59] has demonstrated that our final perception of color at any point in a scene is dependent on colors perceived in other parts of the scene, and that in complex scenes we can perceive colors that cannot be exactly reproduced by a simple mixture of the three primary colors (e.g., highly saturated brown)—in fact, he demonstrated that a mixture of, say, red and white light could induce the human visual system to perceive a realistically colored scene. Other possible problems with the until recently dominant Young-Helmholtz theory includes the fact that the

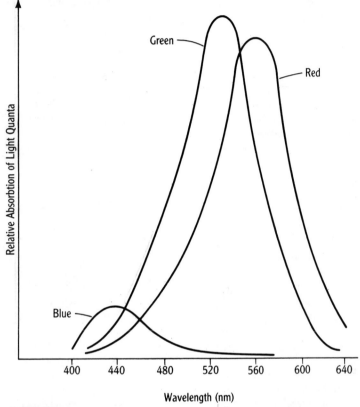

FIGURE 8-17
Absorption of Light Energy by Three Populations of Cones in the Human Eye.

Only the nominal shape of the absorption spectra is shown here. More precise values can be found in G. Wald. *Science* 145; 1007-1017, 1964.

"blue" (short wavelength) pigmented cones are not spatially distributed in the same manner as the red and green cones—they are not as common and are actually absent from the central fovea.[5] The above results imply that any account of color vision based strictly on local stimulation of retinal nerve cells is doomed to fail—color perception involves processes occurring at higher levels in the brain. Nevertheless, we can

still profit by understanding the local sensory apparatus the eye employs to detect and encode the spectral attributes of incident light.

[5]The blue cones seem to be distinguished from the red and green cones in many other important respects, e.g., they do not contribute to the perception of boundaries between differently colored regions, and make little, if any, contribution to the total luminance signal.

The photosensitive part of the eye is a mosaic of rod and cone receptor cells as described in the main text and Box 8-2. Only the cone cells are directly involved in color vision; there are approximately 6 million such cells distributed over each retina, but they are most densely concentrated in the fovea of the eye where there are no rod cells. The rod-free region of each eye (2 degrees in diameter) contains approximately 50,000 cones.

The retinal image consists of a pattern of light energy. This image is transformed into a pattern of nerve activity by the presence of photosensitive pigments in the rods and cones that absorb part of the incident light energy. The rod pigment, rhodopsin, has been successfully extracted and studied. While not as well understood, all the cones appear to be anatomically alike (although their connections differ), and are distributed into at least three populations with distinct spectral responses (see Fig. 8-17). Some recent theories of color vision suggest the presence of receptors with a fourth spectral response, possibly implying an indirect role in color perception for the rod cells.

8-2

Stereo Depth Perception and the Structure of the Human Visual Cortex

With the exception of about two percent of the population, the normal human visual system can convert the overlapping flat images projected onto the retinas of its two eyes into a three-dimensional model of the surrounding environment. We see the world in depth, a luxury shared with most other primates and many predators, e.g., predatory birds. In contrast, many two-eyed animals, such as the rabbit and the pigeon, have panoramic rather than stereo vision: their eyes are placed primarily to look in different directions, rather than to provide the overlapping coverage needed for binocular depth perception.

If we can match corresponding points or objects in the two retinal images, then simple geometric triangulation can be employed to compute the distance (depth) to these objects.[6] The machinery that the human visual system employs to perform the stereo function, while not completely understood, appears to be organized as described below.

Each retinal ganglion cell has a receptive field (the patch of retinal receptor cells supplying the ganglion cell) that consists of an excitatory center and an inhibitory surround. Thus, each such ganglion cell responds best to a roughly circular spot of light of a particular size in a particular part of the visual field. The path from the receptor cells in the retina to the cells in the visual cortex is indicated schematically in Fig. 8-18.

The first of the two major transformations performed by the visual cortex is the integration of information from the retinal ganglion cells so that the cortical cells respond to specifically oriented line segments rather than to spots of light. Depending on the particular cell, its maximum response will be triggered by a moving bright line on a dark background, or the reverse, or it may be a moving boundary between light and dark regions. The orientation of the line, as well as its speed and direction of motion, are also important; note that head and eye movement will cause even a static object in the scene to move across the retina. There appears to be a hierarchy of cell types, with simpler ones feeding the more complex cells. Neurons in the visual cortex with orientation specificity vary in their complexity. "Simple" cells appear to obtain their inputs from a line of retinal cells, and the far more numerous "complex" cells behave as though they receive their input from a number of simple cells, all with the same receptive field orientation, but differing slightly in the exact location of their fields.

The second major transformation performed by the visual cortex is to combine inputs from the two eyes; aside from seeing things in depth, we see a single world, even though the two eyes provide slightly different views of this world. The cells in the visual cortex receiving direct input from the retinas (through the lateral geniculate "relay stations") are all simple "monocular"

[6]Computer stereo techniques are discussed in Chapter 9, Box 9-5.

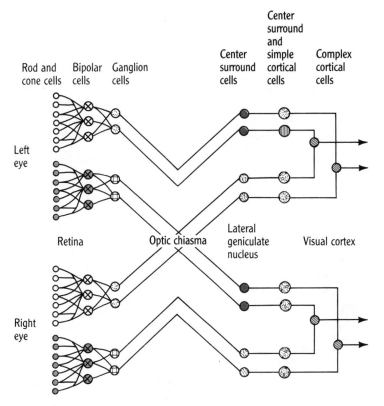

Rod and
cone cells　Bipolar　Ganglion
　　　　　cells　cells

Center
surround
cells

Center
surround
and
simple
cortical
cells

Complex
cortical
cells

Left
eye

Right
eye

Retina　　　　Optic chiasma

Lateral
geniculate
nucleus

Visual cortex

features lying in roughly corresponding regions on each retina can be assumed to correspond to the same real-world object. Since the right and left visual fields depict objects at a variety of different depths in the world, these fields cannot be coherently superimposed, and there is evidence [Pettigrew 79] that "disparity-specific" complex binocular neurons (for a range of disparities) provide local depth information.

The visual cortex is subdivided into roughly parallel columns of tissue, (swirled as in Fig. 8-19, rather than planar, as shown in the simplified schematic drawing of Fig. 8-20), approximately normal to the surface of the cortex. Each column is partitioned into 50 micrometer-thick slabs containing neurons with like receptive field orientation; adjacent slabs have 10 degree shifts in their line orientation. Slabs are arranged into coherent blocks with each block containing a right eye dominant column, and a left eye

FIGURE 8-18
Schematic Diagram of the Path from Receptor Cells to the Visual Cortex in the Human Stereo System.

Approximately half of the complex cells are binocular and the other half monocular; almost all of the center-surround and simple cells are monocular.

cells that receive stimulation from exactly one of the two eyes, but not both. About half of the complex cells are monocular, and the rest are binocular, i.e., they can be influenced independently by both eyes. The left and right receptive field inputs to a binocular complex cell are generally identical in all respects, except that the stimulation ability of one eye typically dominates

the other; all degrees of dominance can be found.

The highly specific stimulus pattern requirements for the firing of "complex" binocular neurons could provide a means for identifying the parts of the left and right images corresponding to the same features. Because the number of identical features in any local region of the image is likely to be small, similar

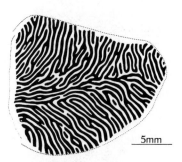

5mm

FIGURE 8-19
Section of Monkey Brain Showing Ocular-Dominance Columns.

(From D. H. Hubel and T. N. Wiesel. *Proceedings of the Royal Society* 198; 35, 1977. Reprinted with permission.)

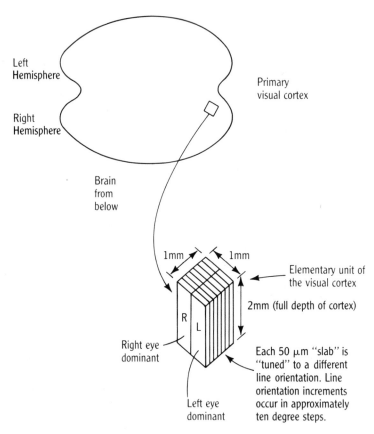

FIGURE 8-20
Schematic Depiction of the Elementary Unit of the Visual Cortex.

- "Aerial perspective" in which distant objects tend to be hazy and assume a bluish tint
- More distant objects which generally appear higher up in the visual field
- "Linear perspective," i.e., convergence of parallel receding lines
- Shading and texture gradients, as shown in Fig. 8-21, which encode depth information.

Nevertheless, the speed, reliability, and accuracy of binocular stereo cannot be matched by the above monocular approaches. One additional advantage of binocular stereo over monocular vision occurs in recognizing patterns. Even when each individual eye fails to see a camouflaged object, a binocular stereo system can still fuse local cues into a clearly visible depth image, [Julesz 74].

(a)

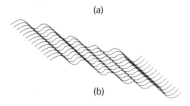

(b)

FIGURE 8-21
Obtaining Depth From Shading and Texture Cues.

(a) Depth from shading (photo by O. Firschein); (b) Depth from texture.

dominant column. Blocks near the center of gaze have small receptive fields; blocks corresponding to receptive fields of increasing eccentricity (further out in the visual field) have large receptive fields.

As we show in the following chapter on computational vision, binocular stereo is not the only method for obtaining depth from two-dimensional images. A single imaging sensor, e.g., a single eye, can recover depth information by viewing a sequence of images, and even a single image offers many depth cues. For example, objects at different depths produce retinal images that move at different speeds when the head is moved, a phenomenon known as *head movement parallax*. Other monocular depth cues include:

- The muscular tension needed to bring different objects into focus, *accommodation*
- Occlusion of more distant objects by near ones

9

Computational
Vision

Computational vision (CV), a subfield of artificial intelligence, is concerned with developing an understanding of the principles underlying visual competence in natural and artificial systems, and with providing a machine with some of the capabilities of the human visual system. Such capabilities include the ability to describe a scene based on data provided by imaging sensors, and to produce an understanding of the function, purpose, and intent of recognized objects. Table 9-1 summarizes the functional requirements of a general purpose vision system.

The challenge for computational vision is twofold: (1) The computing device should be capable of simulating physical experiments, such as *imagining* the movement or rearrangement and distortion of objects in the scene to solve a problem or compare the scene with reference scenes stored in memory, and (2) the computer should have some way of physically interacting with, and sensing, the outside world to build up a database of knowledge and experience. Without physical interaction, there is no reasonable way to capture and store in computer memory a suitably complete model that reflects all the complexity and detail of a real-world scene.

In other areas of AI, we have already observed the appropriateness of the saying, "If you are a hammer, everything

---

> **Table 9-1** ■ Functional Requirements for a General-Purpose Vision System
>
> **Geometric modeling.** Determine the three-dimensional configuration of the surfaces and objects in a scene, including the location of the viewer (sensor) with respect to the scene being viewed.
>
> **Photometric modeling.** Determine the location and nature of the illumination sources and the corresponding shadowing and reflectance effects induced in an image of the scene.
>
> **Scene segmentation.** Partition the scene into meaningful or coherent subunits which can be independently analyzed and identified.
>
> **Naming and labeling.** Identify the objects visible in a scene as either members of known object classes, or as known individuals. Determine the physical attributes (size, material composition, etc.) of recognized objects.
>
> **Relational description and reasoning.** Determine the relationships among the objects in a scene, e.g., the appearance of the scene just prior to the time an image was acquired, and how the scene will appear immediately afterward. How can the objects in a scene be rearranged to achieve some given purpose?
>
> **Semantic interpretation.** Determine the function, purpose, intent, etc., of objects in a scene.

looks like a nail." For computational vision, this can be paraphrased as, "If you are a digital computer, then everything looks like a number or a symbol." Thus, for a digital computer to deal with the visually perceived world, the signals acquired by the imaging sensors must first be converted into numbers and ultimately into symbols. We are therefore led to the *signals-to-symbols* paradigm described in the next section. The rest of this chapter discusses some of the techniques[7] involved in deriving symbolic descriptions from the sensed signals. The sections are sequenced to reflect the increasing complexity and abstraction of the corresponding techniques, beginning with the *low-level* representations and algorithms, and proceeding through the *intermediate* and *highest* levels.

A noteworthy difference between many computational vision representations and those of general AI is that in vision we often use arrays of picture elements (*pixels*) or other iconic (picturelike) representations that mirror the sensed image and thus retain a more direct correspondence to the real world. The accuracy and adequacy of any of the representations in the signals-to-symbols hierarchy is judged by how faithfully it portrays the real world scene that was originally sensed — i.e., the primary concern is with physical modeling of the world. This is in contrast to conventional AI systems which typically do not have a perceptual component, and thus work within a complete, consistent, and closed model of reality. The basic questions we address in this chapter are:

- What is the nature of the computer's symbolic description of the visual world, and how is it obtained?

---

[7]We attempted to select techniques that are both representative and can be understood without the need for an involved mathematical presentation.

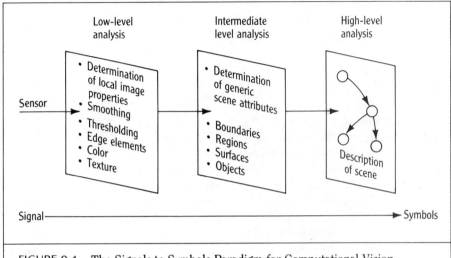

FIGURE 9-1   The Signals-to-Symbols Paradigm for Computational Vision.

Raw sensed data are transformed into a description of the scene by a series of inductive steps.

- What are the representations used in the signals-to-symbols paradigm?
- What algorithms exist for obtaining these representations and extracting information from them? How can we build a machine that can recognize objects and re-create scene geometry from the data provided by two-dimensional images?
- What are the few key ideas and major assumptions that underlie most of the current computational vision algorithms?

We conclude the chapter with a critical look at the signals-to-symbols paradigm, and indicate the requirements that must be satisfied by a computer if it is to achieve human-level competence in visual perception.

SIGNALS-TO-SYMBOLS PARADIGM

Computational vision (CV) is that body of theory and techniques that represents our present understanding of how competence for visual perception can be implemented in computing hardware. The dominant paradigm, signals-to-symbols, is one in which the raw sensed data is transformed into a meaningful and explicit description of the corresponding scene by a series of inductive steps employing progressively more abstract representations (Fig. 9-1). These steps can be partitioned into three categories, based on the nature of the modeling required to carry out the analysis: low-level scene analysis is based on local image properties, intermediate-level scene analysis uses generic geometric and photometric models, and high-level scene analysis is based on goal-oriented semantic models and relationships.

LOW-LEVEL SCENE ANALYSIS (LLSA)

At the lowest levels of the processing hierarchy, the representations and transformation techniques tend to be independent of any final purpose. Concern here is with physical and statistical modeling of the generic local properties of the visible surfaces in the scene and their appearance in the image. Low-level scene analysis (LLSA) is also concerned with the processes of transforming continuous sensor-derived signals into discrete digital representations, and the reduction of noise and distortion introduced by the sensing process. Inputs to this stage of processing are the raw signals from one or more sensors, and the output is typically a set of registered arrays, with each array corresponding to a particular scene attribute such as local surface orientation, surface reflectance, edge point location, etc. LLSA techniques have been developed to:

- Reduce imaging noise and unwanted scene detail without seriously degrading information needed for recovery of higher-level scene description.
- Disambiguate, i.e., separate the contributions of the illumination, surface reflectance, and surface orientation to the brightness of a point in the image (in a sense, to *invert* the imaging process).
- Detect local homogeneities and discontinuities that can be used to partition the

image into regions corresponding to coherent objects in the scene.
- Detect distinguished local image features that are important markers and delimiters of scene features.
- Deduce local surface geometry (three-dimensional depth and orientation) from shading, texture, stereo analysis, and the analysis of a continuous sequence of images ("optic flow").

The analysis usually deals with local phenomena, using models based on such general concepts as continuity (or discontinuity) of intensity, texture, or color. While LLSA provides an interpretation of real-world physical phenomena for use by the integrative and reasoning mechanisms comprising intermediate- and high-level scene analysis, the LLSA techniques themselves have few (if any) of the attributes characteristic of reasoning. LLSA techniques are almost always based on the general position and the continuity assumptions: (1) that the image was taken from an essentially random location in space, and no deliberate attempts were made to make separated and discontinuous things look continuous in the image, or to align shadow and occlusion boundaries, or to make a curved line look straight, etc.; and (2) that because the scene is largely composed of continuous surfaces, the geometric, photometric, and physical properties measured at any point in the image are good predictors of the values appearing in the neighborhood of that point.

We first describe the image-acquisition process, and the preprocessing operations used to improve the quality and utility of the image. We then describe the various methods for detecting local discontinuity and homogeneity. Determination of scene geometry from single and from multiple images completes the discussion of low-level analysis.

Image Acquisition (Scanning and Quantizing)

The computational vision process begins either with an existing image (e.g., a picture taken at some previous time), or a scene currently being sensed by a television camera–type of sensor. To translate scene illuminance information into a form suitable for computer processing, it must first be converted into an array of numbers that represents the intensity of reflected light at each point in the scene.

If we start with an image, rather than the actual scene, we can obtain the intensity data by moving a small aperture or *window* over the image so that the average light intensity level of the image within the window is sensed by a photo-

sensitive device. This scanning process can be carried out using a mechanical device that physically moves a sensor over the image in a regular and exhaustive manner, or by using a *flying spot scanner* that moves a beam of light sequentially over the image and senses the reflected (or transmitted) light from the image. (Such exhaustive scanning is in contrast to the selective scanning employed by the human visual system, as illustrated in Fig. 9-2.)

The continuous electrical signal that results from the mechanical scanning process must still be converted into an array of numbers by sampling the signal at regular time intervals (corresponding to regular spatial intervals over the image), and then approximating the measured voltage by the closest integer in some predefined range of numbers, as shown in Fig. 9-3. With current technology for storing, processing, and displaying pictorial data, a set of values for sampling and

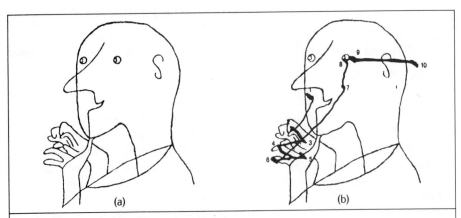

FIGURE 9-2   Adaptive Scanning of a Scene by the Human Eye.

(a) Original picture. (b) Picture with human eye scanning path shown. (From Norton and Stark, *Scientific American*, June 1971, with permission.)

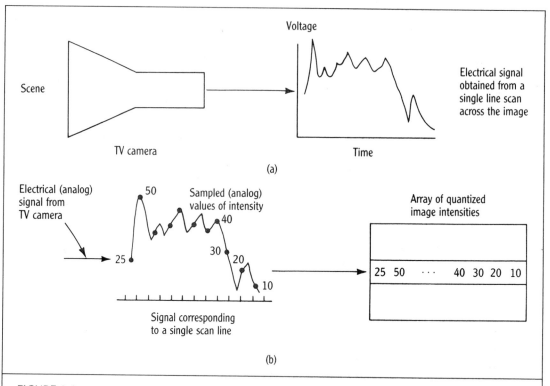

Voltage

Scene

TV camera

Electrical signal obtained from a single line scan across the image

Time

(a)

Electrical (analog) signal from TV camera

50

Sampled (analog) values of intensity

40

25

30

20

10

Signal corresponding to a single scan line

Array of quantized image intensities

25 50   · · ·   40 30 20 10

(b)

FIGURE 9-3
The Image Acquisition Process: Representing a Scene by an Electrical Signal and Then an Array of Numbers.

(a) Obtaining an electrical signal corresponding to intensities from a scene. (b) Converting an analog signal to sampled and quantized intensity values.

digitizing an image is typically a 256 × 256 grid with 256 possible intensity levels at each such grid point.

An important issue is the fidelity with which the actual scene appearance is captured by the array of integers that is extracted to describe it. In all of the digitizing approaches, the scene intensity is spatially sampled. The smallest image distance that can be tolerated between intensity samples depends on the charac-

teristics of the lens system, on the sensitive surface of the sensor, and on the system used to convert the signals from spatially continuous to discrete quantities. The sampled intensities are further quantized into digital values to satisfy practical constraints on the memory or register word size of the computer. How much information is lost in this digitization process; i.e., how faithfully can we reproduce the original image from the derived finite array of numbers? Amazingly enough, the continuous image can be exactly re-created from its sampled (but unquantized) representation if the sample spacing is less than a value determined by the maximum spatial rate of change of intensities in the image. When the sampled analog signal values are converted to integer quantities, some amount of *quantization noise* is introduced in the analog-to-digital conversion which generally cannot be completely removed. However, a sufficient number of levels of quantization can be selected to insure that amplitude noise already introduced by the sensing process is not significantly increased. Thus, we conclude that the process of converting a continuous image into an array of integers does not cause any fundamental loss of information.

Image Preprocessing (Thresholding and Smoothing)

Image *preprocessing* uses operations that are relatively independent of scene content to alter the stored values in the digital array representing the scene. Preprocessing operations are generally intended to remove noise, enhance certain aspects of the image (e.g., edges), and induce other changes that will simplify the higher-level processing steps. It is assumed that image intensities are spatially continuous over most of the image, and that this continuity can be approximated, for example, by a low-order polynomial. An important goal in preprocessing is to avoid eliminating existing edges or introducing false edges.

Typical preprocessing operations are (1) *thresholding*, which reduces the digi-

tally quantized image containing one of many possible integer intensity values at each image location to a binary picture containing one of only two possible values at each location, and (2) *smoothing*, the use of various filtering operations to enhance or suppress certain aspects of a scene.

1. *Thresholding.* The thresholding operation achieves image partitioning at an early stage in the analysis, reduces noise in the image, and simplifies later processing steps. The concept of thresholding is a simple one: we assume that pixels in a coherent region of the image all have an intensity greater than (or less than) a certain value. An intensity threshold is chosen, and all pixels whose intensity level is below this threshold are assigned one value ("black"), and all those above this threshold are assigned another value ("white"). Techniques for automatic threshold selection are discussed in Box 9-1.

2. *Smoothing (filtering).* Smoothing operations (1) remove noise and illumination artifacts that were introduced into the image during the sensing and image-acquisition process; (2) enhance edges and other selected image features; and (3) degrade unwanted detail below the level of resolution at which image interpretation is to be carried out (see Fig. 9-5). Smoothing is usually accomplished by replacing the intensity value of each pixel with a new value based on the intensity values of pixels in the immediate neighborhood of the given pixel. The problem that

BOX 9-1   Image Thresholding

Thresholding transforms a *gray-level* image, whose pixels can have any of a continuous range of intensity values, into a binary image in which each pixel is either black or white. Thresholding achieves a simple form of image partitioning, reduces noise in the image, enhances certain image features, and simplifies later processing steps. In some situations different thresholds may be used in different portions of the image to compensate for some known or deduced illumination variation or change in local scene contrast. A person interactively adjusting the threshold and viewing the effect of each such threshold setting can choose a threshold value that best achieves some desired effect. Automatic threshold selection is usually based on the following techniques:

• **Effect on image.**   An iterative procedure for threshold selection can be based on the number, area, and stability of the regions generated by different thresholds—a good threshold setting should produce mostly large well-separated regions which retain

FIGURE 9-4

An Intensity Contour Map of an Image.

(Photos courtesy of SRI International, Menlo Park, Calif.)

their shape under small variations of the selected threshold value. An intensity contour map for an image can make apparent the effect of different thresholds on the final partitioning of the image (Fig. 9-4).

• **Histogram analysis.**   The intensity histogram is a graph whose x axis shows the range of possible intensity values, and whose y axis shows the number of pixels in the image that have each of these intensities. An image and its associated histogram are shown in Color Plate 3. Note that there are several peaks in the histogram, indicating the intensities that are most common in the image. An appropriate threshold setting for an image can automatically be determined by analyzing the histogram shape, often under the assumption that individual peaks of the histogram correspond to coherent (relatively constant intensity) regions of the image, and that the background is the lightest or darkest of these regions.

arises in the smoothing operation is how to avoid throwing the baby out with the bath water, i.e., how to avoid eliminating essential data in trying to accomplish the goals stated above. The basic issue is how to select the appropriate image subsets to process

coherently without crossing boundaries separating different scene entities. For example, since the smoothing function usually consists of operations in a window centered around the pixel being modified, how can one keep from blurring edges when

FIGURE 9-5
Need to Degrade Unwanted Detail.

Look at this picture from a distance. From far enough away, the texture elements disappear and this looks like a normal photograph. Now look at this picture through a narrow tube from the same distance at which the texture elements originally disappeared—the texture elements should become visible again, showing that under appropriate conditions, the human visual system deliberately degrades low-level detail. (Courtesy of SRI International, Menlo Park, Calif.)

pixels interior and exterior to the object fall in the same window? There is no single best smoothing algorithm. Some of the common approaches to smoothing and the implicit assumptions made for each are described in Box 9-2.

Detection of Local Discontinuities and Homogeneities (Edges, Texture, Color)

No reasonable semantic description or interpretation is possible if every point in a scene is unrelated to its neighbors. However, most of the scenes we encoun-

---

 ## BOX 9-2   Image Smoothing

Image smoothing is employed to reduce noise, to enhance selected image features, and to degrade unwanted image detail. Most smoothing techniques fall into three broad categories: (1) local averaging, (2) model-based smoothing, and (3) geometric smoothing.

Smoothing via Local Averaging

Smoothing based on local averaging operations assumes that the *intensity surface* is continuous over most of the image. This assumption is a special case of the more general assumption that most of the image will depict continuous scene surfaces at an image resolution suitable for interpretation to be possible. In one smoothing approach based on this assumption, we replace the center of a small region around a pixel (typically a square *window*) by the weighted average of the values found within the window; this operation is identical for each pixel of the image. Another approach used to avoid the effect of deviant pixels and to retain edges is to use the median, rather

than the average, of the intensity values in the window.

Smoothing Based On A Priori Models

The following technique is typical of a global approach to smoothing. Suppose we have a model of how the illumination varies in an image. For example, if we know (or assume) that the illumination can be modeled as a quadratic function, we can fit a quadratic surface to the intensity values of the pixels in an extended portion of the image. The intensity of each pixel is then subtracted from the corresponding value of the fitted surface, leaving only the higher-order variations of the underlying signal. We thus prevent a known artifact from interfering with our analysis of the intrinsic information residing in the image.

Geometric Smoothing

Geometric smoothing of an image can be carried out by assuming that very small isolated regions consist of

noise and can be eliminated, and that small gaps between regions are imaging artifacts and can be filled in. Such smoothing can be readily accomplished in binary images using sequences of *shrink* and *grow* operations. In the shrink/grow approach to eliminating small noise regions, we first use a shrinking operation in which black pixels that are not completely surrounded by black are set to white. The shrinking operation can be iteratively applied several times. A growing operation can now be used in which all black pixels that are not completely surrounded by black pixels are provided with surrounding black pixels. Any small black noise regions will have been eliminated by the shrinking operations, and the larger regions will be left unaltered if the number of shrink and grow operations are equal. If the sequence of grow operations is applied first (followed by the shrink operations) small gaps in black objects or between adjacent objects will be filled, but the shapes of the objects will generally be unaltered.

ter can be decomposed into coherent objects or regions that are relatively homogeneous with respect to one or more of the following attributes: intensity, color, texture, distance, motion, material composition, physical cohesion, etc. Correspondingly, there are places in an image where there are sharp discontinuities in some of the above attributes; e.g., across an edge that occludes another part of the scene. Identifying homogeneous regions and discontinuities greatly simplifies the problem of analyzing the image in two important ways: (1) discontinuities are typically associated with the edges of objects, and locating the edges makes object shape explicit; and (2) identifying portions of an image corresponding to coherent objects allows us to analyze those portions in isolation if desired.

Some methods for finding such discontinuities and homogeneities are given below. Some of the techniques are independent of the objects in the scene, while others assume certain characteristics of specific real-world objects.

Local Edge Detection. It has long been recognized that the detection of the edges of the objects appearing in an image is an essential step in scene analysis, and for this reason there has been considerable effort devoted to developing effective edge detection algorithms. One class of such algorithms, local edge detectors (LEDs), assigns an edge value to individual pixels, but does not link pixels together to form an extended edge segment. Therefore, an additional association or linking step must still be carried out in the computer to obtain an internal representation of the connected edge segment. Edge linking is an intermediate level operation, and is

discussed later. LED algorithms can be grouped into the following categories:

Local gradient operators: These algorithms are based on characterizing an edge as a local intensity discontinuity. The intensities in a local region of the image are examined and an edge value (and sometimes an edge orientation) is assigned to a picture element based on the change of intensity within that local region.

The simplest and most commonly employed gradient type LEDs have the following characteristics (e.g., the Sobel edge detector; see Fig. 9-6): They *convolve* a set of small digital *operator* arrays (e.g., a 3 × 3 pixel square) with the image array.[8] Each such operator array evaluates the intensity gradient in one particular direction at the image location corresponding to the center of the operator array (Fig. 9-6b). An approximate gradient can be computed by applying the operator in two orthogonal directions and employing vector addition (Fig. 9-6c). Better results are obtained by running the operator at a large number of angular orientations and selecting the maximum value obtained as the gradient magnitude at the given location, and the corresponding direction as the gradient direction. Edge pixels are determined by thresholding the gradient image.

The simple gradient-type LEDs, such as described above, ignore a number of considerations relevant to real imagery. First, most real images have extended

---

[8]In convolution the operator array is moved across the image, and at each placement the elements of the operator array are multiplied by the corresponding image elements. All the products are summed, and the result is assigned to the image location beneath the current center of the operator array.

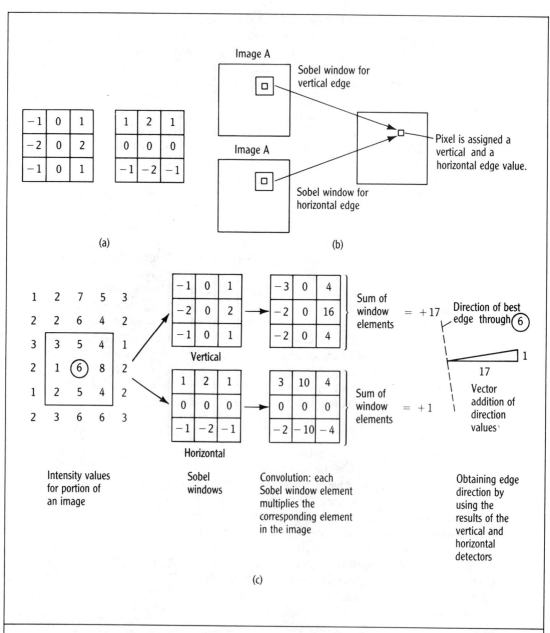

FIGURE 9-6   The Sobel Edge Detector.

(a) Sobel windows. (b) Applying Sobel windows to an image. (c) Example of Sobel edge detector used to find direction of edge through circled element in image array. (See Fig. 9-10 for example of application of Sobel detector to a real photograph.)

smooth gradients that are artifacts of the illumination and imaging processes. There is no reasonable way to set an absolute threshold on the local gradient (e.g., as required by the Sobel LED) to distinguish intensity discontinuities (edges) from these extended smooth gradient artifacts. We are thus faced with the problem of how to detect low contrast edges (using a fixed threshold gradient operator) without being deluged by false alarms arising from smooth gradients. There is also the problem that the intensity discontinuities corresponding to different edges in an image can vary over a range of widths (resolutions); a single size convolution mask (even at multiple orientations) is not adequate. Box 9-3 presents an approach to local edge detection which is better able to deal with these problems.

Generic model fitting: These algorithms are based on modeling an edge as a specific extended intensity profile. Within some local search area, a single best fit is selected to this specified intensity profile . The generic model-fitting approach is very specific about the type of discontinuity it is searching for, in contrast to the local gradient approach which is satisfied by a wide variety of intensity discontinuity types.

It is often acceptable to describe an edge as being a geometrically straight intensity step discontinuity over some local extent of the image. In such a case, we can move a small window over the image and find the best fit of the above model to the intensity pattern viewed through the window at each of its stopping locations. The *Hueckel edge detector* is the most commonly employed operator of this type. It accepts the digitized light intensities within a small disc-shaped

subarea (containing at least 32 pixels) and yields a description of the most edgelike (brightness discontinuity) occurrence found within the disc.

Semantic model fitting: The algorithms based on "semantic edge models" use specific characteristics of the objects of interest to detect the edges. For example, various objects such as roads or rivers in an aerial photograph, or ribs in a medical x-ray film, have edge properties that are dependent on the nature of the objects themselves. The algorithms in this category are therefore tailored to search for the edges of a particular class of objects. For example, to detect roads in low resolution aerial images, the Duda road operator (Fig. 9-7) specifically requires

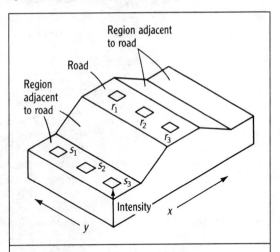

FIGURE 9-7   The Duda Road Operator.

The general idea is (1) adjacent pixels along a road should have similar intensities, and (2) adjacent on-road and off-road pixels should have different intensities. If these two conditions are satisfied, a high road score results.

Score = $f(r)/g(r,s)$. $f(r)$ is high if the differences between r_1, r_2, r_3 are small; $g(r,s)$ is low if (r_1-s_1), (r_2-s_2), (r_3-s_3) differences are large. For a road, $f(r)$ is high and $g(r,s)$ is low, resulting in a high score.

BOX 9-3   Local Edge Detection Based on Lateral Inhibition

Organic visual systems universally employ a mechanism, called *lateral inhibition*, that offers some relief from the edge-finding problems encountered by using the simple gradient-type LED. Computationally, lateral inhibition involves setting the edge "signature" of a picture element (pixel) to be the weighted difference of the average intensities of two differently sized masks centered on the pixel. In some simple implementations, each mask is a uniformly weighted rectangular box. In more sophisticated versions, and especially as found in biological systems, the masks have a gaussian, bell-shaped weighting, rather than a uniform weight distribution (see Fig. 9-8). Applying such an *operator* to a region of an image in which there is a uniform gradient, no matter how strong, will result in a zero response everywhere (assuming that the sum of the weights in the two masks are equal). If there is a sharp intensity discontinuity superimposed on the uniform gradient, then as the operator is moved along a path normal to the discontinuity, its value will be zero until the larger (outer) mask of

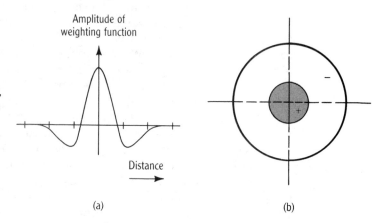

(a)

(b)

FIGURE 9-8

Lateral Inhibition using "Zero-Crossing" Detector based on Difference of Gaussians.

the operator crosses the discontinuity. Then the value returned by the operator will increase until the smaller (center) mask intersects the discontinuity. At this point the value returned by the operator will rapidly decrease, becoming zero when the smaller mask is exactly centered on the discontinuity. Continuing, we now obtain a symmetrical response

to what we had approaching the discontinuity, but with reversed sign. The edge is detected by locating the "zero-crossing" of the operator's response over some portion of the image (not just a zero value). The strength and direction of the edge must be determined by analyzing the response of the operator in the vicinity of the *zero-crossing*.

that a road fragment have relatively constant width and intensity values along a line segment in addition to the generic requirement of high intensity gradient normal to the direction of the segment.

The results obtained by applying several LED algorithms to the same scene are presented in Fig. 9-10. The Duda

operator, specifically designed to detect roads, produces a more intuitively obvious result than the other more generic edge operators.

Analysis of Local Homogeneity.   The identification of homogeneous regions is generally accomplished by first labeling

BOX 9-3 *(continued)*

To determine very sharp intensity discontinuities in an essentially noise-free image, the central mask can be one pixel in diameter, and the outer mask just slightly larger; however, if the intensity discontinuity is "blurred" over a number of pixels, and if the image is noisy, then the outer mask must have a diameter larger than the width of the edge transition region. In fact, the best response in terms of the magnitude and slope of the reversal on which the zero-crossing occurs will be obtained if the outer mask is made as big as possible without making it so large that it simultaneously covers more than one edge. Increasing the diameter of the central mask smoothes the response of the operator, but also decreases the amplitude and slope of the section on which we are looking for the zero-crossing. Choosing an optimal size for the central mask is a complex issue, but it probably should not be larger than the diameter of the edge transition. To deal with a complex scene, a set of zero-crossing operators with graded sizes of the central mask is required to detect edges of varying widths (Fig. 9-9).

FIGURE 9-9   Use of Zero-Crossing Operators to Find Edges at Different Scales of Resolution.

The diameter of the zero-crossing operator was varied to obtain these results. (Courtesy of SRI International, Menlo Park, Calif.)

each pixel in the image with the values of attributes such as texture and color.

Texture analysis. Although there are many fascinating biological and computational aspects of texture perception/detection, we are concerned here only with the limited question of how analysis of texture can be used to partition an image into homogeneous regions. Since the human visual system can easily recognize different types of textures, it may come as a surprise to find that there is no generally accepted definition of texture and thus no agreement as to how it can be measured. It is not easy to formally characterize the basis of our perception

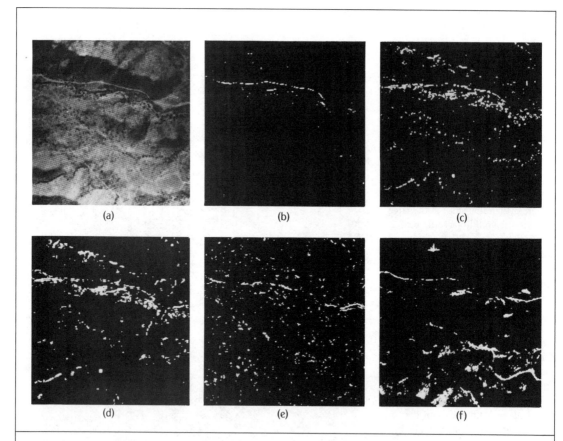

FIGURE 9-10   Result of Various Edge Operators Applied to the Same Scene.

(Operator scores are thresholded to highlight the locations assigned the best scores.) (a) Original image; (b) Duda road operator; (c) Roberts' cross gradient; (d) Sobel-type gradient; (e) Hueckel line operator; (f) Intensity. (Courtesy of SRI International, Menlo Park, Calif.)

of texture described by terms such as "fine," "coarse," "smooth," "granular," "random," "mottled," etc. We know intuitively that texture involves a statistical or structural relationship between the basic elements, and for figurative (cellular, macrostructure) textures such as a brick wall or a tiled floor, our visual system can detect the underlying patterns that make up the texture design, and we can describe the relationship of the elements (Fig. 9-11a). For microstructure texture, such as the fields seen in aerial photographs, or the texture of cloth, the underlying patterns are no longer obvious and it is difficult for the human to describe

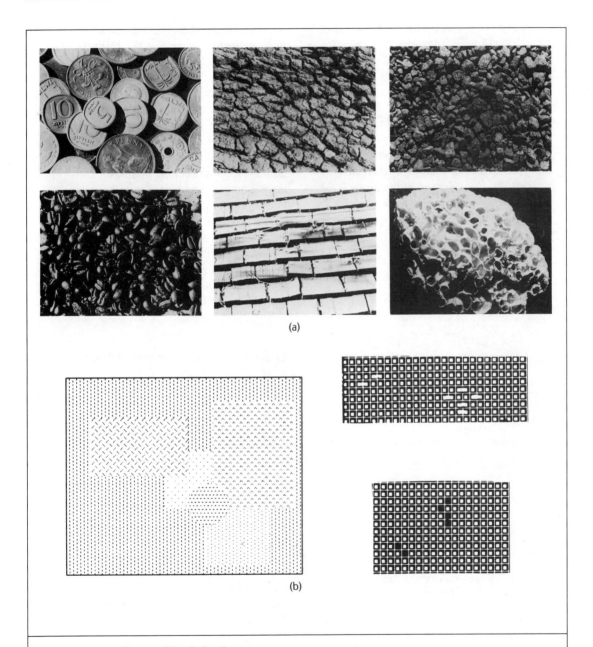

FIGURE 9-11   Texture Discrimination.

(a) Examples of macro- and microtextures. (Photos by O. Firschein.) (b) The human visual system has no trouble partitioning images containing various types of texture patterns.

(but not to recognize!) the texture (Fig. 9-11b). Analysis of micro- and macrostructured textures is discussed in Box 9-4.

Color. A colored image is typically represented in the computer as three separate arrays of numbers, with each array corresponding to a primary color, and the value of a pixel representing the intensity of the primary color component at the corresponding location (see Fig. 9-12). Each element of the image is therefore represented by a triple of values. Although all three images are usually obtained simultaneously using a *color vidicon,* the arrays can also be obtained by sensing the scene three times, each time through a different color filter. Sometimes the spectral (color) component of an image is relatively constant over large areas of the surface of a single object, while total intensity may change more erratically due to uneven direct illumination and local reflections. Thus color can be used to help find homogeneous regions in an image by grouping together neighboring pixels with similar color attributes. Errors may still occur due to the fact that objects will be colored by reflections from other colored objects, because of shadows, and because the basic assumption of homogeneity is not always valid.

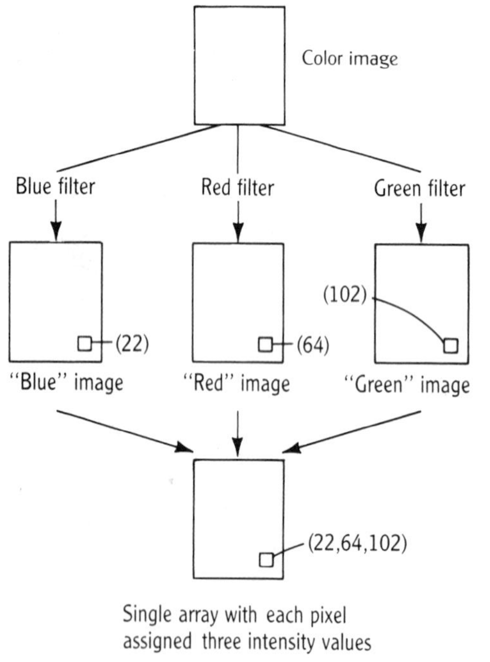

FIGURE 9-12

Color Represented as a Triple of Values.

(Color Plate 3 shows a color photograph and the "blue" image extracted from it.)

Local Scene Geometry from a Single Image (Shape from Shading and Texture)

We know that the shading and texture present in a single image can produce a vivid impression of three-dimensional structure (Fig. 9-13). What is the computational basis of this effect? A crucial source of information about three-dimensional structure is provided by the spatial distribution of surface markings in an image. Since projection distorts texture geometry in a manner that depends systematically on surface shape and orientation (see Fig. 9-14), isolating and measuring this projective distortion in the image allows recovery of the three-dimensional structure of the textured surface. This is not a straightforward task because the projective distortions encoding surface orientations are confounded in

BOX 9-4   Analysis of Micro- and Macrostructured Texture

Texture analysis is a basic operation in scene partitioning. It attempts to formalize our intuitive notion of surface appearance.

Microstructured Texture

Two general approaches can be taken to the analysis of microstructure textures, (1) analysis on the basis of microstructure regularity as detected by statistical or power spectrum techniques, and (2) the use of techniques that model the original surface that produced the texture patterns.

Statistical features approach. Because the basic units of microstructure are small, techniques that detect regularity in short sequences of pixels can be used to partition microtextured scenes. The basic strategy is to form a feature space based on measurements in a neighborhood about each pixel in the image. Segmentation of the image can be accomplished by assigning pixels to one or another region on the basis of the location of that pixel in the feature space.

- **Co-occurrence approach.** The spatial gray-level relationships can be expressed as $S(i,j|d,A)$, the number of times a pixel of intensity i appears within d pixels and an angle A of a pixel of intensity j, in some neighborhood of the pixel to be classified. One can use functions of S as the components of a feature space. Typical of such

functions is *energy*, formed by summing the square of S over all i and j, for given values of angle A and distance d.
- **Fourier analysis approach.** Regularity in gray level pattern shows up in the Fourier transform taken in various directions around a pixel. The set of Fourier measures, obtained by convolving a set of weighted windows over the image, then forms the components of a feature space. Each pixel in the image has an associated set of Fourier energy measurements, and can be represented in the feature space.

Modeling approach. In a *process-modeling* approach to texture analysis, one attempts to describe things in the world in terms of how they arose, e.g., man-made, growing, or *wearing-down* processes (as in a canyon). Using this point of view, it is possible to predict how natural surfaces will produce the texture patterns in an image. A technique based on *fractal functions* can model image textures arising from physical processes that alter the terrain via a sequence of small changes; the corresponding image turns out to have measurable statistical properties that are invariant over linear transformations of intensity and transformations of scale. The fractal dimension, D, of a surface corresponds roughly to our intuitive notion of jaggedness. Thus if we

were to generate a series of scenes with increasing fractal dimension D, we would obtain what could be described as (1) a flat plane for $D=2$, rolling countryside for $D=2.1$, a worn, old mountain range for $D=2.3$, a young, rugged mountain for $D=2.5$, and finally, a stalagmite-covered plane at $D=2.8$ (see Color Plate 2, a synthetic scene generated using fractal textures.) It is possible to measure the fractal dimension of imaged data, and discover whether the corresponding three-dimensional surface is rough or smooth. This information can be used to partition the image into regions of homogeneous surface character, as follows. The fractal dimension is computed for each (say) 8×8 block of pixels in an image, and a histogram of the fractal dimensions is computed for the entire image. This histogram is then broken at the valleys between the modes of the histogram, and the image is segmented into regions belonging to one mode or another.

Macrostructured Textures

Techniques for dealing with macrostructure textures have met with only limited success. Macrostructure texture analysis is quite difficult because one must identify both the primitive(s) and the spatial relationship between them. Perspective effects add to the difficulty by changing the size and shape of the primitives depending on their position in the two-dimensional image.

FIGURE 9-13
Three-Dimensional Structure from Shading
and Texture.

(*Study of a Female Nude* by Pierre-Paul Prod'hon.
Collection of Henry P. McIlhenny.)

natural assumption is that textures do not "conspire" to mimic projective effects or to cancel these effects. Thus it is reasonable to assume that what looks like projective distortion really is such distortion.

FIGURE 9-14
Effects of Projective Imaging on
Regular Texture Patterns.

the image with the properties of the original texture on which the distortion acted.

If the texture is simple and regular, such as a square tile pattern, the change in shape of the rectangles in the image can be measured to derive the surface shape. However, in most situations, there is not a simple, regular texture pattern. An effective technique for recovering surface orientations from general images must rest on texture descriptors that can actually be computed from such images. A

As much as possible of the observed variation is therefore attributed to projection—
the surface orientation that best explains
the data in an image is the best guess for
the actual orientation of the surface in the
scene.

The appearance of surface markings
in the image is subject to two simple geometric distortions: (1) As a surface recedes
from the viewer, its markings appear
smaller (the *railroad track effect*); and
(2) as a surface is inclined off the frontal
plane, its markings appear foreshortened
or compressed in the direction of inclina-
tion (a tilted circle projects as an ellipse).
Thus, any method for recovering surface
orientation from texture must be expressed in terms of some concrete description of the image texture that is
sensitive to these two types of distortion.

When a plane texture is viewed at an
unknown orientation, the original texture
and the orientation of the plane with
respect to the observer cannot be unam-
biguously recovered from the image. However, it is possible to produce a set of
candidate reconstructions by applying an
inverse projective transform at all values
of tilt and slant angle, each associated
with a particular orientation of the planar
surface. The problem of recovering surface orientation can therefore be recast
into that of choosing a "best" or most
likely member from a set of possible reconstructions, by ordering the candidate
reconstructions by some criteria of likelihood. For example, the ordering can be
based on the assumption that all edge
directions are equally likely in the scene.
First, the edge pixels and their orientation
in the image are found, and then one
finds the best combination of tilt and slant

angles of a plane on which these edges
project so as to satisfy the "randomness of
edge direction" assumption. The planar
technique is extended to curved surfaces
by finding a planar estimator to a circular
region surrounding each image point.
Repeated over the image, this method
provides estimates of local surface orientation, but its validity depends on a randomness assumption which is frequently
violated.

The human can perceive convoluted
three-dimensional surfaces on the basis of
the projective distortions imposed on
complex and subtle textures; computational vision is a long way from duplicat-
ing this ability.

Local Scene Geometry from Multiple Images (Stereo and Optic Flow)

All of the previously described LLSA
techniques operate on a single image.
Below we discuss two techniques, stereo
and optic flow, that recover scene information based on analyzing a sequence of
images.

- *Stereo*. Stereoscopic vision allows a
  three-dimensional model of a scene to
  be derived from two sensors that observe the scene from slightly different
  viewpoints. The relative difference in the
  position of objects in the two images is
  called *disparity*, and is caused by the
  slight difference in angle from any given
  object to each sensor. In some conjec-
  tured, but still unknown manner, our
  brain measures this disparity and estimates the absolute distances between
  objects and the viewer (see Appendix 8-2).
  From experiments employing synthetic

BOX 9-5 Stereopsis

Our two eyes form slightly different images of the world because their spatial separation causes them to be at different spatial orientations with respect to objects in the scene. The relative difference in the position of an object on the two retinas is called "disparity," and can be used to estimate the distance of an object from the viewer. "Stereopsis," "binocular vision," and "stereo vision" are the terms used to describe the ability of a vision system to carry out this analysis.

Figure 9-15 shows a simplified two-dimensional example of a stereo system. Two lenses, separated by a distance, d, project a point, P, to the respective retinas at P_1 and P_2. P is distance h from the line of the lenses. The distance from the lens to the retina is f, the "focal length."

The disparity, the shift of the point's position in one image relative to the point's position in the other image, is $(a+b)$. The distance h is given by $h = (fd)/(a+b)$, where the focal length f and the distance between lenses d is a constant for a particular lens pair. If fd is unknown but a constant, then if we can find the disparity between points in the images, the relative distance of objects from the image plane can be determined. Measuring disparity requires that we first identify corresponding points in the two images; people are able to solve this correspondence

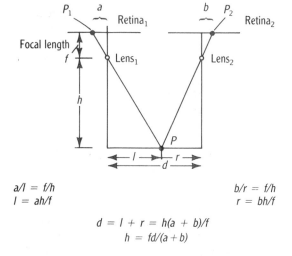

$$a/l = f/h \qquad\qquad b/r = f/h$$
$$l = ah/f \qquad\qquad r = bh/f$$

$$d = l + r = h(a + b)/f$$
$$h = fd/(a + b)$$

FIGURE 9-15   Stereo Geometry.

problem even when the points to be matched are randomly scattered in the images and there is no edge or other obvious structure. The major problem in computer stereo analysis is the solution of the correspondence problem.

images composed of random dots, [Julesz 71], we know that the human does not depend on detection of recognizable features in each individual image to fuse a stereo pair of images, i.e., to recover the depth information. In computational vision, a stereo pair of images is obtained by using two separated cameras or by moving a single camera to two locations (*motion stereo*). The critical and difficult step is determining correspondences between points in the two images so that the disparity

can be determined. Once this has been accomplished, straightforward geometric analysis can be used to compute the three-dimensional location of points in the scene (see Box 9-5). Figure 9-16 shows a stereo pair of images, and an artificially constructed view of the corresponding scene obtained by deducing the scene geometry using stereo analysis. The only scene information employed in this reconstruction was obtained from the stereo image pair shown in Fig. 9-16(a).

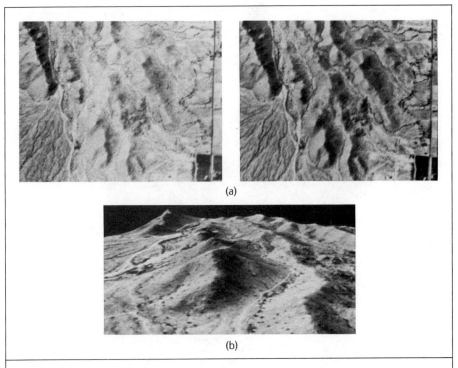

(a)

(b)

FIGURE 9-16   Three-Dimensional Scene Modeling using Stereo Analysis.

(a) Stereo pair of images. (b) An artificially constructed view of the scene depicted in (a), obtained by stereo analysis. (Courtesy of SRI International, Menlo Park, Calif.)

- *Optic flow*. Suppose we have an imaging sensor moving through a scene. As the sensor moves forward, scene points will move in the image plane along curves known as *optic flow curves*. By analyzing these flow curves it is possible to determine the distance from points in the scene to the sensor. These distances can then be used to construct a three-dimensional model of the scene just as in the case of employing stereo analysis. If the sensor is moving forward with pure translational motion, the optic flow curves will be straight lines that con-verge at a point known as the *focus of expansion* (FOE) (Fig. 9-17). (If the sensor moves backward, the lines would converge at a *focus of contraction*.) If the FOE can be located in the image plane, and the distance moved by the sensor from frame to frame is known, then the distance from a point in the scene to the sensor can be found. If it is known only that the motion of the sensor was constant, but not how far the sensor moved, then the relative depth of points in the scene can be obtained (see Box 9-6). This is often sufficient,

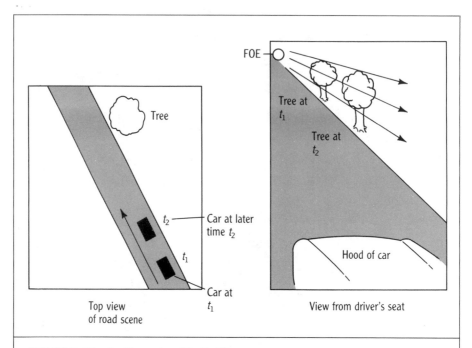

FIGURE 9-17   An Example of Optic Flow.

Seen from the driver's eyes, the hood of the speeding car is perceived as stationary, but the features of the tree-lined road appear to be moving along straight lines radiating from the focus of expansion (FOE).

for example, to partition the scene. If the motion of the sensor is more general, then the optic flow curves must be decomposed into rotational and translational components. Only the translational component contributes to the depth computation. One approach used is to analyze small regions of the image, using the disparities to obtain a trial FOE for each region. For portions of the image in which the rotational effects are strong, the flow segments will not converge to a FOE. If enough portions of the scene do provide a consist-

ent FOE, then the translational portion can be separated from the rotational portion of the disparities. Optic flow is an interesting alternative to stereo because it offers a method for three-dimensional scene modeling that is not dependent on a solution to the matching problem.

INTERMEDIATE-LEVEL SCENE ANALYSIS (ILSA)

Intermediate-level scene analysis (ILSA) is concerned with integrating local or point

BOX 9-6   The Computation of Depth from Optic Flow

Assume a camera with center of perspective at point F is moving with constant velocity v along its principal axis, z, relative to some point P in three-dimensional space. Assume a focal length of one unit with the image plane parallel to the y axis, as shown in Fig. 9-18.

Let P^1 be the image of P. Then

$$y^1 = y/z \text{ and } v = dz/dt,$$

and w, the image plane velocity of

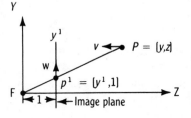

FIGURE 9-18
Geometry of Optic Flow.

P^1, is:

$$w = dy^1/dt = -(y/z^2)v = -y^1v/z$$
$$\text{and } z = -y^1v/w$$

Thus $d^2 = y^2 + z^2 = z^2[(y^1)^2 + 1]$, and d is approximately equal to $(y^1)^2v/w$. This means that if the camera velocity is known, and the image velocity of a point can be measured, then the distance from the camera to the point in space can be found.

---

features into global constructs, e.g., forming edge points into continuous contours, partitioning the image into coherent regions, assigning semantic labels to detected scene entities, evaluating sensor parameters (e.g., determining the spatial location of the sensor), deriving a model of the illumination sources, etc. Distinct representations and techniques are required for intermediate-level scene analysis because it is not possible to extend techniques employed in LLSA to the more complex global phenomena required to understand and interpret natural imagery. ILSA is primarily involved with the selection of models and the assignment of values to these models ("instantiation"). The models employed are of both a generic and scene- or domain-specific nature; ILSA cannot be completely divorced from final purpose.

As indicated in Chapter 8, vision in organic systems involves reasoned intelligent behavior. Where do these intellectual functions appear in the CV paradigm?

Certainly not in the low-level analysis which has a largely mechanical flavor. Even though the achievements of CV are still, at best, comparable to those of fairly primitive organic systems, we will see that many of the intermediate- and high-level techniques described in this and the following sections satisfy the basic criteria for reasoning presented in Chapter 4. In particular, the representations used in intermediate- and high-level analysis, e.g., graphs and relational nets, are similar to those used in the cognitive areas of AI. The techniques are typically designed to perform an efficient search over potentially infinite solution spaces, and many of the methods have associated validation procedures which determine when an acceptable solution has been found. We will describe the following ILSA integration tasks:

1. *Image/scene partitioning*—the problem of breaking the image into coherent or meaningful units

2. *Edge linking and drawing a sketch—* organizing individual pixels that have been identified as candidate line or edge elements into contiguous segments; transforming primitive line drawings into more abstract representations of shape

3. *Recovering three-dimensional scene geometry from line drawings—*using the constraints between edges and surfaces to deduce three-dimensional scene geometry from a two-dimensional line drawing

4. *Image matching—*determining the correspondences between two images

5. *Object labeling—*assigning labels or class names to image structures

6. *Model selection and instantiation—* selecting a model with generalized parameters, and assigning values to these parameters to fit a given set of image data

Computational techniques currently used for some of these integration tasks are given in Appendixes 9-1 to 9-3.

Image/Scene Partitioning

A point-by-point description of a scene, such as that obtainable using LLSA techniques, is too complex and thus relatively useless (in that form) for most purposes. To produce a useful description, one of reasonable complexity in which higher-level scene attributes have been made explicit, the scene must be partitioned into meaningful or coherent components. How can this be accomplished without prior knowledge about the given scene?

It is conceivable that the human visual system first makes global judgments about the scene, and then decomposes this gestalt into a structured description using linguistic or visual primitives to describe localized regions in the image or scene. Except in the simplest cases, we have no notion of how to duplicate this approach in a practical manner with the computational techniques currently at our disposal.

Within the signals-to-symbols paradigm, a common approach to image partitioning is *image space clustering* (Box 9-7), the grouping of pixels based on both spatial contiguity, and homogeneity of attributes that can be measured by LLSA techniques. This approach is often implemented by requiring that regions be composed of adjacent pixels, where each pixel has an intensity value that does not differ from that of its neighbors by more than some specified amount. Other partitioning techniques, employing the same general strategy, include: (1) *feature space clustering*, grouping of pixels located anywhere in an image based on homogeneity of locally measured attributes, and (2) *boundary analysis/contouring* in which a region of an image is considered to be determined by its boundary; the partitioning algorithm links locally detected edge points into closed contours.

An image such as Fig. 9-22 (where a gestalt or overall impression is obtained from the interplay of a myriad of small, relatively meaningless intensity patches) cannot be meaningfully partitioned into regions by any of the above techniques. Isolating the small patches does not help in recovering the global aspect of the image. Further, many images do not yield a unique partitioning since the goal or purpose of the subsequent analysis can play an important role. A single image can

BOX 9-7 Partitioning via Image Space Clustering

Pixels in an image can be grouped into a common region if they have the same local characteristics, e.g., gray level or color, and satisfy a distance or connectivity criterion. Techniques for region or cluster finding can be based on the fact that good criteria for cluster separation can be defined in terms of connectivity of a graph. The first step in such approaches is to form a graph by (1) connecting each point to its k nearest neighbors (only pixels with some distinguished set of attributes are involved), or (2) by connecting any pair of points whose distance is less than a threshold distance. Each edge of the graph can be labeled with the distance between the two points. A typical graph is shown in Fig. 9-19.

One approach for partitioning a graph into separate clusters is to look for "cut points," nodes whose removal would disconnect the graph (e.g., see Fig. 9-20), or "bridges,"

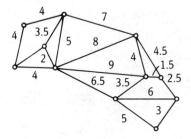

FIGURE 9-19

Typical Graph used to Cluster Pixels.

Distances are actual image distances between pixels. Each node is an image point having a desired characteristic or label.

edges whose removal would disconnect the graph. Another graph approach to partitioning is based on the concept of the *minimum spanning tree* (MST), the tree that connects all the nodes and whose sum of distances on edges is minimal. The general approach to partition-

ing data points represented by a MST is to look for edges that are long with respect to some average of lengths on both sides of the edge. For example, Fig. 9-21(a) shows a set of points formed into a graph, Fig. 9-21(b) shows one of the possible spanning trees of the graph, and Fig. 9-21(c) shows the minimum spanning tree. The long edges in the tree correspond to the gaps between the perceptually obvious clusters.

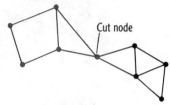

FIGURE 9-20
Use of Cut Nodes to Obtain Clusters.

Elimination of cut node (arrow) would disconnect the graph, and define two separate clusters.

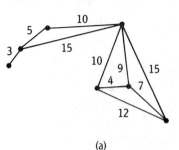

(a)

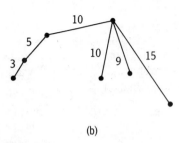

(b)

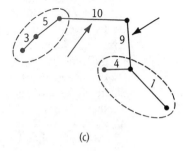

(c)

FIGURE 9-21   Minimum Spanning Tree.

(a) Original graph. (b) One of the spanning trees that connect all the nodes. (c) Minimum spanning tree of original graph; long edges (arrows) indicate possible separation of clusters.

FIGURE 9-22
The "Dalmatian," an Image with a Myriad of Small, Meaningless Regions.

It is possible to find a dalmatian in the approximate center of this picture. (Photo © Ronald C. James with permission.)

also be partitioned in more than one way based on the level of detail desired, or on the point of view of the observer. Figure 9-23 shows a satellite image and the different partitionings made by experts having different disciplinary interests. Figure 9-24 shows an object that is partitioned differently by most people, depending on whether it is viewed right side up or upside-down.

In an important sense, image/scene partitioning is the creative step in visual perception that makes the rest of the descriptive process feasible. It not only decomposes the analysis problem into manageable units, but also provides the necessary structuring needed to index into a knowledge base of stored models. The partitioning techniques described above lack the competence for the type of performance required. What other approaches are possible?

Two of the issues that must be addressed by any partitioning scheme are:

1. What is the nature of the primitive vocabulary if it is not simply the set of locally measurable point attributes?

2. Without using domain-specific knowledge, how can we judge the merits of a proposed partition, or compare two alternative partitions?

There is significant evidence from psychological experiments ([Julesz 83],

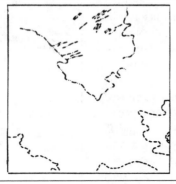
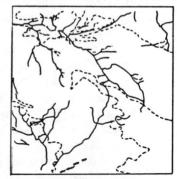

FIGURE 9-23   Different Line Drawing Interpretations of a Single Satellite Photograph Made by Experts in Different Disciplines (Geology, Forestry, and Hydrology).

(From *Ecological Surveys from Space*. NASA Office of Technological Utilization, NASA SP-230, 1970, with permission.)

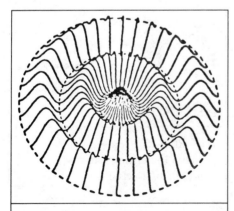

FIGURE 9-24
Different Partitionings based on Orientation of the Figure.

(After Hoffman and Richards, *Cognition* 18:65–96, 1985.) A cosine surface, which observers almost uniformly see organized into ringlike parts. A part stops and another begins roughly where the dotted circular contours are drawn. But if the figure is turned upside down the organization changes such that each dotted circular contour, which before lay between parts, now lies in the middle of a part.

[Treisman 85]) to indicate that groupings of certain primitive features can be detected almost instantaneously regardless of where they occur in the human visual field (e.g., see Fig. 9-11). Such features, called textons by Julesz and Bergen, consist of elongated blobs (especially line segments) distinguished by such properties as angular orientation, width, length, and color; ends of lines and crossings of line segments are also textons. Julesz hypothesizes the existence of a separate "preattentive" human visual system that can distinguish between different types of textons, and different densities of textons, but is unable to process information about positional relationships between different textons. Positional information essential for form perception can be extracted by a time-consuming process, called "focal attention," which is only available to the normal visual system.

There is still much debate about the nature of the primitives that are first extracted from the raw sensed data. Beyond lines or edges, and regions homogeneous in some local attribute, it is difficult to defend any higher-level construct as having sufficient utility to serve as a primitive for a general purpose vision system. It is certainly possible that most of the primitives employed (in human vision) for partitioning are not universal, but are derived for each scene domain based on some general set of principles. For example, if some pattern of points, or particularly shaped region or line segment appears often enough in a given scene, then such an entity would be a good candidate as a primitive for describing that scene, assuming it could be discovered in some reasonably efficient way.

How can we evaluate a proposed partition, or compare two competing decompositions of the same scene? If we recognize the fact that scene partitioning is an implied explanation of how the image was constructed, then in the absence of any absolute validity checking procedure or criteria, we must use various measures of believability as the basis for evaluation or comparison. A believable explanation should be complete, concise (*Occam's razor*), and stable:

- *Completeness*. One way of measuring completeness is to require that deviations of the data from the hypothesized explanation (partition, model, etc.) have the characteristics of random noise; i.e., that all of the correlations and detectable patterns in the data are explicitly addressed in the explanation. For example, suppose we must decide if a *single* straight line is a good description of the data points shown in Fig. 9-25(a), i.e., is this data set coherent or should it be partitioned? We would tend to reject the straight-line explanation since succes-

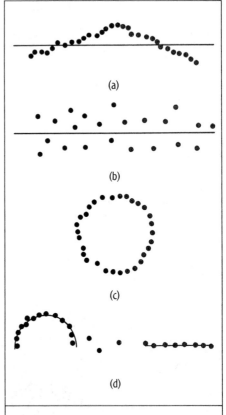

(a)

(b)

(c)

(d)

FIGURE 9-25
Criteria Underlying Effective
Partitioning Decisions.

sive deviations of data points from the hypothesized line are highly correlated. On the other hand, even though the deviations are larger in Fig. 9-25(b), a straight line is a more believable explanation here because of the random nature of the deviations.

- *Conciseness*. Conciseness or simplicity of explanation can be measured by the "length" of the explanation assuming that the vocabulary is appropriate for the given problem domain. For example, if our vocabulary consisted only of the terms "circular arc," "straight line segment," and "image point," and we wished to construct a believable description of the object shown in Fig. 9-25(c), then the single term "circle" is a simpler explanation than a description composed of a concatenation of points or line segments. The object shown in Fig. 9-25(d) is decomposed into the shortest (simplest) description possible in terms of our given primitives (assuming a reasonable "cost" for each point, straight line segment, and circular arc).

- *Stability.* Believable explanations should be stable under slight changes of viewing conditions or of decision procedure parameters. For example, to protect against interpretation mistakes due to viewing an object from an unusual perspective, the "story should remain unchanged" when the relationship between the viewer and the object is slightly perturbed. (If you remember, the story was indeed changed in the impossible triangle of Fig. 8-12.)

A simple computational example of how the stability criterion leads to correct interpretations is illustrated in the problem of attempting to distinguish *intensity quantization boundaries* from *true* boundaries denoting actual scene content. If we shift the quantization thresholds slightly, the intensity quantization boundaries will typically shift spatially while the true boundaries will remain stationary.

Edge Linking and Deriving a Line Sketch

One of the main purposes of ILSA is to take clues about the nature of a scene, as discovered by LLSA, and compile them into more meaningful and abstract structures. The line sketch is one of the most natural and effective abstractions available for representing scene content. For example, some of the earliest expressions of human art are essentially line sketches (Fig. 9-26). The ability to depict structure with a few line strokes, however, is a creative ability only possessed by the most talented artists (Fig. 9-27). What are the computational approaches and problems

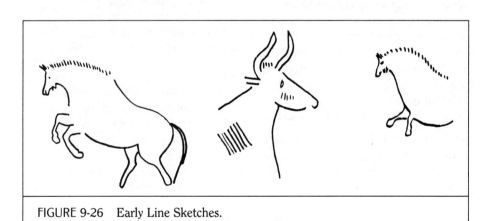

FIGURE 9-26   Early Line Sketches.

FIGURE 9-27

Sketch by Matisse that Captures the Nude Form in a Few Line Strokes.

(© Spadem, Davis/Vaga, New York 1986, with permission.)

to be dealt with in attempting to transform a gray-level image into a line sketch abstraction of the corresponding scene?

The human visual system is so good at interpreting line sketches that it is easy to overlook the fact that such sketches employ the same iconic symbol (the line symbol) to represent three completely different types of information, objective edges, subjective edges, and skeletons:

- *Objective edges.* These are the directly visible edges of regions or objects, e.g., locations in the image at which there are measurable discontinuities of intensity, color, or texture. Even if we restrict our attention to objective edges, there

are usually many distinct ways to link the edge pixels found by low-level techniques. It is therefore generally necessary to appeal to some purpose or value function to provide a criterion for selecting one interpretation over others. An optimization technique for edge linking is described in Appendix 9-1. A more general solution, which is not a function of purpose or semantic constraints, is possible for simple scenes, i.e., those for which almost any observer would produce the same line sketch. The general idea is to find all the edge points in some contiguous region of the image and link these points using a *minimum spanning tree* algorithm (see Box 9-7). Long continuous paths extracted from the tree correspond to the perceptually obvious line structures in the image. This approach is illustrated in Fig. 9-28. The process involves extracting linear feature points based on local intensity characteristics (Fig. 9-28b); separating the extracted points into coherent clusters and linking the points in each cluster into a minimum spanning tree (Fig. 9-28c); pruning the tree of spurious and insignificant branches (Fig. 9-28d); and superimposing the major linear segments, as obtained above, on the original image (Fig. 9-28e).

- *Subjective edges.* These are edges known or deduced to be present in the scene, but not directly visible in the image, i.e., edges not represented by measurable local discontinuities (see Fig. 9-29). Edge linking cannot be expected to produce a complete line sketch. In many realistic situations, points associated with a particular edge will be too scattered (because of low

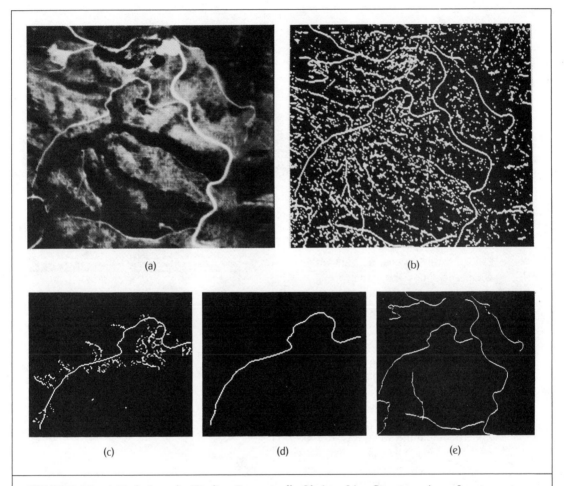

FIGURE 9-28   A Technique for Finding Perceptually Obvious Line Structures in an Image.

(a) Original image. (b) Extracted linear feature points. (c) A single cluster of feature points. (d) Linear segment extracted. (e) Line structures found in the image. (Photos courtesy of SRI International, Menlo Park, Calif.)

contrast, occlusions, and interference from adjacent but distinct edges) to be correctly linked by a simple contiguity criterion. Inferring the presence of subjective edges seems to require deduction from an assumed model, rather than inductive reasoning based on local evidence. For example, in the picture of the Dalmatian (Fig. 9-22), we must assume at some point in the analysis process that the image contains a dog, and then deduce the presence of the edges that form its outline. When there are no contextual constraints on what

FIGURE 9-29   Examples of Subjective
Edges.

(See also Fig. 8-13.)

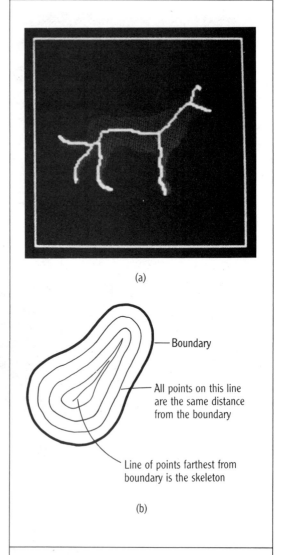

(a)

Boundary

All points on this line
are the same distance
from the boundary

Line of points farthest from
boundary is the skeleton

(b)

FIGURE 9-30

"Stick Figures" Automatically Produced by
a "Skeleton" Generating Technique.

(a) Example of stick figure derived from image of a dog.
(b) Method for obtaining a skeleton by generating a
nested sequence of contours. A "distance transform"
algorithm for this purpose is described in [Fischler and
Barrett 80].

can appear in a scene, it is difficult to
comprehend how the human visual
system is able to select appropriate
models from an infinity of possible
alternatives.

- *Abstract lines or skeletons*. These are
  the centerline, or spine, of long, thin
  objects; e.g., as in the use of stick figures to represent shapes (see Fig. 9-30).
  There may be locally detectable image
  structures corresponding to the abstract
  lines, but often this will not be the case.
  In simple scene domains, especially
  where the image information is essentially binary, the complete contours of
  isolated objects can be extracted to
  obtain a primitive line drawing representation of the image content. However, a
  human-produced sketch of the same
  image would almost certainly be a more
  abstract representation. For example,
  in the case of printed material, the
  width of the characters would be suppressed and only the skeleton would
  be provided. Techniques are available
  for extracting and using skeletons
  as the basis for both two- and three-
  dimensional shape representation.

If it is desired to represent a natural scene by a line sketch, it is generally necessary to eliminate all but a small subset of the detected and inferred edges as the final abstraction. The initial linking, insertion of abstract edges, and subsequent elimination process must be based on purpose or semantic knowledge of the scene domain and a depth of reasoning well beyond the capabilities of our current paradigm.

Recovering Three-Dimensional Scene Geometry from a Line Drawing

A person looking at a two-dimensional line sketch of a three-dimensional scene can usually partition the sketch into its coherent components and describe the corresponding scene. Given that the sketch is indeed two-dimensional, and thus an ambiguous representation of the three-dimensional world, what is the basis for this rather remarkable ability? In this subsection we will describe some computational techniques that attempt to achieve similar performance for a limited class of scenes.

It is possible to transform a gray-level image of a three-dimensional scene into a line drawing using edge analysis methods of the type discussed in preceding sections. We will assume for the present that unbroken lines representing actual edges are obtained, i.e., a perfect line drawing. We will further assume that the scene only contains objects with planar surfaces and that no more than three surfaces meet at one point in space. Given these *blocks-world* assumptions, it is possible to achieve close to human-level partitioning of the scene with relatively simple algorithms.

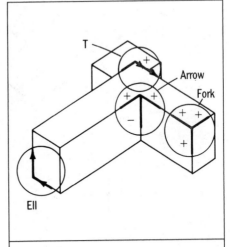

FIGURE 9-31
Three-Dimensional Shape from Line Drawings: Obtaining Junction Labels.

The simple but powerful idea is to assign one of three labels to each line in the image; these labels correspond to three types of three-dimensional edges: + (for a convex edge), − (for a concave edge), and → (for an occluding edge). Further, only four label types are needed to distinguish nodes based on the entering edge types, an ell, a fork, an arrow, and a T, as shown in Fig. 9-31. A good way to derive the complete set of physically realizable node (junction) labels is to view a simple solid figure from various viewpoints, as shown in the figure. If this approach is repeated for all possible viewing angles, the complete set of eighteen legal node labels shown in Fig. 9-32 is obtained.

This labeling scheme can be used to analyze a blocks-world line drawing. An iterative procedure is used in which we begin with all possible labels attached

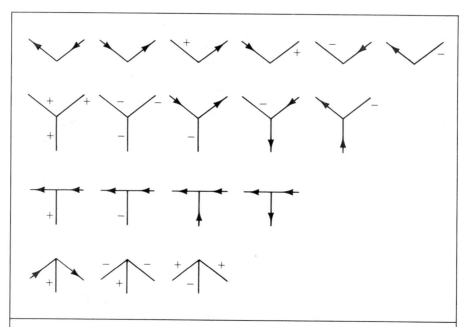

FIGURE 9-32

Three-Dimensional Shape from Line Drawings: Legal Junction Labels.

(From P. H. Winston. *Artificial Intelligence*. Addison-Wesley, Reading, Mass. 1984, with permission.)

to each edge, but by using the dictionary of legal junction types we can eliminate invalid labels. The key idea is that since an edge must have the same label at both of its end points, it imposes a constraint on the two nodes it joins. A globally consistent labeling will often produce a unique label for each edge. It is possible to obtain several different labelings for a given line drawing, but this is to be expected since, when we view a line drawing, we can often see the three-dimensional scene in more than one way, e.g., the stairway illusion (Fig. 9-33) that can be seen in two different ways.

   The labeling approach does indeed determine that the object shown in Fig.

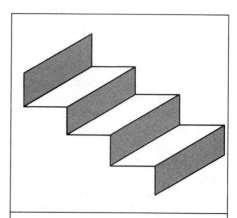

FIGURE 9-33   Stairway Illusion.

Are these stairs being viewed from above or below?

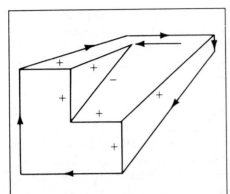

FIGURE 9-34   Impossible Figure.

An impossible object. The indicated ell junction is not among the legal ones. (From P. H. Winston. *Artificial Intelligence*. Addison-Wesley, Reading, Mass., 1984, with permission.)

9-34 is impossible. However, other cases exist for which a depicted object cannot exist in the real world, but we are still able to find a legal set of labels. This failure has caused researchers to look for representations that can more adequately handle impossible objects, and can deal with more complex objects and imaging conditions. In the case of the blocks world, rather complex scenes—even scenes containing cracks and shadows—can be correctly analyzed, (Fig. 9-35), and necessary and sufficient conditions do exist to determine if a perfect line drawing corresponds to a physically realizable object, but these results have not yet been extended to more realistic scene domains or imperfect delineations.

FIGURE 9-35
A Scene Typical of the Type that can be Correctly Analyzed and Partitioned by Existing Techniques.

(From D. I. Waltz. In P. H. Winston (editor), *The Psychology of Computer Vision*. McGraw-Hill, New York, 1975, with permission.)

Image Matching

It is difficult to conceive of a more basic perceptual act than determining whether two images depict the same scene content, and more precisely, the specific or local correspondences. In the case of human stereo vision, the correspondences between the two almost identical images provided by our two eyes allows the brain to create a depth map of the scene, probably using a technique equivalent to simple trigonometric triangulation (see Box 9-5).

When the views to be matched are almost identical (say, differing only in translation and possibly scaled in intensity), then a simple computational solution to the matching/correspondence problem is area correlation, in which small fixed-size patches of the two images are compared. More generally, we are often faced with the problem of matching images that represent significantly different views of the scene. Such images may differ in three respects: (1) the viewing conditions may have changed—view angle, perspective distortion, occluded surfaces, illumination, shadows, highlights, and atmospheric conditions may be significantly different; (2) physical changes may have occurred in the scene—new or altered features such as roads, buildings, floods, or seasonal changes may be present, or objects may have moved, such as cars in a parking lot; and (3) the image acquisition and processing system may have changed—the sensors may have different noise and distortion characteristics, resolutions, spectral response, and the representations produced may be the result of different nonreversible transformations (e.g., an intensity array converted to a line sketch).

In registering one image to another, we wish to find the transformation between either the images or the sensor models, taking full advantage of the known or deduced physical characteristics of the scene and the viewing situation. If the nature of the variation of such characteristics cannot be quantified, then the variable describing these characteristics must be eliminated from the decision process. The matching process is based on the selection of the *features* to be matched, the *control strategy* that specifies how to search for potential matches, and the *criteria* for evaluating the match or selecting a best match.

Correlation approach. The traditional approach to image matching is based on signal processing and statistical decision theory concepts. Each image is treated as a (context-free) signal, with all known distortions, viewing and illumination artifacts, etc., removed prior to the matching step; the images (signals) to be matched are assumed to have some common area of overlap in which the only difference is nominally describable as additive gaussian noise. The matching technique is generally some form of *area correlation* in which the features to be matched are small fixed-size patches of the image. We search for matches by "comparing" a patch in the first image with all the patches in the second image that are potential match candidates, and we select the match that produces the highest "correlation coefficient."

Feature matching approach. As our ability to model the distortion and illumination differences between the two scenes decreases, we are motivated to extract descriptions that ignore the detailed (pixel-by-pixel) intensity variations in the images, and concentrate instead on selected measurable features (or attributes) and relations that are relatively invariant to viewing conditions and sensor variations. For example, intensity discontinuities, or edges, are more likely to remain invariant across two views of the same scene than the absolute intensity values whose differences produced the edges.

We often employ a *signal-processing* approach in determining if two images represent the same scene, by comparing the values of a set of feature measurements made on each of the images. Typical features might include area, perimeter length, spectral energy distribution, etc. The descriptions used for matching purposes in this case are the feature vectors, and the measure of similarity of the two images is the distance between the feature vectors in a Euclidean space defined by the features (see Chapter 3 and Appendix 9-1).

Relational matching approach. To establish detailed correspondences between the images, and to increase the reliability of the matching process beyond that possible using feature measurements, we must explicitly include geometric relationships between selected components of the scene in both the image descriptions and in the matching process. The image descriptions now are conceptually equivalent to a graph, where the nodes represent features or objects in the scene, and the branches represent relations; the matching process (called structural matching) involves the comparison of two graphs, or part of one graph with another.

The matching techniques discussed above (correlation, feature, and relational matching) form a natural ordering in two respects. First, there is an ordering based on the descriptive power of the representation. In area correlation the representation is the intensity array, and there is no *language* for introducing semantic information or for modeling view or sensor-related factors that cause changes in image appearance. The representation for feature matching is the feature vector, and there is no mechanism for introducing information about relations between features. However, the semantic net representation for structural matching potentially offers the full descriptive power of natural language.

The second ordering characteristic is that of modeling difficulty. As the descriptive power of the matching techniques increases, there is a corresponding requirement to define an enlarged vocabulary (names for additional features and objects) and a set of relationships between these vocabulary primitives. However, this brings with it the difficult requirement of detecting the presence or absence of these primitive linguistic constructs in an image to create the desired description.

The image-matching problem is fundamental to all of machine vision, and is therefore typical of what appears to be a pervasive difficulty facing us in all aspects of machine vision under the current paradigm: Our more powerful techniques are based on a symbolic formulation in which large amounts of low-level information are successively integrated into more global and abstract descriptions. Currently, we are limited in our ability to obtain relevant low-level information of suitable quality because our analysis depends on weak descriptive formalisms and a local perspective that is too restrictive to avoid ambiguity and error. If we attempt to use more global *primitives*, the number of such primitives necessary to provide descriptive completeness grows exponentially, and the level of modeling required for each such primitive makes such an endeavor impractical.

Object Labeling

This and the next section discuss the problems of assigning names to objects. Two forms of this problem are: (1) given a specific reference object, find instances of it in an image, and (2) label the objects in an image according to the generic classes to which they belong:

1. *Labeling specific objects.* In the simplest form of specific object labeling we assume that image shape does not differ significantly from reference shape; it is therefore easy to obtain a description suitable for matching. An example of this situation is the recognition of alphabetic characters of a given font, where the number of free parameters is limited, and we can use an attribute space in which the reference pattern and the unknown pattern appear as points. An unknown pattern is assigned to that reference pattern whose representative point is closest to it in the attribute space. However, finding suitable descriptions for complex objects becomes a significant problem. An example here is finding a specific person in a crowd. Since a person can assume various shapes when sitting, standing, or bending, a simple description will not suffice. The description must indicate

the relationship between parts, the constraints in movement, the shape of parts, and the ability of the parts themselves to change shape (e.g., the shape of the mouth); we are also faced with the problem of how to structure the descriptions so that the reference objects can be compared to the descriptions derived for the sensed objects. The matching procedure must be able to deal with occlusion and flexibility of objects. Objects are often occluded by their own parts, by other objects, or by shadows, so that the derived descriptions will only partially match the reference descriptions.

2. *Labeling generic objects.* An example of generic labeling is finding all instances of a road in an image. Note that we are not looking for a known road whose description is available. Instead, a generic description of "roadness" is required. In more difficult problems, one might want to label objects with terms such as "tree," "bush," "meadow," etc. We are not asked to find a specific tree whose measurements are known. The reference object is now much more difficult to describe in terms that permit simple matching. In addition, there is a chicken and egg situation: How can we be sure that the shape of part of an unknown object corresponds to a branch, if we are not sure that the object we are attempting to identify is a tree? Most of our techniques depend on producing a description from image measurements, retrieving relevant models from our stored database (possibly) containing an immense number of such models,

and making the indicated comparison. If we do not know that we are looking at a tree in the first place, then the effort required to examine all components of all models in the database becomes exorbitant. Complete generic labeling of arbitrary scenes is well beyond the present state of the art. Labeling procedures now require that the number of generic classes be limited. One way of accomplishing this is by specifying the context of the image to the program, e.g., "outdoor scene," " office scene," etc., so that the program can select descriptions from its database that are appropriate to this context.

Model Instantiation

Visual perception is based on selecting models that are relevant to the analysis of a sensed scene, and then determining the values of the parameters of these models based on scene content (*instantiating* the model). In intermediate-level vision, typical models of interest are:

- *Geometric models*: e.g., lines, curves, polygons, planes, and surfaces
- *Illumination models*: equations that relate the light sources, surface reflectances, and image intensities
- *Sensor models*: equations that define the camera (sensor) orientation and location parameters, for a given image, in terms of a coordinate system tied to the sensed scene
- *Semantic models*: descriptions of objects and events that might appear in an image (e.g., person, building)

The model instantiation process works as follows: Once it has been determined that a particular model is appropriate for a given image, e.g., a triangle, the system could identify lines in the image that might be the sides of a triangle, find their lengths, and the angles between contiguous lines. If the model is that of a person, the appropriate instantiations could be size of the person, or male or female. In intermediate-level vision, model instantiation often results in numerical values for the model parameters.

There are three approaches to assigning values to the parameters of a model based on observed or experimental data. The classical approach is to use an optimization technique, such as *least squares*, to solve an *overconstrained* set of equations in order to define an instantiated model that best fits *all* the data, i.e., all the data is used simultaneously to solve for the parameters of the model. Problems arise when the data contain gross errors or intermixed data from multiple objects. For example, even a single measurement error, if large enough, can cause least squares to fail, and there is no general method for reliably eliminating such gross errors.

A second approach (e.g., the *Hough transform*, see Appendix 9-1) takes one data point at a time and finds all the parameters of the model consistent with this data point; i.e., we solve an *underconstrained* set of equations to find all solutions compatible with the given data point. The set of solutions determined for each data point is used to "vote" for all the corresponding parameter values. After all the data points have been processed, those parameter values receiving the most votes are taken as the desired solution.

The third approach (e.g., *random sample consensus* [Fischler 83]) randomly selects just enough data points to solve the model equations, and then attempts to confirm this instantiated model by testing it against the remaining data. If such confirmation fails, the process is repeated with another random selection of data points. This approach is surprisingly efficient, as well as robust, under a fairly wide range of reasonable conditions.

The determination of the appropriate model (discussed in the previous section), as opposed to the instantiation of the model, is a problem in detection or classification. One must utilize the evidence accumulated as the result of low level analysis to make this determination. People have a remarkable ability to select the appropriate model from what amounts to an almost infinite set of models. For example, in Fig. 9-36, how do we know that this is a picture of Paris when we have never seen the city from this particular viewpoint? In the case of computer vision, the designer is currently forced to indicate some small set of models to which the system can direct its attention.

FIGURE 9-36   Recognizing a Scene: What City is Depicted Here?

(Drawing by Oscar Firschein.)

HIGH-LEVEL SCENE ANALYSIS (HLSA)

High-level scene analysis (HLSA) invokes the full body of AI techniques (e.g., symbolic logic, expert systems theory) and representations (e.g., relational nets) to provide a description of an image, or the corresponding scene, in terms of some given set of semantic models and linguistic relationships. Currently, there is little direct coupling between the information that can directly and automatically be obtained from our LLSA and ILSA techniques and the input needs of available HLSA systems. The problem here is that high-level scene analysis is strongly coupled to semantic knowledge and final purpose—a tremendous amount of knowledge is needed to bridge the gap between what is immediately visible in an image, and what can be deduced about the corresponding scene.

In trying to derive a symbolic description of a scene, one realizes that the saying, "A picture is worth a thousand words," may be too conservative. As a striking example of HLSA consider the political cartoon: The viewer is expected to recognize the participants, the topic under consideration, and the editorial view of the cartoonist, all from a simple line drawing. When we view a political cartoon from the 1800s we may no longer have the required world knowledge to understand its message.

Image/Scene Description

Having a human produce a natural language description of objects and their relationships in a scene would seem to be straightforward, and we might expect that the meaning of the natural language expression should also be readily determined. For example, the meaning of "The hat is in the box" should be derivable by having a dictionary entry for "in" that says "X is *in* Y if Y spatially includes most of X." It turns out, though, that the meaning of the word "in" is more subtle than that. Expressions such as those given below indicate quite different spatial characteristics, some of which are not captured by a simple definition of inclusion:

- The water *in* the vase (we mean the contents of the vase and not water composing the vase material)
- The crack *in* the vase (crack in the surface of the vase)
- The block *in* the circle (a block resting on a surface on which a circle is drawn
- The bird *in* the tree (a bird on a branch within the bounding region of the tree)

In addition, there are peculiarities of use, such as being able to talk about the table being in the garden, but not that the table is in the lawn. It is acceptable to draw a line in the margin, but not to draw a line in the blackboard. Some locative expressions are context dependent. Thus, given the scene:

$$B$$
$$A$$

we would say that B is to the right of A. But if the scene changes to:

$$B$$
$$A \qquad C$$

we would be hesitant to make the unqualified assertion that B is to the right of A.

Natural language constructions such

as these are not merely curiosities: if we expect a robot to use descriptions prepared by nontechnical people to navigate in the real world or to carry out commands, it is important that the robot be able to decode these expressions to derive the meaning intended by the person. Thus, a person would be dismayed if the command "Get the box under the bush" resulted in the robot's digging into the ground to get under the bush, presumably to find a second, not yet visible box!

Recent studies in the semantics and pragmatics of expressions involving location [Herskovits 85], have revealed remarkable nuances of use, some of which were illustrated above.

We can gain insight into the difficulty of automatic preparation of a high-level description of a gray-level image by examining descriptions prepared by human subjects. Such descriptions depend on the background of the person, the goal of the description, and the complexity of the photograph. The descriptions can be in terms of natural language, or in the form of line drawings that extract the *essence* of the image. The importance of the background and point of view of the person preparing the description was illustrated in Fig. 9-23, where a satellite photograph was described in terms of three completely different line drawings by a geologist, a hydrologist, and a forestry expert.

An example of a natural language description of an aerial photograph, Fig. 9-37, by a layman is as follows: "The picture is an aerial photograph of a land

FIGURE 9-37 Aerial Photograph of an Industrial Area.

(Supplied by O. Firschein and M. A. Fischler.)

area invaded by a three-pronged fork-shaped waterway. Wharves line the sides of the waterway. A bridge, probably for auto traffic, but possibly for rail traffic, crosses the handle of the waterway. The land is used primarily for industry: many large low buildings and fluid storage tanks, such as those used to store oil or water are on the land. The area depicted has dimensions of perhaps one to two miles; the photo exhibits a significant parallax effect. The waterway, perhaps a river or canal, is perpendicular to the line of sight of the camera; its average width is about a quarter mile."

In examining this description, we note (1) probabilistic terms, "seems," "perhaps"; (2) many objects and relations between objects; (3) inferences, "probably for auto traffic"; and even (4) information about the camera viewing location. In addition to the sophisticated reasoning needed to derive such descriptions, to store them in a database for future retrieval purposes, we must represent information in a way that captures all the different aspects of entities being described, i.e., the knowledge representation problem, as discussed below.

Knowledge Representation

If the description, *A bridge crosses the waterway*, is in the database and the question is asked, *What spans the waterway?*, there must be some equivalence established between *crosses* and *spans* for a retrieval match to be made. In addition, if we have stored *A is part of B* and *B is part of C*, we need some mechanism for deducing that A is part of C. Thus, in representing knowledge about a scene, we

are faced with the classic representation questions: (1) What formalism should be used for relating facts and drawing deductions from a collection of facts?; and (2) What basic relationship and descriptive words should be used in the formalism? A good image representation should have the additional important characteristic of capturing some of the implicit iconic information, e.g., objects that are near in the image should be *near* each other in the representation. Of the two representations described below, frames and semantic nets, only the semantic nets retain some of the iconic aspects of the original image.

Frame representations. In the chapter on language we discussed frames, scripts, and scenarios, an attempt to capture the components of typical situations for use in understanding natural language. Similarly, it is possible to develop frames applicable to image analysis, with each frame representing a stereotyped situation or object that might be found in a scene. The frames supply needed information and indicate what image data is relevant. For example, an *office frame* might specify what constitutes an office, e.g., desk, telephone, etc., and this frame can be used to provide the image analysis system with an expectation as to what objects might be in such a scene.

Semantic networks. The semantic network, as described in Chapter 3, has been used for HLSA. In image description applications of semantic networks, objects in the scene are represented by nodes, and the arcs from node to node represent the relations between the objects. A basic set of primitives is chosen to describe objects and relationships, and all descrip-

The picture is a black and white aerial photograph of a land area invaded by a triton-shaped or three-prong-shaped waterway. Wharves line the sides of the waterway. . . .

Concept kernels of the description fragment	Concept classes
The picture is a black and white aerial photograph	Picture property
Photograph is of a land area	Attribute
Land area is invaded by a triton-shaped, i.e., a three-prong-shaped, waterway	Operative
The waterway has sides	Set membership
The sides are lined with wharves	Attribute

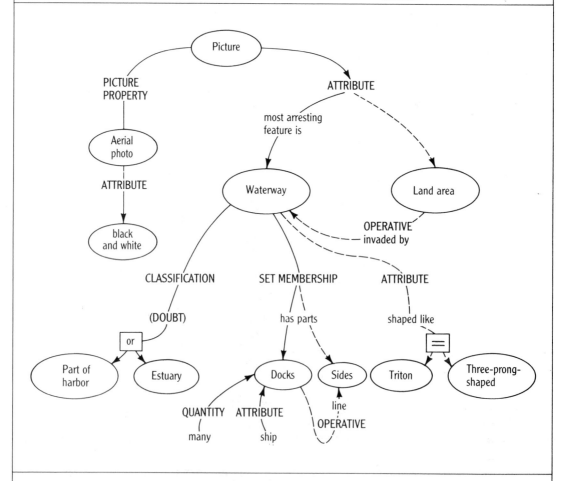

FIGURE 9-38   Semantic Network used for Image Description.

------   Denotes description
fragment given above.

_____   Denotes additional descriptive
information about scene.

tions are converted into compositions of these semantic primitives. The number and type of primitives that form the basic vocabulary is important because the choice of primitives will determine the expressive power of the representation. A semantic network for a portion of the description of the aerial photograph (Fig. 9-37) is shown in Fig. 9-38.

Care must be taken to separate generic concepts, such as *bridges* from a specific token such as the George Washington Bridge, otherwise errors in deductions can result. For example, if we have the following network:

$$A \rightarrow \text{is part of} \rightarrow B$$
$$B \rightarrow \text{is part of} \rightarrow C \ ,$$

then we can follow the links to deduce that A is-part-of C. However, linking can result in incorrect deductions if the generic and specific nodes are intermingled, or if the inheritance characteristics are not carefully isolated. For example, if we have a generic description of a bridge as something that spans a road or body of water, then a specific highway bridge that is in the state of construction must not inherit the characteristic "spanning," if only the abutments have been constructed.

The semantic network representation is not a formal mathematical system with unifying principles. Its use tends to be rather *ad hoc*, with various researchers employing different net interpretation schemes based on the same general concepts.

The Problem of High-Level Scene Analysis

There is no program at the present time that can automatically create a descrip-

tion of a scene at a human level of performance. Further, existing programs for converting from a natural language description to a semantic network are of a rudimentary nature, and work only in very limited domains of discourse. The basic difference between describing a document and describing an image is that a textual document is usually created in accordance with some specific objective of the author. While a potential user may be more interested in a tangential fact of the document, the use cannot be too far removed from the intended theme of the document. Most images, on the other hand, have no central or organizing theme, and a description of the same object from two different points of view may be completely unrelated.

Reasoning About a Simple Scene

Given the scene shown in Fig. 9-39, we are able to reason about what has happened and what is likely to happen next: we use our knowledge of how physical objects behave in the world to deduce that the young woman has pushed the man, causing him to lose his balance, and we predict that he will fall into the well.

Little work has been carried out in obtaining programs that can reason about scenes. Funt [Funt 80] developed a program called WHISPER that reasons about simple line drawings of objects to predict the behavior of a structure constructed from blocks. The program generates calls to a low-level analysis program to determine what shapes are involved and how the shapes make contact. Some of the questions that the vision program must be able to answer are: (1) Do shapes A and B

FIGURE 9-39

Example of Reasoning about a Scene: What Actions do we Expect will Follow?

(From S. Appelbaum. *Advertising Woodcuts from the 19th Century Stage*. Dover Publications, New York, 1977.)

touch? (2) Is shape C symmetrical around a given axis? (3) Where is the center of the area of shape D? (4) How far can shape E rotate around a given point before it will intersect some other shape?

The high-level reasoner consists of procedures which reason about the physical world in such common-sense terms as, "If a block is hanging over too far, it will topple." To determine that a block is hanging over too far, the high-level reasoner must generate calls to the sensor, and the reasoner then assigns domain-dependent meanings to the answers returned. In the case of Fig. 9-40, WHISPER would find that the top rectan-

gular block will fall, and will collide with the block balanced on the triangle, causing it to fall.

Note that in this program, rather than employing a strictly *data-driven* formalism, specific sensor-based observations are called for by the reasoner, and the interpretation of these observations depends on the goals and purposes of the reasoner.

DISCUSSION

We began this chapter with a description of the signals-to-symbols paradigm, and

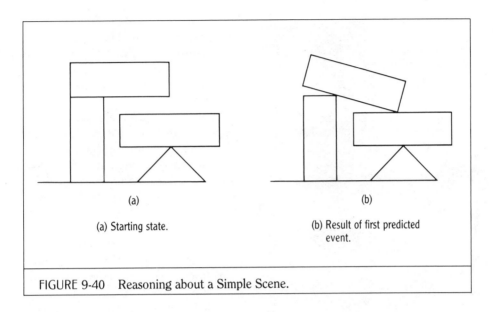

(a)

(a) Starting state.

(b)

(b) Result of first predicted event.

FIGURE 9-40   Reasoning about a Simple Scene.

then described the various assumptions and techniques that represent the current realization of this paradigm. We now take a critical look at this entire approach. The questions we want to address here are: (1) Is signals-to-symbols an adequate paradigm? In particular, what are its weaknesses?, and (2) What are the attributes required by a machine vision system if it is to be capable of human-level performance?

A Basic Concern About Signals-to-Symbols

The signals-to-symbols paradigm was presented in a hierarchical manner: from low- through intermediate- to high-level representation and analysis. In actual practice, the processing will rarely follow such a linear route; we really do not know how to impose an effective control structure on a computational vision system that must contend with images from unconstrained scene domains. For example, very few of the low-level techniques we described would be meaningful in helping to extract the information needed to perceive the Dalmatian shown in Fig. 9-22. On the other hand, if we tried to guide our processing by guessing what was present in the image, there would be an effective infinity of possible guesses. Finally, even knowing that we want to look for a Dalmatian, it is not clear how we bypass the lack of meaningful low-level information to achieve the final perceptual gestalt.

The signals-to-symbols paradigm is the only game in town given today's digital computers which can only process numbers or symbols. However, by employing a representation without an iconic or isomorphic component, we incur the following penalties:

Limited vocabulary. We are forced to

FIGURE 9-41   A Scene Difficult to Describe.

(Photo courtesy of Joseph Firschein.)

describe a scene as a network of relation-ships among a relatively small number of discrete named entities. Thus, we must describe a perceptually continuous scene with a description based on a limited vocabulary—the result is often a weak and inadequate description, or an unusably complex one. The driftwood shown in Fig. 9-41 is an example of a scene that is difficult to describe adequately with even the full power of natural language.

Loss of iconic representation. We lose the constraints and innate spatial relation-ships of the image when we go to a sym-bolic representation that does not have a corresponding innate spatial structuring. We have gone from an *iconic* to a *non-*

isomorphic representation. In the iconic representation relationships are innate; in the nonisomorphic symbolic repre-sentation we must explicitly express rela-tionships such as "near," "to the right of," etc.

Available iconic representations, suitable for computer implementation, are quite primitive. Typically, the image is stored as an array of numbers represent-ing a local attribute of a scene, such as intensity. Implicit information about the shapes, relative positions, and proximity of objects is inherent in this pictorial template representation. However, the pictorial template and its currently known generalizations fall considerably short of what will probably be required for a gen-eral solution to the problem of modeling real-world vision.

There is a large volume of experimen-tal evidence to indicate that humans use a sophisticated iconic representation in at least some of their visual tasks. For exam-ple, Roger Shepard [Shepard 71] has shown that when subjects are asked to mentally transform the spatial orientation of solid figures, they perform mental oper-ations that are highly analogous to the transformations used to reorient the cor-responding physical objects in space. Kosslyn [Kosslyn 80] has shown that the stored mental images used by human subjects appear to preserve distance: operations such as scanning took longer when the objects mentally searched for were farther apart.

Necessary Attributes of a Machine Vision System

Almost all computer vision research to date has dealt with the problem of identifying objects and describing their geometric relationships based on their appearance in an image. However, this mode of analysis represents a small subset of the reasoning employed by humans in interpreting a scene. Equally important is the ability to answer to such questions as:

Function. What are the objects in the scene doing?

Purpose. What are the objects supposed to be doing?

Competency. What are the objects able to do?

Intent. What does each object intend to do?

Anomaly. What is unusual or "wrong" with the scene?

Event analysis. What has happened?

Prediction. What is going to happen?

Evaluation. Why did the event happen?

The size and sophistication of the appropriate database, and the deductive apparatus needed to carry out the above type of analysis is far beyond what we are currently capable of doing with available techniques.

Summary

Key points that are implied in the above discussion can be summarized as follows:

Iconic representation. Many vision problems cannot be adequately described in a purely abstract formalism; this implies the need for employing some sort of iconic representation, as well as a computing device capable of supporting such a representation.

Learning. We cannot, in a practical sense, make explicit all of the knowledge needed to create a system capable of general purpose vision; some learning ability must be provided.

Need for experimentation. Because of limited understanding of the visual world, many vision problems will have to be solved by a process resembling physical experimentation; where the complexity of the problem environment prevents us from modeling it at a suitable level of detail, the *experimental space* of a device capable of general purpose vision may have to be extended out to the real world. Thus there must be an active interplay between sensing and interpretation.

Appendixes

9-1

Mathematical Techniques for Information Integration

Intermediate-level scene analysis was defined as the aggregate of operations in which local or point events are integrated into global phenomena. For example, edge points are connected to form continuous contours and semantic labels are assigned to detected scene entities. This appendix describes some of the mathematical techniques used to perform these integration operations:

- *Relaxation.* Local values or labels are adjusted to be *compatible* with neighborhood values or labels. The adjustment process continues until all values are compatible with their neighbors. The nature of the solution is determined by specified consistency and boundary conditions which remain unaltered during the computation.

- *Combinatorial optimization.* Given a set of objects, and a "cost" associated with each subset or configuration of these objects, the problem is to select a subset that satisfies a set of constraints, and at the same time minimize or maximize the value of a function of the costs. An optimal solution is selected by organizing the computation so that only the most promising alternative choices are pursued.

- *Model instantiation.* The *free* parameters of a model are assigned those values that permit the model to best describe a given set of data.

- *Statistical classification.* Objects are to be assigned to N predesignated classes. Each object is represented by a vector whose components correspond to measurements made on the object. Vectors corresponding to *ideal* measurement sets are specified for each of the N classes. Objects are classified by some function of their feature (measurement) space *distance* to the ideal measurement vectors.

Relaxation

The labeling or assignment process is a basic one in scene analysis. For example, assigning an edge strength and edge direction to a pixel is a form of labeling. On a higher level, we might label a line in an image with a code that indicates concavity or convexity of the edge it represents in the three-dimensional world. Intuitively, we know that if global information is used we can obtain a better assignment of labels than if we only use local information. A major problem is that of computational cost, since the larger the region used as the basis for establishing the labeling, the more time-consuming and complex the computation.

Relaxation techniques for scene analysis use iteration (repeated tries) as a means of obtaining a global interpretation by using only local understanding and local operations. Multiple passes are made through the image, and the labeling results are modified in each pass based on constraints, or compatibility of the current assignment of the labels at each pixel and those of its neighboring pixels. The intent is to have the local information propagate globally by means of label modification.

Forms of Label Assignment. In order to implement a relaxation process, we must have some way of making an initial assignment of labels to each pixel. For example, in edge analysis this can be done by using multiple masks, each representing a distinct edge orientation. At every pixel, those masks that produce a response greater than a certain threshold

value cause a corresponding label to be assigned to that pixel. Labels can appear in two forms: (1) *discrete labeling* that does not involve probability assignments, and (2) *probabilistic labeling* in which a strength or score is assigned to the labels. An example of discrete labeling is the set of labels *vertical, horizontal, diagonal, no edge*, that can be assigned to a pixel. Probabilistic labeling would be the assignment to a pixel of probability of horizontal=0.6, probability of vertical=0.2. In the discrete labels approach, successive iterations eliminate labels that cause compatibility problems with a neighbor, while in the probabilistic case the probabilities for each label of each pixel are modified.

Relaxation with Discrete Labels. The relaxation process used with discrete labels can be best presented by an example. Suppose that we are labeling pixels in edge analysis, that the possible labels are horizontal (H), vertical (V), and none (N), and that compatibility rules require: (1) An H pixel must have H neighbors to the left or right; (2) a V pixel must have V neighbors above or below; (3) an N pixel must have N labels in three out of four of its neighbors.

Suppose we have the following situation at a pixel, P, labeled with H and N, and surrounded by four neighbors:

$$V\ H$$

$$H\ N \qquad H\ N \qquad H\ V$$

$$V\ N$$

We see that the N label of P does not satisfy compatibility requirement 3, since we cannot find three neighbors having an N label. The N label would therefore be dropped from the center pixel. (In most discrete relaxation approaches, once a label is deleted there is no mechanism for regenerating it at a later stage of computation.) The H label does satisfy condition 1 that requires H labels on either side, so the H label would be retained.

The iterative procedure terminates when there are no pixels that have more than one label or when no additional changes occur in one complete iteration. Note that it is possible to reach a situation in which all the labels at a pixel are deleted because none of the labels satisfy the required compatibility conditions.

Relaxation with Probabilistic Labels. As indicated previously, a preprocessing operation must provide the initial set of labels and their probabilities. A revised probability for each label at each pixel is typically obtained by an updating expression of the form shown in the box below.

The support for k around pixel i is a number between -1 and $+1$, with -1 indicating that the presence of label k is incompatible with the neighborhood labeling. This support value is a function of the *compatibility* between label k and the label L of each neighbor and the probability that L is a valid label for each neigh-

bor. The normalizing factor is used to keep label probabilities between 0 and 1.

Although appealing intuitively, this type of updating rule has no absolute justification, and its convergence properties are not generally well understood; in many examples, results first improve and then degrade if too many iterations are used.

Discussion. Relaxation is a computational mechanism that attempts a global analysis by using local consensus and iterating the procedure many times. Relaxation is attractive because the local operations can proceed in parallel, and the technique therefore has the potential for high-speed mechanization. Relaxation has also been suggested as the computational mechanism employed by biological systems [Feldman 85]. As currently employed, relaxation procedures tend to be *ad hoc*; their mathematical and semantic properties are poorly understood.

Combinatorial Optimization

Perception can be defined as finding a best interpretation of sensed data in terms of a set of *a priori* models. The term "best" often implies some sort of optimization, i.e., a selection from a set of alternatives.

Almost all optimization problems dealt with in scene analysis are either of (1) a statistical nature, e.g.,

a statistical measure, often in a feature space, is used to make a selection of the best set of entities, or (2) combinatorial optimization in which selection from a set of alternatives is made on the basis of maximizing or minimizing some objective function. We discuss statistical optimization below; here we describe some of the combinatorial techniques that have been employed in computational vision. The general approach is to transform the original vision problem into a problem in which a *cost* or figure of merit can be assigned to each possible combination of elements. Although the best combination could be found by evaluating the cost for every possible combination and selecting the configuration with the lowest cost, the large number of combinations makes this exhaustive approach infeasible. The optimization techniques organize the computation so that combinations that are not good candidates for solution are not considered.

Optimization Problems in ILSA. Examples of ILSA optimization problems are (1) finding the best way of linking pixels, as in edge finding, and (2) image matching.

1. **The edge-linking problem.** Suppose we have a technique that assigns a cost to each pixel in an image to indicate the likelihood of the presence of a road (or edge or line) at each pixel location. The costs are

$$\text{Revised probability of label } k \text{ at pixel i} = \frac{(\text{Previous probability}) (1+\text{support for k})}{\text{Normalizing factor}}$$

assigned so that a low cost indicates a high likelihood of a road. Given this array of cost values, we would like to find a path through this array such that the sum of the costs along this path is minimized. In the image, this minimum cost path would then be marked as the road. Note that the resulting solution assures continuity of the global structures as well as the best collection of locally "roadlike" elements.

2. **The image-matching problem.** We are given a reference image consisting of blobs of various shapes, and a sensed image that we would like to match with this reference image. If the sensed image is a distorted version of the reference image, then we cannot use a straight-forward correlation technique in which we move the sensed image over the reference image, looking for the best match. Instead, we imagine the sensed image to be on a transparent rubber sheet, so that blobs can be displaced from one another by stretching and compressing the rubber sheet. We now perform a matching operation by laying the sensed image over the reference map and stretching and compressing the rubber sheet to obtain the best possible match of the various blobs. In this matching operation we use a cost which is the weighted sum of two components: (1) a cost based on individual comparison of blobs in the sensed and reference images, and (2) a cost based on the amount of stretching or compressing required. The problem is to find the stretch and match combination that results in the smallest overall cost.

An Edge-Linking Algorithm. An approach to combinatorial edge linking is to use two arrays: (1) a local cost array that provides a measure of the edge likelihood at each pixel location, and (2) a *total path cost array*, that stores the lowest cost of the path from a starting point to each pixel. The total path cost array stores the results of each iteration, and the computation ends when no further changes can be made to this array.

We begin with a set of initial values stored in the total path cost array. All the elements are set to a very high value except that element that we would like to be start point of the path. We assign the start pixel its local cost array value. Appendix 9-2 shows an algorithm in which, for each pixel, P, we form the sum of each of its neighbor's total path cost array value plus the local cost array value of P. If the minimum of these eight sums, SMIN, is less than the current total path cost array value of P, we replace P by SMIN. The iteration is repeated until no changes occur in the total path cost array. All paths and their costs can be determined directly from the final configuration of the total path cost array.

An Image-Matching Algorithm. Suppose we have a reference image consisting of N components, and these components are constrained in position with respect to one another. For example, the pieces could be lines constrained to form an approximate rectangle. The image-matching algorithm must find an optimal fit of the reference figure to a structure visible in the sensed image.

An example of such an algorithm can be described using the rectangle example (see Appendix 9-3). First, each component of the reference is matched separately with the sensed image and a list is kept of acceptable match positions and the quality of the match at each position. We order the list so that the component most likely to be correctly matched appears at the top of the list, followed by the next most reliable, etc.

We now use the most reliable piece, A, and its best match locations in the sensed image, MA1, MA2, ..., and the next most reliable piece, B. Since we know the constraint relationship between A and B, we know for each of the MA1, MA2, ..., the approximate locations where the MB matches should be. We can use the list of best matches for B and determine the maximum stretch for each MB entry which satisfies the positional constraint condition relative to an MA entry.

If the combined score of the original MB match plus the stretch cost is too great, then that MB point will be eliminated from further consideration. If, for some MAn there is not at least one MBk, then we eliminate the MAn match point from further consideration. After one has formed all the acceptable

(MAn,MBk) pairs, then the next piece, C, on the list is examined for MC points that satisfy the constraints with regard to A and B components. Unmatched (MAn,MBk) pairs are eliminated and the procedure continues to D, the last piece on the list.

Discussion. The design of the cost function is crucial in the optimization approach, since it will determine the complexity of the computation and will affect the quality and characteristics of the solution. For example, in the path finding problem, adding a constant bias to each cost value tends to smooth and straighten the optimal path. This effect occurs because, as the bias increases, the length of the track becomes relatively more important in comparison to the local quality as defined by individual pixel costs. Similarly, raising each cost to a power introduces a very strong inhibition against going through a point with a high cost. Thus, the designer can introduce *a priori* knowledge (e.g., a preference for curving roads in mountainous regions, or straight roads in flat terrain) by suitable tailoring of the cost function.

Classification and Model Instantiation

This section presents some classification and model fitting techniques that have the common characteristic of using a "parameter" or "attribute space" as the underlying representation. A parameter space associates a different parameter with each coordinate axis (or possibly the same

parameters from two different images). We map from the image space representation to parameter space to assign labels to individual pixels in the image, or to find those collections of pixels in an image that satisfy a model such as "house," "airport," etc. A simple example of a parameter space is the intensity histogram of an image, in which intensity is used as one axis and the other axis is the count of pixels in the image for each intensity value.

We will discuss three types of parameter space decision problems:

1. *Supervised classification,* in which the location of an "ideal" for each class in parameter space is known, and location of unclassified points in parameter space relative to the ideal points is used to make the classification assignments (statistical decision theory).
2. *Unsupervised classification,* in which point clusters in parameter space are assumed to correspond to meaningful or coherent image structures.
3. *Model instantiation,* in which point clusters in parameter space are used to find the parameters of a modeled object visible in a given image.

Supervised Classification. An example of supervised classification arises in the analysis of images acquired by earth resources satellites. A multispectral image, i.e., a set of N registered images corresponding to N different frequency bands, is obtained for some portion of the earth's surface. Each picture element then has N associated measurements. The classification

problem is to assign a class label, e.g., "corn," "water," "rock," to each pixel.

If we use an N dimensional parameter space whose axes correspond to the N frequency bands, then the measurement vector at each pixel location can be mapped as a point in this measurement space. To classify the pixel, we must specify in the parameter space a set of *ideals*, points that are typical of each class. Classification then consists of assigning a pixel to the class of the *closest* ideal.

Unsupervised Classification. An example of unsupervised classification is finding a set of intensity thresholds to partition a gray-level image into coherent objects by feature space clustering. Such a procedure, based on histogram analysis, is described in Appendix 9-3.

Model Instantiation. Parameter space clustering can be used to assign values to the parameters of a model of some scene entity appearing in an image. For example, suppose we are searching for straight lines in an image. The parameters in a model for a straight line might be the slope, m, and the y intercept, b, in the relation $y = mx + b$.

We form a parameter space, (m,b), so that any line through a particular pixel will be mapped into a point in (m,b) space. If we pass a set of k lines of k different slopes through a pixel x,y in image space, we will get k different points mapped in the m,b space. If this is done for each pixel in the image that has some minimum value of *edge* strength, then we have the situation in which each such pixel *votes* for the *m,b* combination that represents possible lines passing through it. After all *N* edge pixels are mapped into *k*×*N* points in *m,b* parameter space, the point in parameter space that receives the most votes represents the best instantiation of the underlying model. Rather than using quantized histogram *buckets* to count the number of points satisfying a particular *m,b* combination, we could use a cluster analysis technique in a nonquantized space.

In practice, the *m,b* parameterization for straight lines is not suitable because *m* and *b* can become infinite. A better choice of parameters is the normal to the line , and the angle of this normal, as shown in Fig. 9-42(a). The his-

togram in (normal line, angle) space for lines passing through the point x_1,y_1 is shown in Fig. 9-42(b). Fig. 9-42(c) shows how a dominant line can be determined using this histogram.

Note that this approach results in a mapping of many points to the parameter space for each pixel in the image. We are essentially trying out many possible instances of the model (in this case a straight line), and relying on the clustering in parameter space to obtain the best value of the parameters for the model. This approach, called the *Hough transform*), can be extended to general shapes, as described below.

If the object we are searching for is an arbitrary shape, as shown in Fig. 9-43, we select an arbitrary point, *P*, interior to the region and

draw the vector from this interior point to points on the boundary.

For each point on the boundary, we have two vectors, the vector *R* to the interior point, and the tangent vector at the boundary point. We now form an *R*-table containing each tangent vector and its associated *R*-vector. The *R*-table is used as follows. For each point in a given image that is a strong edge point we find the edge orientation, i.e., the tangent vector at that point. We then use this vector as a look-up entry into the *R*-table and find the one or more *R*-vectors that are associated with this tangent vector. Thus, for each edge point in the image we now have one or more *R*-vectors.

Now for each edge point, position the tail of its one or more *R*-vectors at the edge point. Note where the head of each *R*-vector falls and plot this *R*-vector-head point in a histogram whose axes have the same *x* and *y* values as the image. If the modeled object is visible in the image, then we will get a clustering of *R*-head points in this histogram corresponding to point *P* in the model. If a strong cluster does exist, then we have found the location of point *P* and can also locate the boundary of the object in the image.

As another example of mapping each image pixel into many histogram points, consider the following problem. Suppose we have two images taken of the same area but having different intensity characteristics due to illumination changes. Suppose, moreover, that there is some *x,y* displacement between the images. We would like to find both the spatial displacement and the intensity mapping function.

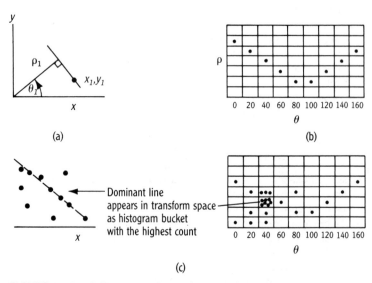

FIGURE 9-42   A Parameter Space for Straight Lines.

(a) ρ, θ parameters.
(b) ρ, θ histogram for lines passing through point x_1, y_1.
(c) Determining dominant line.

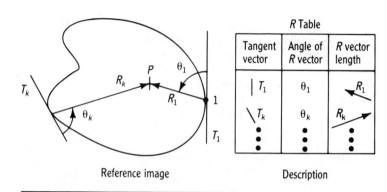

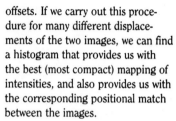

Tangent vector	Angle of R vector	R vector length
T_1	θ_1	R_1
T_k	θ_k	R_k
• • •	• • •	• • •

R Table

Reference image   Description

offsets. If we carry out this procedure for many different displacements of the two images, we can find a histogram that provides us with the best (most compact) mapping of intensities, and also provides us with the corresponding positional match between the images.

Using the R Table

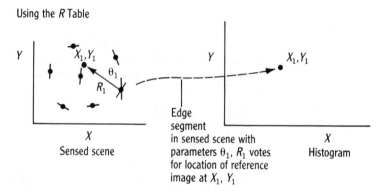

Sensed scene

Edge segment in sensed scene with parameters θ_1, R_1 votes for location of reference image at X_1, Y_1

Histogram

FIGURE 9-43   Hough Transform for General Shapes.

Statistical Classification

We have previously discussed the concept of constructing a feature space whose axes correspond to measurements made on an object. We have also indicated that when an unknown object is represented as a point in this space, there are several methods for assigning it to a class by using its distance from an ideal point of that class, or by noting where the unknown point falls in a previously partitioned feature space. In this section we will discuss how statistical theory can be used to provide the distance metric or the partitioning criteria.

We can proceed by forming a histogram in which one axis represents the intensity of a pixel in image 1, and the other axis represents the intensity of a corresponding pixel in image 2, as shown in Fig. 9-44. We show two different placements of image 1 over Image 2. For each placement we obtain a histogram of the number N for each combination (intensity 1, intensity 2) that represents the number of overlapped pixels in the images that have this intensity combination. For one of the x,y offsets we find that we obtain a better (more compact) clustering in its histogram than for the other

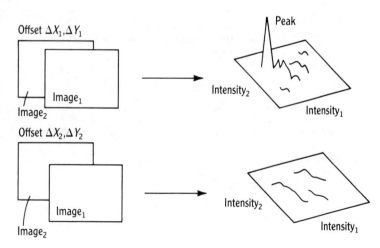

FIGURE 9-44   Image Matching using a Two-Dimensional Histogram.

The components of the statistical classification process are shown in Fig. 9-45. On the right is a *classifier* that assigns an unknown object to a class based on the classifier parameters and a set of measurements made on the object. On the left is shown the design or *training* process for obtaining the parameters of the classifier. To determine these parameters, we must know or assume the *a priori* probability of occurrence of each class, the variation in each measurement for each class (the probability density function, PDF, for each class), and the cost of misclassification (the cost of assigning an object actually of class X to class Y.)

In the discussion below, we use a single measurement and two classes for clarity, but the expressions can be extended to any number of measurements and classes.

The Conditional Probability Density Function (PDF). A typical PDF for a single measurement, *weight*, and two classes, *man* and *woman*, are shown in Fig. 9-46. We use the term *conditional PDF* and the notation p(weight measurement|woman) to denote the probability of a weight measurement, given that we are dealing with the class "woman." Note that in this example each PDF has a single peak. For most objects of practical concern, a PDF with more than a single pronounced peak indicates that the choice of measurement is not a good one.

The process of estimating the PDFs using a given set of labeled reference objects is known as *training* and will be described later.

Bayes's Theorem. We can use Bayes's theorem to modify the given or *a priori* probability of a class, by using the conditional PDF and the measurement obtained for the unclassified object:

$$p(C_i|m) = \frac{p(m|C_i)p(C_i)}{\text{normalizing factor}}$$

where $p(C_i|m)$ is the probability of class C_i given measurement m (called the *a posteriori* probability); $p(m|C_i)$ is the conditional PDF-supplied value, given measurement m and assuming class C_i; and $p(C_i)$ is the *a priori* probability of class C_i. The normalizing factor is used to make the set of *a posteriori* probabilities sum to unity.

Given two classes C_1 and C_2, we classify an unknown object as being a member of C_1 when the probability of class C_1 given measurement m is greater than that of class C_2, i.e., $p(C_1|m) > p(C_2|m)$. From Bayes's theorem this becomes, choose C_1 when $p(m|C_1)p(C_1) > p(m|C_2)p(C_2)$, otherwise choose C_2. If the PDFs are given as histograms derived from a reference set of measurements made on *ideal* objects representing each class, we would scale each histogram based on the *a priori* probability of its class, and assign the unknown object to the class that had the largest resulting value for measurement(s) m.

We note that since $p(C_1)$ and $p(C_2)$ are constants, and the $p(m|C_i)$ are single peaked functions for the example shown in Fig. 9-46, the decision criteria in this case amount to assigning all persons with mea-

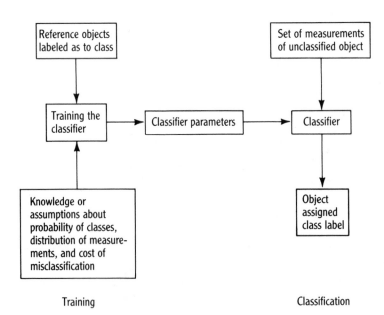

Training

Classification

FIGURE 9-45

Components of the Statistical Classification Process.

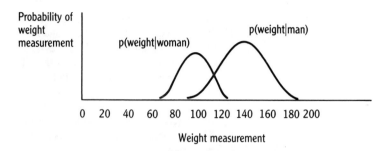

FIGURE 9-46
Conditional PDFs of Weight Measurements for Two Classes.

Training. The heart of the statistical classification approach is the conditional PDF. Either *parametric* or *nonparametric* classifiers can be designed, based on what is known about the PDF and what must be estimated. A parametric classifier assumes a functional form of a PDF based on some knowledge about the objects being classified. Statistical procedures are used on the reference set to estimate parameters such as the mean and variance of the assumed PDF. In a nonparametric classifier we do not know enough about the objects to assume a PDF and therefore the PDF form is estimated from the reference data. This requires much more reference data than the parametric case. The process of estimating the PDFs using the reference objects is often referred to as *training*, and if the reference objects have been labeled (classified) by the designer, the term *supervised training* is used.

sured values of m less than some value, M^*, to the class *woman* and all persons with values of m greater than M^* to the class *man*. Thus, the decision criteria based on statistical arguments can be interpreted as a simple partitioning of feature space into two regions separated by a simple boundary. For a multidimensional feature space the partitioning is performed using multidimensional planes (hyperplanes) or multidimensional surfaces (hypersurfaces). An alternative interpretation is to consider the statistical analysis as altering the initial Euclidean distance metric in such a way that any point can be assigned to the class corresponding to the nearest ideal point.

9-2

A Path-Finding Algorithm

This appendix presents a dynamic programming approach to finding the lowest cost path in a cost array. The example array is given in Fig. 9-47(a) and the numbers represent the local cost of having the path go through that element. In this example, we want to traverse the array from the lower left (start element) to the upper right (end element) so that the sum of the path elements will be minimum.

The algorithm uses a "path cost array" that specifies the total cost of the path from the starting point to each element of the array. We begin the process by initializing the path cost array with high values for all elements except that element we wish to make the start of the path; this element is assigned its local cost array value. In our example we want the start of the path to be in the lower left hand corner, so we assign that element the value 3, its value in the local cost array. All other elements are assigned the suitably large arbitrary value 100, as shown in Fig. 9-47(b).

A revised path cost array value is obtained by adding the local value of an element in L and the path cost array value of one of its neighbors;

(a)

```
9 8 2 2 1
8 3 7 8 8
7 2 6 3 8
7 8 3 8 2
9 8 7 6 2
3 2 2 2 8
```

(b)

```
100 100 100 100 100
100 100 100 100 100
100 100 100 100 100
100 100 100 100 100
100 100 100 100 100
  3 100 100 100 100
```

(c)

```
100 100 100 100 100        100 100 100 100 100
100 100 100 100 100        100 100 100 100 100
100 100 100 100 100        100 100 100 100 100
100 100 100 100 100         18  19  14  22  24
 12  11  18  24  26         12  11  12  13  11
  3   5   7   9  17          3   5   7   9  17
```

(d)

```
100 100 100 100 100        100 100 100 100 100
100 100 100 100 100         24  19  23  25  25
 25  16  20  17  25         23  16  20  16  21
 18  19  14  19  13         18  19  14  19  13
 12  11  12  13  11         12  11  12  13  11
  3   5   7   9  17          3   5   7   9  17
```

(e)

```
28  27  21–23–24
24  19  23  24  24
23  16  20  16  21
18  19  14  19  13
12  11  12  13  11
 3   5   7   9  17
```

(f)

```
81  64   4   4   1         100 100  58–62–63
64   9  49  64  64         100  54  81  96  96
49   4  36   9  64          94  45  68  32  87
49  64   9  64   4          94 100  41  83  23
81  64  49  36   4          84  67  56  47  19
 9   4   4   4  64           3 – 7–11–15  79
```

FIGURE 9-47   Arrays used in the Path Computation.

(a) Local cost array (L). (b) Initial path cost array (P). (c) Results of first (left) and second (right) iterations. (d) Third (left) and fourth (right) iterations. (e) Fifth iteration, showing solution path. (f) Effect of squaring the local cost array on solution path: Squared local cost array (left) and solution path cost array (right).

we perform this computation for each of its eight neighbors, and if one of these sums, SMIN, is less than the element's current path cost, T, we replace T by SMIN (in P). We show in Fig. 9-47(c) the result of performing this operation while sweeping through each row from left to right, and processing rows from bottom to top.

Notice in the first iteration how change spreads from the lower left corner. The repeated bottom-to-top sweeping rule we are using here is not an efficient one, since change is generated at the bottom of the array; a better strategy would have been to start at the bottom, but to reverse the sweep direction at each additional iteration. Continuing the iterations we obtain the array shown in Fig. 9-47(d). Notice that no changes are occurring in the bottom rows. The final result is obtained on the fifth iteration, Fig. 9-47(e).

To obtain the minimal cost path, we start with the final element of the path (the end element), and look for the neighboring element having the lowest value. Thus we thread through the array with the path 24–23–21–19–16–14–11–3. To illustrate the relevance of the *cost* assignment process, note what happens when the computation is repeated, but with the local cost array squared, i.e., a monotonic transformation of the cost function. Since the differential between low and high costs has become more extreme, it now pays to lengthen the path to avoid high-cost pixels, and we obtain a longer and more "wiggly" path, as shown in Fig. 9-47(f).

The path is now 63–62–58–54–45–41–32–23–19–15–11–7–3.

9-3

Relational (Rubber Sheet) Image Matching

This appendix shows how dynamic programming can be used to solve a problem in image matching. We have a reference image

$$6 \ 4$$
$$3 \ 5$$

and we want to find the best match in the sensed image:

$$5 \ 2 \ 8 \ 8$$
$$7 \ 5 \ 1 \ 3$$
$$8 \ 1 \ 5 \ 7$$
$$4 \ 3 \ 2 \ 4$$

If the reference image was "rigid," then we would move the sensed image over the reference image looking for the location where the sum of the absolute differences between the sensed and reference elements was smallest. (The absolute difference of corresponding pixel values is the local cost function chosen for this example.) In the present situation, we are willing to allow a certain amount of "give" between the reference elements; however, a penalty will be paid for such stretching. For reference purposes, we will label the reference image

$$A \ B$$
$$D \ C$$

We will assume that springs exist between pairs (B,A),(C,B), and (D,C) , and that there are the following costs to stretching:

- Element A has no spring cost
- Element B to element A: B adjacent to right of A costs nothing
  B displaced one unit to the right costs 1
  Other movements of B from A cost infinity
- Element C to element B: C adjacent below B costs nothing
  C displaced one unit down from B costs 1
  Other movements of C from B cost infinity
- Element D to element C: D adjacent to left of C costs nothing
  D displaced one unit to left costs 1
  Other movements of D costs infinity

For convenience, we display below the cost of match for each reference element. Each array was obtained by taking the absolute difference of a reference element with each element of the sensed array.

The arrays on page 300 show the results of the computational sequence. The leftmost arrays show the placement of element A. Looking at A's cost matrix, we choose the lowest cost positions, those having a cost of 1. For clarity we have drawn a separate array for each best location of A. For each best placement of A we then consider the best placements of B. For example, B can be placed adjacent to the first placement of A for a cost of $1+2+0$ units, or B can be stretched for a cost of $1+4+1$. The first term is A's best cost, the next term is B's match cost, and the third term is the stretch cost. Once A and B have been placed, we have a total cost for the A,B combination. In our example, we choose the lowest cost in each array to determine the positioning of the corresponding component. In actual practice we could carry along more than one position for each component.

In the placement of element C on the first row of arrays, given the best placement of A and B costing 3 units, we can place C for $3+0+0$ or $3+4+1$ units, as shown. The placement that results in 3 units of cost is chosen, and is used in the rightmost column to obtain a placement of D at a cost of $3+4+0$ units.

A match cost	B match cost	C match cost	D match cost
1 4 2 2	1 2 4 4	0 3 3 3	2 1 5 5
1 1 5 3	3 1 3 1	2 0 4 2	4 2 2 0
2 5 1 1	4 3 1 3	3 4 0 2	5 2 2 4
2 3 4 2	0 1 2 0	1 2 3 1	1 0 1 1

Cost Arrays

Placement A	Placement A,B	Placement A,B,C	Placement A,B,C,D
1 - - -	A 3 6 -	A B - -	A B - -
- - - -	- - - -	- 3 - -	7 C - -
- - - -	- - - -	- 8 - -	- - - -
- - - -	- - - -	- - - -	- - - -
- - - -	- - - -	- - - -	- - - -
1 - - -	A 2 5 -	A B - -	A B - -
- - - -	- - - -	- 6 - -	- - - -
- - - -	- - - -	- 5 - -	6 C - -
- - - -	- - - -	- - - -	- - - -
- 1 - -	- A 4 3	- A - B	- A - B
- - - -	- - - -	- - - 5	- 8 7 C
- - - -	- - - -	- - - 5	- 6 6 C
- - - -	- - - -	- - - -	- - - -
- - - -	- - - -	- - - -	- - - -
- - 1 -	- - A 4	- - A B	- - A B
- - - -	- - - -	- - - 5	- 6 6 C

Thus, the lowest cost placements have a value of 6 and they are the following:

- - - -	- - - -	- - - -	- - - -	- - - -
A B - -	- A - B	- A - B	- - - -	- - - -
- - - -	- - - -	- - - -	- - A B	- - A B
D C - -	- D - C	- - D C	- D - C	- - D C

In actual practice the computations would be in tabular form. Note that if we add the additional constraint that D must be in the same column as A, then only three solutions are valid.

Epilogue

We began this book with the question: *To what extent is it possible to model intelligence as an information processing activity that can be carried out by a machine?* This epilogue restates and summarizes the most important views and arguments relevant to this *computational hypothesis*, and examines whether it is possible to construct an "intelligent machine" that can function in the world. A discussion of the possibility of a robotic entity is appropriate because such a device would have to draw on the entire range of intelligent capabilities, from reasoning to language to vision, and the problem of integrating these capabilities brings to the fore many of the deep questions that arose in the individual chapters.

The human brain, a three-pound lump of biological tissue, is perhaps the most amazing object in the universe—it sees, hears, thinks, creates, and even seeks an explanation for its own existence. Can it really be the case that in spite of its remarkable properties the brain is simply a "machine" that carries out complex computational procedures? This question has been the basis of the intellectual quest that we have pursued in this book. An affirmative answer seems to degrade the concept of humanity to a point unacceptable to most people despite the fact that we are generally willing to accept the idea that other living creatures may indeed be very sophisticated machines. If we refuse to accept the computational hypothesis, then only mysticism is left, a situation unacceptable to most scientists.

PHILOSOPHICAL AND CONCEPTUAL QUESTIONS

In this epilogue we deal with major questions raised at various points in the book, some of which reflect a basic concern about the brain as a machine, some that concern the machine as it affects society, and some about the field of artificial intelligence in general. For each question we will first summarize our beliefs and the points of view of others in the field, and then indicate the impact of the question on the possibility of creating a humanlike autonomous robotic device.

Because we are dealing with ultimate limits of an intelligent machine, we quickly find ourselves delving into rather deep philosophical questions that concern such topics as understanding, consciousness, language, and mind. These questions arise when the behavior of a machine causes us to ask, "Does the *behavior* of the machine mean that the machine is *really* capable of X," where X is understanding, consciousness, thinking, etc. Some of the questions that have been discussed for thousands of years have taken on a new interest and importance due to artificial intelligence (AI).

True Understanding

Can a machine truly understand?

One point of view concerning machine understanding is stated by Simon [Simon 81]: "At the root of intelligence are symbols, with their denotative power and their susceptibility to manipulation." Such symbol manipulation can be carried out by a brain or by various forms of computers. Simon therefore sees no reason why machines should not be capable of human forms of understanding the world. In Chapter 6 we discussed the strongest attack on this point of view, Searle's Chinese room metaphor [Searle 84], which asks whether one can ascribe "understanding" to mere symbol manipulation. An important point of the Chinese room metaphor is to show that when we limit a person's role to strict symbol manipulation, this activity adds nothing to the person's ability to truly understand the task at hand. Although Searle makes no attempt to supply an operational definition of understanding (or even a set of necessary conditions), what makes the metaphor so powerful is that we ourselves would not require or attain an understanding of Chinese if placed in this situation. If we, as conscious thinking creatures do not exhibit understanding in the presence of such formal symbol manipulation, how can a machine?

Even though he does not make the explicit point, Searle appeals to the idea that consciousness plays a prime role in human understanding. (In a slightly modified way, this is Descartes' mind-body problem again; see Chapters 1 and 2.) Consciousness seems to be some coherent *whole* that cannot be decomposed into electronic switches, or computer instructions, or even subsystems, and thus is not subject to the type of reductionist analysis often used in science. Why do we have the introspective ability called "consciousness?" Minsky [Minsky 68] believes that the evolutionary role of consciousness has been to give access to otherwise inaccessible modules, so as to debug, reprogram, or retrain them. He suggests that an organism would be better able to survive if it has a model of itself. Dennett [Dennett 84] imagines the development of consciousness as follows. People found that they could get advice on future actions by asking other people. At some point it was found that even if nobody is around, a person's problem solving activity is aided by asking questions out loud. Gradually, it was realized that the same effect can be achieved by internally asking the questions,

> Under what conditions would the activity of asking oneself questions be useful? . . . Crudely put, pushing some information through one's ears and auditory system may stimulate just the sorts of connections one is seeking, may trip just the right associative mechanisms, tease just the right mental morsel to the tip of one's tongue. One can then say it, hear oneself say it, and thus get the answer one was hoping for.

One additional function that consciousness appears to serve is that of a high-level executive, or even an external observer, who monitors the performance of the body in relation to its high-level goals, and makes appropriate suggestions, e.g., as in the case of a runner verbally "telling himself" to go faster (See Box 2-3).

Sometimes if we know the structure of a machine or the background of a person we can make a decision concerning the nature of the understanding involved. For example, suppose we know that we are dealing with a person who has been blind from birth and has never experienced color. He has been provided with an instrument that senses color and communicates the results in Braille. The person can point the sensor at objects, and can then report color as well as a sighted person. No matter how good his operational performance is, we still feel that he has no understanding of what it means to see the world in color.

Sloman [Sloman 85] would not agree with the above point of view. He argues that there is no clear boundary between things that do, and things that do not understand symbols. He feels that our ordinary concept of "understanding" denotes a complex cluster of capabilities, and different subsets of these may be exhibited in different people, animals or machines; to ask "Which are necessary for *real* understanding?" is to attribute spurious precision to a concept of ordinary language. Thus, in the example above, Sloman would say that a congenitally blind person may attach meanings to color words not too different than a sighted person, because much of the meaning resides in the rich interconnection with concepts shared by both.

The potential role of "consciousness" in a robotic device is uncertain. Certainly, it is possible for each subsystem of a robot to signal its status and goals to other subsystems and to attain the external appearance of conscious behavior, but what have we lost by implementing the *appearance*, but not the *substance*, of conscious awareness? For example, is it imaginable that such an implementation would be capable of autonomously conceiving of, and printing, the message "I think (compute?), therefore I am"?

The issue of understanding is a crucial one in the robotic domain, since it brings to the fore the basic question as to whether "true understanding" is required to achieve high levels of performance, i.e., to give explicit shape to high-level goals in an uncertain environment, and whether robotic devices are responsible enough to take their place in society, as discussed in the following paragraphs.

Societal Aspects

Can a machine take a role in society as if it were a person?

Suppose we reach a point in time when a robotic entity can be placed in a position to carry out decision making in government, banking, medicine, law, or the military. Could the robot perform as if it were a person. No! answers Weizenbaum [Weizenbaum 76], who points out that knowledge about a society "is acquired with the mother's milk and through the whole process of socialization that is itself so intimately tied to the individual's acquisition of his mother tongue. It cannot be explicated in any form but life itself." Thus, an American judge, no matter what his intelligence and fairmindedness, could not sit in a Japanese family court. His intelligence is simply *alien* to the problems that arise in Japanese culture. "Whatever intelligence a computer can muster, however it may be acquired, it must always and necessarily be absolutely alien to any and all concerns." This question is not a theoretical one, for we already have medical and business decision making programs in use that affect human health and welfare.

Weizenbaum and many others believe that true understanding can only be gained by actually experiencing the world and thereby developing an internal database that represents these experiences. A child builds up knowledge of the world by exploring and learning. Similarly, it is necessary for a robotic device to build up its database of world knowledge by learning about its environment, since manual entry of sufficient relevant information about the world is impractical. While present-day machine learning consists merely of determining the specific parameters and relationships for a representation that has been chosen by the designer of the machine, we have no reason to suspect that machines are inherently incapable of the more powerful forms of learning needed to counter Weizenbaum's criticisms.

If we change the question in this subsection to, *Can a machine play a useful role in society?* rather than requiring the machine to function as a person, then the strict requirements for deep understanding of the society indicated by Weizenbaum can be relaxed. The designer has a much simpler task, and quite useful devices can be constructed. Weizenbaum would still feel that society must carefully control the use of such devices, and avoid applications where the consumer might ascribe more intelligence to the device than is warranted.

The Frame Problem

How can a computer focus its attention on just those aspects of a given problem that are relevant to its solution?

This is the *frame problem*: How can an intelligent system, in trying to solve a problem or carry out an action, know what information in its database should be ignored, and what is relevant to the problem at hand? The question, "What was Benjamin Franklin's telephone number?," given in Chapter 3, is a relevant example. Somehow people know that they must invoke the relevant information of Franklin's date of birth and the date of the invention of the telephone to solve the problem.

To fully represent the conditions for the successful performance of an action, an impractical and implausible number of qualifications would be required. McCarthy [McCarthy 80] gives as an example the many qualifications that would have to be supplied for the simple act of a boat crossing a river—the oars and oarlocks must be present and unbroken, the boat cannot have a hole in it, cannot be filled with rocks, etc. Since many other qualifications can be added, the rules for using a rowboat become almost impossible to apply unless some focusing mechanism is available.

The frame problem is of crucial importance to an autonomous robot. It must "think before it leaps," coming up with reliable but not necessarily foolproof expectations of the effects of its actions. This process must be carried out in an acceptable amount of time, taking into account everything in its database that is relevant to the proposed action. The big problem is knowing what is indeed relevant, since the time constraints will not permit examination of the implication of every fact in the database. Many AI systems have the unfortunate characteristic that increasing the amount of knowledge in their database degrades, rather than improves, their performance.

There are currently several approaches that try to deal with the frame problem. One scheme uses the attention-focusing ability of stereotypes, such as the Schank script approach described in Chapter 6. A script attempts to define and organize all of the relevant information for a given situation, but there is still the problem of knowing which of many possible scripts is relevant to a complex situation. McCarthy has proposed [McCarthy 80] *circumscription*, a form of nonmonotonic reasoning augmenting ordinary first-order logic as a mechanism that can be used for "jumping to appropriate conclusions." Circumscription conjectures that the only entities that can prevent an action are those whose existence follows from the facts at hand. Loosely speaking, it is a "don't-go-looking-for-trouble" approach. In the example of the boat, if no lack of oars or other circumstance preventing the use of the boat has already been deduced, then conclude that the boat is usable. A program must contain heuristics for deciding what circumscriptions to make and when to withdraw them.

It may be that the frame problem is an artifact arising from the symbolic representations used in AI. Such representations eliminate the implicit connections that exist between objects in the world, and much effort is required to "put Humpty Dumpty back together again." In particular, the logic formalism does not capture the implicit relationships between things in the world nor permit the type of approximation that seems to be required for everyday reasoning [Pentland 83]. The seriousness of the frame problem is stated by Dennett [Dennett 84a]:

> It appears at first to be at best an annoying technical embarrassment in robotics, or merely a curious puzzle for the bemusement of people working in AI. I think, on the contrary, that it is a new, deep epistemological problem—accessible in principle but unnoticed by generations of philosophers—brought to light by the novel methods of AI, and still far from being solved.

The frame problem is closely related to the decomposability question discussed below.

Decomposing Intelligence

Is intelligent behavior decomposable?

As indicated in Chapter 3, most formal analysis begins by decomposing a problem into manageable portions (see also the discussion of the partitioning problem in Chapters 8 and 9 and the necessity for the independence assumption in both formal and probabilistic reasoning, Chapter 4). We often assume that the whole is made up of its parts and that such decomposition can be carried out for even the most complex of situations. But suppose, in fact, that much of intelligent behavior is not decomposable, and that in partitioning behavior for mechanization purposes, one is incorrectly making an assumption of independence of the parts. Until we are able to deal with the entire unpartitioned problem, we would not be able to achieve human performance for such tasks. Dreyfus [Dreyfus 79] has stated,

> . . . . all aspects of human thought, including nonformal aspects like moods, sensory-motor skills, and long-range self-interpretations, are so interrelated that one cannot substitute an abstractable web of explicit beliefs for the whole cloth of our concrete everyday practices [p.54] . . . . Since intelligence must be situated it cannot be separated from the rest of human life [p.62] . . . . If one thinks of the importance of sensory-motor skills in the development of our ability to recognize and cope with objects, or of the role of needs and desires in structuring all social situations, or finally of the whole cultural background . . . . the idea that we can simply ignore this know-how while formalizing intellectual understanding as a complex system of facts and rules is highly implausible [p63].

In a more intuitive sense, the naturalist John Muir noted that everything in the universe is attached to everything else. If it turns out that it is not possible to decompose many of the processes required for an entity to function in the world, then non-learning robotic devices will be limited as to the type of reasoning and problem solving they can carry out (because of practical limits on what can be designed into them). In particular, if intelligence is not decomposable, it is not incrementally achievable: the idea of building a partially intelligent robot would make as much sense as digging half a hole.

Again we must stress that we are talking about highly intelligent entities. Once we relax that criterion, then it is surely possible to develop useful devices based on reductionist principles.

Language and Thought

What is the relationship between language and thought?

This question has been discussed for thousands of years, and the final answers have still not been found. In many myths about the creation of man, language is taken to be one of man's inherent characteristics like vision or hearing.[1] Some of the many theories about the relation of language and thought include:

1. *Thinking is a form of subvocal speech.* John B. Watson, the father of the psychological school known as behaviorism, believed that all thinking was a form of motor behavior that had been conditioned to stimuli. When challenged that no motor behavior can be seen while thinking, he claimed that thinking was subvocal speech i.e., motor behavior that could not be noticed. Thus, people who were engaged in thinking activities were just softly talking to themselves [Watson 30]. This point of view was discredited in 1947 by an experiment in which a subject was able to think despite complete paralysis of his musculature [Smith 47].

2. *Language influences a person's thinking and his perception of the world,* the Whorfian hypothesis [Whorf 56]. This hypothesis was discussed in Chapter 6. No definitive experiment has proved or disproved this hypothesis because it is difficult to design an experiment that is not subject to the many cultural and environmental factors that bear upon language. Thus, each experiment that supposedly proves or disproves Whorf's hypothesis can be attacked by opponents who cite confounding factors such as the environment in which the subjects grew up, possibility of misunderstandings of the experiment by the subjects, or similar performance by an entirely different type of subject.

3. *Language is shaped to fit the prelinguistic thoughts that are to be communicated,* a point of view argued as long ago as Aristotle. In the seventeenth century John Locke wrote that man's organs were fashioned to "form articulate sounds" and he was given the ability to "use these sounds as signs of internal conceptions and make them stand as marks for the ideas within his own mind." This view says that thinking comes before speech, and that our language is shaped by the thoughts that we want to convey. Studies that support this theory attempt to find a structural commonality in language structure among the world's languages that would indicate that language is shaped by thought. For example, Greenberg [Greenberg 63] showed that for 98 percent of the world's languages the subject precedes the object—an indication that in constructing linguistic structures, we use a word order that first establishes what the sentence is about.

4. *Language mechanisms of the brain are unlike those of any other cognitive skill,* has been an important theme in Chomsky's work. This theory says that language, like vision, uses genetically determined special neural structures [Caplan 82, Lenneberg 67]. Since language is species-specific to man, it is not possible, as in vision, to carry out animal experiments to gain insight as to the relation between linguistic stimulation and neural structure. Therefore, the advocates of this position must reason from the following basic facts: (1) children rapidly learn language by being immersed in a linguistic environment, (2) modern linguistics has shown how difficult sentence comprehension really is, and (3) children will learn the particular

---

[1]The history of the biological basis of language by Otto Marx, given in Appendix B of E. H. Lenneberg's *Biological Foundations of Language* [Lenneberg 67] makes fascinating reading.

language of their environment. Thus advocates postulate special brain structures for language that somehow have the power to deal with the complexity of language, and yet have the *plasticity* so that there is no bias toward any one particular language. Opponents feel that learning a language is a special case of very general cognitive ability, and that language learning is merely the application of general learning procedures to the special case of learning to talk [Anderson 80]. At the present time the conflict is not resolved. As Marshall states: "We just do not know whether the neurons, synapses, transmitter substances, patterns of connectivity, and so forth in the language area of the brain differ in important respects from those characteristic of other parts [Marshall 80]."

It is interesting that most of the discussions about thought and language give short shrift to thought and image. If it turns out to be the case that thinking involves languagelike processes, as suggested by Luria [Luria 73], then our present-day approach to robotic reasoning based on symbol manipulation would be justified. Yet, there is the nagging thought that animals, who do not have the language facility of humans, are obviously able to reason, survive, and to achieve goals. Can it be that they are using image-based reasoning? A discussion of the "representation of thought" question is continued below.

Representation in the Brain

What is the nature of representation used by the brain?

Fodor [cited in Miller 83] states: "I suspect that the representational system with which we think, if that's the right way to describe it, is so rich that if you think up any form of symbolism at all, it probably plays some role in thinking." The mind apparently uses two major representations, propositions and images (or at least representations that are isomorphic to images) (see Chapter 1). These two representations have been used in AI, and there are strong advocates of each approach. For example, Nilsson [Nilsson 83] asserts that AI is the study of how to acquire and represent knowledge within a logiclike propositional formalism, and the study of how to manipulate this knowledge by use of logical operations and rules of inference; he does not see a need for additional (iconic) representations. Some feel that this point of view is extreme. Pentland and Fischler [Pentland 83] stress that multiple representations are necessary. Weaknesses in the propositional formalism can sometimes be eliminated through the use of an auxiliary isomorphic representation, since a representation whose structure "mirrors" (is *isomorphic* to) some properties of the domain being represented is able to *implicitly* represent those properties preserved by the isomorphism. "How is it that an isomorphism-based reasoning process can succeed where the theorem-proving approach fails? The trick is that the isomorphic approach makes use of the *semantics* of the problem domain 'built into' the representation to express useful *approximations*, . . . while logical systems admit no such *approximations* [Pentland 83]." However, Fodor [cited in Miller 83] has observed that one problem about imagery is its limited "expressive capacity," in comparison with language: "There is, for example, no difficulty in *saying* of a man that he is not scratching his nose, however difficult it may be to have an *image* of his not doing so."

The *connectionist* approach of Feldman [Feldman 82] is another possible computational alternative to logical reductionism. The fundamental premise of connectionism is that individual neurons do not transmit large amounts of symbolic information. Intead, they compute by being appropriately connected to large numbers of similar units. This approach employs a representation for expressing local constraints and uses a parallel computational process based on *relaxation* (see Appendix 9-1) to achieve some overall goal.

A robotic device will certainly use both propositions and iconic representations, since each serves best to solve distinct types of problems. However, as discussed in Chapters 8 and 9, progress has been slow in understanding how to effectively represent iconic knowledge in the machine.

Future Prospects

What are the future prospects for AI?

We are a long way from having an integrated robotic system that can function in the real world, even at the level of a five-year-old child. Depending on one's level of optimism or pessimism, this can be viewed either as offering much exciting future research potential, or of indicating that "we may never get there from here." A recent paper brought together comments from various experts in the field of AI [Bobrow 85]. Some of these are given below:

> *Bernard Meltzer*: With very few exceptions, all of AI until now has been concerned with what Freud termed secondary processes of the mind, that is, those concerned with logical, rational, reflexive or potentially reflexive, commonsense thinking; it has neglected the primary processes, that is those concerned with apparently non-rational, non-reflexive thinking that results for instance in new metaphors, shafts of wit, jokes, dreams, poems, brain-waves, neuroses and psychoses.

> *Nils Nilsson*: [I predict] better understanding of the relationships between perception and reasoning, codification of a large and useful store of commonsense knowledge, significant progress on such conundrums as the frame problem and nonmonotonic reasoning, and large-scale systems based on the "belief-desire-intention" model of intelligent agents.

> *Terry Winograd*: There are two quite different starting points to define AI—the dream and the technology. As a dream, there is a unified (if ill-defined) goal for duplicating human intelligence in its entirety. As a technology, there is a fairly coherent body of techniques that distinguish the field from others in computer science. In the end, this technology base will continue to be a unified area of study with its special methodology. We will recognize that it is not coextensive with the dream, but it is only one (possibly small) piece. . . .

A SUMMARY

We have completed our intellectual journey. Some might feel that they only retain snap-shots as a result of their travels—and that they bring back no coherent story. We could have attempted to provide such a story by organizing all of intelligent behavior under a single theory as the "logic imperialists" have suggested [Nilsson 83, Pentland 83]. Or we might have presented a collection of subtheories, such as those of Marr [Marr 82] in vision, or Chomsky in language [Chomsky 75]. Alas, none of these more encompassing theories are believable in the light of our current knowledge. One might be tempted to use the robot as an integrating framework, but here, again, there is no encompassing theory: robotics at present is an application domain for the computational techniques we have presented, rather than a primary source of intellectual ideas. Therefore in this final chapter we tried to weave together the various separate threads that were exam-ined earlier in the book, using major intellectual questions as a focusing mechanism.

Finally, it should be emphasized that in this epilogue we were mostly dealing with questions of the *ultimate* role of the computer as an intelligent device. Thus there may have been a tone of pessimism in some of the views presented here. However, in the near term, for limited domains and less ambitious goals, we are confident that efforts to achieve these goals will result in advances that will both contribute to and quite likely revolutionize society, even if humanlike robots are not created.

Bibliography

[Alford 78] D. K. H. Alford. The demise of the Whorfian hypothesis. In *Berkeley Linguistic Society Proceedings*, pages 485–499. Berkeley Linguistic Society, Berkeley, Calif., 1978., volume 4.

[Allport 80] D. A. Allport. Patterns and actions: Cognitive mechanisms are content-specific. In G. L. Claxton (editor), *Cognitive Psychology: New Directions*. Routledge & Kegan, London, 1980.

[Amarel 68] S. Amarel. On representations of problems of reasoning about actions. In D. Michie (editor), *Machine Intelligence 3*. American Elsevier, New York, 1968.

[Anderson 81] J. R. Anderson (editor). *Cognitive Skills and Their Acquisition*. Lawrence Erlbaum Associates, Hillsdale, N.J., 1981.

[Anderson 83] J. R. Anderson. *The Architecture of Cognition*. Harvard Press, Cambridge, Mass., 1983.

[Anderson 85] J. R. Anderson. *Cognitive Psychology and Its Implications*. W. H. Freeman., San Francisco, 1985, 2nd edition.

[Andrews 70] H. C . Andrews. *Computer Techniques in Image Processing*. Academic Press, New York, 1970.

[Appelt 85] D. Appelt. Planning English referring expressions. *Artificial Intelligence* 26:1–34, 1985.

[Arbib 72] M. A. Arbib. *The Metaphorical Brain*. Wiley, New York, 1972.

[Arnheim 69] R. Arnheim. *Visual Thinking*. University of California Press, Berkeley, Calif., 1969.

[AI 84] Artificial Intelligence. Special Volume on Qualitative Reasoning about Physical Systems. *Artificial Intelligence*. 24, 1984.

[Asher 66] H. Asher. *Experiments in Seeing*. Fawcett Publications, Greenwich, Conn, 1966.

[Aslin 83] R. N. Aslin, D. P. Pisoni, and P. W. Jusczyk. Auditory development and speech perception in infancy. In M. M. Haith and J. J. Campos (editors), *Handbook of Child Psychology: Infancy and Developmental Psychobiology*. Wiley, New York, 1983.

[Atkinson 68] R. L. Atkinson and R. M. Shifrin, Human memory: proposed system and its control process. In K. W. Spence and J. T. Spence (editor), *The Psychology of Learning and Motivation: Advances in Research and Theory*. Academic Press, New York, 1968.

[Ballard 81] D. H. Ballard. Generalizing the Hough transform to detect arbitrary shapes. *Pattern Recognition* 13:111–122, 1981.

[Ballard 82] D. H. Ballard and C. M. Brown. *Computer Vision*. Prentice-Hall, Englewood Cliffs, N.J., 1982.

[Banks 83] M. S. Banks and P. Salapatek. Infant visual perception. In M.M. Haith and J. J. Campos (editor), *Handbook of Child Psychology: Infancy and Development Biology*. Wiley, New York, 1983.

[Barlow 53] H. B. Barlow. Summation and inhibition in the frog's retina. *Journal of Philosophy* (London) 119:69–88, 1953.

[Barrett 79] W. Barrett. *The Illusion of Technique*. Anchor Books, New York, 1979.

[Barrow 78] H. G. Barrow and J. M. Tenenbaum. Recovering intrinsic scene characteristics from images. In A. R. Hanson and E. M. Riseman (editors), *Computer Vision Systems*. Academic Press, New York, 1978.

[Barrow 81] H. G. Barrow and J. M. Tenenbaum. Computational vision. *Proceedings of the IEEE* 69:572–595, 1981.

[Beck 83] J. Beck, B. Hope, and A. Rosenfeld (editors). *Human and Machine Vision*. Academic Press, New York, 1983.

[Begbie 73] G. H. Begbie. *Seeing and the Eye*. Anchor/Doubleday, New York, 1973.

[Binford 81] T. O. Binford. Inferring surfaces from images. *Artificial Intelligence* 17:205–245, 1981.

[Biological 68] Biological Sciences Curriculum Study Group (C. A. Welch, D. I. Arnon, H. Cochran, F. C. Erk, J. Fishleder, W. V. Mayer, M. Pius, J. Shaver, and F. W. Smith, Jr.). *Biological Science: Molecules to Man* Houghton Mifflin Co., Boston, 1968.

[Block 81] N. Block (editor). *Imagery*. MIT Press, Bradford Books, Cambridge, Mass., 1981.

[Bobrow 68] D. G. Bobrow. Natural Language Input for a Computer Problem-Solving System. In M. Minsky (editor) *Semantic Information Processing*. MIT Press, Cambridge, Mass., 1968, Chapter 3.

[Bobrow 85] D. G. Bobrow and P. J. Hayes. Artificial intelligence—where are we? *Artificial Intelligence* 25:375–415, 1985.

[Boden 77] M. A. Boden. *Artificial Intelligence and Natural Man*. Basic Books, New York, 1977.

[Boden 81] M. A. Boden. *Minds and Mechanisms*. Cornell University Press, Ithaca, N.Y., 1981, chapter 11.

[Boolos 80] G. S. Boolos and R. C. Jeffrey. *Computability and Logic*. Cambridge University Press, Cambridge, England, 1980. 2nd edition.

[Brachman 85] R. J. Brachman and H. J. Levesque (editors). *Readings in Knowledge Representation*. Morgan and Kaufmann Publishers, Los Altos, Calif., 1985.

[Brady 82] M. Brady. Computational approaches to image understanding. *Computing Surveys* 14:3–71, March 1982.

[Brooks 81] R. A. Brooks. Symbolic reasoning among 3-D models and images. *Artificial Intelligence* 17:205–244, 1981.

[Brown 58] R. Brown. *Words and Things*. The Free Press, New York, 1958. chapter 7.

[Brown 77] R. Brown. *A First Language: The Early Stages*. Harvard University Press, Cambridge, Mass., 1977.

[Brown 80] J. W. Brown. Language, brain, and the problem of localization. In D. Caplan (editor), *Biological Studies of Mental Process*. MIT Press, Cambridge, Mass., 1980.

[Brownston 85] L. Brownston, R. Farrell, E. Kant, and N. Martin. *Programming Expert Systems in OPS5*. Addison-Wesley, Reading, Mass., 1985.

[Buchanan 78] B.G. Buchanan and E.A. Feigenbaum. DENDRAL and METADENDRAL—Their applications dimensions. *Artificial Intelligence* 11:5–24, 1978.

[Buchanan 84] B. G. Buchanan and E. H. Shortliffe. *Rule-Based Expert Systems*. Addison-Wesley, Reading, Mass., 1984.

[Bundy 83] A. Bundy. *The Computer Modeling of Reasoning*. Academic Press, New York, 1983.

[Bundy 85] A. Bundy, B. Silver, and D. Plummer. An analytical comparison of some rule-learning programs. *Artificial Intelligence* 27(2):137–181, November, 1985.

[Butcher 73] B. T. Butcher. *Human Intelligence*. Harper and Row, New York, 1973.

[Butter 68] C. M. Butter. *Neurophysiology: The Study of Brain and Behavior*. Brooks/Cole Publishing Co., Belmont, Calif., 1968.

[Caplan 82] D. Caplan and N. Chomsky. Language development. In D. Caplan (editor), *Biological Studies of Mental Process*. MIT Press, Cambridge, Mass., 1982.

[Carroll 56] J. B. Carroll. *Language and Thought.* Prentice-Hall, Englewood Cliffs, N.J., 1956.

[Castleman 79] K. R. Castleman. *Digital Image Processing.* Prentice-Hall, Englewood Cliffs, N.J., 1979.

[Chang 73] C. Chang and R. Lee. *Symbolic Logic and Mechanical Theorem Proving.* Academic Press, New York, 1973.

[Changeux 85] J.- P. Changeux. *Neuronal Man.* Pantheon Books, New York, 1985.

[Cheeseman 85] Peter Cheeseman. In defense of probability. *Proc. of the Ninth International Joint Conference on Artificial Intelligence,* August 1985, Los Angeles. Calif. Morgan Kaufmann, Los Altos, Calif.

[Chomsky 75] N. Chomsky. *Reflections on Language.* Random House, New York, 1975.

[Clocksin 81] W. F. Clocksin and C. S. Mellish. *Programming in Prolog.* Springer-Verlag, Berlin, 1981.

[Cohen 82] P. R. Cohen and E. A. Feigenbaum (editors). *Handbook of Artificial Intelligence.* William Kaufmann, Los Altos, Calif., 1982. Volume 3, chapters 12 and 13.

[Cornsweet 70] T. N. Cornsweet. *Visual Perception.* Academic Press, New York, 1970.

[Courant 41] R. Courant and H. Robbins. *What is Mathematics?* Oxford University Press, London, 1941.

[Cox 46] R. Cox. Probability, frequency, and reasonable expectation. *American Journal of Physics* 14:1–13, 1946.

[Crane] H. Crane. *Beyond the Seventh Synapse.* SRI International, Menlo Park, Calif. (forthcoming).

[Crossley 72] J. N. Crossley, C. J. Ash, C. J. Brickhill, J. C. Stillwell, and N.H. Williams. *What is Mathematical Logic?* Oxford University Press, Oxford, England, 1972.

[Cunningham 72] M. Cunningham. *Intelligence: Its Organization and Development.* Academic Press, New York, 1972.

[Davis 82] R. Davis and D. B. Lenat. *Knowledge-Based Systems in Artificial Intelligence.* McGraw-Hill, New York, 1982.

[Dawkins 76] R. Dawkins. *The Selfish Gene.* Oxford University Press, New York, 1976.

[De Groot 65] A. D. De Groot. *Thought and Choice in Chess.* Basic Books Inc., New York, 1965.

[De Kleer 84] J. De Kleer. A qualitative physics based on confluences. *Artificial Intelligence* 24:7–84, 1984.

[De Kleer 84a] J. De Kleer. How circuits work. *Artificial Intelligence* 24:205–280, 1984.

[Dennett 78] D. C. Dennett. *Brainstorms: Philosophical Essays on Mind and Psychology.* Bradford Books, Montgomery, 1978.

[Dennett 84] D. C. Dennett. Cognitive wheels: the frame problem of AI. In C. Hookway (editor), *Minds, Machines, and Evolution.* Cambridge University Press, Cambridge, England, 1984.

[Dennett 84a] D. C. Dennett. *Elbow Room: The Varieties of Free Will Worth Wanting.* MIT Press, Cambridge, Mass., 1984.

[Dennett 85] D. C. Dennett. Can machines think? *In How We Know (Nobel Conference 20),* pages 121–145. Harper and Row, New York, 1985.

[Deregowski 74] J. B. Deregowski. Pictorial perception and culture. In *Image, Object, and Illusion.* W. H. Freeman, San Francisco, 1974.

[Dewdney 84] A. K. Dewdney. Computer Recreations. *Scientific American* 250:19–26, 1984.

[Dewdney 84] A. K. Dewdney. Computer Recreations: A computer trap for the busy beaver. *Scientific American* 251:19–23, 1984.

[Dewdney 85] A. K. Dewdney. Computer Recreations. *Scientific American* 253:23–24, September, 1985.

[Dretske 85] F. Dretske. Machines and the Mental. In Americal Philosophical Association Proceedings, pages 23–33. *American Philosophical Association,* Chicago, 1985.

[Dreyfus 79] H. L. Dreyfus. *What Computers Can't Do.* Harper & Row, New York, 1979, revised edition.

[Duda 73] R. O. Duda and P. E. Hart. *Pattern Recognition and Scene Analysis.* Wiley, New York, 1973.

[Duda 75] R. O. Duda and P. E. Hart. Use of the Hough transform to detect lines and curves in pictures. *Communications of the Association for Computing Machinery* 15:11–15, 1975.

[Duda 76] R. O. Duda, P. E. Hart, and N. J. Nilsson. Subjective Bayesian methods for rule-based inference systems. *Proc. AFIPS, National Comp. Conf.* 45:1075–1082, 1976.

[Duda 79] R.O. Duda, J. Gaschnig, P. E. Hart. Model design in the PROSPECTOR consultant system for mineral exploration. In D. Michie (editor), *Expert Systems in the Micro-electronics Age.* Edinburgh University, Edinburgh, 1979.

[Duda 83] R. O. Duda and Edward H. Shortliffe. Expert

System Research. *Science* 220:261–268, 1983.

[Duke-Elder 58] W. S. Duke-Elder. *System of Ophthalmology (Vol. 1, The Eye in Evolution)*. C. V. Mosby Co., St. Louis, 1958.

[Dyson 79] F. Dyson. *Disturbing the Universe*. Harper and Row, New York, 1979.

[Earley 70] J. Earley. An efficient context-free parser. *Communications of the Association for Computing Machinery* 13:94–102, 1970.

[Eccles 70] J. C. Eccles. *Facing Reality*. Springer-Verlag, New York and Berlin, 1970.

[Eimas 75] P. D. Eimas. Infant perception: from sensation to perception. In L. B. Cohen and P. Salapatek (editors), *Developmental Studies of Speech Perception*. Academic Press, New York, 1975.

[Epstein 84] R. Epstein. *Bird Insight*. Nature, March, 1984. Cited in Science News, March 17, 1984, "Tracking bird-brained insight," page 171.

[Ernst 69] G. W. Ernst and A. Newell. GPS: A Case Study In Generality And Problem Solving. *Academic Press*, New York, 1969.

[Evans 68] T. G. Evans. A program for the solution of a class of geometric analogy intelligent-test questions. In M. Minsky (editor) *Semantic Information Processing*. MIT Press, Cambridge, Mass., 1968.

[Eyseneck 81] H. J. Eyseneck and L. Kamin. *The Intelligence Controversy*. Wiley, New York, 1981.

[Falmagne 75] R. J. Falmagne (editor). *Reasoning: Representation and Process in Children*. Lawrence Erlbaum Associates, Hillsdale, N.J., 1975.

[Feldman 85] J. A. Feldman. Connectionist models and parallelism in high level vision. *Computer Graphics and Image Processing* 31:178–200, 1985.

[Feller 50] B. W. Feller. *Probability Theory and Its Applications*. Wiley, New York, 1950.

[Fikes 85] R. Fikes and T. Kehler. The role of frame-based representation in reasoning. *Communications of the ACM* 28(9):904–920, Sept. 1985.

[Findler 79] N.V. Findler. *Associative Networks: The Representation and Use of Knowledge by Computers*. Academic Press, New York, 1979.

[Fingerman 69] M. Fingerman. *Animal Diversity*. Holt, Rinehart, and Winston, New York, 1969.

[Fischler 73] M. A. Fischler and R. A. Elschlager. The representation and matching of pictorial structures. *IEEE Transactions on Computers* 22:68–92, January 1973.

[Fischler 81] M. A. Fischler and R. C. Bolles. Random sample consensus: a paradigm for model fitting with applications to image analysis and automated cartography. *Communications of the ACM* 24:381–395, 1981.

[Fischler and Barrett 80] Fischler, M.A. and P. Barrett, "An Iconic Transform for Sketch Completion and Shape Abstraction," Computer Graphics and Image Processing, 13:334–360, 1980.

[Flavell 63] J. H. Flavell. *The Developmental Psychology of Jean Piaget*. D. Van Nostrand, New York, 1963.

[Flavell 85] J. H. Flavell. *Cognitive Development*. Prentice-Hall Inc., Englewood Cliffs, N.J., 1985, 2nd Edition.

[Fodor 64] J. A. Fodor and J. J. Katz. *The Structure of Language*. Prentice-Hall, Englewood Cliffs, N.J., 1964.

[Fodor 74] J. A. Fodor, T. G. Bever, and M. F. Garrett. *The Psychology of Language*. McGraw-Hill, New York, 1974.

[Fodor 75] J. A. Fodor. *The Language of Thought*. Crowell, New York, 1975.

[Fodor 83] J. A. Fodor. *The Modularity of Mind*. MIT/ Bradford Books, Cambridge, Mass., 1983.

[Forgus 66] R. H. Forgus. *Perception*. McGraw-Hill, New York, 1966.

[Forgy 77] C. Forgy and J. McDermott. OPS, a domain-independent production system language. In *Proceedings of the 5th International Joint Conference on Artificial Intelligence*, pages 933–939. Cambridge, Mass. August, 1977. William Kaufmann, Los Altos, Calif., 1977.

[Fox 82] R. Fox and C. McDaniel. The perception of biological motion by human infants. In *Science* 218:486–487, 1982.

[Frisby 80] J.P. Frisby. *Seeing—Illusions, Brain and Mind*. Oxford, Oxford, England, 1980.

[Fu 74] K. S. Fu. *Syntactic Methods in Pattern Recognition*. Academic Press, New York, 1974.

[Funt 80] B. V. Funt. Problem-solving with diagrammatic representations. *Artificial Intelligence* 13:201–230, 1980.

[Gallup 77] G. Gallup. Self-recognition in primates: a comparative approach to bidirection properties of consciousness. *American Psychologist* 32:329–338, 1977.

[Gardner 63] E. Gardner. *Fundamentals of Neurology*, W. B. Saunders Co., Philadelphia, 1963, 4th edition.

[Gardner 69] A. R. Gardner and B. T. Gardner. Teaching sign language to a chimpanzee. *Science* July 15, 1969.

[Gardner 82] H. Gardner. *Art, Mind, and Brain*. Basic Books Inc./Harper, New York, 1982. Chapter 26.

[Gardner 83] H. Gardner. *Frames of Mind: The Theory of Multiple Intelligences*. Basic Books, New York, 1983.

[Gardner 85] H. Gardner. *The Mind's New Science*. Basic Books, New York, 1985.

[Garey 79] M. R. Garey and D. S. Johnson. *Computers and Tractability*. W. H. Freeman, San Francisco, 1979.

[Garvey 81] T. D. Garvey, J. D. Lowrance, and M. A. Fischler. An inference technique for integrating knowledge from disparate sources. In *Proceedings of the 7th International Joint Conference on Artificial Intelligence*, Vancouver, August, 1981. William Kaufmann, Los Altos, Calif. 1981.

[Gazzaniga 85] M. S. Gazzaniga. *The Social Brain*. Basic Books, New York, 1985.

[Gedamer 76] H.- G. Gedamer. *Philosophical Hermeneutics*. University of Calif. Press, Berkeley, Calif., 1976.

[Gentner 83] D. Gentner and A. L. Stevens (editors). *Mental Models*. Lawrence Erlbaum Associates, Hillsdale, N.J., 1983.

[Georgeff 84] M.P. Georgeff. An expert system for representing procedural knowledge. *In Joint Services Workshop on Artificial Intelligence in Maintenance, Volume 1*, Boulder, Color., 1983.

[Geschwind 79] N. Geschwind. Specializations of the brain. *Scientific American* 243:180–199, 1979.

[Gibson 50] J. J. Gibson. *The Perception of the Visual World*. Houghton-Mifflin, Boston, 1950.

[Gibson 66] J. J. Gibson. *The Senses Considered as Perceptual Systems*. Houghton Mifflin, Boston, 1966.

[Gibson 79] J. J. Gibson. *The Ecological Approach to Visual Perception*. Houghton Mifflin, Boston, Mass., 1979.

[Gilchrist 79] A. L. Gilchrist. The perception of surface blacks and whites. *Scientific American* 240:88–97, 1979.

[Gloess 82] P. Y. Gloess. *Understanding LISP*. Alfred Publishing, Sherman Oaks, Calif., 1982.

[Gombrich 61] E. H. Gombrich. *Art and Illusion: A Study in the Psychology of Pictorial Presentation*. Princeton University Press, Princeton, N.J., 1961.

[Gonzalez 77] R. C. Gonzalez and P. Wintz. *Digital Image Processing*. Addison-Wesley, Reading, Mass., 1977.

[Gould 81] S. J. Gould. *The Mismeasure of Man*. W. W. Norton, New York, 1981.

[Greenberg 63] J. H. Greenberg. Some universals of grammar with particular reference to the order of meaningful elements. In J. H. Greenberg (editor), *Universals of Language*. MIT Press, Cambridge, Mass., 1963.

[Gregory 70] R.L. Gregory. *The Intelligent Eye*. McGraw-Hill, New York, 1970.

[Gregory 78] R. L. Gregory. *Eye and Brain: The Psychology of Seeing*. McGraw-Hill, New York, 1978. revised edition.

[Griffin 84] D. Griffin. *Animal Thinking*. Harvard University Press, Cambridge, Mass., 1984.

[Grosz 80] B. J. Grosz. Utterance and objective: issues in natural language communication. *AI Magazine*. 1:11–20, 1980.

[Grosz 82] B. J. Grosz, N. Haas, G. Hendrix, J. Hobbs, P. Martin, R.Moore, J. Robinson, and S. Rosenschein. *DIALOGIC: A Core Natural-Language Processing System*. Technical Report Technical Note No. 270, SRI International, Menlo Park, Calif. 94025, November 1982.

[Guilford 67] J. P. Guilford. *The Nature of Human Intelligence*. McGraw-Hill, New York, 1967.

[Gunderson 85] K. Gunderson. *Mentality and Machines*. University of Minnesota Press, Minneapolis, Minn., 1985. 2nd Edition.

[Guzman 69] A. Guzman. Decomposition of a visual scene into three-dimensional bodies. In A. Grasseli (editor), *Automatic Interpretation and Classification of Images*. Academic Press, New York, 1969.

[Hanson 78] A. R. Hanson and E. M. Riseman (eds). *Computer Vision Systems*. Academic Press, New York, 1978.

[Harmon 73] L. D. Harmon. The recognition of faces. *Scientific American* 229:71–82, 1973.

[Haugeland 85] J. Haugeland. *Artificial Intelligence: The*

Very Idea. MIT Press/Bradford, Cambridge, 1985.

[Haugeland 85a] J. Haugeland. *Mind Design*. MIT Press, Cambridge, Mass., 1985.

[Hayes 77] J. R. Hayes. Psychological differences among problem isomorphs. In D. B. Castellan, D. B. Pisoni, and G. R. Potts (editors). *Cognitive Theory*. Lawrence Erlbaum Associates, Hillsdale, N.J., 1977.

[Hayes 85] P. Hayes. The second naive physics manifesto. In: *Formal Theories of the Commonsense World*. J. Hobbes and R. Moore (editors). Ablex., Norwood, N.J., 1985.

[Hayes-Roth 83] F. Hayes-Roth, D. Waterman, and D. Lenat. *Building Expert Systems*. Addison-Wesley, Reading, Mass., 1983.

[Hegner 59] R. W. Hegner and K. A Stiles. *College Zoology*, Macmillan Co., New York, 1959, 7th edition.

[Heidegger 62] M. Heidegger. *Being and Time*. Harper and Row, New York, New York, 1962.

[Held 72] R. Held and W. Richards (editor). *Perception: Mechanisms and Models*. W.H. Freeman, San Francisco, 1972.

[Held 74] R. Held and W. Richards (editors). *Image, Object, and Illusion*. W. H. Freeman, San Francisco, 1974.

[Held 76] R. Held and W. Richards (editors). *Recent Progress in Perception*. W. H. Freeman, San Francisco, 1976.

[Hendrix 78] G. G. Hendrix. Developing a natural language interface to complex data. *ACM Transactions Database Systems* 3:105–147, 1978.

[Herbrand 30] J. Herbrand. Recherches sur la theorie de la demonstration. *Trav. Soc. Sci. Lettres Varsovie, Classe III Sci. Math. Phys.* (33), 1930.

[Herrnstein 73] R. J. Herrnstein. *IQ in the Meritocracy*. Atlantic, Little, Brown, & Co., Boston, Mass., 1973.

[Herskovits 85] A. Herskovitz. Semantics and pragmatics of locative expressions. *Cognitive Science* 9:341–378, 1985.

[Hilgard 75] E. R. Hilgard, R. C. Atkinson, and R. L. Atkinson. *Introduction to Psychology*. Harcourt Brace Jovanovich, Inc., New York, 1975, 6th edition.

[Hinchman 83] J. H. Hinchman and M.C. Morgan. Application of artificial intelligence to equipment maintenance. In *Proceedings of Joint Services Workshop on Artificial Intelligence in Maintenance. Volume 1*.

Boulder, Colo., 1983.

[Hobbs 85] J. R. Hobbs. *Formal Theories of the Commonsense World*. Ablex Publishing Corp., Norwood, N.J., 1985.

[Hochberg 78] J. Hochberg. *Perception*. Prentice-Hall, Engelwood Cliffs, N.J., 1978.

[Hodges 83] A. Hodges. *Alan Turing: The Enigma*. Simon and Shuster, New York, 1983.

[Hoffman 85] D. D. Hoffman and W. Richards. Parts of recognition. *Cognition* 18:65–96, 1985.

[Hofstadter 79] D. R. Hofstadter. *Godel, Escher, and Bach*. Basic Books, New York, 1979.

[Hofstadter 83] D. R. Hofstadter and D. C. Dennett (editors). *The Mind's I*. Basic Books, New York, 1983.

[Holland 83] J. H. Holland. Escaping brittleness. In *Proceedings of the International Machine Learning Workshop*. University of Illinois, Urbana, Ill., 1983.

[Hookway 84] C. Hookway (editor). *Minds, Machines, and Evolution*. Cambridge University Press, Cambridge, England, 1984.

[Horn 74] B. K. P. Horn. Determining lightness from an image. *Computer Graphics and Image Processing* 3:277–299, 1974.

[Horn 77] B. K. P. Horn. Understanding image intensities. *Artificial Intelligence* 8:201–231, 1977.

[Horvitz 86] E. Horvitz and D. Heckerman. A framework for comparing alternative formalisms for plausible reasoning. In *AAAI-86*. Philadelphia, Penn. 1986.

[House 63] R. W. House and T. Rado. An approach to artificial intelligence. In *Proc. IEEE Winter General Meeting*, pages 111–116. IEEE, February, 1963.

[Hubel 78] D. H. Hubel. Anatomical demonstration of orientation columns in macaque monkey. *Journal of Comparative Neurology* 177:361–380, 1978.

[Hubel 79] D. H. Hubel and T. N. Wiesel. Brain mechanisms of vision. *Scientific American* 241:150–162, September, 1979.

[Hueckel 73] M. Hueckel. A local visual operator which recognizes edges and lines. *Journal of the Assoc. Comput. Machinery* 20:634, 1973.

[Hummel 83] R. A. Hummel and S. W. Zucker. On the foundations of relaxation labeling processes. *IEEE Trans. on Pattern Analysis and Machine Intelligence* PAMI-5:267–287, 1983.

[Hutchins 66] R. E. Hutchins. *Insects*. Prentice-Hall,

BIBLIOGRAPHY

Englewood Cliffs, N. J., 1966.

[Jacobs 81] G. H. Jacobs. *Comparative Color Vision.* Academic Press, New York, 1981.

[Jaynes 77] J. Jaynes. *The Origin of Consciousness in the Breakdown of the Bicameral Mind.* Houghton-Mifflin, Boston, Mass., 1977.

[Johnson-Laird 77] P. N. Johnson-Laird and P.C. Wason. A theoretical analysis of insight into a reasoning task. In P. N. Johnson-Laird and P. C. Wason (editors), *Thinking: Readings in Cognitive Science.* Cambridge University Press, Cambridge, England, 1977.

[Jolly 85] A. Jolly. A new science that sees animals as conscious beings. *Smithsonian* 15:65–75, 1985.

[Jones 74] J. R. Jones. Recursive Undecideability. *American Mathematics Monthly* 81:724–738, 1974.

[Julesz 71] B. Julesz. *Foundations of Cyclopean Perception.* University of Chicago Press, Chicago, Illinois, 1971.

[Julesz 74] B. Julesz. Cooperative phenomena in binocular depth perception. *American Scientist* 62:32–43, 1974.

[Julesz 75] B. Julesz. Experiments in the visual perception of texture. *Scientific American* 232:34–43, 1975.

[Julesz 83] B. Julesz and J. R. Bergen. Textons, the fundamental elements in preattentive vision and perception of textures. *Bell System Technical Journal* 62:1619–1645, 1983.

[Kahneman 82] D. Kahneman and A. Tversky. On the study of statistical intuitions. *Cognition* 11:123–141, 1982.

[Kanade 80] T. Kanade. Region segmentation: signal vs. semantics. *Computer Graphics and Image Processing* 13:279–297, 1980.

[Kaniza 79] G. Kaniza. *Organization in Vision.* Praeger Publishers, New York, 1979.

[Kaufman 74] L. Kaufman. *Sight and Mind.* Oxford, Oxford, England, 1974.

[Kay 73] M. Kay. The MIND system. In R. Rustin (editor), *Natural Language Processing.* Prentice-Hall, Englewood Cliffs, N.J., 1973.

[Kelly 55] G. A. Kelly. *A Theory of Personality.* W. W. Norton, New York, 1955.

[Kemeny 55] J. Kemeny. Man viewed as a machine.
Scientific American 192:58–67, 1955.

[Kender 78] J. P. Kender. Shape from texture: a brief overview and a new aggregation transform. In *Image Understanding, Proceedings of a Workshop.* Science Applications, Washington, 1978.

[King 63] B. G. King and M. J. Showers. *Human Anatomy and Physiology.* W. B. Saunders Co., Philadelphia, 1963.

[Kline 80] M. Kline. *Mathematics, The Loss of Certainty.* Oxford University Press, New York, 1980.

[Knuth 73] D. Knuth. *The Art of Computer Programming: Fundamental Algorithms.* Addison-Wesley, Reading, Mass., 1973.

[Koestler 69] A. Koestler. *The Act of Creation.* Dell, New York, 1969.

[Kondratov 69] A. Kondratov. *Sounds and Signs.* MIR Publishers, Moscow, USSR, 1969.

[Kosslyn 80] S. M. Kosslyn. *Image and Mind.* Harvard University Press, Cambridge, Mass., 1980.

[Kosslyn 83] S. M. Kosslyn. *Ghosts in the Mind's Machine.* W. W. Norton & Co., New York, 1983.

[Kowalski 79] R. Kowalski. *Logic for Problem Solving.* North Holland, New York, 1979.

[Kuffler 76] S. W. Kuffler and J. G. Nicholls. *From Neuron to Brain.* Sinauer Associates, Inc., Sunderland, Mass., 1976.

[Kuipers 84] B. Kuipers. Commonsense reasoning about causality: deriving behavior from structure. *Artificial Intelligence* 24:169-204, 1984.

[Kripke 72] S. Kripke. Naming and necessity. In D. Davidson and G. Harmon (editors). *Semantics of Natural Language.* Reidell, Dordrecht/Boston, 1972.

[Land 59] E. H. Land. Experiments in color vision. *Scientific American* 200:84–99, 1959.

[Land 77] E. H. Land. The retinex theory of colour vision. *Scientific American* 237:108–128, 1977.

[Lane 85] H. Lane. *When the Mind Hears: A History of the Deaf.* Random House, New York, 1985.

[Larkin 81] J. Larkin. A model for learning to solve textbook physics problems. In J. R. Anderson (editor), *Skills and Their Acquisition.* Lawrence Erlbaum Associates, Hillsdale, N. J., 1981.

[Lenat 77] D. Lenat. On automated scientific theory formation: a case study using the AM program, pages 251–286. In *Machine Intelligence.* Halstead Press,

New York, 1977, Volume 9.

[Lenat 84] D. B. Lenat and J. S. Brown. Why AM and Eurisko appear to work. *Artificial Intelligence* 23:269–294, 1984.

[Lenneberg 67] E. H. Lenneberg. *Biological Foundations of Language*. Wiley, New York, 1969.

[Lettvin 59] J. Y. Lettvin, R. R. Maturana, W. S. Mc-Colloch. What the frog's eye tells the frog's brain. *Proc. Inst. Radio Engineers* 47:1940–1951, 1959.

[Levine 85] M. Levine. *Vision in Man and Machine*. McGraw-Hill, New York, 1985.

[Linden 74] E. Linden. *Apes, Man, and Language*. Saturday Review Press, New York, 1974.

[Linden 86] E. Linden. *Silent Partners: The Legacy of the Ape Language Experiments*. Times Books, New York, 1986.

[Lindsay 72] P. H. Lindsay and D. A. Norman. *Human Information Processing*. Academic Press, New York, 1972.

[Lipkin 70] B. S. Lipkin and A. Rosenfeld (editors). *Picture Processing and Psychopictorics*. Academic Press, New York, 1970.

[Lowe 85] D. Lowe. *Perceptual Organization and Visual Recognition*. Kluwer, Boston, Mass., 1985.

[Luria 73] A. R. Luria. *The Working Brain: An Introduction to Neuropsychology*. Basic Books, New York, 1973.

[Lythgoe 79] J. N. Lythgoe. *The Ecology of Vision*. Clarendon Press, Oxford, England, 1979.

[MacLean 73] P. D. Maclean. *A Triune Concept of Brain and Behavior*. University of Toronto Press, Toronto, Canada, 1973.

[MacWorth 73] A. K. MacWorth. Interpreting pictures of polyhedral scenes. *Artificial Intelligence* 4:121–137, 1973.

[Malotki 83] E. Malotki. Hopi time: a linguistic analysis of the temporal concept in the Hopi language. *Trends in Linguistics, Studies and Monographs*. Number 20, Mouton, Berlin, 1983.

[Mandelbrot 82] B. B. Mandelbrot. *The Fractal Geometry of Nature*. Freeman, San Francisco, Calif., 1982.

[Mandler 83] J. M. Mandler. Representation. In J. H. Flavell and E. M. Markman (editor), *Handbook of Child Psychology: Cognitive Development*. Wiley, New York, 1983.

[Marcus 80] M. P. Marcus. *A Theory of Syntactic Recognition for Natural Language*. MIT Press, Cambridge, Mass., 1980.

[Marr 76] D. Marr. Early processing of visual information. *Philosophical Transactions of the Royal Society* 275(Series B):483–524, 1976.

[Marr 76] D. Marr and T. Poggio. Co-operative computation of stereo disparity. *Science* 194:283–287, 1976.

[Marr 78] D. Marr and H. K. Nishihara. Visual information processing: artificial intelligence and the sensorium of sight. *Technology Review* 81:1–23, 1978.

[Marr 82] D. Marr. *Vision*. W. H. Freeman, San Francisco, 1982.

[Marshall 82] J. C. Marshall. Biology of Language Acquisition. In D. Caplan (editor), *Biological Studies of Mental Processes*. MIT Press, Cambridge, Mass., 1980 (paperback edition 1982).

[Martin 78] W. N. Martin and J. K. Aggarwal. Dynamic scene analysis. *Computer Graphics and Image Processing* 7:356–374, 1978.

[McCarthy 80] J. McCarthy. Circumscription—A form of non-monotonic reasoning. *Artificial Intelligence* 13:27–39, 1980.

[McDermott 80] J. McDermott and C. Forgy. R1: An expert in the computer systems domain. In *Proceedings of the First Annual National Conf. on Artificial Intelligence*, pages 269–271, Stanford, Calif. August 1980, American Association for Artificial Intelligence, Menlo Park, Calif. 1980.

[McDermott 81] J. McDermott. R1: The Formative Years. *AI Magazine* 2:21–29, 1981.

[McKeithen 81] K. B. McKeithen. Knowledge organization and skill differences in computer professionals. *Cognitive Psychology* 13:307–325, 1981.

[McKim 72] R. McKim. *Experiences in Visual Thinking*. Brooks/Cole, Monterey, Calif., 1972.

[McNaught 75] A. B. McNaught and R. Callander. *Illustrated Physiology*. Churchill Livingstone, Edinburgh, 1975. 3rd edition.

[Miller 83] J. Miller. *States of Mind*. Pantheon, New York, 1983.

[Milne 72] L. Milne and M. Milne. *The Senses of Animals and Men*. Atheneum, New York, 1972.

[Minnaert 54] M. Minnaert. *Light and Color*. Dover, New York, 1954.

[Minsky 67] M. Minsky. *Computation: Finite and Infinite*.

Prentice Hall, Englewood Cliffs, N.J., 1967.

[Minsky 68] M. Minsky. Matter, mind and models. In M. Minsky (editor) *Semantic Information Processing*. MIT Press, Cambridge, Mass., 1968.

[Mitchell 83] T. M. Mitchell, P. E. Utzoff, and R. B. Banerji. Learning by experimentation: acquiring and refining problem-solving heuristics. In R. S. Michalski, J. G. Carbonell, T. M. Mitchell (editors), *Machine Learning, An Artificial Intelligence Approach*. Tioga Press, Palo Alto, Calif., 1983.

[Mitchell 83] T. M. Mitchell. Learning and problem solving. In *Proceedings of the 8th International Joint Conference on Artificial Intelligence*, Karlsruhe, West Germany, August 1983, William Kaufmann, Los Altos, Calif., 1983.

[Moore 81] R. C. Moore. Problems in logical form. In *Proceedings of the 19th Annual Meeting of the Association for Computational Linguistics*. Stanford, Calif., June-July 1981.

[Moore 85] R. C. Moore. A formal theory of knowledge and action. In R. Hobbs and R. C. Moore (editors). *Formal Theories of the Common Sense World*. Ablex Publishing, New York, 1985.

[Mowskowitz 76] A. Mowskowitz. *The Conquest of Will—Information Processing in Human Affairs*. Addison-Wesley, Reading, Mass., 1976.

[Mueller 66] C. G. Mueller and M. Rudolph. *Light and Vision*. Time Inc., New York, 1966.

[Nagel 58] E. Nagel and J. R. Newman. *Gödel's Proof*. New York University Press, New York, 1958.

[Nagel 74] T. Nagel. What is it like to be a bat? *Philosophical Review* 83:435–451, 1974.

[Navatia 82] R. Navatia. *Machine Perception*. Prentice-Hall, Engelwood Cliffs, N.J., 1982.

[Neisser 67] U. Neisser. *Cognitive Psychology*. Appleton-Century-Croft, New York, 1967.

[Nelson 73] K. E. Nelson, G. Carskaddon, and J. Bonvillian. Syntax acquisition: impact of experimental variation in adult verbal interaction with the child. *Child Development* 44:497–504, 1973.

[von Neumann 56] cited in: *Theory of Self-Reproducing Automata*. A. W. Burks (editor). University of Illinois, Urbana, Ill., 1956.

[von Neumann 56a] J. von Neumann. Probabilistic logics and the synthesis of reliable organs from unreliable components. In *Automata Studies Number 34*. Princeton University Press, Princeton, N.J., 1956.

[Newell 72] A. Newell and H. Simon. *Human Problem Solving*. Prentice Hall, Englewood Cliffs, N.J., 1972.

[Newell 73] A. Newell. Production systems: Models of control structures. In W. G. Chase (editor) *Visual Information Processing*. Academic Press, New York, 1973.

[Newman 82] E. A. Newman and P. H. Hartline. The infrared "vision" of snakes. *Scientific American* 246:116–127, 1982.

[Nilsson 71] N. J. Nilsson. *Problem-Solving Methods in Artificial Intelligence*. McGraw-Hill, New York, 1971.

[Nilsson 80] N. J. Nilsson. *Principles of Artificial Intelligence*. Tioga, Palo Alto, Calif., 1980.

[Nilsson 83] N. J. Nilsson. Artificial intelligence prepares for 2001. *AI Magazine* 4(4), Winter 1983.

[Norman 81] D. A. Norman (editor). *Perspectives in Cognitive Science*. Ablex Publishing, Norwood, N.J., 1981.

[North 76] R.C. North. *The World That Could Be*. The Portable Stanford, Stanford Alumni Association, Stanford, Calif., 1976.

[Ohlander 78] R. Ohlander, K. Price, and D. R. Reddy. Picture segmentation using a recursive splitting method. *Computer Graphics and Image Processing* 8:313–333, 1978.

[Olds 67] J. Olds. Emotional Centers in the Brain. *Science Journal* 3:87–92, Associated Lliffe Press, London, 1967.

[Ornstein 73] R. E. Ornstein. *The Nature of Human Consciousness*. W. H. Freeman, San Francisco, 1973.

[Parzen 60] E. Parzen. *Modern Probability Theory*. Wiley, New York, 1960.

[Patterson 78] F. Patterson. Conversations with a gorilla. *National Geographic*, October 1978.

[Pavlidis 77] T. Pavlidis. *Structural Pattern Recognition*. Springer-Verlag, Berlin, 1977.

[Pavlidis 82] T. Pavlidis. *Graphics and Image Processing*. Computer Science Press, Rockville, 1982.

[Pearl 84] J. Pearl. *Heuristics: Intelligent Strategies for Computer Problem Solving*. Addison-Wesley, Reading, Mass., 1984.

[Penfield 78] W. Penfield. *The Mystery of the Mind*. Princeton University Press, Princeton, N.J., 1978.

[Pentland 83] A. P. Pentland and M. A. Fischler. A more rational view of logic. *AI Magazine* 4(4), Winter 1983.

[Pettigrew 72] J. D. Pettigrew. The neurophysiology of binocular vision. *Scientific American* 227:84–95, 1972.

[Piaget 52] J. Piaget. *The Origins of Intelligence in Children*. International Libraries Press, New York, 1952.

[Pirenne 67] M. H. Pirenne. *Vision and the Eye*. Barnes and Noble, New York, 1967.

[Polya 54] G. Polya. *Patterns of Plausible Inference*. Princeton University Press, Princeton, N.J., 1954.

[Popper 77] K. R. Popper and J. C. Eccles. *The Self and the Brain*. Springer-Verlag, London, 1977.

[Pratt 76] W. K. Pratt. *Digital Image Processing*. Academic Press, New York, 1976.

[Pribram 71] K.H. Pribram. *Languages of the Brain*. Prentice-Hall, Englewood Cliffs, New Jersey, 1971.

[Putnam 75] H. Putnam. The meaning of meaning. In H. Putnam (editor) *Mind, Language, and Reality: Philosophical papers*, Vol. 2, Cambridge University Press, Cambridge, England, 1975.

[Pylyshyn 78] Z. W. Pylyshyn. Imagery and artificial intelligence. In Ned Block (editor), *Readings in Philosophy of Psychology*. Harvard University Press, Cambridge, Mass., 1981.

[Pylyshyn 73] Z. W. Pylyshyn. What the mind's eye tells the mind's brain: A critique of mental imagery. *Psychological Bulletin* 80:1–24, 1973.

[Pylyshyn 80] Z. W. Pylyshyn. The causal power of machines. *The Behavioral and Brain Sciences* 3:442–444, 1980.

[Rado 62] T. Rado. On non-computable functions. *Bell Systems Technical Journal* 41:877–884, 1962.

[Raphael 76] B. Raphael. *The Thinking Computer*. W. H. Freeman, San Francisco, 1976, chapter 6.

[Ratliff 72] F. Ratliff. Contour and contrast. *Scientific American* 226:90–101, 1972.

[Restak 79] R. Restak. *The Brain, The Last Frontier*. Warner Books, New York, 1979.

[Restak 84] R. M. Restak. *The Brain*. Bantam Books, New York, 1984.

[Reynolds 78] A. G. Reynolds and P. W. Flagg. *Cognitive Psychology*. Winthrop, Cambridge, Mass, 1978.

[Richardson 72] K. Richardson, D. Spear, and M. Richards (editors). *Race and Intelligence*. Penguin Books, Baltimore, 1972.

[Richie 84] G. D. Richie and F. K. Hanna. AM: A case study in AI methodology. *Artificial Intelligence* 23:249–268, 1984.

[Rips 77] L. J. Rips. Supposition and the analysis of conditional sentences. In M. A. Just and P. A. Carpenter (editors) *Cognitive Processes in Comprehension*. Lawrence Erlbaum Associates, Hillsdale, N.J., 1977.

[Robinson 65] J. A. Robinson. A machine-oriented logic based on the resolution principle. *Journal of the ACM* 12:23–41, 1965.

[Robinson 73] D. N. Robinson. *The Enlightened Machine*. Dickeson Publishing Co., Belmont, Calif., 1973.

[Robinson 82] J. J. Robinson. DIAGRAM: A grammar for dialogues. *Communications of the ACM* 25:27–47, 1982.

[Rock 85] I. Rock. *The Logic of Perception*. MIT Press, Cambridge, Mass., 1985.

[Romer 55] A. S. Romer. *The Vertebrate Body*. W. B. Saunders, Philadelphia, 1955.

[Rosch 77] E. Rosch. Classification of real world objects: origins and representations in cognition. In P. N. Johnson-Laird and P. C. Wason (editors), *Thinking: Readings in Cognitive Science*. Cambridge University Press, Cambridge, England, 1977.

[Rosenfeld 76] A. Rosenfeld and A. Kak. *Digital Picture Processing*. Academic Press, New York, 1976.

[Rosenschein 83] S. Rosenschein. Natural language processing: crucible for computational theories of cognition. In *International Joint Conference on Artificial Intelligence*, pages 1180–1186. Karlsruhe, West Germany, William Kaufmann, Los Altos, Cal., August, 1983.

[Ross 80] G. S. Ross. Categorization in 1- to 2-year-olds. *Developmental Psychology* 16:391–396, 1980.

[Sacks 86] O. Sacks. Mysteries of the deaf. *New York Review of Books*, March 27, 1986.

[Sagan 78] C. Sagan. *The Dragons of Eden*. Ballantine Books, New York, 1978.

[Salapatek 77] P. Salapatek. Stimulus determinants of attention in infants. In B. B. Wolman (editor), *International Encyclopedia of Psychiatry, Psychology, Psychoanalysis, and Neurology*. Van Nostrand Reinhold, New York, 1977.

[Samuel 67] A. L. Samuel. Some studies in machine learning using the game of checkers II: recent progress. *IBM Journal of Research and Development* 11:601–617, 1967.

[Schank 81] R. Schank and C. R. Riesback. *Inside Computer Understanding*. Lawrence Erlbaum Asociates, Hillsdale, N.J., 1981.

[Scientific 72] Scientific American. *Perception: Mechanisms and Models*. W. H. Freeman, San Francisco, Calif., 1972. (Readings from the *Scientific American*; paperback.)

[Scientific 72a] Scientific American. *Communication*. W. H. Freeman, San Francisco, 1972. (Readings from the *Scientific American*; paperback.)

[Scientific 74] Scientific American. *Object and Illusions*. W. H. Freeman, San Francisco, 1974. (Readings from the *Scientific American*; paperback.)

[Scientific 76] Scientific American. *Progress in Perception*. W. H. Freeman, San Franscisco, 1976. (Readings from the *Scientific American*; paperback.)

[Scientific 79] Scientific American. *The Brain*. W. H. Freeman and Co., San Francisco, CA., 1979. (Readings from *Scientific American*; paperback.)

[Scribner 77] S. Scribner. Modes of thinking and ways of speaking: culture and logic reconsidered. In P. N. Johnson-Laird and P. C. Wason (editors), *Thinking: Readings in Cognitive Science*. Cambridge University Press, Cambridge, England, 1977.

[Searle 69] J. R. Searle. *Speech Acts: An Essay in the Philosophy of Language*. Cambridge University Press, London, 1969.

[Searle 83] J. R. Searle. Minds, brains, and programs. In D. R. Hofstadter and D. C. Dennett (editors) *The Mind's I*. Basic Books, New York, 1983.

[Searle 84] J. R. Searle. *Minds, Brains and Action*. Harvard University Press, Cambridge, Mass., 1984.

[Sebeok 80] T. A. Sebeok and D. J. Umiker-Seboek (editors). *Speaking of Apes: A Critical Anthology of Two-Way Communication with Man*. Plenum, New York, 1980.

[Sejnowski 86] T. J. Sejnowski and C. R. Rosenberg. *NETtalk: A Parallel Network That Learns to Read Aloud*. Tech. Report JHU/EECS-86/01, The Johns Hopkins University Electrical Engineering and Computer Science Dept., Baltimore, 1986.

[Shafer 76] G. A. Shafer. *A Mathematical Theory of Evidence*. Princeton University Press, Princeton, N.J., 1976.

[Shafer 85] G. A. Shafer and A. Tversky. Weighing evidence: the design and comparison of probability thought experiments. *Cognitive Science* 9:309–339, 1985.

[Shanon 85] B. Shanon. The role of representation in cognition. In J. Bishop, J. Lockhead, D. N. Perkins (editor), *Thinking*. Lawrence Erlbaum Associates, Hillsdale, New Jersey, 1985.

[Shepard 71] R. N. Shepard and J. Metzler. Mental rotations of three-dimensional objects. *Science* 171:701–703, 1971.

[Shepard 82] R. N. Shepard and L. A. Cooper. *Mental Images and Their Rotations*. MIT Press, Cambridge, Mass., 1982.

[Shifrin 77] R. M. Shifrin and W. Schneider. Controlled and automatic human information processing II: perceptual learning, automatic attending, and a general theory. *Psychological Review* 84:127–190, 1977.

[Shirai 75] Y. Shirai. Generating schematic descriptions from drawings of scenes with shadows. In P. H. Winston (editor), *Psychology of Computer Vision*. McGraw-Hill, New York, 1975.

[Shortliffe 76] E. H. Shortliffe. *Computer-based Medical Consultations: MYCIN*. Elsevier Publishing Co., New York, 1976.

[Simon 81] H. A. Simon. *Cognitive Science: The Newest Science. Perspectives on Cognitive Science*. Ablex Publishing, Norwood, N.J., 1981.

[Skinner 57] B. F. Skinner. *Verbal Behavior*. Appleton-Century-Crofts, New York, 1957.

[Sloman 85] A. Sloman. What enables a machine to understand? In *Proceedings of the Ninth International Joint Conference on Artificial Intelligence*, Los Angeles, August 1985, Morgan Kaufmann, Los Altos, Calif., 1985.

[Smith 47] S. M. Smith, H. O. Brown, J. E. P. Toman, and L. S. Goodman. The lack of cerebral effects of d-tubercurarine. *Anesthesiology* 8:1–14, 1947.

[Smith 72] C. U. M. Smith. *The Brain, Towards an Understanding*. Capricorn Books, New York, 1972.

[Smith 85] C. G. Smith. *Ancestral Voices*. Prentice-Hall, Englewood Cliffs, N.J., 1985.

[Smith 83] R. G. Smith, and J. D. Baker. The dipmeter advisor system: a case study in commercial expert system development. In *Proceedings of the 8th International Joint Conference on Artificial Intelligence*, pages 122–129. Karlsruhe, West Germany, August, 1983. William Kaufmann, Los Altos, Calif.

[Soloway 80] E. M. Soloway. *From Problems to Programs Via Plans*. Technical Report COINS Technical Report 80-19, University of Mass., Amherst, Mass., 1980.

[Spelke 82] E. S. Spelke. Perceptual knowledge of objects in infancy. In J. Mehler, E. C. T. Walker, and M. Garrett (editor), *Perspectives in Mental Representation*. Lawrence Erlbaum Associates, Hillsdale, N.J., 1982.

[Spence 83] A. P. Spence and E. B. Mason. *Human Anatomy and Physiology*. Benjamin Cummings Publishing Co., Menlo Park, Calif., 1983, 2nd edition.

[Springer 85] S. P. Springer and G. Deutsch. *Left Brain, Right Brain*. W. H. Freeman, San Francisco, Calif., 1985, revised edition.

[Sternberg 82] R. J. Sternberg (ed). *The Handbook of Human Intelligence*. Cambridge University Press, New York, 1982.

[Svedja 79] M. Svedja and D. Schmid. The role of self-produced locomotion on the onset of heights on the visual cliff. *Paper presented at the meeting of the Society for Research in Child Development*, San Francisco, March, 1979.

[Szlovits 82] P. Szlovits (editor). *Artificial Intelligence in Medicine*. Westview, Boulder, Colo., 1982.

[Terrace 81] H. S. Terrace. *Nim: A Chimpanzee Who Learned Sign Language*. Knopf, New York, 1980.

[Thompson 84] H. Thompson and G. Ritchie. Implementing Natural Language. In T. O'Shea and M. Eisenstadt (editors) *Artificial Intelligence: Tools, Techniques, and Applications*. Harper and Row, New York, 1984.

[Thorpe 65] W. H. Thorpe and M. E. W. North. Origin and significance of the power of vocal imitation: with special reference to the antiphonal singing of birds. *Nature* 208:219–222, 1965.

[Tou 74] J. T. Tou and R. C. Gonzalez. *Pattern Recognition Principles*. Addison-Wesley, Reading, Mass., 1974.

[Treisman 85] Treisman, A., "Preattentive Processing in Vision," Computer Vision, Graphics, and Image Processing, 31(2):156–177, August 1985.

[Turing 50] A. A. Turing. Computing machinery and intelligence. *Mind* 59:433–460, 1950.

[Turner 85] R. Turner. *Logics for Artificial Intelligence*. Halsted/Wiley, New York, 1985.

[Tversky 74] A. Tversky and D. Kahneman. Judgment under uncertainty: heuristics and biases. *Science* 185:1124–1131, 1974.

[Ullman 79] S. Ullman. *The Interpretation of Visual Motion*. M.I.T. Press, Cambridge, Mass., 1979.

[Walls 42] G. Walls. *The Vertebrate Eye and Its Adaptive Radiation*. Cranbrook Institute of Science, Bloomfield Hills, Michigan, 1942. (also Hafner, New York 1942).

[Waltz 75] D. I. Waltz. Generating schematic descriptions from drawings of scenes with shadows. In P. H. Winston (editor), *The Psychology of Computer Vision*. McGraw-Hill, New York, 1975.

[Wang 60] H. Wang. Toward mechanical mathematics. *IBM Journal of Research and Development* 4:2–22, 1960.

[Wasserman 73] A. O. Wasserman. *Biology*. Appelton-Century-Crofts, New York, 1973.

[Watson 30] J. Watson. *Behaviorism*. W. W. Norton, New York, 1930.

[Weinreb 84] E. L. Weinreb. *Anatomy and Physiology*. Addison-Wesley, Reading, Mass., 1984.

[Weiss 79] S.M. Weiss and C.A. Kulikowski. EXPERT: A system for developing consultation models. In *Proceedings of the 6th International Joint Conference on Artificial Intelligence*, pages 942–947, Tokyo. William Kaufmann, Los Altos, Calif., 1979.

[Weissman 67] C. Weissman. *LISP 1.5 Primer*. Dickenson, Belmont, Calif.,1967.

[Weizenbaum 66] J. Weizenbaum. ELIZA, a computer program for the study of natural language communication between man and machine. *Communica-*

tions of the Association for Computing Machinery 9:36–45, 1966.

[Weizenbaum 76] J. Weizenbaum. *Computer Power and Human Reason*. W. H. Freeman and Co., San Francisco, 1976.

[Wells 68] M. Wells. *Lower Animals*. McGraw Hill, New York, 1968.

[Wertheimer 61] M. Wertheimer. *Productive Thinking*. Tavistock, London, 1961. (Original edition 1945, Harper & Bros., New York)

[Whorf 56] B. L. Whorf In J. B. Carroll (editor). *Language, Thought, and Reality: Selected Writings of Benjamin Lee Whorf*. Wiley, New York, 1956.

[Wigglesworth 72] V. B. Wigglesworth. *Principles of Insect Physiology*. Chapman and Hall, London, 1972. 7th edition.

[Wilensky 84] R. Wilensky. *LISPcraft*. W. W. Norton, New York, 1984.

[Winograd 70] T. Winograd. *Procedures as a Representation for Data in a Computer Program for Understanding Natural Language*. PhD thesis, MIT, Cambridge, Mass., August, 1970.

[Winograd 74] T. Winograd. *Five Lectures on Artificial Intelligence*. Report STAN CS 74-459, Computer Science Department, Stanford University, September 1974.

[Winograd 83] T. Winograd. *Language as a Cognitive Process: Syntax*. Addison-Wesley, Reading, Mass., 1983.

[Winograd 86] T. Winograd and F. Flores. *Understanding Computers and Cognition*. Ablex Publishing Co., Norwood, N.J., 1986.

[Winston 75] P. H. Winston. Learning Structural Descriptions from Examples In P. H. Winston (editor). *The Psychology of Computer Vision*. McGraw-Hill, New York, 1975.

[Winston 84] P. H. Winston. *Artificial Intelligence*. Addison-Wesley, New York, 1984. 2nd edition.

[Winston 85] P. H. Winston and B. K. Horn. *LISP*. Addison-Wesley, New York, 1985. 2nd edition.

[Wittgenstein 68] L. Wittgenstein. *Philosophical Investigations*. Macmillan, New York, 1968.

[Woods 77] W. A. Woods. Lunar rocks in natural English: explanations in natural language question answering. In *Linguistic Structures Processing*. A. Zampoli (editor). North-Holland, Amsterdam, 1977.

[Wos 84] L. Wos, R. Overbeek, E. Lusk, and J. Boyle. *Automated Reasoning: Introduction and Applications*. Prentice Hall, Englewood Cliffs, N.J., 1984.

[Wright 69] D. Wright. *Deafness*. Stein and Day, New York, New York, 1969.

[Yonas 81] A. Yonas. Infant's response to optical information for collision. In R. N. Aslin, J. R. Alberts, and M. R. Peterson (editor), *Development of Perception: Psychobiological Perspectives*. Academic Press, New York, 1981.

[Young 68] J. Z. Young. *Doubt and Certainty in Science*. Oxford University Press, New York, 1968.

[Young 76] R. M. Young. *Seriation by Children: An Artificial Intelligence Analyis of a Piagetian Task*. Birkhauser, Basel, Switzerland, 1976.

[Zahn 71] C. T. Zahn. Graph-theoretical methods for detecting and describing gestalt clusters. *IEEE Transactions on Computers* C-20:68–86, 1971.

[Zucker 76] S. Zucker. Region growing: childhood and adolescence. *Computer Graphics and Image Processing* 5:382–399, 1976.

[Zucker 77] S. W. Zucker, R. A. Hummel, and A. Rosenfeld. An application of relaxation labeling to line and curve enhancement. *IEEE Transactions on Computers* C-26:394–403, 1977.

Index